Approaches to Teaching the Works of Sor Juana Inés de la Cruz

Approaches to Teaching World Literature

Joseph Gibaldi, series editor

For a complete listing of titles, see the last pages of this book.

Approaches to Teaching the Works of Sor Juana Inés de la Cruz

---

Edited by

Emilie L. Bergmann

and

Stacey Schlau

The Modern Language Association of America
New York 2007

Library of Congress Cataloging-in-Publication Data
Approaches to teaching the works of Sor Juana Inés de la Cruz / edited by Emilie L. Bergmann and Stacey Schlau.
p. cm.—(Approaches to teaching world literature ; 98)
Includes bibliographical references and index.
ISBN: 978-0-87352-815-3 (hardcover : alk. paper)
ISBN: 978-0-87352-816-0 (pbk. : alk. paper)
1. Juana Inés de la Cruz, Sister, 1651–1695—Criticism and interpretation.
2. Juana Inés de la Cruz, Sister, 1651–1695—Study and teaching. I. Bergmann, Emilie L., 1949– II. Schlau, Stacey, 1948- III. Series.
PQ7296.J6Z566 2007
861'.3—dc22 2007022807
ISSN 1059-1133

Cover illustration of the paperback edition:
Sor Juana de la Cruz. By Francisco Vallejo (2005).
Acrylic paint on acrylic plate. Property of the artist.

Published by The Modern Language Association of America
26 Broadway, New York, New York 10004-1789
www.mla.org

CONTENTS

PREFACE TO THE SERIES

In *The Art of Teaching* Gilbert Highet wrote, "Bad teaching wastes a great deal of effort, and spoils many lives which might have been full of energy and happiness." All too many teachers have failed in their work, Highet argued, simply "because they have not thought about it." We hope that the Approaches to Teaching World Literature series, sponsored by the Modern Language Association's Publications Committee, will not only improve the craft—as well as the art—of teaching but also encourage serious and continuing discussion of the aims and methods of teaching literature.

The principal objective of the series is to collect within each volume different points of view on teaching a specific literary work, a literary tradition, or a writer widely taught at the undergraduate level. The preparation of each volume begins with a wide-ranging survey of instructors, thus enabling us to include in the volume the philosophies and approaches, thoughts and methods of scores of experienced teachers. The result is a sourcebook of material, information, and ideas on teaching the subject of the volume to undergraduates.

The series is intended to serve nonspecialists as well as specialists, inexperienced as well as experienced teachers, graduate students who wish to learn effective ways of teaching as well as senior professors who wish to compare their own approaches with the approaches of colleagues in other schools. Of course, no volume in the series can ever substitute for erudition, intelligence, creativity, and sensitivity in teaching. We hope merely that each book will point readers in useful directions; at most each will offer only a first step in the long journey to successful teaching.

Joseph Gibaldi
Series Editor

PREFACE TO THE VOLUME

Known since her own time as the "tenth muse," Sor Juana Inés de la Cruz (1648–95) both stands out, for her erudition and genius, and fits in, into the long history of women intellectuals who, in Europe and elsewhere, wrote from a position that challenged gendered scholastic norms. Over the past thirty or so years, renewed and revisionist scholarly interest in early modern women writers, inspired in large part by feminist concerns about the literary canon as it was traditionally taught and by consequent new theoretical apparatuses, has resulted in the discovery and rediscovery of many such authors. Certainly, research about medieval and early modern women writers such as Sor Juana, Laura Cereta, and Christine de Pizan, to name only a very few, has helped complete the scholarly portrait of Western intellectual history. Literary scholars and historians have worked for more than two decades to illuminate areas traditionally eclipsed by the logical fallacy of mistaking partiality for universality, in terms of both gender and geography.

The position of early modern women writers, and particularly one writing in the relative isolation of a convent in colonial New Spain, provides a unique perspective from that of the centers of power. Sor Juana's cleverly worded critiques of masculinist culture and colonial subjugation, in particular her *Respuesta a sor Filotea* (*The Answer* [1691]), written in response to the bishop of Puebla, are key documents in Western intellectual history, in both style and content. A baroque tour de force in the form of an *apologia pro vita sua* that relies heavily on her training in classical rhetoric, the *Answer* has been misunderstood for almost all of the three hundred years since it was written. Defiantly erudite in its defense of her passion for natural sciences, poetry, and classical learning, the *Answer* sets her apart from other early modern women writers, making her a significant feminist foremother. Like Virginia Woolf's *A Room of One's Own*, Sor Juana's *Answer* represents a significant historical moment in feminist consciousness while it continues to speak to women's condition in the present.

This is a propitious time for publishing a volume on teaching Sor Juana. Because of new scholarship and excellent translations into English of her poetry, prose, and theater, instructors of not only Latin American literature but also women's literature, religious studies, theater, and intellectual history have begun to include her work in course syllabi. Her secular semiautobiographical play *Los empeños de una casa* ("The Trials of a Household") has been translated and produced in English, and English translations of the *loa*, or prologue, to her *auto sacramental* ("morality play") *El divino Narciso* (*The Divine Narcissus*) have been included in anthologies for use in comparative courses on early modern literature, world theater, and literature by women.

Those who have recently discovered the texts Sor Juana authored find themselves astounded by her wit, brilliance, unique grasp of baroque stylistics, and nuanced argumentation. As noted, the *Answer* is a key document in the intellectual history of her times. Her *Primero sueño*, a daring baroque poem shaped by a quest for a methodical approach to knowledge, opens with images of female transgression. The *Dream* challenges the scholastic tradition with a new rationalism and reflects seventeenth-century scientific discoveries and theories as well as traditional views from antiquity. As a late baroque poet, Sor Juana demonstrates the aesthetic practice of imitation and conceptual wit. Her position as a woman born in colonial New Spain, lacking the authority of university-educated male intellectuals and court poets, adds impetus to her emulation and rivalry with her Spanish, Italian, and classical models.

The controversies in recent Sor Juana scholarship present competing stories with potential to empower readers or isolate them from this colonial Mexican nun's exceptional accomplishments. At issue is the biographical narrative of women's literary careers, viewed as doomed and self-destructive since the time of the original tenth muse, Sappho. With particular irony, Sor Juana mocked her own status as the "phoenix," the mythical creature whose immolation is necessary for its rebirth.

This volume addresses the religious, sociocultural, and political context of colonial society. Sor Juana lived in a convent, a community of women whose lives were strictly regulated by the rules of their order (in her case, the Hieronymites). She was subject to the authority of the bishop and other clerics. She lived in the capital of an enormously wealthy colonized region whose vast territority and many inaccessible rural areas created governance nightmares. She participated in a highly stratified colonial society in which class, race, religion, and gender determined performative behaviors to a great extent. She was subject to a power struggle between the secular and religious arms of government, as well as internecine church conflicts. Her ability to throw off some of the weight of restrictions and limitations on a woman of her temperament, vocation, and family background remains truly remarkable.

ELB
SS

ACKNOWLEDGMENTS

The editors are grateful to the University of California, Berkeley, and West Chester University for reassigned time and research funding in support of this project. Our colleagues' prompt and informative replies to the survey and the contributors' gracious collaboration made this volume possible. We especially thank Julia Farmer for many hours of bibliographic, editorial, and technical assistance.

INTRODUCTION

Sor Juana is a dramatic figure, an icon of Mexican culture, whose defiant achievement in the face of ecclesiastical opposition and opprobrium attracts the attention of students. Because of students' fascination not only with Sor Juana's life but also with her work, the instructor's task is not that of motivating them to study the texts but rather that of guiding them through the daunting baroque complexity that dazzled her contemporaries and made her an international intellectual celebrity. Sor Juana wove conceptual networks of meaning that reward the effort required to read her poetry, prose, and theater. The essays in this volume provide resources for navigating those networks.

An internationally renowned woman writer, Sor Juana exemplifies the centrality of the gendered, colonized margin to cultural practices and concepts. Sor Juana's writing reflects the different sense of the world and the word that she developed through the experience of reading as an outsider—self-taught, illegitimate, Creole, female—who perceived herself as part of a long tradition of scholarly women. Although much writing about Sor Juana's life at the viceregal court and in the convent involves some degree of speculation, it is now clear that, exceptional as she was, she occupied contradictory subject positions as an illegitimate *criolla* (Creole woman, Mexican-born of Spanish descent), celebrated writer at the court, and nun whose wit and intellect won her privilege in the convent and a following outside it. To understand the interrelationships among this multiplicity of roles, including that of writer, requires some introduction to seventeenth-century culture.

Bridging two major periods of intellectual history, in the context of which Sor Juana called into question the distinctions between European and American, as well as masculine and feminine, Sor Juana's oeuvre, especially its baroque style and philosophical inquiry, signals the end of the long Middle Ages and the beginning of modern thought. The account of scientific experimentation and insatiable intellectual curiosity in the *Answer* places her at the opening of a new era. Scholars have debated the possibility that she may have read René Descartes and Pierre Gassendi, despite the prohibition on importing their work to New Spain. Her scientific concepts and interpretation of Egyptian mythology can, however, be attributed to the prolific Jesuit Athanasius Kircher, whose work is currently the object of renewed interest (see Findlen). The medieval and Renaissance rhetorical structure and the authorizing strategies she employs in her writing are strong evidence of the continuing intellectual tradition she drew on, and they explain in part her choice of the long poem ("The Dream"), rather than a prose essay, for epistemological exploration. The breadth and depth of reading evidenced in the *Dream* demonstrates both the possibilities and the limits of modern thought in colonial New Spain.

As a colonial subject authorizing her writing through classical and contemporary literary models, Sor Juana participated in almost all the poetic and theatrical genres of her time, utilizing a dazzling array of poetic meters, in courtly Italian and popular Castilian verse forms. She had learned enough Nahuatl to write a poem in that indigenous language of Mexico; other poems imitate the speech patterns of African slaves. Whether or not it is true, as she claimed in the *Answer*, that "The Dream" was the only poem she wrote of her own volition, her wit and the aesthetics of imitation that shaped her poetry require some explanation for students accustomed to valuing originality and autonomy in literature. Sonnet 195, "El hijo que la esclava ha concebido" ("The child the slave-woman has conceived"), which introduced her first volume of poetry, *Inundación Castálida* (1689), comments on her position as *criolla*, dependent on a powerful patron to make her work known outside the convent and eventually to publish it in Spain. Another, different kind of hybrid prose and verse piece, the *Neptuno alegórico* (*Allegorical Neptune*), explains the elaborate symbols decorating an arch commissioned by the cathedral to welcome the new viceroy and his wife to Mexico in 1680. In addition to this unique occasion, Sor Juana was regularly commissioned to write cycles of *villancicos* ("carols") set to music for the cathedrals in Mexico City and Oaxaca. Other poems commissioned by wealthy, powerful patrons celebrate commonplace events in their family life. Her love sonnets are often philosophical, whereas her ballads range from sophisticated humor to ironic or melancholy contemplation of the paradoxes of (her) fame.

Given the limits on access to reading and writing and the restrictive norms for women's behavior, a woman with Sor Juana's intellectual desire and literary renown was destined to conflict with her superiors. She distanced herself from her powerful confessor around 1681 but had the support of the viceroy and his wife until their return to Spain in 1686. This was her most productive literary period. The controversy about her intellectual pursuits and betrayal by her powerful ecclesiastical ally the bishop of Puebla prompted her to write the defense of her pursuit of secular and theological learning in the *Answer* (1691). A second volume of her poems appeared in 1692, three years after the first. Her fame may have exacerbated the ire of her superiors and contributed to the circumstances leading to her statements of humility during the last years of her life. Because Sor Juana wrote very little in the two years before her death, she is often misleadingly depicted as a victim of inquisitorial oppression.

It is clear that Sor Juana was pressured to relinquish her extensive library and her scientific and musical instruments to raise funds for the convent. She signed a general confession in 1693 and a declaration of faith, repentance, and abandonment of her intellectual pursuits, formulaically signed in her own blood, in 1694. These dramatic scenes unfold against the background of convent life in a highly theatrical and coercive society, but since 1995 debates have reopened regarding their effect. In the light of the political, economic, and ecclesiastical crises and corruption of the time, scholars question the particularity and severity of the Mexican intellectual's fate. They no longer ask, Why did she abandon the activities that gave meaning to her life? but rather, To what extent?

A central problem in teaching Sor Juana is the iteration of entrenched narratives based on myths. Students and instructors, for instance, reinforce each other in returning to what Frederick Luciani calls "strategic vignettes of her childhood and youth" in the *Answer* (*Self-Fashioning* 17): hair cutting, refraining from eating cheese, professing as a rejection of marriage, kitchen as chemistry laboratory, desire to cross-dress to attend university, and trailing her older sister to the neighborhood school for girls. The essays in this book, however, expand the possible meanings of the anecdotes by identifying nuances in them using a critical skepticism informed by contemporary theories of subjectivity.

What is known about Sor Juana's biography produces more questions than answers. Sor Juana was self-taught from her grandfather's library in Nepantla, near Puebla, and her precocity brought her to the viceregal court in Mexico City in her early teens. She entered the Hieronymite convent in 1668. In the *Answer* she explains that the decision was made not because she wished to pursue a religious vocation but because it was the best option to continue her intellectual pursuits. Her stated "absolute unwillingness to enter into marriage" and her passionate poetry to two female patrons have given rise to speculation about her sexuality (Arenal and Powell 51). For most of the over three hundred years since her death, critics accepted Diego Calleja's biographical account (1700), which followed a hagiographic model portraying her as the ideal woman religious whose piety overshadowed her erudition. This view was only modified in the 1920s, with the archival research on Sor Juana's conflictive relationship with religious authorities by Dorothy Schons, who called the Mexican intellectual the "first feminist" of the Americas. The next influential critical trend provided a Freudian framework for associating her intellectual pursuits with masculine tendencies. In Ludwig Pfandl's 1946 "psychobiography," she is depicted as a narcissist with a father fixation. Octavio Paz began to challenge this view with a tercentenary article that led to research culminating in his book-length study. Nonetheless, despite recognition of her importance as a Mexican cultural icon, not until Georgina Sabat de Rivers began developing a critical oeuvre on Sor Juana in the 1970s was there a scholarly approach to the intellectual and literary complexity of her poetry. In the 1980s, Electa Arenal and Stacey Schlau's research on writing by early modern Spanish and colonial Spanish American nuns advanced critical frameworks for understanding texts authored by women religious. Publication and controversy about Sor Juana's life and work intensified after the appearance of Paz's *Sor Juana Inés o las trampas de la fe* (*Sor Juana; or, The Traps of Faith* [1982; 1988]). A series of conferences in Mexico City beginning in the 1990s provided a forum for new biographical, historical, feminist, and rhetorical readings of her work.

Approaches to Teaching the Works of Sor Juana Inés de la Cruz represents fully and widely the contemporary approaches that emerge from literary and feminist scholarship, ranging from those based in historical research to those with a focus on cultural studies. The book features discussions not only of the most frequently assigned work of Sor Juana—the *Answer*—but also of most of the important titles from the rest of her oeuvre. It includes articles on teaching the poetry (the long metaphysical poem, "The Dream"; love poems; occasional poetry such as carols, ballads, and sonnets); theater (especially "The Trials of a Household" and the *loa* to the *Divine Narcissus*); and rhetorical prose, especially the *Carta atenagórica* ("Letter Worthy of Athena").

No matter their discipline or approach, instructors of the Mexican nun-author's writings share some issues and concerns. Her work is taught in a wide variety of classroom settings: colonial Latin American literature, women in Hispanic literatures, world women writers, and intellectual and religious history. The study of Sor Juana as a woman writer cannot be disregarded: unquestionably a protofeminist thinker herself, it would be difficult to ignore questions of gendered sexual politics, of sexuality and intellectuality in her work. One purpose of this guide is to help instructors illuminate Sor Juana's highly ironic treatment of gender and sexuality in her own time, as well as to offer studies of contemporary versions of these issues. It is clear that she was well aware of gender norms and the perceived "unnaturalness" of her prodigious intellect. Contemporary interpretations, including María Luisa Bemberg's film "I, the Worst of All" (*Yo la peor de todas* [1990]), and numerous stage plays, operas, and novels about her life have drawn attention to biographical questions, particularly those about her apparent abandonment of intellectual pursuits and about her choice of celibacy and her passionate poems to women. From the transgressive mythological figures at the opening of the philosophical *Dream* to occasional poems celebrating events in her patron the vicereine's family life, a complex approach to the feminine is essential to examining her work.

Two distinct audiences can make use of this volume, those in Hispanic studies classrooms and those who teach Sor Juana in English. While their needs undoubtedly overlap, the two audiences require different kinds of information to fill in the gaps and, in some senses, different kinds of strategies for classroom use. For both, these essays offer essential background in the institutional history of the period: economic, political, and religious relations between Spain and the colonies; church politics; state apparatuses for controlling indigenous, African, and mixed-race populations and the urban poor; tensions between secular and religious authorities; censorship of words and ideas; and the social organization of daily life.

Instructors of world women's literature and women's studies are beginning to read and teach Sor Juana. While anthologies and studies still use the term "early modern women's writing" to refer only to English-language materials, there is a growing awareness among students as well as instructors of the diverse cultural geography of women's contributions to early modern thought. As interest in the roots of feminism drew attention to Christine de Pizan, Louise Labé, Madame de La Fayette, Isotta Nogarola, Laura Cereta, Veronica Franco, Gaspara Stampa, Margaret Cavendish, and Mary Wortley Montagu, among others, scholars not exclusively focused on feminism also found rich areas of literary and cultural history that had been eclipsed for centuries. The Other Voice in

Early Modern Europe series constitutes one important example of the effort to ensure that these women's work becomes a permanent part of the body of knowledge that we call literary studies. Stephanie Merrim's *Early Modern Women's Writing and Sor Juana* (1999) places Sor Juana in the company of Italian, French, and English women intellectuals. The visionary and literary nuns whose writing is collected, translated, and discussed in Arenal and Schlau's *Untold Sisters: Hispanic Nuns in Their Own Works* (1989), as well as the seventeenth-century German Jewish autobiographer Glückl of Hameln, the French missionary nun Marie de l'Incarnation in Canada, and the Dutch scientific illustrator Maria Sibylla Merian in Surinam presented in Natalie Zemon Davis's *Women on the Margins* (1995), populate a world in which Sor Juana is still extraordinary but neither unique nor inexplicable.

For much of the second half of the twentieth century, in the Hispanic literary canon Sor Juana Inés de la Cruz was one of only two early modern women writers normally given academic attention; Saint Teresa of Ávila was the other. They were generally cited as the exceptions to the rule, since it was commonly assumed that there were no early modern women writers worth placing on reading lists for master of arts degrees or syllabi of survey courses. It is no coincidence that both were nuns. Their access to literacy and advanced learning and contemplative religious life made writing possible, while religious institutions preserved their texts. Being a bride of Christ bestowed on both women a rhetorical and conceptual virility, but their strategies and style differed significantly. While Saint Teresa, whose life and work were rooted in mystical experience, cultivated what Alison Weber terms a "rhetoric of femininity" that appeared to conform to gender norms of humility and ignorance, Sor Juana demonstrated a prodigious intellectuality and openly defied those norms with ironic wit.

In classes on Latin American literatures in Spanish, no matter the breadth or depth of the course in which students read Sor Juana, they already understand some basic underlying questions having to do with the circumstances of the conquest and colonization; that is, they will bring to their readings some degree of familiarity with the complexity and diversity of the Spanish American cultural heritage. In survey courses, Sor Juana is used as an example, or, more often, the exemplar of what is commonly called the *barroco de Indias* ("Spanish American baroque"), which incorporates indigenous and African conceptual and lexical elements into European stylistics and literary concerns. In more advanced literary and cultural studies courses taught in Spanish, students and instructors can analyze seventeenth-century themes and techniques in her work in greater depth.

Sor Juana, recognized as the first "great" writer of Latin America, has a secure place in the canon, but only a small fraction of her work is required on course syllabi and graduate reading lists. Sor Juana's ballad "Hombres necios" ("Foolish Men"); a few paragraphs from the *Answer*; and a complex sonnet on the transitory nature of beauty, "Este, que ves, engaño colorido" ("This object which you see—a painted snare"), appear in anthologies of Latin American literature, most often with insufficient notes and discussion. A significant number of scholars study her writing, but the dense philosophical framework and complicated linguistic techniques characteristic of late-seventeenth-century writing have deterred some colonialists from incorporating her texts into their courses. Nevertheless, those of us who have successfully taught Sor Juana know that those difficulties can be not only overcome but even valued as part of the complex fabric of her work.

The essays in this volume furnish students and instructors with the necessary cultural capital to fully decipher Sor Juana's texts. The breadth and depth of historical, rhetorical, philosophical, and theological references evident in all her writings assume a differently formed literacy than most of us come equipped with in the early twenty-first century. Her texts exemplify a kind of lively excess that draws the reader into a dialogue intended to instruct by pointing out new and surprising connections. Reading her work requires an active engagement rather than a reverential view of a cultural relic and thus has the potential to develop students' literary imagination through an encounter with distinctly different aesthetic values. To appreciate the wit and irony, as well as the textured complexity of ideas and themes, Sor Juana's knowledge of Latin, patristic fathers' and other theologians' treatises, baroque and classical stylistics, early and medieval women's intellectual history, and seventeenth-century science has to be taken into account. Contemporary students' admiration of Sor Juana's intellectual and literary strength grows with greater comprehension of these and other elements. We offer these pages to instructors in search of strategies to help students develop competence and enjoyment as readers of her work.

ELB
SS

Part One

MATERIALS

Editions

Spanish Editions

Despite the tradition of recognizing Sor Juana as a Mexican cultural icon, the first critical edition of her writing did not appear until 1951, when Alfonso Méndez Plancarte began publication of the four-volume *Obras completas*, in order to commemorate the tercentenary of what was then thought to be Sor Juana's birth date. Volume one consists of her secular lyric poetry; volume two, the religious poetry; volume three, the religious theater; and volume four, edited by Alberto G. Salceda, contains her secular theater and prose, including the *Respuesta* and documents signed by the nun, such as the vows she renewed toward the end of her life. The edition includes an extensive introduction and copious notes. Although scholarly interest in Sor Juana grew in the 1970s, Alfonso Méndez Plancarte's edition was allowed to go out of print and was not reissued until 1994. A more compact critical edition with selective notes appeared in 2004, edited by Elias L. Rivers and Georgina Sabat de Rivers, entitled *Poesía, teatro, pensamiento: Lírica personal, lírica coral, teatro, prosa.* Their edition updates Méndez Plancarte's and includes recently rediscovered documents such as the *Enigmas ofrecidos a la Casa del Placer* and letters (Alatorre). These materials are also included in the CD-ROM edited by Guadalupe Correa and Tadeo Stein and published by Ediciones Nuevo Hélade in 2004. This valuable CD-ROM, although based on the Méndez Plancarte–Salceda edition, also includes additional introductory materials, notes, digitized facsimiles of early editions, glossaries, and a wealth of images: portraits of Sor Juana, maps, and visual materials from works by Athanasius Kircher.

Editorial Porrúa's 1985 *Obras completas* is cheap and accessible but contains no notes or line numbers. Two editions of Sor Juana's selected poetry are of particular interest for classroom use: the 1992 Cátedra edition of *Poesía lírica*, with introduction and notes by José Carlos González Boixo, and the briefer selection published by Alianza, *Antología poética* (2004), with a succinct introduction by José Miguel Oviedo and selections from *Primero sueño*.

English Translations

Carol Maier

Instructors seeking to teach the work of Sor Juana Inés de la Cruz in English will find a wealth of material. Not all Sor Juana's work has been translated, but the last two decades have seen a growing interest in Sor Juana by North American scholars and readers and a veritable outpouring of translations by enthusiastic and, for the most part, accomplished translators.[1] Before the 1980s, however, few translations had been made, although as early as 1956, Robert Graves had written a laudatory essay about this "woman of poetic genius" (171) and translated several of her poems. Graves's essay and his translations, like the translation of twenty-two of Sor Juana's sonnets that Pauline Cook published in 1950 apparently fell into oblivion. The same could be said of the prose versions of selected poems by Sor Juana that Elias L. Rivers included in his 1966 anthology, although Rivers described *Primero sueño* (*First Dream*) as "philosophically more ambitious . . . than any other poem written in Spanish during the fifteenth and sixteenth centuries" (23).

It was not until 1982, when Margaret Sayers Peden's translation of *La respuesta* in *A Woman of Genius* appeared, that Sor Juana was again seen in English. Other translations followed in close succession: John Campion's translation of *El sueño* appearing in 1983; Peden's bilingual *Sor Juana Inés de la Cruz, Poems* in 1985; and the selections in Kate Flores and Angel Flores's *Defiant Muse*, Luis Harss's *Sor Juana's* Dream, Frank Warnke's selected sonnets, and Amanda Powell's translations (in Arenal's "This life"), all appearing in 1986. The publication of Peden's translation of Paz's *Sor Juana* (see Paz, *Traps*) and its bilingual companion *A Sor Juana Anthology*, edited and translated by Alan S. Trueblood in 1988, introduced Sor Juana to the general public and sparked a much wider readership in English. Since that date, translators have continued to engage with her poetry and prose; translations of her religious and secular theater have also been published as complete versions of individual works and in anthologies.

Sor Juana's poetry has inspired many translations, and there are multiple versions of numerous poems. Her philosophical satire "Hombres necios," for example, has been a favorite of translators beginning with Graves ("Poems" 181–82). It has also been translated by Arenal and Powell (156–59), Willis Barnstone (who translates fragments of the poem, 74–75), Muriel Kittel, Peden (*Sor Juana* 28–33; *Poems* 148–51), Trueblood (111–13), and Warnke (108–13). Of the sonnets, several, such as sonnet 164, have proved most compelling to translators, regardless of the context or approach. (See, for example, Arenal and Powell 154–55; Barnstone 92–93; Cobb 50–51, who has translated all the sonnets; Larkin and Manrique 38–39 [2003]; Peden, *Sor Juana* 63 and *Poems* 180–81; Rivers 327–28; Trueblood 80–81; and Warnke 94–95.) Of Sor Juana's major poem, *Primero sueño*, there are complete translations by Campion, Gilbert Cunningham, Harss, Peden (*Poems*), and Trueblood; and Warnke includes a generous selection. Accompanying most of these translations is at least a brief commentary by the translator. The remarks by Cobb, Harss, and Peden (*Sor Juana*; *Poems*) are especially detailed.

Given such a large number of translators, it is not surprising that, as a poet, Sor Juana appears in multiple guises. Rivers is the only translator who renders her work in prose, but the verse translations vary greatly so that it would be impossible to summarize the differences among them. Most translators suggest in their remarks that they share Peden's belief that contemporary readers and translators "must go to the baroque . . . and attempt to recreate it" on and in its own terms (*Sor Juana* 9; *Poems* vi). However, with the exception of Cook and

Cobb, translators have not worked strictly within the rigorous constraints of baroque style. As Cobb explains, even Peden employs a form that is "almost, but never quite Petrarchan" (1). The same could be said for Warnke (see Warnke 21). Harss and Trueblood have discussed their work as a closeness or "intimacy" with the original (Trueblood xiii), but they both describe that closeness as not overly restrictive. Harss, for example, in his version of *Primero sueño*, "adopted a basic iambic trimeter with random rhymes where chance offered them" (25); Trueblood "retained rhyme where it could be managed without awkwardness" (xiii). Larkin and Manrique undoubtedly offer the freest translations. As Larkin explains, their goal was to achieve the greatest "accuracy of connotation or mood" (79 [2003]). Cobb describes their versions as " 'free verse' summaries of the originals" (2). In fact, however, they are attempts to capture in direct, contemporary English what Larkin refers to as the "elegance and [the] coarseness of Sor Juana's language" (79 [2003])—in Manrique's words, Sor Juana is "one of the most carnal bards of all time" (11 [2003]).

Numerous translations of Sor Juana's prose exist; there are three translations of the letter to Antonio Núñez de Miranda, her confessor (Galván; Paz, *Traps* 495–502, translated by Peden; and Scott, *Madres* 71–81), and three of *La respuesta a sor Filotea de la Cruz* (Arenal and Powell; Peden, appearing in both *Poems* 1–75 and *Woman*; and Trueblood 205–45). Each of these translators has aimed to convey the baroque "flavor" of Sor Juana's prose, although the translations differ, in some ways markedly. Of those versions, it would probably be safe to say that Arenal and Powell's bilingual edition has occasioned the greatest response. Not only did Arenal and Powell provide a detailed introduction to Sor Juana's life and work, they offered a discussion of her work from the perspective of gender and an explanation of their own commitment as feminist translators to make explicit Sor Juana's "spiritual, cultural, social, and female context" (ix). In this way, their translation differs from that of Peden, for example, who also situates *La respuesta* in a gendered context but does not define her practice as a translator in political terms (see Maier).

Translations of Sor Juana's dramatic production have been slower to appear, but there are now three complete translations of her secular play, *Los empeños de una casa*: Catherine Boyle's *House of Desires*, David Pasto's *House of Trials*, and Susana Hernández Araico's *Pawns of a House*. In addition, Peden has translated Doña Leonor's monologue (*Sor Juana* 128–33; *Poems* 240–54). Sor Juana's *El divino Narciso* (*Divine Narcissus*) has been translated in its entirety by Patricia A. Peters and Renée Domeier. Their translation of the introductory *loa* is included in W. B. Worthen's *The Wadsworth Anthology of Drama* (499–507). There are also two additional versions of the *loa*: Willis Knapp Jones and Peden (*Sor Juana* 88–127; *Poems* 194–239). Peden's version is included in Susan Castillo and Ivy Schweitzer's anthology *The Literatures of Colonial America* (151–60).

A discussion of Sor Juana's work in English would not be complete without a mention of the creative pieces based on her life and work. None of them could be considered translations or even adaptations (with the exception of John M. Bennett's "transduction" of *Primero sueño*), but all of them draw on her work in Spanish or in English translation. Because much of the information about her life remains unavailable, to embody her in drama or fiction implies not only projection but also speculation, most commonly about her emotional life and sexuality. Arenal's "dramatic re-recreation" of Sor Juana's "life and thought" ("This life" 164) portrays her as a counterpart to Anne Bradstreet, her North American contemporary; Diane Ackerman has "tried to imagine the most turbulent part of her life" and written a dramatic poem in which she invents a heterosexual relationship for Sor Juana, as does Estela Portillo Trambley. The fiction writers Alicia Gaspar de Alba, a Chicana author, and W. Paul Anderson, a Canadian, have each written a novel based on Sor Juana's life. Gaspar de Alba approaches Sor Juana from a lesbian perspective and in *Sor Juana's Second Dream* constructs for her a "sexuality and politics of location [that] is strictly my own" ("Politics" 163n33). Anderson's *Hunger's Brides* is a mystery novel (and to large extent a meditation on translation) whose main characters, in addition to Sor Juana, are a brilliant young woman obsessed with Sor Juana's life and work and a middle-aged professor who was the woman's instructor and lover.

Given the spectrum of translations and translators, how might an instructor choose the version or versions most appropriate for a particular group of students? Perhaps there are two principal issues to bear in mind. First, despite differences in approach and quality, each translation offers a distinct reading of one of Sor Juana's texts and, in doing so, makes a contribution to our understanding of her work. Because most of the translations are relatively recent and because there is currently a strong interest in Sor Juana's work, all the major translations remain in print. Those, such as Cook's and Warnke's, that are not can be obtained easily through interlibrary loan. Second, the existence of multiple translations occasions not only the need for a choice but also an opportunity to compare readings and discuss them in their own contexts as documents from a given time and place. (See Hunt and Quispe-Agnoli, in this volume, for a detailed comparison of translations.) Since so many of Sor Juana's translators have included some commentary on their work, the amount and nature of that commentary can serve as a guide to instructors, as can essays like Peden's "Building a Translation," which is about translating sonnet 145. Further guidance can be found in reviews of translations, for example in the brief but descriptive comments included regularly in the *Handbook of Latin American Studies*. With respect to translation strategies and feminist translation, Isabel Garayta's dissertation includes a "case study" that is perceptive and illuminating.

In short, English language instructors have access to a large body of material in translation. They will find teaching Sor Juana's work an experience that introduces their students to a highly accomplished writer and a remarkable human being. At the same time, that experience will allow students to glimpse the challenges involved in translating literary works from another country and a distant age.

Editions Used in This Book

All quotations from Sor Juana's work in Spanish are from the four-volume *Obras completas* begun by Alfonso Méndez Plancarte and completed by Alberto G. Salceda. The format of these citations consists of the volume number separated from the page number by a colon. Thus a reference to volume 4, page 22, would be "(4: 22)." The writings of Sor Juana are listed in the works-cited section by editor or translator, when possible, or by title.

NOTE

[1]New translations and retranslations of Sor Juana's work continue to appear. For example, since completion of this essay, Glenna Luschei has published the first English translation of the twenty *enigmas*, along with a brief commentary ("*Enigmas*" and "Translating").

The Instructor's Library

Predictably, almost all respondents to our survey teach the *Answer*. In addition, the shaping of the canon that occurs through textbook anthologies ensures that two sonnets, "Este, que ves, engaño colorido" ("This object which you see—a painted snare") and "Rosa divina" ("Divine Rose"), and the redondillas "Hombres necios" ("Foolish Men") frequently appear on course syllabi. The results of the questionnaire are, however, in some ways startling. Courses in which Sor Juana is taught vary greatly: they encompass survey, special-topic, first- or second-year undergraduate courses and advanced graduate seminars. While the majority are taught in Spanish departments, increasingly Sor Juana appears on the syllabi of comparative and English literature courses. The subject matter of such courses includes early modern theater, Golden Age poetry, women writers, colonial baroque literature and cultural studies, and Latin American culture and civilization. Surprisingly, a wide range of poems are addressed: *romances* ("ballads"), *villancicos* ("carols"), other sonnets, and unusual poetic forms such as the burlesque portrait written in *ovillejos* and the *romance decasílabo* "Lámina sirva el Cielo al retrato" ("May heaven serve as plate for the engraving" [Trueblood 49]). Also taught quite frequently are her secular play, *Trials of a Household*, and the *loa* that accompanies her mystery play, *Divine Narcissus*.

Because there are so many approaches to teaching Sor Juana, and such a variety of courses in which she is taught, the survey showed an almost dizzying array of background readings, both those used by instructors to prepare and those assigned to students. Nevertheless, only a handful were cited repeatedly: Octavio Paz's *The Traps of Faith*, in English and in Spanish; Stephanie Merrim's *Feminist Perspectives on Sor Juana Inés de la Cruz* and *Early Modern Women's Writing and Sor Juana Inés de la Cruz*; Georgina Sabat de Rivers's *En busca de Sor Juana* ("In Search of Sor Juana"); and Electa Arenal and Amanda Powell's *The Answer / La respuesta*.

Background materials on convent life, the colonial baroque, Mexico's place in the empire, seventeenth-century poetics, "new" science and definitions of knowledge, and early modern theology ground the teaching of Sor Juana's writing. Irving Leonard's *Baroque Times in Old Mexico* (1966) is an informative and enjoyable text that has withstood the passage of time. Electa Arenal and Yolanda Martínez–San Miguel provide an overview of colonial Mexican culture in "Refocusing New Spain and Spanish Colonization: Malinche, Guadalupe and Sor Juana" in *A Companion to* The Literatures of Colonial America. For teaching and learning about women religious, convents, and religious women's cultural history in the Hispanic world, Electa Arenal and Stacey Schlau's *Untold Sisters: Hispanic Nuns in Their Own Works* remains, as one respondent said, the "undisputed classic introduction." In addition, Josefina Muriel's *Cultura femenina novohispana* ("New Spain's Feminine Culture") and Asunción Lavrin's many articles, in particular "Unlike Sor Juana?" in *Feminist Perspectives*, are key resources.

For teaching the Hispanic baroque, background knowledge in both the political and religious contexts of the *barroco de Indias* ("colonial Spanish American baroque") and its poetics is indispensable. The classic source about the peninsular baroque is José Antonio Maravall's *La cultura del Barroco* (published in English translation as *Culture of the Baroque*), which emphasizes the period's hegemonic aspects. In contrast, Mariano Picón Salas's "El barroco de Indias" defines the American baroque as a complex and contradictory cultural phenomenon. A recent anthology of essays edited by Nicholas Spadaccini and Luis Martín-Escudillo, *Hispanic Baroques: Reading Cultures in Context*, offers a number of leading critics' perspectives on the baroque in Spain and Spanish America, while the introduction to Alan S. Trueblood's *A Sor Juana Anthology* provides a transatlantic framework for the poetics of the baroque.

Recent critical studies have linked Sor Juana's version of Petrarchism with her profound knowledge of optics and seventeenth-century empirical principles. Drawing on his research on the history of science in New Spain, Elías Trabulse pioneered the contextualization of Sor Juana's understanding of science; "El universo científico de Sor Juana" encapsulates his approach. Ruth Hill's chapter on Sor Juana in *Scepters and Sciences in the Spains* addresses the Mexican intellectual's adaptation of scientific discourses to her literary purposes.

Because of his detailed interweaving of historical context, biographical research, and literary analysis, Octavio Paz's *Sor Juana; or, The Traps of Faith* (1982), in Spanish and English, is the study most often referenced in the questionnaires, although with many caveats. As one respondent points out, his book provides a useful point of departure from which to discuss other critical interpretations. Another notes that Paz situates Sor Juana's work "in an historical and especially cultural context without falling into facile determinisms." Undoubtedly, both as a pedagogical and scholarly tool, *The Traps of Faith* remains valuable. Nonetheless, Paz has been roundly criticized for emphasizing European connections to the detriment of Sor Juana's Mexican framework. No less problematic is his lack of recognition of Sor Juana as a *woman* writer.

Serious scholarship on Sor Juana's writings arose from women's studies rather than Hispanic literary studies. The development of feminist literary criticism in the past quarter century has contributed to burgeoning scholarly interest in the Mexican nun-author. Dorothy Schons anticipated late-twentieth-century feminist approaches, even calling Sor Juana the "first feminist in the New World." Despite its title, Marie-Cécile Bénassy-Berling's *Humanisme y religión en Sor Juana Inés de la Cruz*, published in 1983, constructs a feminist-inflected argument for understanding Sor Juana's thought and production. First published in 1983, Arenal's groundbreaking "The Convent as Catalyst for Autonomy" continues to offer instructors important insights. Josefina Ludmer, in her now-classic 1985 essay, "Las tretas del débil" ("Tricks of the Weak"), argues that silence in Sor Juana is an empowering strategy. Jean Franco's chapter in

Plotting Women, "Sor Juana Explores Space," presents a valuable framework for situating Sor Juana in the gender politics of her society. Respondents to the questionnaire highlighted several essays in Stephanie Merrim's 1991 collection, *Feminist Perspectives on Sor Juana Inés de la Cruz*: those by Arenal ("Where"), Ester Gimbernat González, Ludmer, and Georgina Sabat de Rivers ("Feminist Rereading") were most often cited. Merrim's volume continues to be widely used as a resource that brings together significant feminist approaches and a range of Sor Juana's works. The highly informative study and textual notes that accompany Arenal and Powell's bilingual edition of *The Answer / La respuesta* provide a rich background for teaching the *Answer* and several poetic genres.

Scholarship on Sor Juana has flourished in the past twenty-five years and has produced abundant studies on specific works that are helpful for classroom discussion and instructors' preparation. Martínez–San Miguel's *Saberes americanos* ("American Ways of Knowing") locates *El divino Narciso* amid multiple subalternities—gendered, indigenous, and Creole—and illuminates discussion of Sor Juana's religious theater in the colonial context. The only book-length study in English of Sor Juana's secular theater, Guillermo Schmidhuber de la Mora's *The Three Secular Plays* (in collaboration with Olga Martha Peña Doria) discusses not only *Los empeños de una casa* ("The Trials of a Household") but less well known plays that round out the view of her theatrical imagination. The focus on baroque, colonial, and feminine subjectivities offers new insights on Sor Juana's poetry.

The only poem she claimed to have written of her own volition is also the most challenging, and yet several critics have mapped its labyrinths. Sabat de Rivers's essays "Sor Juana y su *Sueño*: Antecedentes científicos en la poesía española del Siglo de Oro" ("Sor Juana and Her Dream: Scientific Antecedents in Spanish Golden Age Poetry") and "Sor Juana: Imágenes femeninas de su científico *Sueño*" ("Sor Juana: Feminine Images in Her Scientific *Dream*") address the mythological and scientific imagery of the poem. In *En busca de sor Juana*, Sabat de Rivers devotes another essay to portraiture and the visual, a topic also elaborated by Frederick Luciani ("Anamorphosis" and "Emblems"), Luis Avilés, Emilie L. Bergmann ("Optics"), and William Clamurro, the latter two focusing on the much-anthologized sonnet "Este, que ves, engaño colorido." Luciani's *Literary Self-Fashioning* examines the performative and mythmaking aspects of Sor Juana's poetic, dramatic, and prose works. Rosa Perelmuter's rhetorical study of the *Respuesta*, *Los límites de la femineidad en sor Juana Inés de la Cruz* ("The Limits of Femininity in Sor Juana Inés de la Cruz"), also includes chapters on the Mexican nun's lyric poetry and the *Dream*, as well as a history of Sor Juana criticism until 1950. Mario Ortiz's extensive but not exhaustive bibliography reflects the scope of critical productivity about Sor Juana. Of particular interest are his lists of editions in Spanish and English and of literary works based on the poet's life.

Several anthologies of papers from the numerous conferences anticipating and celebrating the tercentenary of Sor Juana's death in 1695 collect diverse studies of contexts and specific works. Among these are *"Y diversa de mi misma entre vuestras plumas ando"* ("Borne on your feather-pens' plumes, my flight is no longer mine"), edited by Sara Poot-Herrera; two separate volumes published by the Universidad del Claustro de Sor Juana in 1995 and 1998 with the same title, *Sor Juana y su mundo: Una mirada actual* ("Sor Juana and Her World: A Contemporary View"), the first edited by Sara Poot-Herrera and the second by Carmen Beatriz López Portillo; *Los empeños: Ensayos en homenaje a Sor Juana Inés de la Cruz* ("Embroilments: Essays in Honor of Sor Juana"), edited by Sergio Fernández and Vicente Quiarte; and *Memoria del Coloquio Internacional Sor Juana Inés de la Cruz y el pensamiento novohispano* ("Proceedings of the International Colloquium on Sor Juana Inés de la Cruz and New Spanish Thought").

Audiovisual and Electronic Resources

Almost unanimously, instructors show at least clips from María Luisa Bemberg's popular film, *Yo, la peor de todas* ("I, the Worst of All"). While respondents to the questionnaire agree that the film effectively dramatizes the circumstances under which Sor Juana wrote, one objects to its enactment of Paz's victimology, and another notes its distortions. The director and translator David Pasto's clever re-creation of *House of Trials* and other videotaped performances of *Los empeños de una casa*, *Amor es más laberinto*, and versions of *El divino Narciso* and its *loa* by various groups from Latin America, Spain, and the United States are available for a minimal rental fee through the Association for Hispanic Classical Theater (www.trinity.edu/org/comedia/catalog.html). The 1999 interpretation titled *Los enredos de una casa*, performed by the Teatro de Repertorio Latinoamericano from Caracas, Venezuela, is particularly witty.

A good place to start searching Internet resources is the Cambridge University site managed by Geoffrey Kantaris (www.latin-american.cam.ac.uk./culture/SorJuana). The site includes clips from "I, the Worst of All" and concise essays on context, knowledge and gender, genre, baroque troping, and differences. It also has a link to the University of Bielefeld's digitized facsimile text of *Fama y obras pósthumas* (www.ub.uni-bielefeld.de/diglib/delacruz/fama). The *Sor Juana Ines de la Cruz Project* (www.dartmouth.edu/~sorjuana), hosted by Dartmouth College, includes searchable texts of the complete works, a brief bibliography, and links to the Bielefeld text. The 2004 CD-ROM of Sor Juana's *Obras completas* (Correa and Stein), as noted above, includes the Méndez Plancarte–Salceda edition and additional notes, glossaries, and visual materials. In addition, various Web sites display one or more of the six portraits of Sor Juana (see Mélendez, this volume).

Part Two

APPROACHES

Introduction

In a quintessentially baroque paradox, awareness of the differences between Sor Juana's time and our own brings her closer to twenty-first-century readers. From that awareness comes a recognition of the historical background and literary techniques necessary to explore the rich complexity of her writing. The essays that follow are intended to guide instructors and students through that process. Because Sor Juana transforms the baroque through her colonial and feminine subjectivity, the most productive strategies are integrative ones that combine European baroque stylistics with colonial cultural and gender studies. Such strategies offer a wide range of theoretical and practical approaches and, as a group, represent significant points of entry.

We have arranged the essays from general overviews to more specific treatments of topics and texts. Thus we open with a section that we consider essential background for contextualizing more detailed studies: Mexican colonial history, women's intellectual history, religious institutions and theology, and ideological connections and differences between Spain and its colonies. In the second section, we bring together readings that situate Sor Juana as a female intellectual in the context of the *barroco de Indias*. Generic analyses constitute the third section, which features articles on theater, poetry, and prose, including the *Answer*. In the final section we offer a series of essays grounded in more recent fields such as queer studies, food studies, applications of visual technology, and interdisciplinary exploration combining literature with musicology.

The essays in the first section frame the gendered, historical, political, and religious contexts necessary for reading Sor Juana's work. They offer diverse perspectives on the peripheral position of the colonial Americas in the cultural, epistemological, and political milieu of the second half of the seventeenth century. A general introductory essay on seventeenth-century New Spanish society opens the section, in order to help instructors understand the cultural limits and possibilities within which Sor Juana exercised her imagination. The remaining essays in the section take up specific aspects of Sor Juana's conflictive relationship with the church, engagement with a tradition of female-centered knowledge production, and contributions to New Spanish epistemologies.

By the late seventeenth century, when Sor Juana was writing, New Spain had developed a distinct identity through its economic structures, system of governance, demographic profile, devotional practices and religious institutions, and cultural production. Asunción Lavrin's essay sets the stage for Sor Juana's role in the intellectual life of the viceregal capital, discussing how the church and the viceregal court, both under the sometimes nominal control of distant European centers of power, largely shaped that identity. Sustained by the exploitation of Mexico's vast silver deposits, the multiethnic and multicultural society of New Spain was highly stratified and had sharply delineated hierarchies of race, class, and gender.

Because Sor Juana saw herself as not only a colonial subject but also a woman, her extraordinary intellect and powerful critique of masculine privilege ensure her continued recognition as a forerunner of feminist thought. Electa Arenal provides a background against which gender ideology, a variation of which continues to this day, explains Sor Juana's paradoxical rhetoric of humility and ambition in the cultural codes of her time.

Nuns held a central, though precarious and ambiguous, place in colonial society. Stephanie Kirk demonstrates how gendered forces made the convent a nexus of conflicting ideologies. Male-authored texts, from a thirteenth-century papal edict to Sor Juana's contemporary Carlos de Sigüenza y Góngora's convent history, reinforce the societal dichotomy between idealization and abjection of women. As women, nuns were the incarnation of sin, but their cloistered life enacted the cultural imperative of female purity, thus solidifying the control and containment of women, especially their bodies. At the same time, the nuns mobilized resistance to the control of ecclesiastical authorities.

Studying the texts, music, art, and crafts of colonial women religious writers contradicts the traditional perception of these women's social and spiritual isolation while providing a more accurate context in which to read Sor Juana's writings. Jennifer L. Eich locates Sor Juana in the company of other women religious, delineating how they influenced and shaped the cultural products of their religious sisters and colonial culture by using correspondence, legal petitions, guides to spiritual practice, conventual chronicles, poetry contests, music, theater, and arts and crafts.

The *Carta atenagórica* ("Letter Worthy of Athena"), whose intricate theological arguments baffle instructors and students of Sor Juana, is important because it sets off a series of text-driven confrontations in the polemic between Sor Juana and her ecclesiastical superiors. Grady C. Wray offers a systematic analysis of Sor Juana's theological position, especially her critique of the sermon by the Portuguese Jesuit Vieira. His essay gives the reader the tools with which to explore not only Sor Juana's deep immersion in the theological currents of her time but also the strategies with which she established her own religious authority.

Often, teaching the "Mexican" aspect of Sor Juana's works is limited to her relationship with Sigüenza y Góngora, comic portrayals of Indians in some poems, and references to Mexico in others. In contrast, Stephanie Merrim opens the "Mexican archive" to trace the New Spain origins of the baroque that Sor Juana knew and, in the process, explains how she appropriated the humanistic curriculum introduced by the Jesuits. Merrim locates Sor Juana's Mexicanness in three aspects of her literary career: her engagement with Creole political issues and writers and with Spanish-born (*radicado*) writers, her production of works for the mass audiences of Europe and of public festivals in Mexico, and the indirect references she makes in her writing to the Virgin of Guadalupe.

Arguing against the depoliticization and dehistoricization of transatlantic and early modern approaches, Yolanda Martínez–San Miguel points out both the potential and limitations of such approaches for understanding the ambivalent discourse of a colonial subject. Using specific poems and the *loa* to *The Divine Narcissus* to exemplify recent disciplinary paradigm shifts, her approach incorporates coloniality as an integral part of conceptualizing modernity without losing a sense of the specificity of Sor Juana's geographic and intellectual location.

Lisa Vollendorf contextualizes Sor Juana within a cohort of Spanish women who represent the first traceable "boom" in Hispanic women's writing. She compares her with two peninsular secular fiction writers, María de Zayas and Mariana de Carvajal, while locating her within a literary religious context that includes the mystic poet Luisa de Carvajal y Mendoza, Sor Catalina de Jesús y San Francisco, and the beata María de Orozco y Luján. Sor Juana and these Iberian counterparts defended women's intellect, manipulated male readers, and criticized women's exclusion from education and justice.

The essays in the second section aim to help teachers familiarize students with the scientific and aesthetic aspects of this colonial Latin American woman's ways of knowing through readings of Sor Juana's poetry as the culmination of the baroque system of signifying tropes. Catherine M. Bryan perceives the poet's prefiguring of feminist studies of visual culture by bringing together the two sonnets "Este, que ves, engaño colorido" ("These lying pigments facing you" [Trueblood 95]) and "Verde embeleso" ("Green allurement" [Trueblood 101]) with responses to her portraits. Through Donna Haraway's notion of "situated knowledge," Bryan illuminates Sor Juana's characteristically baroque preoccupation with the visual in terms of her feminist and colonial consciousness.

Tamara Harvey's trans-American and transatlantic comparison between Sor Juana and other "exceptional" women writers of her time, many of whom were referred to as the "tenth muse," delineates the ways in which Sor Juana and other European and American intellectual women called into question the masculinist, imperial, scientifically objectifying conceptualizations of early modern philosophy. Using the framework of "semantic fields," the next contributor, Rocío Quispe-Agnoli, focuses on Sor Juana's self-fashioning and the topic of fame to make the author's figurative language accessible to students who are confronted with the technical challenge of her poetry for the first time.

Elias L. Rivers's essay offers an introduction to the figurative intricacy of Sor Juana's poetic narration of her epistemological struggle to understand the world in rational terms in *Primero sueño* ("First Dream"). Awareness of Sor Juana's study of scientific, mythological, and theological texts from classical antiquity to seventeenth-century European thought, as well as the *Answer*'s accounts of Sor Juana's keen desire to understand common phenomena, informs this guide to the language, symbols, imagery, and themes of Sor Juana's lyric flight of imagination. Rivers's essay clearly demonstrates that Sor Juana's representation of the transgressive striving of a gender-neutral human mind is as fundamentally feminist a gesture as the *Answer*.

As intellectually challenging as the *Dream*, the *Allegorical Neptune* is an ideal vehicle for studying Sor Juana as a colonial baroque writer. Verónica Grossi explores the central function of allegory with regard to theatricality, interrelations among the arts, and the hybrid nature of seventeenth-century cultural discourses. As Grossi points out, the *Neptune* (1680) is key to understanding the allegorical meanings of Sor Juana's later works, her place in the viceregal court, and the baroque in New Spain. It not only inaugurates her intellectual project but also signifies her triumphal entrance into the public, male-dominated space of fame.

In the section on genre, three essays focus on theater, a form closely linked to Sor Juana's participation in public spaces. First, having translated and adapted Sor Juana's *Los empeños de una casa* as *House of Desires* for the Royal Shakespeare Company, Catherine Boyle traces the development of dramatic language from page to stage, from original text to translation, adaptation, and performance. She provides students with a method of reading that unlocks a series of meanings and performance possibilities. Her account of staging the play unpacks Sor Juana's destabilization of the gendered theatrical conventions of desire and honor.

In the context of a twentieth-century Latin American theater course (in English), Gwendolyn Alker explains that Sor Juana's *loas* are liminal texts that give students a historical sense of *mestizaje* ("racial miscegenation") and creolization in Mexican culture and performance. As an account of the classroom experience, the essay highlights how to teach the subversive possibilities of dramatic composition in a regimented political climate. Kathryn Joy McKnight discusses a Spanish graduate-level research-methods course that considers how Sor Juana challenges existing social and dramatic conventions in *The House of Trials* through the lens of the combined theoretical frameworks of cultural materialism and feminist criticism. Students can apply to other literary and cultural arenas the skills gained in this course: an understanding of the broad textual concept of conventions, how they are embedded in hegemonic discourses, and how authors creatively manipulate these conventions.

Sor Juana undermines literary tradition with particular wit and humor in her poetry. Petrarchism, an authorizing discourse for empire and patriarchy, for instance, became in Sor Juana's hands a platform for critiquing the authorized portrayal of women. Lisa Rabin presents the lyric portrait of Lisarda in the *ovillejos* as an example of the baroque exposé of worn-out, objectifying Petrarchan conventions. Rabin argues that Sor Juana's belatedness to Petrarchan tradition affords her an opportunity for agency, allowing the appropriation of the colonial baroque in the "New World" as a new space for poetry. Daniel P. Hunt's collaborative exercises in translation, paraphrasing, retranslation, and structural analysis of tropes from English back to Spanish assist students in unraveling the complexity of Sor Juana's baroque poetic syntax. His accompanying *PowerPoint* presentations graphically illustrate structures of allusion and conceit in samples of her verse, as well as alert students to the trap of reducing the inherent multivalence of metaphor to any univocal, authorized reading.

Undoubtedly, the most famously unauthorized text of Sor Juana was the *Answer*, one of the earliest and most powerful defenses of women's right to intellectual pursuits. When she writes back to the bishop of Puebla, she privileges her authority over his. Rosa Perelmuter argues that "Sor Filotea's" harsh criticism required a witty but effective response to prove Sor Juana's innocence. While playing along with the fiction of a "sisterly" warning, Sor Juana negotiated authority through letters, a privileged genre for philosophical debate. Perelmuter's essay maps how in the *Answer* Sor Juana uses juridical rhetoric, with its traditional sequence of sections and the disguise of a familiar letter, a learned but disarming humanistic genre.

Nina M. Scott's essay examines the recent discovery of letters and other archival materials by and about Sor Juana that have generated much speculation and controversy regarding her last years. Her ironic defiance in a letter written to her confessor ten years before the *Respuesta*; account books recording her illegal, lucrative investments of convent funds; and an inventory of books and manuscripts in Sor Juana's cell after her death challenge the image of submissive "model nun." With this background, instructors can bring their knowledge of biographical and historical issues up to date. Instructors who wish to pursue Sor Juana's silences in the *First Dream* and the *Answer* while also respecting the irreducible otherness of retreat face a formidable challenge. Geoff Guevara-Geer's articulation of this paradox offers methods of familiarizing students with notions of reading lapses, ellipsis, and withdrawals.

The last section of essays bridges the gap between the seventeenth and twenty-first centuries. It opens new perspectives using theories of gender and sexualities, visual culture and technology, food, and music. Addressing questions of lesbian sexuality in Sor Juana's poetry, Amanda Powell proposes ways to correct previous baffled, prurient, or appropriating—and usually anachronistic—critical treatments that have been (mis)applied to those love poems that Sor Juana wrote specifically to women. The essay contextualizes these brilliant displays of poetic conventions of the period that are written in the framework of a seventeenth-century pan-European fashion for sapphic poetry while analyzing their challenge to heterosexist and gendered paradigms that work to objectify and silence women on the page and in society.

Visual materials, especially those found on the Internet, can make Sor Juana's work more accessible. Mariselle Meléndez discusses the skills needed to critically analyze visual culture in order to demonstrate how images have been historically used to communicate knowledge. As Sor Juana pointed out, visual representation is always a reconstruction of what we would like to see; the technologies of film and the Internet provide even greater potential for such deception and distortion but can also open up new perspectives for pedagogical practices and critical interpretations.

Sor Juana forges gendered links between physicality and scientific inquiry, in opposition to the dominant seventeenth-century split between mind and body; the heightened awareness of this duality is a central theme of both the

Respuesta and *Primero sueño*. John A. Ochoa considers material culture, and especially Sor Juana's literary and philosophical use of food and cooking, as tropes. While outlining methods of avoiding anachronism, he transforms the classroom into a "laboratory" with a set of effective classroom opportunities, taking advantage of recent illustrated cookbooks with updated recipes from conventual archives.

Mario A. Ortiz's two-pronged essay examines both the use that Sor Juana made of music in her work and the ways in which her work has been set to music. Sor Juana draws extensively on early modern cosmology, which depended heavily on music as a structuring metaphor. Ortiz draws on his musicological training to develop active exercises that make that imagery accessible to students without a technical background. In addition, he discusses her *villancicos* ("carols") as lyrics intended for music written by composers from her time to ours.

Emily Hind's cultural critique of popular usages of Sor Juana reveals the irony of the gender-neutral, nonthreatening twentieth- and twenty-first-century image in the light of the poet's dissatisfaction with the limitations imposed by gender. Hind foregrounds the gendered contexts in which Sor Juana, constituted as an icon, continues to be circulated in contemporary Mexican popular culture, as unique and isolated now as in her own time. Sara Poot-Herrera's essay finds Sor Juana's work woven into the very texture of twentieth- and twenty-first-century Mexican women's and Chicana writing. Her voice resonates not only in the writings of the many women authors who have converted the Mexican nun into a literary character but also in the productions of artists who have represented and interpreted her in music, painting, film, theater, collage, and performances of various types.

While we have arranged the essays according to topics that lend themselves easily to preparation for teaching and study, it is possible to frame the groupings by other conceptual categories. Lavrin and Scott shed light on questions of institutional authority: Lavrin in terms of political authority and Scott regarding newly discovered documents that can change our view of Sor Juana's relationship to her ecclestiastical superiors. Eich, Kirk, and Wray provide a context for Sor Juana's religious life and theological exegeses. Arenal, Bryan, Eich, Harvey, and Vollendorf explore the depth and breadth of a female intellectual tradition that positions Sor Juana both among her foremothers and as a foremother to us. A related theme, that of connections among women, shapes Powell's piece, as well as Eich's. Powell and Rabin describe how the poet writes as a woman against the grain of Petrarchism. Comparing and contrasting the European and the colonial baroque, Grossi, Merrim, and Martínez–San Miguel explore ways in which the periphery rewrites the metropolis. Martínez–San Miguel and Vollendorf expose the possibilities and limitations of the transatlantic approach in the baroque. Another series of essays can be constructed around the topic of "Mexicanness": Hind's, Lavrin's, Merrim's, Ochoa's, and Poot-Herrera's essays treat aspects of nationalizing discourses. Lavrin, Merrim, and Ochoa refer to the colonial period, whereas Hind and Poot-Herrera trace the uses of Sor Juana as icon in twentieth- and twenty-first-century Mexican and Chicana pop and "high" culture. Bryan and Meléndez elaborate the possibilities of reading texts against interpretations of visual imagery. Alker, Boyle, Bryan, Grossi, Guevara-Geer, Hunt, Quispe-Agnoli, Rivers, Perelmuter, and Wray examine how specific texts inscribe feminine colonial subjectivity. A specific focus on teaching practices shapes the essays by Hunt, McKnight, Meléndez, Ochoa, Ortiz, and Quispe-Agnoli.

BACKGROUNDS: GENDER, POWER, AND RELIGION IN COLONIAL SOCIETY

Seventeenth-Century New Spain: A Historical Overview

Asunción Lavrin

Sor Juana Inés de la Cruz lived at the height of New Spain's viceregal period. Seventeenth-century Mexico City had evolved from the Tenochtitlán of 1521 into a populous town with rectangular plazas, impressive administrative buildings, and numerous sumptuous churches. In the 1620s some canals that had traversed the Aztec capital still carried traffic to certain areas of the metropolis. A wealthy city, in which the rich competed among themselves to live an ostentatious life, it also had poor quarters for the Indians. Its population comprised an increasing number of persons of mixed blood (*castas*) and poor whites who, along with the Indians, served in a myriad of occupations.

The capital was the political and commercial heart of a society that was largely agricultural in its central and southern areas and that had a vast semiarid but mineral-rich northern territory. The cities of Puebla, Morelia, and Querétaro marked the boundaries of El Bajío, the rich agricultural basin that fed the capital city. Guanajuato, Zacatecas, and San Luis Potosí were hubs that channeled the yield of mining towns such as Fresnillo, Sombrerete, Real de Catorce, and Parral. The wealth of the mines was the backbone of the export economy. Silver bars or coined treasure traveled to Spain in fleets departing from Veracruz at irregular intervals. Some of the wealth stayed in the viceroyalty and sustained a social elite constantly seeking its own aggrandizement through appropriate marital alliances and investments in land and commerce.

Economically and socially, towns dominated the rural areas because they were home to the administrative structures essential to putting into effect policies dictated by the peninsular bureaucracy. Mexico City, which acted as a magnet attracting people and wealth from the provinces, was the site of the only archbishopric in the realm and of one of the two appellate courts (*audiencias*) deciding the most important legal suits. The university and several of the colleges established by the religious orders, as well as the most important printing presses, also made it the intellectual heart of the kingdom.

The roots of a Mexican identity began to appear in the mid–seventeenth century, when a growing consciousness emerged among the elite born in the New World that those coming from the peninsula did not share their customs and regard for the land in which they were born. But there was more to New Spain than the nascent feeling of being "*americanos*" or "criollos." Along with Peru, the Mexican colony was one of the two most important possessions of the Spanish crown in the New World. As such, its wealth and productivity were of the greatest concern for those who ruled it and for those who controlled the key mechanisms of its economy, such as miners, merchants, and landowners. It was almost "natural" that an exceptional woman, such as Sor Juana, born in a small town, would feel the need to travel to the capital where all material and intellectual resources were shared by a small and influential elite.

The indigenous peoples were declared subjects of the king, and they carried out most of the burden of agricultural labor, as well as tasks in the public works, as part of their obligation to pay a head tax either in cash or labor. Having assumed that the indigenous peoples' conversion to Christianity had taken place in the previous century, many churchmen were concerned about the depth and nature of their beliefs. Early in the seventeenth century ecclesiastical investigations had unearthed examples of idolatry still found among some indigenous populations, and it was feared they had not assimilated Christianity as Spaniards practiced it. Despite the alarm created in some minds by these findings, most of the Indian population adhered to Catholicism, at least to its formal public rituals.

Population and Social Hierarchies

To a foreign eye, the most fascinating feature of New Spain was its racial diversity. By mid–seventeenth century the population was a mixture of Indian, Spanish, and African unlike any in Europe. Since the early sixteenth century male Spaniards had mixed with Indian women, producing the first mestizos/as of both races. With the introduction of Africans—mostly slaves—the demography of race mixture began to take a complex route, producing a mosaic of human types eventually known as *castas*. The presence of Africans and their descendants in some key cities of the viceroyalty and the coastal areas of the Pacific and the Gulf of Mexico was significant.

Another important demographic change that took place in the sixteenth century affected the makeup of the population in the seventeenth: a series of lethal pandemics reduced the indigenous populations significantly in the core geographic areas of the viceroyalty. By the middle of the seventeenth century the indigenous population began to grow again, and, while it never regained its preconquest levels, it remained the largest portion of the population. Areas such as Oaxaca and Yucatán were largely Indian. Spanish migration to New Spain continued to strengthen the elite ranks, but Spaniards never achieved the numerical momentum to form more than a slim layer at the top of the social pyramid. Only full-blooded Indians who could claim to have belonged to the ruling elite of native societies were acknowledged in the top layers of society, albeit at a lower level than the white elite.

Spaniards or their descendants and elite Indians kept their distance from each other in the seventeenth century. The period of advantageous alliances between conquering Spaniards and the female indigenous nobility had ended by the last quarter of the sixteenth century. Spaniards found themselves surrounded by a growing number of *castas*, which in urban areas formed the bulk of the working masses. After several generations, those of Spanish descent born in the New World began to acquire a sense of their own identity, calling themselves either *americanos* or criollos. This subtle sense of separateness in the seventeenth century did not create a perceivable political or social rift among people of Spanish descent. Below them in rural and agricultural areas, *castas* and Indians worked alongside African slaves. In short, the population of New Spain was a vast tapestry woven with multicolored threads.

The social consequence of *mestizaje* (racial miscegenation) was the acknowledged ranking of people by color and descent. Because the many racial mixtures had often occurred out of wedlock, the issue of legitimacy of birth was added to that of Spanish lineage (*linaje*) to create a society that placed Spaniards and their descendants in control of the government, ecclesiastical hierarchy, sources of wealth accumulation in trade, and ownership of large estates. The concept of lineage translated into *hidalguía*, or privileged birth. The seventeenth-century elite was built on the consciousness of "purity of blood" (*limpieza de sangre*) and unblemished Spanish descent, which separated the endogamous few from the heterogeneous plebeians in the middle and lower rungs of society. Legitimacy of birth, however, was not race-bound. Plebeians also had a clear sense that a necessary sign of social distinction was to be born in wedlock, as the church prescribed, and they strove to provide their children with that marker as a symbol of compliance with human and religious laws. What this meant for Juana Inés de la Cruz is clear. She was free from any racial admixtures, but, being born out of wedlock, she had something in common with the many whose parentage was certainly not prestigious. This was a fact that had to be discreetly ignored among the viceregal circles in which she moved, as it was for many others—male and female—who had talent or education to offer in exchange. At her religious profession her "defect of birth" was covered with a fictive lineage. A few nuns in that century were allowed to profess despite having born out of wedlock, being the daughters of powerful men whose influence gained them entrance to the convent.

The Ruling Order

The administration of this part of the Spanish empire had consolidated into an imperial bureaucracy with distinct features and traditions. At its top was a viceroy, appointed by the king of Spain and given a significant amount of power to guarantee the fulfillment of the law and the integrity of the royal power that he represented. Justice and the administration of royal policies were in charge of the *audiencias*, whose judges (*oidores*) and attorneys constituted the highest appellate court of the viceroyalty. Throughout the seventeenth century, the aspiring American-born elite began to claim the government of towns as well as appointments to the lower bureaucracy. Appointees for the highest posts came from Spain, including nearly all the bishops and archbishops. Posts in the *audiencias*, however, became available to distinguished criollos; by the end of the century such posts were in the hands of high bidders who paid the crown handsome sums. As scions of wealthy families, Creole men used landownership and the church as their main venues for social mobility. At the municipal level, the sale of offices initiated by Phillip III resulted in channeling those offices into the hands of those who were American-born and whose social prestige was thus enhanced by an informal system of defense that entitled them to raise small militias, bear arms, and call themselves captains.

Indigenous communities had administrations parallel to the Spanish elite, which were also adapted from Spanish models. Through self-government they maintained a considerable degree of social cohesiveness and autonomy in making decisions that affected them at the local level. They retained their own governors and confraternities, but by the seventeenth century the schools founded for them by eager Franciscans in the early years of Christianization had been reduced to a shadow of their earlier selves. For religious purposes indigenous people remained under close supervision of the church, largely represented by the mendicant orders that had undertaken their conversion in the sixteenth century. The secular church, however, was beginning to take a great interest in the Indians and struggled for power with the orders to influence the spiritual life of the Indians. The non-Indian urban population was largely under the ministry of the secular church, although the Jesuits became important spiritual advisers and were held in great esteem as intellectuals. Dominicans and Augustinians competed with Jesuits to provide higher education.

New Spain as a Polity

Spain was a belligerent and powerful state in seventeenth-century Europe. Its wealth in the New World and political stance in a Europe divided by wars of religion attracted enemies to the smaller islands of the Caribbean, from which they raided the coasts of New Spain. The viceroyalty suffered the attacks of pirates interested in snatching the contents of the Seville-bound fleets laden with silver bars, minted coins, and jewels. Throughout the seventeenth century, the coasts of the Gulf of Mexico were vulnerable to such attacks, although pirates were unable to stop the international traffic or make any inroads into the settled areas of the continent. Veracruz was defended by the castle of San Juan de Ulúa, while smaller guard vessels did their best to strengthen the presence of the Spanish flag between Yucatán and the mouth of the Mississippi. New Spain protected Florida and Cuba to safeguard its own shores. On the Pacific coast, the town of Acapulco served as the entrepôt center for trade with the Orient, the source of the silks and luxury items that were in great demand among the well-to-do population.

Throughout the seventeenth century, New Spain expanded its frontier northward, in an effort to establish a firm foothold in the remoter areas of New Vizcaya, Coahuila, New Mexico, and Baja California. The north offered rewards with the discovery of silver mines, but beyond the possibility of finding new sources of mineral wealth was the stark reality of having to defend outlying areas from raids of nomadic or seminomadic tribal Indians who constantly attacked the mining towns. Colonizing the far north was slow and dangerous; the establishment of settlers in the Rio Grande basin was subverted by a general Pueblo rebellion in 1680 that pushed back the settlement effort for another decade. New Mexico was "recolonized" in 1693, although there were further disturbances in subsequent years. The Jesuits and Franciscans undertook the conversion of the "wild" north, reenacting to some extent the missionary activities of the sixteenth century. A system of presidios, a combination of military and religious establishments, began to be put in place in the last decades of the century.

Religion and Piety

The Virgin Mary, as an icon known as Guadalupe, was presumed to have appeared to an Indian sometime in the mid–sixteenth century. The seventeenth century witnessed the expansion of the devotion of the Virgin of Guadalupe and the strengthening of Catholic piety. It was in this period that the story of the apparition took root, laying the foundation for her consolidation as the patron of Mexico in 1747. The origins of the devotion are muddled and subject to much critical historical review. After 1629, when Guadalupe was believed to have helped to relieve Mexico City of a severe flood, worship of her began to grow. In 1648 Miguel Sánchez, a secular priest, wrote the first narrative of the apparition, dating it in 1531. In 1649, Luis Laso de la Vega, the friar of a shrine erected to Guadalupe, wrote her story in Nahuatl (Sousa, Poole, and Lockhart). It has been argued that Guadalupean worship was mainly developed among Creoles, not Indians. However, during the seventeenth century her popularity continued to grow among all ethnic groups and social classes.

Other Marian icons shared the attention of the worshippers. Our Lady of the Rosary was among the most popular, but shrines devoted to local worship of special images of saints and the passion of Christ were widespread throughout Mexico. Most towns had several favorite sites of worship, and the most important pictorial production was of religious images. This was a century of uncontested piety, expressed in a variety of ways: public processions; the foundation of confraternities to support religious feasts; donation of money for masses for the souls of the dead; and pious deeds that established churches, nunneries, and monasteries. The Holy Office of the Inquisition had been introduced in New Spain in 1571 to ensure orthodoxy in the practice of Catholic religion and to prosecute any breach in the observance of the sacrments. In addition to blasphemy, sorcery, solicitation of sexual favors, and bigamy—charges aimed at the non-Indian population—the Inquisition surveyed the activities of Jewish converts (new Christians). When they relapsed into non-Christian practices, which some did, the Inquisition initiated processes to expose them and obtain their return to the "true faith." The pursuit of Judaizers increased in the early years of the century. Between 1600 and 1649, the date of a large auto-da-fé, the Inquisition ordered the execution of fifty persons accused of practicing Judaism. Sor Juana Inés de la Cruz was concerned that one of her works—the *Carta atenagórica* ("Letter Worthy of Athena")—would bring her problems with the Inquisition for unorthodox statements. Throughout this century, the Holy Office exercised strict control of the philosophical and theological content of books published in New Spain. Indigenous peoples were exempted from its surveillance, but the *Provisorato de Indios*, a special religious court, was responsible for judging Indian loyalty to the Catholic Church.

In general, the church maintained strict control over the faith of most inhabitants of New Spain. The cathedrals of Mexico, Puebla, Guadalajara, and other key cities of New Spain were refurbished and maintained with pious deeds. Thirty-five female convents were founded between 1540 and 1700 to channel the religious vocation of hundreds of women. Bishops and the archbishop of Mexico held enormous prestige among the population and became conscious of their power in several confrontations with the authorities or with members of the regular church. The foundation of nunneries incorporated hundreds of women who aspired to live totally dedicated to their faith. The first foundation dates to 1540, when the Order of the Conception opened a convent in Mexico City. Transplanted from Spain, it was one of the leading female orders. Franciscans and Dominicans followed shortly thereafter with foundations in 1576 and 1593. The Convent of San Jerónimo and Santa Paula, where Sor Juana professed, was founded in 1585. The reformation of the Carmelite order by Teresa of Ávila, her death in 1582, and her canonization in 1622 imparted greater prestige to female religious life in Spain. In Mexico, the Carmelite order was approved by papal bull in 1615.

Cities measured their rank by the number of convents founded. Counter-Reformation spirituality encouraged the cloistering of women dedicated to God as brides of Christ. The renunciation of the world and its vanities to search for personal salvation and pray for the rest of humanity was held as the highest form of female spirituality and as a more perfect state than marriage. Nuns were regarded as chosen women who commanded personal and social respect as well as veneration. Throughout the seventeenth century several of them elicited such profound admiration that after their death their followers initiated a process to achieve their beatification, the first step toward canonization; however, none reached that goal. Although Sor Juana was not the type of pious nun who could be nominated, she was nevertheless admired for her literary and intellectual talents.

In New Spain, the daughters and granddaughters of conquistadors and first settlers found themselves in a society in which violence was still real and in which sometimes the option of a good marriage with social equals was not feasible. The lack of suitable spouses, poverty, loss of parents, and the high price of marriage dowries were noted by patrons and founders of convents. These institutions became places to shelter and protect women of Spanish descent, as well as to satisfy their spiritual need to follow a religious life.

Men and women who donated significant amounts of money or property to promote the foundation of a convent were often people of means, although small donors helped solidify many a foundation. In general, large donors—miners, landowners, and merchants with a solid fortune—believed that their patronage helped save their souls. They also believed that nunneries were signs of great spirituality and enhanced the social standing of their families. Often they received special privileges for their patronage, such as the right to be interred in the nunnery's church or the admission of female relatives to the cloister. Some convents had several female members of the same family.

Women played a key role in founding convents; they were patrons of fourteen of the convents founded between 1600 and 1700 in the viceroyalty. The founder of the Convent of San Jerónimo, Isabel de Guevara, for example, obtained papal approval and, with the help of her mother and brother, not only bought the house that would shelter the nuns but also spent over twenty thousand pesos to provide it with all the required furnishings.

Governance and Social Restlessness in Seventeenth-Century Mexico

Loyalty to the Spanish monarchy was unquestioned, but there were many sources of social and economic unrest. Serious problems of governance arose in the seventeenth century, caused by gaps among rich and poor, by the suspicion of the elite toward the *mestizos/as* in their midst, by acknowledged corrupt practices of the members of the bureaucracy, and by struggles for power among members of different branches of government and between lay and ecclesiastical authorities. Around 1612, rumors of a conspiracy of slaves created fear among the authorities of Mexico City; several slaves were hanged. The slave trade continued to add numbers to the labor pools of domestic service in the capital and of the mining and agricultural industries elsewhere. Potential slave rebellions in the rural areas were often squelched when the authorities reached deals that allowed the resettlement of rebels in free towns. Africans and their descendants continued to mix with the rest of the population, and the slave trade declined. The numbers of people of African descent living in Mexico would decline precipitously in the ensuing century.

Spurred by poverty and periodic problems with the corn supply created by droughts, the feeling of marginalization predominant in the majority of the population grew, especially in the cities. Several confrontations among members of the upper classes had an effect on the poorer classes in the capital. Taking sides with one faction or the other allowed those at the social bottom to vent pent-up emotions at a time when "subjects" had little choice but to obey their superiors. During the tenure of Viceroy Diego Pimentel y Enriquez, Marquis of Gelves, the antagonism among the *audiencia*, the archbishop of Mexico, and the viceroy reached a height not witnessed before. Driven by a sense of strict adherence to the law, the marquis carried out a campaign to clean up corruption in the collection of taxes, a move that created resentment among those involved, who were numerous. He also antagonized the archbishop of Mexico, Juan Pérez de la Serna, over matters of treatment of the American-born officials and engaged in conflicts over the jurisdictional powers of viceroy and bishop. A storm about the primacy of the secular over the ecclesiastical arm in matters of governance broke out in 1624, when the viceroy expelled the archbishop from Mexico and ordered that he be deported to Spain; the viceroy also ordered members of the *audiencia* incarcerated. This incident provoked a riot in the city that ended with the deposition of the viceroy by the *audiencia* and left seventy people dead.

Discord among some viceroys, archbishops, and members of the *audiencia* took many shapes throughout the century. The arrival in 1640 of Juan de Palafox y Mendoza as visitator general of New Spain, later bishop of Puebla, and, for a short period, interim viceroy of Mexico had political consequences and created social unrest. Palafox antagonized not only the two viceroys, the Duke of Escalona and the Marquis of Salvatierra, over corruption but also the mendicant orders over control of the indigenous parishes. He was also involved in triggering the most extensive investigation of crypto-Jews in New Spain, in 1642. And he provoked the hostility of the Jesuits over theological and economic issues, seeking to collect tithes from their rural estates. The protracted bickering among the magistrates caused several incidents of public rioting, which obliged the bishop to retreat from public view for some months.

The last and best-known public expression of disorderly unrest in the century took place in 1692. It was significant enough to have involved the savant Carlos de Sigüenza y Góngora, a close friend of Sor Juana's: he struggled to save materials from the burning viceregal palace. The incident took place three years before Sor Juana's death, so she was surely aware of the situation. That year, the price of corn had risen astronomically because of prolonged droughts.

When the restless urban poor began to attack the viceregal palace and the residence of the archbishop, they voiced their dislike of the Spaniards at the helm. In June 1692, a mixed crowd of Indians, *castas,* and whites became incensed by the refusal of both the bishop and Gaspar de la Cerda Sandoval Silva y Mendoza, Count of Galve to pay attention to their demands. Clerical authorities were unable to contain the people, and the viceroy had to escape the viceregal palace. Looting and fire caused panic for several days. In the end, however, this headless revolt had little impact on the rule of the city. Fifteen people were sentenced to death, and public order was restored.

As the century closed, the rule of the house of Habsburg, the most brilliant of Spanish history, saw its demise. With the death of Charles II in 1700 without royal issue, Spain became involved in a war of succession that resulted in the advent of one branch of the French Bourbons to the throne. For New Spain, this remarkable century represented its midcolonial period, a century in which the profile of its population, nature of governance, character of religiosity, and expression of arts and letters became unique, stamping the history of Mexico with an identity of its own.

Sor Juana and Company: Intellectuals and Early Feminists

Electa Arenal

Underlying my teaching is the view of Sor Juana Inés de la Cruz as a product of one of the most culturally diverse places in the world of her time. To help students examine facets of the milieu that nurtured the blossoming of her intense drive and curiosity, I emphasize the variety of locations and communities in which she lived—farm, court, convent—as well as her self-education in philosophy, theology, and letters. Striving to accumulate, remember, and speculate on as much ancient and contemporary knowledge as she could, the young scholar kept in her sights such figures as Homer and Aristotle, King David and Saint Jerome, and the women who surrounded them. At the same time, she studied and wrote in a climate of magnanimous admiration and support on the one hand and of envious and threatening opprobrium on the other. As students become aware of this dramatic wealth of connection, it also becomes plausible to them that Sor Juana's precocious gifts flowered, perhaps precisely because of the multicultural environment in which the frivolities of the court and the orthodox strictures of the church exercised fewer limits on her development than they might have in Europe or in other historical periods.

Thinker, poet, and playwright, Sor Juana displayed a subtle gender consciousness forged from experience and book learning. She began to read in early childhood, avidly gaining an informal education grounded in the Latin classics (including translations from the Greek) she found in her grandfather's library. She grew up in the valley of the snow-capped Popocatepetl volcano not far from Mexico City, hearing Nahuatl and the African accents of enslaved laborers and keenly aware of notions of legitimacy and difference. Her situation as a colonial subject and a Creole woman born out of wedlock afforded her perspectives from the margins that she used to great advantage. As a servant to the innermost chambers of the governing viceroyalty and the church, Sor Juana gained insight into the intricacies of sociohistorical constructions of gender, and, as a precocious learner and composer of verses, she evolved a critique that permeates all of her work and that strikes us as modern.

That she possessed a room of her own and was exempt from having to provide for most of her daily needs was not merely incidental; these have been requisite preconditions that, for many learned males, have been generally taken for granted. In her own library, one of the most extensive in the Western hemisphere at the time, she tirelessly consulted dozens of works, engaging in "reading and still more reading, study and still more study, with no teacher besides my books themselves" (Arenal and Powell 53). What this autodidact lost in personal instruction, she gained in independence of thought and rhetorical strategies. She tells us, "what I do not understand in one author . . . I usually understand in another author who treats what appears to be a very distant subject" (Arenal and Powell 59). Often she would cite opposing representations and opinions that accorded with her needs and circumstances and reframe arguments, gradually confounding readers into ceding textual authority to her, by "engineering in her own writings to be [as] multiple and unseizable" as a literary artist (Merrim, "Hemispheric" 1).

From wide-ranging if solitary studies, a privileged imagination, and acute observations of reality, she culled a keen sense of the prevailing disparagement of women, especially of their minds. The young prodigy grew into a strong feminist and a precursor of the scientific and philosophical paradigm shifts known as the Enlightenment. Reason was her guide. In keeping with the sensibility of her time, her elegant projections of the mind's faculties were baroque in style and figuration. She employed parable, allegory, and the language of mythology to deride misogynist and other sorts of ignorance and narrow-mindedness, and to praise audacity and the free expression of opinion.

One highly effective focus for organizing class sessions to encompass these elements, present throughout her work, is to underscore the gendered sensibility that she displayed in such writings as her satirical ballad "Hombres necios" ("You foolish men"). With students, I contextualize that poem among major feminist responses to the *querelle des femmes*, for example, those by Christine de Pizan and Tullia d'Aragona. In the *Respuesta a sor Filotea* ("The Answer to Sor Filotea"), Sor Juana herself authorizes her writing by citing distinguished female company and defending her theological *Carta atenagórica* ("Letter Worthy of Athena"), which set off a bitter polemic when it was published without her knowledge. Placing Sor Juana's *villancicos* (cycles of religious poetry that were sets of carols) in the similar context of the title pages added in the process of publication displays the contradictions she confronted as a poet and intellectual: while her religious poetry claims her right to learning in terms of the wisdom of the Virgin Mary and Saint Catherine of Alexandria, the title pages frame the poet as an anomaly. In teaching the *Primero sueño* ("First Dream"), I place this epistemological poem among the ambitious cosmological explorations of Anne Bradstreet and Margaret Cavendish. The less-familiar *Neptuno alegórico* (*Allegorical Neptune*) provides unique opportunities for students to research aspects of baroque visual culture and opens possibilities for reexamining and restructuring gendered hierarchies of knowledge in the academic settings in which we study Sor Juana and other women writers.

Pedagogical Strategies

The Woman of Wit and "Foolish Men"

In part because of its very popularity, "Hombres necios," as poem 92 is often called, is sometimes overlooked in critical studies of Sor Juana's poetry. Within its rhymed oppositions and musical form, the author deftly employs witty conceits, tongue-twisting repetitions of sounds, and other poetic devices to contest the sexual double standard. Playfully, she represents the social construction of gender arrangements; mocks childish, self-imposed male fears; defends sex workers; and ends by applying to men the very description used to indict women since the Middle Ages—in them "we have devil, flesh, and world: a man" (Arenal and Powell 159).[1]

Memorized from textbooks by many thousands of school children throughout the Hispanic world in the twentieth century, the poem commands attention. Students nod their heads in assent as they hear or read the first stanza: "You foolish and unreasoning men / who cast all blame on women, / not seeing you yourselves are cause / of the same faults you accuse" (Arenal and Powell 157). Its popularity may be owed "in part to the suppressed anger it reveals in women and the giddy catharsis (as a dispelling of guilt) it permits men" (Arenal and Powell 149). Its apparent simplicity, set to clever effect, makes it a potentially powerful agent of consciousness raising, self-reflection, and recognition of gender insensitivity beyond formal classroom settings.

Sor Juana and the *Querelle des Femmes*

The contemporary resonance of "Hombres necios" is closely linked to the intellectual daring of Sor Juana's feminism. I explore this link in breadth with a series of assigned readings, inviting students to follow the trajectory of the *querelle des femmes*, beginning with Christine de Pizan's spirited defense of her sex in her response to the misogynist *Roman de la rose*. In *Early Modern Women's Writing and Sor Juana Inés de la Cruz*, Stephanie Merrim demonstrates that the *Respuesta* must be included in any serious consideration of the *querelle*.[2] Sor Juana was not an isolated figure in the literary landscape, as we may note in the increasing number of studies in the United States and elsewhere of women writers of the early modern and other periods. Among many who protested allegedly "natural" and "universal" categories that served to exclude all of womankind and most of humanity, she was one of the most brilliant thinkers and outstanding poets.3 Studying the commonalities and divergences in the work of Anne Bradstreet and Sor Juana for my play "This life within me won't keep still" led me to extend the question to other writings of sixteenth- to eighteenth-century English- and Spanish-speaking religious women on both sides of the Atlantic in courses and sessions at conferences.

When the erudite Mexican poet is seen within a long tradition of scholarly women, a tradition she herself felt part of, it is easier to comprehend her frequent insistence, often laced with irony, on perceiving that women are as greatly endowed (if not better) with reason as men.

The sixteenth-century philosopher and poet Tullia d'Aragona (1510–56), author of the *Dialogo della Signora Tullia d'Aragona della infinità di amore* ([1547] *Dialogue on the Infinity of Love*), exemplifies this position. Elizabeth Pallitto addresses d'Aragona's "important but overlooked contribution to period debates on Neoplatonism and the 'questione della donna' (woman question)," asserting that the philosopher-poet's *Dialogue* "questions received ideas about the social and ontological status of women; reassigns the roles of body and soul, revising the position held by most Florentine Neoplatonists . . . and reexamines period interpretations of Plato's *Symposium*" ("Laura's Laurels" 34). While evidence that Sor Juana read the work of this earlier (proto)feminist is lacking, the two writers' strategies are strikingly similar. A century before Sor Juana's birth, d'Aragona responded in prose and verse to sixteenth-century debates regarding the "intellective, rational, and appetitive aptitudes of the souls of women . . . — that is, regarding whether they were fully human" (Pallitto, "Laura's Laurels" 56). The following lines from a poem in her *Rime*, dedicated to a friend, Piero Manelli, demonstrate d'Aragona's eager ambition and her dispute with the concept of female inferiority:

> Since (like you) by Nature I was wrought
> . . . .
> my dear Manelli, do you think the desire for honor
> was not given me as well—and capacity for lofty thought?
> . . . .
> that like you I labor, aspire to the firmament,
> and to leave my name renowned on earth. ("Laura's Laurels" 56)[4]

As I have observed, Sor Juana becomes less isolated, less a *rara avis*, when placed among the numerous other outstanding figures of the early modern period, including d'Aragona. Like many of them, she appropriated and subverted the style of eminent male predecessors, Petrarch and Vergil among them.

In a course I taught on Christine de Pizan, Sor Juana Inés de la Cruz, and Mary Wollstonecraft, the students, enthusiastic about being introduced to Christine's *The Book of the City of Ladies* (1403–04), Sor Juana's *Respuesta a sor Filotea de la Cruz* (1691), and Mary Wollstonecraft's *A Vindication of the Rights of Women* (1792), were nevertheless dismayed because they had never heard of these authors in their general humanities, philosophy, political science, and history courses. Seeking validation and redress, they eagerly undertook projects exploring the contours of the three writers' thought and their relation to other women and men of the fifteenth, seventeenth, and eighteenth centuries. The student researchers had difficulty engaging with Christine's piety and promotion of self-abnegation in marriage and her seeming acceptance of patriarchal insistence on women's purity and virtue. They were able, however, to appreciate her book's structure and allegorical conceits, since they contrasted the manner in which the three writers countered common misogynist slander against women through allegory, parody, satire, and revisionary exposition. Collaborative projects among students of various specializations and disciplines help acquaint them with the breadth and complexity of Sor Juana's thought and art. Relating her works to those of her contemporaries and of women writers of other times and countries constitutes a rich field for exploration in both graduate and undergraduate assignments.

Sor Juana as Veiled (Feminist) Theologian

Sor Juana repeatedly expressed exasperation at hearing "merits called faults"—that is, disrespect for intelligence and derision of women for the same qualities that were praised in men. Cloaking her complaints in complex allegory, she consistently countered power with knowledge, identifying with saints and sinners, students and sages, heavenly constellations and the metamorphosing symbols of scientific and esoteric wisdom. One of the studious Sor Juana's merits is to have been able to both rewrite and make intellectual history as she uncovered and (re)invented knowledge formations distinct from those of the patriarchal order. Vying with the city of lettered men, she located and mapped routes to knowledge through female lineages and circumvented male-dominated citadels.

The *Respuesta a sor Filotea de la Cruz*, her answer to the bishop of Puebla who wrote disguised as "Sister Filotea," creates a Chinese box puzzle. For centuries the bishop's epistolary prologue to her *Carta atenagórica* was interpreted as friendly, and her response to it taken at close to face value. Readers missed many of the exquisite intricacies of Sor Juana's multivalenced reply. She pokes at seemingly unchallengeable orthodoxies and then veils her jabs. In a rarely commented-on passage that follows a bold, anger-tinged declaration of the right to freedom of opinion, even in theological matters, Sor Juana promoted the pursuit of science with stark certainty.

Hiding her voice behind that of Juan Díaz de Arce, rector of the university, she tucks in the proscience remark almost parenthetically, between entirely orthodox praise of two Mexico City nuns. He reports that one of the nuns astonished people with her memory for scripture and the other thrilled listeners with biblical and liturgical readings and translations. Sor Juana observes, "y se duele de que tales talentos no se hubieran empleado en mayores estudios con principios científicos" ("and [Arce] grieves that such talents should not have been set to higher studies, guided by principles of science" [4: 469; Arenal and Powell 93]). Arce's Arenal and Powell daring assertion is followed by two protective moves. Sor Juana adds that he does not name the nuns, nor does she know these sisters, her contemporaries. Then she strategically returns to the theme of sacred letters and the permissibility of older women studying and teaching in private.

A few pages earlier she had affirmed: "yo no quiero ruido con el Santo Oficio" ("I want no trouble with the Holy Office" [4: 444; Arenal and Powell 47]). That very fear kept her, she tells us, from engaging in theological writing. The claim was only partly disingenuous; the poetic rhetorical forms in which she expressed religious concerns caused their theological arguments to be overlooked for centuries. Only at the end of the twentieth century did religious scholars, seminarians, and divinity schools begin to include in their curricula her *villancicos*; *autos sacramentales* (one-act Corpus Christi plays, especially *The Divine*

Narcissus); *loas* (short theatrical preludes to plays); and other poems and religious "exercises," in addition to the long prose critique of Antonio Vieira's sermon. Students of religion are now discovering how these texts constitute a body of feminist theology. Further studies of its wide scope may surprise us with the ecumenical—and, for some, controversial—inclusiveness of Sor Juana's religious ideas.

Using a variety of contemporary theoretical framings, comparative analyses of Sor Juana's writings and her critics will promote the mainstreaming of women's contributions to literature and the humanities in general, as well as richer readings of the work of many women writers.[5] Detailed analyses that include the gendered dimensions of men's and women's lives and works require larger, panoramic, and systemic views of culture, which will enable us to more finely trace the commonality of resistance to exclusion—repeatedly crushed, repeatedly renewed—that accompanies women's artistic expressions across the globe and across historical periods. Developing strategies; attempting to confound in the interest of escaping conformity; expressing doubt, grief, confidence, these writers become vocal critics of patriarchal culture. Through their works some of them stride into public spaces from which, through custom and rule, they have been banished. On this theme Sor Juana wrote telling lines in *El divino Narciso* (*The Divine Narcissus*).[6] She knew that:

> que acostumbrados insultos
> con dificultad se olvidan,
> no habiendo quien del discurso
> os esté siempre borrando
> con encontrados asuntos
> de diferentes recuerdos. (3: 82)
>
> insults to which we are accustomed
> are forgotten with difficulty
> in the absence of someone
> who from speech erases them
> with opposing matter [themes]
> different in residue. (my trans.)

Sor Juana made a different sense of the world and the words that express it by defining and placing women at the center of knowing and being.

Epistemology and *Primero sueño*

In her epistemological pursuits, Sor Juana was a disciple of Athanasius Kircher, the most prominent of the seventeenth-century Jesuits who attempted to pursue science without falling into heresy by devising a necessarily synchretic encyclopedism. Sor Juana charmingly but cautiously explained and defended her thirst for scientific knowledge in some of the more famous and often anthologized passages of *La respuesta* (*The Answer*). She had, some years before, in her major philosophical poem, *Primero sueño* ("First Dream"), given free rein to an imagination formed by the richest of visual and literary experiences. The poem creates a post-Cartesian compendium, a woman-centered epistemological quest of daunting ambition. It is "a Baroque concerto, a dialogue with the texts of its times and a prefiguring of twentieth-century modes" (Arenal qtd. in Merrim, *Feminist Perspectives* 8).

Reflecting and appropriating the rich structure of the emblematic engravings, paintings, and myths that were her everyday fare, Sor Juana moves from the female body to the cosmos and back. She elaborates, especially in the areas of optics and mechanics, her interest in new scientific inventions, empirical observation, methodologies, and modes of cataloging (Gaos; Pascual Buxó, " 'El sueño' "; León; Trabulse, "El universo"). In her chapter entitled "The New Prometheus," Merrim groups Sor Juana with Anne Bradstreet and Margaret Lucas Cavendish, showing how in distinct yet analogous ways these self-taught women revise the script for scaling the heights to steal the fire of the gods and goddesses (*Early Modern* 211–48). She also makes a convincing case for the emergence of feminism from outrage at the seventeenth-century reversals of sixteenth-century advances in intellectual tolerance and encouragement. Along with Sor Juana, among those involved in trying to remedy the educational crisis, Merrim includes Mary Ward, Bathsua Maken, Hannah Wooley, Mary Astell, Margaret Fell, Anna Maria van Schurman, Marie de Gournay, Poulain de La Barre, and María de Zayas (*Early Modern* 199–204).

The Baroque and the Visual in Sor Juana's *Neptuno alegórico*

It is extraordinary to have the opportunity to devote an entire semester to Sor Juana, and even rarer to focus on a single work, but the experience of a semester-long graduate course on Sor Juana's *Allegorical Neptune* demonstrated how valuable such an experience can be. One particular seminar challenged me to undertake cracking the codes of that compendium of seventeenth-century humanism. The graduate students and I divided up her erudite references to other authors. Each member of the class took major responsibility for twenty Latin citations. Besides turning into a valuable research methodology practicum, the course inspired the students to discover for themselves how the baroque intertwined verbal and visual culture. At the same time we began exploring how visual as well as verbal culture may have affected Sor Juana's intellectual and psychological gestalt. Study of the relations among emblematic iconography and literature, art, architecture, political rituals, and festivals including royal ceremonies and other public spectacles is essential to this exploration.

Graphic images were staple ingredients of the kitchen in which Sor Juana concocted her revised intellectual economy. Through her revitalizing interpretations of these images, in the *Neptune* and other works, she transformed symbolically rendered females into (potentially) real-world women, guides, leaders, speakers, teachers—all highly reasoning, contesting, and actualizing participants in history and society. Quill in hand, she was able to redraw the cosmos and the polis, in the decoration of an arch that would be on view for a short time and then dismantled, although the text describing and explaining it remains. The *Neptuno* thus transposes representations of material reality with symbolic images and then spirals, metamorphosing those Greco-Roman legendary images back into Sor Juana's own bustling Mexico City.

The Feminist *Villancicos*, Religious Verses Set to Music

The *Neptuno* was produced in 1680, at the height of Sor Juana's literary career. Ten years later, when Sor Juana reached her early forties, in the wake of increasing literary fame, and perhaps because of her success as convent treasurer, Sor Juana was gradually forced to behave in a manner more befitting a nun. Still, she continued to compose several important texts for events witnessed by a wide public audience, including her last and most blatantly feminist set of *villancicos*, those to Saint Catherine of Alexandria, sung in the presence of thousands of the faithful in the Cathedral of Oaxaca in 1691. With sections addressed to those from the most and the least educated levels of society, this paean to a woman's courageous perseverance, mental acuity, and ethical spirituality reached everyone in attendance.

The printed panegyrics that accompany the publication of these *villancicos* in Puebla exemplify the contradictions typical of ecclesial misogyny and show how, despite having provoked members of the reigning echelons of Catholic Mexico, Sor Juana continued to retain many friends in the church. With characteristically baroque hyperbole on the title page and in the dedication, supporters refer to her "erudición sin segunda y admirable entendimiento" (2: 431) ("peerless erudition and awe-inspiring intelligence" [my trans.]) and describe Sor Juana as a "Prodigio de la Naturaleza . . . Oráculo de toda la América . . . Mujer Fuerte" (2: 431) ("Prodigy of Nature, Oracle of all the Americas, Powerful Woman [my trans.]).[7]

By the time she found it necessary to keep a nearly total silence, Sor Juana had been writing for over twenty years and produced almost 1,000 pages of prose and verse, much of it sung and performed. Like other artists who embody their own time and place and yet transcend them, Sor Juana created works that provide keys to her own "baroque times in old Mexico" (Leonard) while inviting ever new readings.

Transforming the Academy with Sor Juana

The opportunity for my first contact with and fascination by Sor Juana came in the 1950s at Barnard, a women's college where one of our required courses was Man and His World. For many of us Spanish majors, her ideas stirred sympathies with the not-so-distant suffragist past. Sor Juana's notions regarding knowledge, being, and power do indeed make her a significant precursor to the field of women's studies and feminist research, but that fact could not be recognized, of course, before the second-wave women's movement emerged through the process of consciousness raising—that is, before the the field itself was established.

We all learned to contextualize differently through decades of teaching and research. Beginning in the early 1970s, with undisciplined and multidisciplinary discussions and debates raging, the search for lost and forgotten texts by women (and for more perspicacious readings of canonical figures such as Sor Juana, María de Zayas, Saint Teresa of Ávila, and Madre Castillo) helped many of us apply new directions in theory and engage in shaping the first women's studies courses (Arenal, "What Women Writers?"). While exploring Sor Juana's role as a feminist foremother, I am still increasingly impressed by the fluidity of her concepts of gender.

Almost three hundred years before the field we now call women's studies developed, Sor Juana presaged its emergence. Through delving into the texts themselves in seminars and other classrooms, we have scrutinized such topics as her ideas on women's history, her view of belief systems as a product of discourse, and her respect for creeds of earlier times and other peoples. In addition, her critiques of male violence (sexual, political, military) and praise of peace; self-fashioning as a teacher; reconceptualizations of motherhood, maternity, and birth and rejection of marriage; and gendered contradiction on the level of vocabulary and grammar have stimulated untold collaborative projects and individual scholarship.

Although women's history and culture are still an invisible framework in many critical works, courses, and textbooks, in others Sor Juana is now situated in the context of centuries of monastic women (founders, leaders, authors, musicians, artists, and advisers to kings and local communities); of other writers of the Spanish colonies, especially the Mexican and Peruvian viceroyalties; and of early modern European women writers, scientists, and artists.[8]

Most particularly, she emulated and parodied the stylistic conventions carried into and established during the Renaissance and baroque periods, as she projected herself and others through extremes and excess—hyperbolic heights and abject lows. If she was an "ignorant" woman (Arenal and Powell 47), and even, as she says in her final confession and retraction, "the most unworthy" (a locution common among monks and nuns), she also trumpeted her uniqueness, presenting herself in the guise of both female and male paragons of wisdom—Isis, Athena, Saint Catherine, Saint Thomas Aquinas, Mary, and Christ. This paradoxical rhetoric of humility and of arrogance mystifies many students and is a good entry point for teaching the past as multifariously different, as, in effect, another language.

Over the years I have found that many students are ultimately grateful to have been jolted into rethinking assumptions regarding progress and history and into reconsidering a gender ideology that became codified millennia ago as it traversed the globe with all the major religions. Understanding that variations of the same ideology still permeate daily life, especially in religio-social arenas, making some environments inhospitable to females with a penchant for learning—and comprehending their complicated intersection with race and class issues—takes time and teaching. That advances and regressions have been historically cyclical and anything but monolithic is also a concept that requires Socratic dialogue and learning. Sor Juana is always a good place to begin.

NOTES

I want to thank Kathleen Zane for skillful and laughter-filled editorial midwifery.

[1]A new edition of *The Answer / La respuesta*, edited by me and Amanda Powell, will be published in 2008.

[2]Merrim amplifies earlier views of the *querelle des femmes,* situating Sor Juana's *Respuesta* [1691] beside Marie de Gournay's *Egalité des homes et des femmes* ("The Equality of Men and Women") (1622) and *Grief des femmes* ("The Ladies' Grievance") (1626).

[3]See *Women Imagine Change: A Global Anthology of Women's Resistance from 600 B.C.E. to Present.* The editors DeLamotte, Meeker, and O'Barr and their collaborators document dozens of other voices. Albert Rabil and Margaret L. King's series The Other Voice in Early Modern Europe, published by the University of Chicago Press, focuses on the early modern period; over fourteen volumes have been published, with dozens more projected. In the Hispanic field anthologies of women playwrights and poets have begun to appear.

[4]Original: "Poi che mi die natura a voi simile / . . . / Non pensate ch'anc[h]or disio d'honore / Mi desse, & bei pensier, MANEL gentile? / . . . / . . . ch'anch'io / Fatico ognihor per appressarmi al Cielo, / E lasciar del mio nome in terra fama." The poem also appears in Pallitto, *Sweet Fire* 60–61.

[5]Among already published studies in these areas, see Merrim's *Feminist Perspectives* and *Early Modern Women's Writing*; Perelmuter, *Límites*, especially chapter 8; Bergmann, "Sor Juana"; Franco, *Plotting Women*; Arenal, "Monjas"; Castillo and Schweitzer's companion reader to their anthology, which includes an essay by Arenal and Martínez–San Miguel on Malinche, Guadalupe, and Sor Juana.

[6]This play has recently been receiving increased attention—in seminaries as a theological text—for its extraordinary appropriation of the myth of Narcissus to reallegorize the Christian sacrament of transubstantiation.

[7]On Sor Juana as "tenth muse" see Harvey, in this volume.

[8]See Arenal and Schlau on Hispanic nuns-authors from the fifteenth through eighteenth centuries; Sabat de Rivers ("Amarilis") on Sor Juana and Peruvian counterparts; Arenal and Martínez–San Miguel on Malinche, the Virgin of Guadalupe, and Sor Juana and the formation of Mexican identity; Merrim ("Hemispheric") on Sor Juana in the context of hemispheric colonial studies.

Power and Resistance in the Colonial Mexican Convent

Stephanie Kirk

To unravel the densely packed sociocultural moment in which Sor Juana wrote, we must leave aside the marginal role the convent plays in today's secular society and enter the fervid religious world of the Latin American baroque. Students need to become aware of the pivotal role the convent held in New Spain and to understand how the study of convent communities sheds light on the role of women in colonial Mexican society. For a sense of the size, location (in the center of the city), and grandeur of these spaces, I show images of convents in class.[1] The sheer number demonstrates their importance: during the colonial period, twenty-one—some of which housed hundreds of women—were founded in Mexico (Holler 5).

Once students have understood the centrality of the convent in New Spanish society, the next step is to make them aware of the nexus of conflicting gender ideologies that converged on this space. Nuns held an ambiguous and precarious role in society. As cloistered women they were the guardians of purity and the expiators of society's sins. As women, however, they were also the very incarnation of sin. I explain to my students the fragility of the border between Mary and Eve, between the virgin and the prostitute, in colonial Latin American gender ideology. An excellent point of departure for contextualizing the complex and conflicting web of ideologies that focused on the nun is the thirteenth-century papal edict *Periculoso*, which promulgated the first law to mandate universal enclosure for all women religious. The text is very short, and an excellent English translation is available (Makowski 135–36). Students need only read the opening paragraph, especially the first line, for a sense of the historical and cultural trajectory of the gender controls operating in the convents in Sor Juana's day: "Wishing to cast off the dangerous and abominable situation of certain nuns, who, casting off the reins of respectability and impudently abandoning nunnish modesty and the natural bashfulness of their sex, sometimes rove about outside of their monasteries" (Makowski 135). From this brief document, students are able to sense the fear of the uncontained female body that led the church to enclose religious women.[2] Ironically, once nuns were enclosed, however, the church was faced with the problem of its own making: there were many potentially sinful and dangerous female bodies confined together under the same roof without a normalizing male presence.

The ecclesiastical authorities' need to control the convent at all cost brings our discussion to the concepts of *holocausto* and *sacrificio*. The words *holocausto* (in its meaning of "burnt whole" from the Greek) and *sacrificio* are not perhaps the first words that come to mind when thinking about convent life in seventeenth-century New Spain. Yet these are two words that the church most frequently employed in dictating how to lead an exemplary life in the convent.[3] As symbolic concepts, they illuminate the ecclesiastical authorities' view of the model nun—one who denied self, mind, and body to give herself completely to God. The nun was encouraged to think of herself as both empty vessel and sacred offering and to engage in a type of living death, waiting for the moment when she would finally join her divine husband. My students are surprised to learn that Mexican clerics generated a huge number of didactic and proscriptive works, including manuals dictating convent behavior and inspirational religious biographies of exemplary nuns. These texts formed a discursive network that tried to impose tight controls on every aspect of convent behavior and to ensure that community life conformed to the exact specifications of the church. Carlos de Sigüenza y Góngora's *Paraíso occidental* ("Western Paradise") is an available primary-source text that elucidates for students the complex models of discourse and discipline that the authorities employed in their attempt to dictate nuns' behavior.[4] This text also exposes the untenable duality the nun's body held as both incarnation of sin and guardian of purity. Published in Mexico City in 1684, it tells the story of the founding of the convent of Jesús María. The author describes the importance of this foundation—the first in the New World—to the virtuous young women of Mexico City who were "longing with fevered anxiety to consecrate themselves to God in virginal holocaust" (57).[5] He also incorporates the biographies of nuns and other women in the convent into his history. Different factors come together to make this text compelling for students. His connection to Sor Juana, as her contemporary and friend, led to Sigüenza y Góngora's writing the now-lost eulogy, *Oración funébre* ("Funeral Oration"), upon her death (Paz, *Trampas* 89). Furthermore, *Paraíso occidental*, with its baroque excesses, allows students a glimpse into the mentalities of the time. Such glimpses can simultaneously provide a culture shock and entertain. In *Paraíso occidental* a sinful female body, exposed to the dangers inherent in the convents, is the subtext that emerges clearly, framed in the vehement rhetoric and metaphors of aberrance and illness typical of the baroque era.

Sigüenza y Góngora's history of the convent of Jesús María in Mexico City, written to commemorate its one-hundredth anniversary, is ostensibly a book written for women. In the "Prólogo al lector" Sigüenza y Góngora describes his aim: "to write a history of women for women" (45).[6] The book does indeed portray the lives of many women, incorporating the *vidas* ("lives") of various exemplary nuns and other figures associated with the convent to tell their stories. Kathleen Ross, however, describes how Sigüenza y Góngora manipulates and appropriates these texts to further his own ideological aims (151).[7] She warns us not to "accept at face value Sigüenza y Góngora's stated intention" (12) but instead advises an examination of "the different levels of discourse" on which the text operates (14). One of these levels of discourse constitutes a warning against what Ross calls "the dangers of female flesh and the need to securely control woman's desire" (11). Sigüenza y Góngora emphasizes that women are weak and mutually incite one another to deviate from the path of perfection. Consequently, he highlights the dichotomy of the convent: women are separated from society to conserve their purity yet are then susceptible to the bad influence of an all-female, weak-willed community. He counsels his reader to be aware of "the nature of a community of women, among whom there is always one who blinds herself with the light through a love of the shadows" (317). I encourage my students to think of this text, indeed to consider the mind-set of the ecclesiastical authorities, in terms of chiaroscuro, of light and shadows. Sigüenza y Góngora may tell tales of exemplary women but none is untouched by the trope of *escarmiento* or "chastising example" to convey the moral of his tale.

I assign only short sections of Sigüenza y Góngora's text to my students, since even advanced undergraduates may find the dense baroque prose difficult to decipher. However, taking students carefully through selections with an eye to reading the above-mentioned subtexts is worthwhile because it opens their eyes to the way in which this patriarchal society viewed the nun. Selections from book 2, which Sigüenza y Góngora dedicated in its entirety to the life of Madre Marina de la Cruz, work especially well in the classroom. In those pages he shows how the subject of this exemplary tale suffered for her faults, only to eventually emerge victorious on the path to the religious perfection that church authorities prescribed. In telling her tale, he stresses how the nun must be faithful to her heavenly husband and must not distract herself with secular affections, such as those with other nuns in the convent, thus highlighting one of the rhetorical mainstays the ecclesiastical authorities employed to control communities of religious women. Students can view an example of the textual excesses with which writers approached this topic in Sigüenza y Góngora's account of the death of Marina's twelve-year-old daughter (141–47). This young woman (or girl) had accompanied her mother into the convent she entered after being widowed for the second time, purportedly to fulfill a lifetime dream. The author rails against the close mother-daughter bond, explaining how it was wrong of Marina to lavish so much attention on her daughter, since this distracted her from the true love of God, to whom he addresses himself in the following: "how can you permit that those souls, who are now your brides, gravely sin, attaching their affections to human creatures?" (144). Sigüenza y Góngora also denounces the "monster of worldly affection" (143) and "loathsome particular friendships" (283), which constitute the root of all evil in the convent, damning those who engage in them to "perpetual death" (143). In the convent women were said to be *muerta al mundo* ("dead to the world") and, as Sigüenza y Góngora's tirade against convent relationships shows, dead also to life in the convent community.[8]

Sigüenza y Góngora also extravagantly describes the extremes of self-mortification to which some women pushed themselves. He does so with a relish and attention to detail that always startles students. What better way, I ask my students, to ensure control over the convent population than through a life-denying rhetoric that encouraged self-inflicted suffering? Church authorities encouraged extreme manifestations of penitence such as these acts of self-mortification and abjection as long as the confessor first granted permission. The acts exemplified two tenets of the Christian experience for women in the Hispanic baroque: pain and obedience (Ibsen 71). Clearly, the mortification of the body appealed to the baroque society's fascination with the grotesque. The female body was an ideal site for this transformation to occur. Ecclesiastical authorities taught nuns that this was the model to which they must aspire, with the hope that "control over their bodies—and their minds—was ensured at all times" (Ibsen 75).

In *Paraíso occidental*, Sigüenza y Góngora describes Marina's fight to reach religious perfection in the face of the temptations and torments that the devil sent her way. The nun's body must be punished in order for her to reach perfection. Sigüenza y Góngora describes Marina's daily penitence as consisting of three "severe disciplines, two made of leather strips and bands, and the other made from the thin strands of a chain, to do penance, as she used to say, for her sins" (195). In the same section he describes how she would move around the convent "on all fours like an animal and dragging heavy stones that injured her in such a way it is impossible to articulate" (195).

Selections from Sigüenza y Góngora's history help students begin to understand how patriarchal discourse portrayed life in the convents, and they really begin to engage with the material and appreciate the gender biases of the period. Depending on the time allotted for the study of convent culture, students can also read selections from Octavio Paz's *Las trampas de la fe* (*The Traps of Faith*), which, although it contains some useful historical information, also uncritically recuperates fragments from *Paraíso occidental*, taking them out of context to depict the convent as a perverse and aberrant space populated by maladjusted women who were little more than prisoners of male control (159–83). Another text that goes even further in its misuse of Sigüenza y Góngora's baroque tales is Fernando Benítez's *Los demonios en el convento* ("Demons in the Convent"). The author's imagination seems to have run riot since his representation of life in the convent, with its sadistic overtones, far exceeds Paz's. Readings such as these help students plot a historical trajectory and realize the fear and fascination that convent space has inspired throughout history.

The above-mentioned texts establish the patriarchal view of convent culture as well as the principles that governed the ecclesiastical authorities' desire to control and contain female religious women. But, as I tell my students, this is only half the story. It is essential to counterbalance this viewpoint by introducing a pedagogical strategy that emphasizes how, despite the authorities' wishes, nuns were not simply the passive victims of male control—consumed in *holocausto* and *sacrificio*—but were able to carve out spaces of resistance for themselves. In class discussions students identify the anxiety that seems to inform the ecclesiastical authorities' control over the convent, leading us to a discussion of power. If the church fathers' power is so absolute, I ask the class, why then do we sense this anxiety? I invite students to explore the ways that they believe people exercise power and, in turn, how they exercise resistance to power. To establish a theoretical framework from which to best consider this problem,

I introduce my students to Michel Foucault's model of power and resistance. Foucault theorizes that power is not possessed; it is exercised. Where there is power, moreover, there is also always resistance. In discussion most students will offer the idea that power is exercised from the top down and is usually enforced through the willful and often violent suppression of individual freedom. After reading Foucault, however, students begin to see constellations of power as omnipresent in all areas of society and as productive rather than repressive. They grasp that people do not have power implicitly; instead, power is a technique or action in which individuals can engage—even those who appear at first sight not to have agency. So equipped, students are able to deconstruct traditional concepts of power and therefore understand that colonial male ecclesiastical control was not monolithic. Nuns could and did exercise resistance within a multiplicity of discursive force relations, particularly those involving the control and distribution of ideas in texts and conversations.

Foucauldian theory may seem a tall order for undergraduates. I have found, however, that students respond well to this model for understanding power. An investigation that focuses on power as acquired rather than inherent helps free up the convent terrain for a questioning of what, at first sight, may seem like historical givens—nuns as passive victims of male control, for example. Students learn to see how resistance exercised in small ways can be construed as a challenge to a power, which, despite appearances to the contrary, is not all-encompassing. Some of Foucault's writings on power are more accessible than others. I have found that his essay "The Subject and Power" in *The Essential Foucault* works particularly well in the undergraduate classroom because it provides a clear and concise overview of his ideas. Of course, the addition of a study guide prepared by the instructor can also be a great help for students to engage with Foucault.

Once students understand that the convent space was not a male-controlled prison, they begin to analyze the different ways that resistance was exercised against the patriarchal fictions that underlay female containment. The challenge lies in finding the means to show students that resistance was common in convents. Here, nuns' writings offer us the paradigm of resistance we are seeking. In her feminist reading of Foucault, Jana Sawicki has talked about the importance of establishing "a historical knowledge of resistance and struggle" and of retrieving "subjugated knowledges" (57). According to Foucault, "subjugated knowledges" are experiences or beliefs that have traditionally been "disqualified as inadequate to their task, or insufficiently elaborated: naive knowledges, located low down in the hierarchy, beneath the required level of cognition or scientificity" (qtd. in Sawicki 26). This definition sums up the way the ecclesiastical authorities dealt with women's writing in the convent. As I tell my students, it was not easy for women to penetrate the official channels of communication in colonial Mexico. Male authorities controlled access to the written word and decided which records were kept. If women did gain access to the written word, they were not often permitted to write their opinions or feelings openly.

As both scholars and teachers, we are often faced with the difficult task of reading between the lines to crack the code of female writing. As teachers, we can facilitate access for our students to these subjugated knowledges through texts written by women that have been obscured for centuries by the master narratives of history. Different reading strategies—ones that use tools from critical theory grounded firmly in sociocultural contextualization—can, however, open up women's worlds in the classroom.

Sor Juana was, of course, unique because of her immense talent and fame. It is vital, however, for students to understand that other women also took up the pen in a bid for agency in the face of male control. Texts written by nuns themselves best enable us to view their resistance to the paradigms of patriarchal control. These works give us a very different view of convent life than that which emerges from male-authored texts. Convents—with their hierarchies, conflicts, and factionalism—were not female utopias. However, nuns' writings also show the solidarity and friendship that came from communal living in an all-female space. Furthermore, letters, poetry, convent chronicles, and religious autobiographies demonstrate that, through the act of writing, women rejected the role of victim and awarded themselves authority through the text. Their works testify to acts of resistance through solidarity and community because nuns wrote many of these texts for their sisters or to enshrine the singularity of their convent's history—often a source of pride and identity. Of course nuns were also "escritoras por obediencia" ("writers through obedience"), composing their *vidas* at the behest of male confessors who attempted to carefully control their texts (Myers, *Neither Saints* 14). These texts too, however, were spaces in which nuns resisted and subverted male control. Through the unearthing of these subjugated knowledges, students begin to see Sor Juana as a member of a network of resisting nuns and as part of a writing community.

In the last few years scholars have done much work to recover from the archives texts written by colonial nuns, and thus students have access to some of these voices through editions of nuns' writings. An excellent resource is of course the pioneering *Untold Sisters: Hispanic Nuns in Their Own Works, works*, edited by Electa Arenal and Stacey Schlau. Reading brief excerpts of some of the texts they have included (which are available in the original Spanish and in English translation by Amanda Powell), students can identify this textual resistance. As Arenal and Schlau write in their introduction, "the prose of women in the convent was always an act of defiance although it purported to be an act of obedience" (16). Another useful text is Elisa Sampson Vera Tudela's *Colonial Angels*, which includes an appendix with previously unpublished archival material written by nuns. Sampson rejects the conclusion that most nuns' texts are insignificant because they do not conform to expected aesthetic models. She shows the resistance to power structures that women's authorship implies, claiming that these texts possess a "negotiated originality" in which authors "negotiated with priests, with literary traditions, with cultural values" and that these strategies in turn produce texts that are "dynamically creative" (xii).

Before students read brief passages of nuns' texts, I introduce them to concepts such as Josefina Ludmer's "tricks of the weak" or Ann Rosalind Jones's idea of "negotiation," which allow students to grasp the subtleties of women's challenging of patriarchal power through the written word. They begin to identify strategies that show women undercutting the power they claim to obey so unquestioningly. I often assign an excerpt from the autobiography of María de San José (Arenal and Schlau 378–87). In class we explore how María uses but subverts the conventions of patriarchal discourse. She refers constantly to her own weaknesses as a writer, but reading between the lines we can see how she is in fact promoting her rights as an author. Following the dictates of the ecclesiastical authorities, María claims she only writes because her confessor orders it: "My confessor commanded me to write during every minute of the time I had at my disposal" (383).[9] At the same time that she professes ultimate obedience, her writings show the confessor to be a volatile despot: "He came one day into the confessional and ordered me to write nothing at all, nor should I so much as take the pen in my hand, . . . and I obeyed him in this matter also, without a single word of protest" (383). The confessor then takes all María's writings away from her, never telling her what was to become of them (386). Despite claiming blind acceptance of his decisions, María in fact cleverly circumvents the confessor's authority by showing she is protected by someone far more powerful than he. One day while gazing on a statue of "the glorious Saint Teresa de Jesús," the mystic hears the "holy Mother" speak directly to her, promising her she will "care for [her] writings" (387). With these holy female powers protecting her, she insinuates she is invulnerable to the cruel idiosyncrasies of her confessor and thus free, she implies, to control her own narrative.

As students read and discuss texts such as María's, they see the resistance that nuns offered to the power that colonial church authorities attempted to wield over them. These women were not sacrificial victims consumed in the symbolic fires of religious *holocausto* but astute actors operating in the interstices of power. Both the colonial convent and its inhabitants come to life through their writings. Authors-nuns offer a discursive textual network that challenges the view of convent life that emerges from male texts. Students can see the possibility of female resistance to what, at first glance, seems to be an all-powerful male ecclesiastical establishment. Reading Foucault alongside nuns' works, students understand that convents were places where female agency could be mobilized to resist masculine power and extinguish the fires of *holocausto*.

NOTES

[1]An excellent resource for images of convents is the lavishly photographed book *Conventos de monjas: Fundaciones en el México virreinal*, edited by María Concepción Amerlinck de Corsi and Manuel Ramos Medina.

[2]In the Middle Ages some male houses were also founded with the goal of withdrawal from a sinful world (Duby 232–33). However, male orders in New Spain—first the Fran-

ciscans, Augustinians, Dominicans, and later the Jesuits—came charged with an apostolic mission. There were no cloistered male houses in the viceroyalty (Rubial Garcia, "Varones").

[3]According to Margo Glantz, patriarchal society viewed nuns in the seventeenth century as being like the vestal virgins of old "offered in holocaust," and she likens the ceremony of profession to being "burned alive by a priest during a ceremonial ritual" ("Cuerpo" 178).

[4]Carlos de Sigüenza y Góngora, the professional scholar, scientist, and writer, was one of the leading Mexican intellectuals of his day. He was intimately connected to the ruling power structures, both secular and religious. Although expelled from the Jesuits for improper behavior while a student in 1668, he nonetheless remained close to the order (Paz, *Trampas* 198). Although his petition for readmission to the Jesuits was refused, in 1677 he was granted absolution from expulsion (Leonard, *Baroque Times* 196). He was also close to Francisco de Aguiar y Seijas, the powerful archbishop of Mexico (1682–98). Aguiar y Seijas, who was Sor Juana's nemesis, bestowed various favors and sinecures on Sigüenza y Góngora, including the chaplaincy of the Hospital del Amor de Dios (Paz, *Trampas* 483).

[5]All translations are mine unless otherwise noted. Another example of the preponderance of this rhetoric can be found in the works of Sor Juana's erstwhile confessor, Antonio Núñez de Miranda. Of the twenty-nine religious works he wrote between 1664 and 1695 eleven were addressed directly or indirectly to nuns. Núñez liked to liberally pepper his texts with the words "holocausto" and "sacrificio." A typical example comes from his *Plática doctrinal que hizo el Padre Antonio Núñez de la Compañia de Jesús en la profesión de una señora religiosa del convento de San Lorenzo* ("Doctrinal Address Given by Father Antonio Núñez of the Society of Jesús on the Profesión of a Religious Lady in the San Lorenzo Convent"), in which he likens the nun's profession to a human sacrifice: "A virgin sacrifices everything to God, her body, soul, power, feelings, habits, and desires, without keeping a single thing for herself, nor for society, neither flesh nor blood; instead she sacrifices everything for God in the holy fire of his charity" (*Plática* 3).

[6]All references to Sigüenza y Góngora refer to *Paraíso*.

[7]In most cases, Sigüenza y Góngora's text is the only access we have to the nuns' *vidas*. However, in the case of the texts of Mariana de la Encarnación, who wrote a chronicle of the founding of the Carmelite convent of San José, Ross was able to compare the original with Sigüenza y Góngora's excerpts. She shows how Sigüenza y Góngora "writes over" (161) the original text to make it conform to *Paraíso occidental*'s overall discursive plan.

[8]Sor Juana's confessor Antonio Núñez de Miranda had a more extreme way of espousing this viewpoint. Addressing himself directly to nuns he warns them to be "shrouded by your veil" and "cut off, alone and silent in your corner" (*Plática* 124, 56).

[9]Translation by Powell in Arenal and Schlau.

Women's Spiritual Lives: The History, Politics, and Culture of Religious Women and Their Institutions in Colonial Society

Jennifer L. Eich

Early modern Spanish and colonial Spanish American women's social and cultural lives were organized by institutions and traditions that encouraged their spirituality and depended on personal and societal pious practices. Indeed, the religious calendar regulated the observance of regular and special liturgical days as well as social events affected by religious rites such as weddings, baptisms, and funerals. The church, therefore, structured people's lives in a preset and visible manner, especially in urban areas; in rural areas the church's role tended to be more circumstantial. A burial would take place soon after death, yet the enactment of the funeral rite depended on the schedules of circuit-riding priests or friars. Other delayed official ceremonies included marriages and baptisms, which could follow the actual union or the children's births by months or even years. The secular documentation of a domestic change depended on whether a male family member had the energy and time available to travel to the nearest urban center and record it. Thus, dates on official certificates often conflicted with the actual event. The discrepancy in the year originally given by her biographer Diego Calleja for Sor Juana Inés de la Cruz's birth (1651 versus the actual 1648), for instance, is more likely a bureaucratic matter than a moment of vanity.

Sor Juana's varied contributions to the social and cultural milieu of both Spanish America and Spain are impressive in their artistic range and intellectual power. Her contemporaries clearly recognized her brilliance, which is evidenced by the publication of multiple editions of her collected works within ten years of her death in 1695. The "cartas de aprobación," or "letters of approval," and prefatory poetry at the beginning of her collected works—the first two volumes published in different cities in Spain in her lifetime and the third posthumously—further illustrate her popularity. Indeed, the prefatory poems, many of them by female Spanish poets, taunt their American cousins for failing to properly value this woman whom they call the "tenth muse."

Yet Sor Juana was neither unique nor unaccompanied by other women in her creative and intellectual endeavors. Carlos Sigüenza y Góngora's *Paraíso occidental* ("Occidental Paradise"), a conventual history of the Convento Real de Jesús María in Mexico City, chronicles the lives of many notable nuns, especially Marina de la Cruz. The extraordinary spiritual life of America's first universal patron, Rose of Lima (1586–1617), elicited several biographies about the Dominican tertiary: among the first was Leonhard Hansen's lengthy composition in Latin verse, swiftly translated into several European languages. Others based on Hansen's text were written for religious events in Spain and Spanish America following the beatification and subsequent canonization of America's first saint.

The lives of Sor Juana's cerebral and religious sisters have also been recorded by secular historians. Asunción Lavrin sheds light on this active intellectual sisterhood in "Unlike Sor Juana?: The Model Nun in the Religious Literature of Colonial Mexico," an essay included in an excellent compilation that focuses on Sor Juana and other early women writers. Lavrin and Josefina Muriel, especially Muriel's *Cultura femenina novohispana* ("New Spain's Feminine Culture"), offer invaluable evidence and details about the lives and works of these and other religious women intellectuals.

Nevertheless, whereas Sor Juana and Francisca Josefa de la Concepción de Castillo, known as Madre Castillo, are seldom absent from literary discussions of colonial Spanish American cultural life, the creative contributions of their less familiar sisters often are omitted from undergraduate curricula. These women's lives and works were significant; I suggest we can include religious women whose daily activities and practices reflected—yet resisted—patriarchally established boundaries for feminine participation in the social and cultural life of colonial Spanish America. I propose to show how undergraduate curricula, readings, and research can include the lives and works of Sor Juana's spiritual sisters, who contributed significantly to the religious and secular events structuring the cultural, political, and social lives of colonial Spanish Americans.

Lavrin's and Muriel's historical works heralded others by literary scholars, especially Electa Arenal and Stacey Schlau's unequaled bilingual edition and critical work *Untold Sisters: Hispanic Nuns in Their Own Works*, which serves both students able to read in the original Spanish and those restricted to English-only texts. Critical studies and editions of the spiritual autobiographies of four Spanish American nuns and mystics accessible to Spanish readers recount the lives of the Colombian Poor Clare Jerónima Nava y Saavedra (1669–1727), the Mexican Augustinian María de San Joseph (1656–1719 [Myers, *Word*]), the Chilean Dominican Úrsula Suárez (1666–1749), and the Peruvian Carmelite María Manuela de Santa Ana (1695–1793 [Armacanqui-Tipacti]). A selection can be made from chapters treating similar themes in the biographies of Rose of Lima, Isabel de la Encarnación (1594–1633 [Salmerón]), Catarina de San Juan (c. 1607–88 [Ramos; Castillo Grajeda]), Anna Guerra de Jesús (1639–1713 [Siria]), María de San Joseph, and María Anna Águeda de San Ignacio (1695–1756 [Bellido]). The lives of these mystics contrast nicely with Calleja's biography of Sor Juana.

Works accessible to English-only readers include selections of San Joseph's spiritual journals by Kathleen Myers and Amanda Powell, *A Wild Country out in the Garden*; Luis Martín, *Daughters of the Conquistadores*, which studies

Peruvian women religious; and Elisa Sampson Vera Tudela, *Colonial Angels*, which includes translated primary documents from New Spanish sources. Muriel's *Cultura femenina novohispana* is the fundamental historical text in Spanish; it contains extensive passages of selected primary materials. *The Cambridge History of Latin America*, edited by Leslie Bethell, and studies by historians Susan Migden Socolow, *The Women of Colonial Latin America*, and Kathryn Burns, *Colonial Habits*, are key texts for Spanish and English-only readers.

Critical studies of Spanish American religious women writers that include bibliographies and offer thematic studies include Jennifer L. Eich, *The Other Mexican Muse*; Kristine Ibsen, *Women's Spiritual Autobiography in Colonial Spanish America*; Kathryn McKnight, *The Mystic of Tunja*; and Kathleen Myers, *Neither Saints nor Sinners*. Each has an introduction studying historical, social, and cultural events shaping religious women's lives and references for primary and secondary sources.

I have divided the contributions made by colonial Spanish American nuns and female religious according to types of documents and material and included suggestions for assignments to accompany readings and stimulate discussion. Unless a bilingual text such as Arenal and Schlau's is used, the instructor must create a substantial course packet or prepare the course on an Internet-driven resource such as *Blackboard*. Students must have time to read and discuss their classmates' creative and analytic compositions, and the use of in-class brainstorming in groups is helpful in achieving cogent and well-documented papers. Prereading exercises about themes or characteristics of these texts distinguish between "before" and "after" impressions and emphasize acquired knowledge. These can be done at the course's beginning, halfway through, and as a final evaluative exercise. Students then value their intellectual and creative growth and can appreciate their historical and literary comprehension of the works. A reflective narrative preceding a portfolio of selected writing assignments and exams encourages a remarkable final-evaluation project.

I also recommend that any course treating artistic contributions by colonial Spanish American nuns and female religious include a brief study both of the conventual architecture and of female monastic art, especially nuns' profession and death portraits, contained in the convents and in female monasteries. Contrasting death portraits with colonial-era caste paintings differentiating social status illuminates the social and cultural concerns and values of the period. Finally, instructors may wish to present Sor Juana and her Spanish American precursors or contemporaries in a comparative framework with their European or American intellectual sisters, such as Hildegard of Bingen, Christine de Pizan, Catherine of Siena, Marie de l'Incarnation, Anne Bradstreet, and María de Jesús de Ágreda. Again, this approach yields opportunities to compare literary, architectural, and artistic endeavors of religious women and their contemporaries and successors. It also permits comparison with the lives and deeds of biblical women and their secular counterparts.

Themes

There are religious and secular themes, rhetorical formulas, and tropes that recur in the autobiographical writings of and biographical texts about nuns and female lay religious. These include conflicts between good and evil, struggles with the devil's torments, physical illnesses and their accompanying suffering, a woman's capacity for and specific practices of self-mortification, spiritual struggles overcome by devotional exercises, and disputes with or obstacles created by family members and conventual sisters or superiors who do not understand an individual's religious vocation. Two strikingly contradictory characterizations of female religious depend on the genre: an autobiographer almost always describes herself as a "nothing" or "worm," whereas biographers tend to establish their subject's status as "the virile or heroic woman." Both textual paradigms also present the woman as chosen by God, another thematic convention.

These tropes and their religious rhetorical formulas offer topics and approaches for comparative, literary, and cultural studies that can organize an entire curriculum or a single section of a course. The devil and his many and noisy minions who appeared to Encarnación compare nicely with Madre Castillo's visions of him as a woman, an Indian, and an African and with Suárez's descriptions of him as a black man or an Indian. Obstacles placed in a woman's path to profession include San Joseph's difficulties with her elder brother's resistance, Suárez's battles with her mother, and Guerra's physical struggles with her husband and with Satan, who repeatedly tries to kill her. These case stories have roots in Job's struggles to retain his faith in God. The Song of Songs serves as the template for vocabulary used in descriptions of mystical union or as a means for achieving it as is described in many of these ecstatic women's lives. Accounts chronicling events in the life of a female religious that show her as God's servant are significant opportunities to highlight cultural and social norms. The sense of being God's chosen or having to obey his will is even more salient if we compare the accounts with Sor Juana's intellectual defense, the *Respuesta a sor Filotea de la Cruz.*

By examining the writing styles, narrative emplotment, and cultural resonances of not only colonial secular but also religious writings, students can see how narratives vary with the writer's ambitions and attentive readers will perceive how the author reveals her personal beliefs and cultural context.

Religious and Secular Epistolary

Conventual and female monastic correspondence, which often occupied the prioress/abbess and her secretary, is perhaps the clearest example of texts that show how religious women participated in matters affecting people's lives. Letters between a female religious institution and the extramural religious and secular worlds sometimes included accounts of notable women's religious, spiritual, and physical lives as a means of inspiration to the addressee or community. Other bureaucratic missives, such as petitions for increases in the institution's financial resources and physical improvements reveal significant economic arrangements that affected the social and cultural lives of the region. Although archival research has not yet yielded the type of prolific correspondence between Spanish king and nun exemplified by the Spanish María de Jesús de Ágreda and Philip IV, there are cases where Spanish American nuns did enter political and religious arenas. Occasionally conventual correspondence included resistance to ecclesiastical and civil authorities' control, such as requests to remove a corrupt or incompetent majordomo.

Archival research yields documents substantiating that conventual and monastic inhabitants were circumscribed by secular and religious cultural practices. Founding a convent or female monastery in the Americas, for example, required letters from every local political, economic, and religious institution. Petitions to the king of Spain required proof that such an institution's founding neither offended nor demeaned any area religious and secular authorities. The Archive of the Indies in Seville houses an unpublished petition for the founding of the Convent of Santa Rosa in Puebla that states that a second collection of the obligatory letters from the leaders of regional religious institutes is included, some emphasizing that the new convent would greatly help with attending to the growing secular populace's spiritual needs (Petition). The supplicant's request also states that this second petition resulted from previous paperwork being lost at sea, most likely when the ship bearing it was attacked by pirates.

Other conventual correspondence comprises more operational matters. An abbess or prioress had to inform her ecclesiastical superiors of the death of a religious sister, and this type of correspondence was typically factual, routine, and short. Yet some of these obligatory letters also recount the deceased's biography and reveal the author's effort to highlight the dead woman's pious qualities and spiritual uniqueness. Reading these epistolary obituaries lends itself to writing assignments. An assignment asking students to write a similar letter could indicate that they can write an obituary for themselves or for a family member or friend. Grading these letters can be difficult; it must be stressed that specific formal elements must be present that would demonstrate their comprehension of the inherent ideological and rhetorical structures in a religious epistle. This creative project permits students to analyze what is personally and culturally important to them and their peers.

Guidebooks

After the Counter-Reformation, the Roman Catholic Church kept an active and vigilant eye on women's personal and communal spiritual practices since women were deemed the primary source for their children's Christian upbringing. In an effort to regularize behavior and monitor women's attitudes and to assist priests with their pastoral duties, ecclesiastical officials, including confessors and spiritual directors, composed confessional manuals and guidebooks for religious comportment. Sor Juana's spiritual director, Antonio Núñez de Miranda, wrote two such books that he dedicated to his unnamed yet acknowledged "spiritual daughters." This types of guidance could also appear as a sermon delivered to commemorate the profession or death of a nun from a socially significant family. Sermons composed for and delivered at the funerals of two eighteenth-century nuns from prominent families, Sebastiana Josepha de la Santissima Trinidad and Sebastiana Mariana del Espíritu Santo, include thematic metaphors in their titles. These religious topoi indicate the guiding principles behind the sermons' composition, and their delivery at the nuns' convents and subsequent publication ensured their delivery to both conventual and secular audiences. Núñez de Miranda's two most comprehensive guides, *Distribucion de las obras ordinarias y extraordinarias* ("Distribution of Ordinary and Extraordinary Acts") and *Cartilla de la doctrina religiosa* ("Letter of Religious Doctrine"), were published and reprinted in Mexico in the decade following his death—in the same year as his most noted spiritual daughter, 1695. Written specifically for religious women who had requested spiritual and physical guidance, they contain several eye-opening sections. Despite the Jesuit priest's stilted style, his warning about the dangers of allowing young women to read books of chivalry and comedies, referring to them as "la peste de la juventud" ("the pestilence of youth"), triggers lively class discussions on censorship, reading lists, and movie ratings.

Nuns and female religious also wrote guidebooks, generally for their conventual and monastic sisters, which were not printed. Águeda de San Ignacio wrote a guidebook on how to perform the conventual offices with spiritual benefit, although the text itself has been lost. Her biographer, Joseph Bellido, and funeral eulogist, José de Villa Sánchez, praise and cite passages from her work, and it was given to all area convents and monasteries.

Once a convent or female monastery was established, daily life, whether following the *vida común* ("common life") or *vida particular* ("separate life"), included certain daily sacrifices, many appearing in women's confessional or spiritual narratives. The constrained nature of institutionalized religious life meant that some pious women, such as Guerra de Jesús, chose to live outside conventual walls, although Guerra de Jesús allied herself with the Jesuits. Other women such as Sor Juana entered a convent or female monastery and later left, deciding to enter a less restrictive religious environment. In every case, however, the women's physical and spiritual lives were prescribed in ways that made clear the dangers of failing to observe the limits imposed by ecclesiastical authorities who wielded daily influence. Undergraduates understand this all-encompassing control easily after viewing María Luisa Bemberg's *Yo, la peor de todas* ("I, the Worst of All"). A more contemporary nun's life is recounted in the Audrey Hepburn film titled *Nun's Story*, based on the novel by Kathryn Hulme. This film and Hulme's book provide an enlightening look at issues of social justice and a woman's right of self-determination, especially when her religious vocation and the development of her talents require a choice similar to Sor Juana's.

Conventual and Monastic Chronicles

A particularly interesting opportunity for historical and creative writing assignments arises from the biographies or vitae based on hagiographic works of the Middle Ages, which also often form part of conventual and monastic foundational chronicles. Sor Juana's biography by Calleja is an innocuous narrative by a Spanish playwright that leaves out more than it tells. Some more compelling as well as revealing works recount the earthly and spiritual lives of female mystics: action-packed biographies of mystics include the lives of María de Jesús Tomelín (1579–1637), Encarnación, Águeda de San Ignacio, and Guerra de Jesús. Students particularly enjoy reading selections from the Jesuit Antonio de Siria's biography of the Guatemalan female lay religious, especially chapters in which Siria recounts miracles that saved Anna Guerra de Jesús from death even before her birth. Pairing these with Saint Teresa of Ávila's decision to leave home and fight in the crusade offers an opportunity for students to reflect on their understanding of contemporary Christian beliefs and mythologies as well as how their religious faith and personal spiritual practices shape their lives. It also triggers discussions of supernatural phenomena as the students have experienced them through television, movies, and readings. This is not necessarily a nonliterary exercise: just as some colonial Spanish American women were affected by the secular and religious stories (especially those of female saints) they heard recounted and read, our students depend on visual media for much of their knowledge of what is defined as supernatural, extraordinary, or inappropriate.

Other vitae are autobiographical. Sor Juana's intellectual autobiography provides an in-depth model to spur students' imaginations in writing their own history as a final project. The confessional narrative of Suárez provides an earthly and accessible paradigm in her *Relación autobiográfica* ("My Life"), especially if the instructor selects excerpts in which she complains about her mother and of her family's neglect of her education and upbringing. Nava de Saavedra's autobiography is filled with mystic imagery, much of which can be compared with Madre Castillo's mystical poetry.

Both biographies and autobiographies chronicle personal stories while simultaneously recording cultural and social customs. An instructor could ask students to keep a journal in which they record important events in their lives or those of their family or classmates. As part of the text's final presentation, they should be asked to analyze their entries and indicate the social or cultural customs they find. A less personal assignment would be to write the biography of someone who played a significant role in the growth of the student or his or her family. This assignment is particularly fruitful in areas where students' families have recent immigrant roots. It also avoids the lack of objective perceptiveness into which many students fall when writing about their lives.

Poetry Contests

Unfortunately, many Spanish American religious women chose to enter poetry competitions either under an assumed name or anonymously, making the task of identifying the individual or her talent difficult. Muriel's *Cultura femenina novohispana* includes a number of compositions entered in poetry contests for special occasions whose female authors won. These poems, however, are difficult for students to follow; their constrained thematic focus makes them more appropriate for a special-topic seminar.

Asking students to write poems on special topics has brought home the difficulty of writing this kind of poetry, yet offering the opportunity to present a collection of poems as a final project or in-class presentation has resulted in the publication of my students' efforts in journals. Classes have presented their translations of favorite poems, and comparing their different translations of the same piece has been exciting.

Music

Spanish American nuns and female religious composed and performed music, although their efforts did not always yield authorial attribution or publication. Much liturgical music composed and sung by New Spanish women is extant. Mexican and French groups have recorded compositions, at times in collections of music by international women composers. Muriel discusses in *Cultura femenina novohispana* the inauguration of scholarly research into the archives of different music conservatories in Mexico created or used by female religious or their students and refers to types of musical genres and instruments. She also points out that women were renowned singers and composers, mentioning, among others, Inés de la Cruz Castillet, Juana de Santa Catarina, and the Peruvian Ana Arias Rivera. We cannot forget Sor Juana's study of musical theory titled "El Caracol" ("The Nautilus"). Before playing recordings of her *villancicos* ("feast day songs"), I have students read these poems aloud to foreground their sense of music. Doing so permits students to be conscious of the songs' contrapuntal nature. Poems by Sor Juana have been set to music (see Ortiz, this volume).

Theater

Sor Juana's *Festejo de los empeños de una casa* ("Festival of the Trials of a House") stands alone as a dramatic work composed by a Spanish American religious woman writer. Yet her secular cloak-and-dagger play, featuring the theme of unrequited and obstructed love and its attendant emotional troubles, contrasts effectively with Agustín Moreto y Cavana and Francisco Lanini y Sagredo's saints play treating a young man's efforts to obtain the carnal love of Rose of Lima.

Giving historical and thematic background before identifying multiple levels of "play" (cultural, amorous, political, and verbal) in baroque drama is helpful, as are schematic presentations of love triangles or cultural intricacies relating to the defense or possession of honor. A review of the thematic structure of unrequited love as it is related to personal and family honor and contrasting it with students' current sense of what is romantically "right" and "wrong" facilitate class discussion. I focus on themes rather than vocabulary, except where words exhibit play or permit them to see the drama's originality. Short period poems, baroque music, and even contemporary songs (especially *corridos*) featuring the themes of honor and love can help students understand these plays.

Iconography and Architecture

The profession and death portraits of nuns in Spanish America permit an instructor and her or his students to explore colonial and early modern religious iconography. Comparing the portraits of mystic nuns, often included in their vitae, with paintings of Sor Juana reveals striking differences. Josefina Muriel and Manuel Romero de Terreros offer a fascinating view of the habits worn by New Spain nuns and female religious, as does Alma Montero Alarcón in her *Monjas coronadas* ("Crowned Nuns"). Hispanic religious habits, seen in art and historical studies of female institutions, contrast nicely with the monastic and conventual costumes of the European Middle Ages and Renaissance.

A review of European Renaissance and baroque paintings and sculptures and of works from the Spanish and American baroque and churrigueresque era—such as sculptures of Jesus, Mary, saints, and the founders of orders, convents, and feminine monasteries (e.g., Rose of Lima, Teresa of Ávila, and Catherine of Siena)—gives a visual and plastic sense of the world in which female religious worked and prayed. These works of art also show differences between the influences and styles of the two worlds. Muriel and Alicia Grobet present an architectural study of a New Spain convent while Francisco de la Maza (*Arquitectura*) focuses specifically on the architecture of the choirs used by nuns in Mexico and traces the architecture and institutions marking Sor Juana's life. A literature course does not permit a lengthy study of the plastic arts, yet briefly focusing on them facilitates exploration of the artistic resources and influences, cultural interests, religious symbolism, and classical mythology found in the products of these women's intellectual and artistic labors.

Contemporary fictional works in Spanish and English that feature Hispanic nuns or female religious writers are on the increase. Spanish American female religious can be opportunely paired with fictionalized women appearing in

Ángeles de Irisarri, *América*; Gaspar de Alba, *Sor Juana's Second Dream*; Edna Pozzi, *El ruido del viento* ("The Noise of the Wind"); and Gustavo Sáinz, *Retablo de inmoderaciones y heresiarcas* ("Retable of Immoderations and Heresy"). Valuable literary, critical, and political studies exist: Jean Franco, *Plotting Women*; Stacey Schlau, *Spanish American Women's Use of the Word*; Nina Scott, *Madres del verbo / Mothers of the Word*; and Hilda Smith and Berenice Carroll's *Women's Political and Social Thought: An Anthology*. The works and lives of Sor Juana's European and American precursors or contemporaries, such as Hildegard of Bingen, Christine de Pizan, Catherine of Siena, Marie de l'Incarnation, and Anne Bradstreet, when paired with Sor Juana and her spiritual sisters such as Rose of Lima, Teresa of Ávila, Madre Castillo, Águeda de San Ignacio, Jerónima del Espíritu Santo, Suárez, María de Jesús de Ágreda, San Joseph, and Sebastiana Mariana del Espíritu Santo, have profound resonances and cadences.

The lives and works of the nuns and female religious demonstrate that the physical, social, spiritual, and personal boundaries of religious life did not immobilize women or eliminate their participation in the social and cultural life of colonial Latin America. Nuns and female lay religious contributed to religious and secular communities. They wrote religious and secular texts, maintained correspondence with religious and civil authorities, filed legal petitions, fabricated and sold goods and food products, composed music, created and produced regional arts and crafts, and even mobilized resistance to civil and ecclesiastical authorities' control. Studying the achievements of Sor Juana and her spiritual sisters is vital in comprehending conventual and monastic culture and politics. It also allows us to more completely understand the history, psychology, literature, spirituality, gendered politics, and institutions of the sixteenth, seventeenth, and eighteenth centuries. By studying the cultural products of colonial female religious writers, we challenge traditional perceptions of these women's social and spiritual isolation and provide a more accurate context to appreciate Sor Juana's extraordinary spirit and literary works. Indeed, in exploring the creativity, imagination, and intellectual interests of Sor Juana and her spiritual sisters, we see how they influenced and shaped the cultural products of their societies. By including more women's works and lives in our curricula, we help current and future students recognize and acknowledge spiritual women's roles in secular and religious customs and literary traditions as well as a woman's proper place in social, political, economic, and cultural histories.

Sacred Allusions: Theology in Sor Juana's Work

Grady C. Wray

In her *Respuesta de la poetisa a la muy ilustre sor Filotea de la Cruz* ("The Poet's Answer to the Most Illustrious Sor Filotea de la Cruz" [1691]), Sor Juana Inés de la Cruz writes that she aspired to study theology because she felt she would have failed as a Catholic if she had not spent her life trying to understand the divine mysteries (4: 447). Her desire to achieve an understanding of theology causes those who teach her works and have an interest in her literary production to question where this theological aspiration presented itself in her other, less autobiographical texts. One approach to understanding Sor Juana's use of theology begins with her most overtly theological work, the *Carta atenagórica* ("Letter Worthy of Athena" [1690]), or, as she titled it on its second publication, *Crisis sobre un sermón* ("An Opinion on a Sermon" [1692]).[1] The *Carta* shows Sor Juana's familiarity with theological writing and her self-taught ability to contribute to theological argument. In the following pages, I not only provide pedagogical advice and activities that will help teachers and students better approach Sor Juana's *Carta*, but I also present the *Carta* as a point of departure for the study of other works that draw on her theological knowledge. To begin I offer some pedagogical precautions for teaching Sor Juana's *Carta* and related texts, as well as some ways to incorporate them into syllabi. I suggest some basic texts to which teachers and students should have access in order to make threading through the theological labyrinth as beneficial as possible. I follow with a brief summary of the history of the *Carta*, and I review the base text from which the *Carta* grows: Antonio Vieira's sermon on Christ's *finezas*, or favors or demonstrations of love. Finally, I dedicate several sections to how Sor Juana contests each part of the sermon and continues to add her opinion of divine *finezas*. Throughout, I supply activities that help teachers and students approach the *Carta*, as well as other theologically focused texts of the period.

Pedagogical Precautions

The *Carta* and its related texts are complicated, theological, baroque narratives. The success of those who delve into these multifaceted works depends heavily on prereading activities and information. The more instructors and students know about the context and content of these pieces before examining them, the more rewarding the initial reading will be. In fact, the strategies that teachers and students use to decipher these theological intricacies greatly enhance their ability to approach other baroque works.

The Carta *in Syllabi*

Certainly, the *Carta* can stand alone and serve as an excellent example of seventeenth-century theological commentaries, debates, and, to a certain extent, sermons. Therefore, it may be included as a representative work in religious studies and history curricula as well as in literary studies. A study of the *Carta* also works well as a precursor or an epilogue to an analysis of the *Respuesta*. If read as preparation, the *Carta* sets the historic scene for Sor Juana's apologia, or, if read afterward, it presents a clearer picture of why Sor Juana responded to "Sor Filotea" as she did. If time allows, the *Carta* can be an integral part of the study of the epistolary literature surrounding Sor Juana. Other letters that could be treated in a study of this magnitude include Sor Juana's letter to Father Núñez [c. 1682; Tapia Mendez]), *Carta de sor Filotea de la Cruz* ("Filotea de la Cruz's Letter" [25 Nov. 1690]), *Carta de Serafina de Cristo* ("Serafina de Cristo's Letter" [1 Feb. 1691; Trabulse]), and the *Respuesta* (1 Mar. 1691). Invaluable critical readings for understanding and debating the controversies surrounding these documents include Antonio Alatorre's "La Carta de sor Juana al P. Núñez (1682)," Alatorre and Martha Lilia Tenorio's *Serafina y sor Juana*, Sara Poot-Herrera's "Una carta finamente calculada, la de Serafina de Cristo" and "La caridad de Serafina, fineza de Sor Juana," Nina M. Scott's "'If you are not pleased to favor me,'" and Elías Trabulse's "El silencio final de sor Juana." No matter how instructors include the *Carta* in a syllabus, the *Diccionario de autoridades* and the Douay-Rheims version of the Bible may serve as basic reference texts that make initial readings more comprehensive. For a deeper understanding of context, teachers and students also should consult Antonio Vieira's *Sermón del padre Antonio Vieira en la Capilla Real, año 1650*; Saint Gregory the Great's homilies; and the original texts on Christ's *finezas* by Saint Augustine, Saint Thomas Aquinas, and Saint John Chrysostom.

History of the Carta atenagórica

Sor Juana composed the *Carta atenagórica* in response to the request of the bishop of Puebla, Manuel Fernández de Santa Cruz, that she comment on a sermon by Vieira, a renowned Portuguese Jesuit. She wrote a commentary and sent it to the bishop, who titled it and published it without Sor Juana's permission in 1690. The *Carta*'s publication set in motion a chain of events that scholars only began to decipher in the last decades of the twentieth century. In the *Carta* Sor Juana took issue with Vieira's opinions about Christ's final *finezas*. While on the surface she criticized Vieira's statements, at the same time she indirectly challenged her ex-confessor, Antonio Núñez de Miranda, also a Jesuit, who, before Sor Juana wrote the *Carta*, had published a piece on a similar theme, the *Comulgador Penitente de la Purissima* ("The Most Pure Virgin's

Penitent One Who Receives Communion"), and dedicated it to Bishop Fernández de Santa Cruz. We know that Sor Juana directed the *Carta* not only against Vieira but also against her ex-confessor Núñez de Miranda because of the discovery of another letter directed to Bishop Fernández de Santa Cruz dated 1 February 1691, the *Carta de Serafina de Cristo*. Sor Juana risked much more with the *Carta atenagórica* than with her other theological writings because it aggravated a rift between her and the archbishop, Francisco Aguiar y Seijas, who wished to reform New Spanish convents according to his vision, forcing nuns to follow strict discipline. Sor Juana included the *Carta* under her own title, *Crisis sobre un sermón*, in the second volume of her works in 1692. The archbishop strongly disapproved of Sor Juana's theological ventures, and in April of 1693 his vicar-general, Antonio de Aunzibay y Anaya, began a secret episcopal process that accused her of heresy, disrespect for authority, and activities incompatible with her monastic state (Trabulse, "Silencio" 146). The main objective of the episcopal process was to stop her writing altogether, whether theological or secular.

Using this history as a starting point, graduate students in literature and religious studies can trace the relationship between Núñez de Miranda's *Comulgador Penitente de la Purissima* and the *Carta atenagórica*, as well as both Sor Juana's and her contemporaries' other writings surrounding the *Carta*. Those interested in archival research could investigate the history of the relationship between Vieira, Núñez de Miranda, Bishop Fernández de Santa Cruz, and Archbishop Francisco Aguiar y Seijas, as well as the secret episcopal process aimed at Sor Juana that began in 1693. A close analysis of Elías Trabulse's "El silencio final de Sor Juana" provides a point of departure for considering this process, a relatively uncharted area.

Father Vieira's Sermon

In the *Carta atenagórica* Sor Juana bases her arguments on the *Sermón del padre Antonio Vieira en la Capilla Real, año 1650* in which Vieira proclaims he will present the greatest of Christ's final *finezas* during Christ's last days on earth. Vieira preached this sermon on Maundy Thursday for the ceremony of the washing of the disciples' feet.[2] He also pledges that no one will be able to refute his selection and explication of Christ's greatest *fineza*. Saint Augustine, Saint Thomas Aquinas, and Saint John Chrysostom had already contributed to the literature on the *finezas* theme, but Vieira reexamines their writings and takes issue with their opinions (see app. A, cols. 1 and 2). He then argues for what he perceives as the irrefutably greatest of Christ's final *finezas*: Christ's desire that humankind repay him by loving one another with the love he had for humankind (4: 690). As biblical support for his opinion, Vieira quotes John 13.14: "You also ought to wash one another's feet."[3] He points out that Christ has changed the natural order of love. Instead of love representing a reciprocal action between lover and beloved, he argues that both love and the reciprocal correspondence of love should be redirected to the beloved. The lover (Christ) gives love but does not receive. The beloved (humankind) can only repay the lover by loving others. Vieira presents this obligation on the part of the beloved as a debt that humankind must continually pay. Loving others is an infinite debt because it is modeled on divine love, which is infinite and must be paid infinitely. As proof, he relates Christ's words in John 13.34 (the same chapter that recounts the washing of the disciples' feet): "A new commandment I give unto you: That you love one another, as I have loved you, that you also love one another" (see app. B for a complete list of the biblical quotes Vieira uses as support for this final argument).

Because Vieira's sermon is at times difficult to follow, undergraduate students can benefit from creating charts or lists similar to those I provide in the appendixes that compare Augustine's, Aquinas's, and Chrysostom's opinions of Christ's final *finezas* with Vieira's and Sor Juana's opinions and with the biblical references and proofs used by Vieira and Sor Juana. These activities do not require much extratextual research, and they sharpen students' abilities to decipher arguments in a theological text. Graduate students can take this project further and consult the texts of these saints in order to see if Vieira or Sor Juana manipulates them to aid their arguments.

Sor Juana's Critique

Sor Juana responds to Vieira's sermon by preparing her commentary with the aid of the saints' arguments that Vieira critiques (see app. A, col. 3). She begins with Vieira's suggestion that when Christ left humankind he performed a greater *fineza* than when he died (4: 414). Disagreeing with Vieira, she sides with Augustine and reiterates that dying represents the greatest *fineza* because life and honor are the most estimable to humankind and because Christ gives them both in death (4: 415). As part of this argument, she adds that Christ's death repeats three benefits: the Creation (it restores grace), preservation of temporal life (Christ dies so humankind may live, and he leaves his flesh and blood to sustain life), and the Incarnation, (the first incarnation united Christ's flesh with his mother's; in death(Christ's blood unites all humankind [4: 417–18]). Sor Juana ends her first refutation claiming that Vieira incorrectly assumes that Christ left humankind because, before Christ's death, at the Last Supper, he left himself in the sacraments. She completes the argument with the assertion that Christ's absence is part of his death (4: 420).

Sor Juana also agrees with Aquinas's description of Christ's *fineza*: Christ remains with humankind in the sacraments (4: 420 [see app. A, col. 3]). She finds fault with Vieira because he constructs a genus-to-species instead of a genus-to-genus argument (4: 420–21). Vieira argues that Christ concealed himself without senses in the sacraments rather than merely remaining unconcealed and aware of his surroundings (4: 678–79). Sor Juana contends that the way in which Christ remains in the sacraments is of little importance as long as he remains. If Vieira had contested the mystery of the sacraments, which implies that Christ remained on earth, as opposed to another divine mystery such as the Incarnation or the Immaculate Conception, he would have met the logical standard for a genus-to-genus argument. However, a change within the sacraments (species) does not change the mystery of the sacraments (the genus itself). A genus-to-genus argument would examine whether the sacraments themselves represent *finezas*, but a species-to-species argument would explore how Christ remained within the sacraments (concealed or not, with or without senses). Not content to simply dismiss Vieira's argument as illogical, Sor Juana proves that even a species-to-species argument using Vieira's example would not furnish evidence of a greater *fineza*. She maintains that Christ performs less of a *fineza* when he remains in the sacraments without the use of his senses than when he remains with senses and suffers the insults that come from experiencing the lack of respect for the sacraments.

Not surprisingly, Sor Juana discounts Vieira's disagreement with Saint John Chrysostom, who writes that Christ performed his greatest *fineza* when he washed the feet of the disciples (see app. A, col. 3). Vieira opines that the greater *fineza* was when Christ washed Judas's feet. Christ had no cause to wash the feet of Judas, a traitor whose heart was possessed by the devil and whose actions would yield thorns instead of fruit (4: 689). Therefore, Christ's greatest *fineza* was washing Judas's unworthy feet without a reason. In Sor Juana's retort, she proposes that Vieira places too much emphasis on the cause, or lack thereof, for the feet washing instead of the effect (4: 422). She states that the cause (Christ's love, for example) was implicit in the effect (Christ's washing of the disciples' feet) and therefore that the effect expresses the cause. As part of her rebuttal she rhetorically questions why Chrysostom would think that Christ did such an action without cause (4: 422). It is clear to her that the saint could not have thought as such. She stresses that Chrysostom emphasizes Christ's actions (washing the feet of his disciples) in order for humankind to infer more greatness about the possible causes. An unfathomable cause is better expressed by its effect. Christ's actions magnify and better explain the reasons behind them.

After refuting all the arguments that Vieira had made against the saints, Sor Juana tackles Vieira's opinion of Christ's greatest *fineza*: Christ's desire for humankind to repay his love by loving one another. She disagrees with Vieira's inference that Christ does not want humankind to respond directly to him for his love but rather to respond indirectly by loving one another. Instead she contends that Christ demands correspondence. Basing her proof on the precepts and instances in scripture that command humankind to love God (see app. C), she also calls for her reader to remember that when someone, in this case Christ, requests that an act of love be done for another, the one who performs the action (humankind) must love the one who requests the action (Christ [4: 425]). According to Sor Juana, humankind should love in Christ and for Christ; in other words, humankind should love Christ first (4: 425). She uses scriptural references 2–7 in app. C to describe how Christ prohibits intimate relationships if they compete for his love (4: 426). She presents God as jealous of the others whom humankind loves (app. C, references 8–9).

Sor Juana differentiates between a human and a divine capacity for demonstrating love. Not to want correspondence is a human *fineza*, because human beings want correspondence (4: 430). To want correspondence is a *fineza* of Christ because Christ is not interested in humankind's correspondence (4: 430). Human beings can perform certain *finezas* for Christ such as resisting and fearing temptations; however, because Christ cannot be tempted or fear the dangers of sin, he cannot offer the same *fineza* (4: 429). Christ lacks nothing, and to solicit our correspondence when he has no need for it is his *fineza* (4: 430). Sor Juana emphasizes the difference between Vieira's argument and hers: for Vieira, Christ does not want correspondence for himself but for humankind (4: 430); for Sor Juana, Christ wants correspondence for himself but the usefulness, or utility, that results from the correspondence should go to humankind (4: 430–31). Christ finds the utility of the correspondence unnecessary, not the correspondence. She cites the example of Christ's asking Saint Peter if Peter loved him. After Saint Peter responds affirmatively, Christ tells him to feed his sheep (John 21.17). Saint Peter should give his love to Christ, but he should give his utility to Christ's sheep (4: 431). Christ asks for love because loving him takes the form of usefulness for humankind (4: 431–32). What, then, can humankind do to give service to God? Sor Juana's response requires that humankind ask God for more; God will receive that request as payment (4: 432). God wants humankind's love to benefit humankind, not God (4: 432). Sor Juana concludes her critique of Vieira's sermon with a biblical example as proof of how one looks to give the utility or benefits of love to another instead of to oneself. She recounts the story of Absalom, Amnon, David, and Joab and asserts that David clearly wanted the correspondence of his love to go to Amnon and not to himself (4: 434).[4]

Aware of her gender and possibly expecting some retribution, Sor Juana adds an epilogue to her argument against Vieira's opinion in which she excuses herself as an unknowing woman, far removed from theological study. At the same time she references her biblical foremothers, Judith and Deborah, who surpassed the restrictions of gender on the battlefield and in the court (4: 435). The reference to Sor Juana's foremothers foreshadows those who will appear later, in the *Respuesta*, after "Sor Filotea" chastises Sor Juana for such theological daring.

Given that Catholic teachings provide the foundations for these texts, students of literature and language, of history, and of religious studies at the undergraduate level can enhance their comprehension of Catholic doctrine by defining and describing the history of specific terminology as it relates to the seventeenth century, such as *fineza*, theology (especially its status as a science), the Incarnation, the Immaculate Conception, and the sacraments as related to Sor Juana's theological works. Graduate students may use these defining activities to further investigate the theological issues that arise in Sor Juana's texts in general and how her other works relate to her *Carta*. History students may analyze the function of genus-to-genus and species-to-species arguments. In the seventeenth century was it acceptable to argue from genus to species? Also, how does one structure a cause-and-effect argument? Can an argument based only on effect successfully express the cause?

Sor Juana's Opinion/Sermon

Bishop Fernández de Santa Cruz also requested that Sor Juana expand on the greatest *fineza* of divine love as part of her commentary. As Sor Juana fulfills this request, her personal interpretation of theology surfaces. She no longer limits herself to Vieira's sermon or to her own opinion of Christ's final *finezas*; rather, she slightly shifts the focus of her text to the benefits that humankind receives from God. She sets up her own argument; in essence, she writes a brief sermon. Stating that God's ability to stop giving gifts because of humankind's ingratitude is God's greatest *fineza* (4: 436), she continues with an explanation of the difficulty with which God withholds love, since God's natural condition liberally gives love. Again, she depends on scriptural references to support her contentions, as well as on a reference to Saint Gregory the Great (see app. D). She notes Judas's poor reaction to God's gifts (app. D, reference 4) and also mentions God's decision to destroy the earth because of the evils of humanity (app. D, reference 5). Sor Juana exclaims that God's greatest *fineza* is not to give benefits and expresses great exasperation at humanity's dull-wittedness and blindness for not recognizing the negative type of benefit that God bestows (4: 438).

Approaching Sor Juana's Personal Theological Interpretations

The *Carta atenagórica,* which disputes the sermon of a famous Jesuit priest, reflects Sor Juana's familiarity with seventeenth-century theological discourse. Her experience and personal struggles as a New Spanish nun and woman of genius influence her interpretation of God's relationship with humankind. A gifted daughter of the church, she recognizes the talents God has given her. She also knows the responsibility and problems that such gifts bring. She even likens the possession of God's gifts to punishment. The benefits of fortune or natural talents only serve as great burdens and objects of envy.[5] She felt how others envied her prowess, and she could possibly have sensed a plot to squelch what she claims are her God-given talents. Through the *Carta,* she suggests that others should not criticize those who have received talents from God because the receipt of a benefit requires a responsible correspondence. Those who respond with appropriate gratitude and responsibility deserve more praise and receive more benefits than those who squander or reject what God has given them. This implied concern could be directed to certain members of New Spanish society, but her well-formulated theological argument of support for the church forefathers, Augustine, Aquinas, and Chrysostom, should have protected her from retaliations by New Spanish church officials. However, because Vieira was admired by Bishop Fernández de Santa Cruz, her ex-confessor Núñez de Miranda, and Archbishop Aguiar y Seijas, who was attempting to reestablish stricter rules in convents, she risks the persecution that soon ensues.

Sor Juana does not imply that God retains all benefits. In fact, she portrays God as already having given everything through the gift of Jesus, the only begotten; however, humanity does not properly accept God's gifts. Therefore, she emphasizes that God's greatest *fineza* is restraint: God's greatest demonstration of love occurs when God does not demonstrate love (4: 439). Naturally God does not withhold good, but God understands human nature and knows that humans work harder and strive more without gifts. God's negative benefits become positive in humans. At the end of her *Carta*, she asks God for the grace to recognize *finezas* and correspond to them accordingly. She wants the discussion of God's *finezas* not to remain in speculative discourse but to lead to practical service and gratitude for God's gifts (4: 439). For Sor Juana, showing appropriate gratitude and giving to God yields greater rewards from God.

Aside from the possible embedded criticism of the New Spanish religious hierarchy, the *Carta* provides a closer look at Sor Juana's theological interpretations. Although she claims, in standard humble and obedient discourse, that Bishop Fernández de Santa Cruz asked her to prepare the work (4: 435), she goes beyond refuting points that others have established and presents a separate opinion about a related but different matter (4: 436). Through her examination of *finezas* in the contexts of God and of Christ's last days, she reiterates the necessity of properly showing appreciation, or correspondence, for divine favors or demonstrations of love. Stylistically, emotion and bewilderment intensify when she confronts humanity's failure to appropriately respond to Christ's or God's love. The theological message of proper correspondence, gratitude, and appreciation for divine *finezas* echoes throughout her complete works and provides a point of departure for excursions to places where Sor Juana's readers can reap the benefits of her own intricately crafted *finezas*.

NOTES

[1]The bishop of Puebla, Manuel Fernández de Santa Cruz, originally publishes and titles the work *Carta atenagórica* in 1690 without Sor Juana's permission. Sor Juana changes the title to *Crisis sobre un sermón* when she includes it in her second volume of works in 1692. Although the best contextual English translation of *crisis* may be "opinion," it is intriguing that Sor Juana's "opinion" signaled a "crisis."

[2]The sermon is also known as "Sermón Tercero del mandato en la Capilla Real, año 1650" ("Third Sermon of the Mandate in the Royal Chapel, 1650"). For more information on its publication history see the note for line 73 in Juana Inés de la Cruz, *Obras* 4: 633.

[3]This and all subsequent quotations of the Bible, in the essay and appendixes, come from the Douay-Rheims version, translated directly from the Latin Vulgate with which Sor Juana was familiar.

[4]2 Kings 13–19, esp. 18.5 and 33.

[5]The subject of envy also appears in the *Respuesta* (4: 440–75), *Romance* 51 (1: 158–61), and sonnet 146 (1: 277–78), as well as other texts.

APPENDIX A
Christ's *Finezas*

Church Fathers' Opinions according to Sor Juana	Vieira	Sor Juana
Saint Augustine: Christ dies for humankind.	Christ leaves humankind (absents himself), which represents a greater *fineza* than dying.	Christ did not leave (absent himself) because he remained in the sacraments.
Saint Thomas Aquinas: Christ remains with humankind and, at the same time, leaves.	Christ conceals himself in the sacraments, which represents a greater *fineza* than remaining with humankind.	Vieira's argument is illogical because it argues species (how Christ remains in the sacraments) instead of genus (whether or not the sacraments represent a *fineza*).
Saint John Chrysostom: Christ washes the disciples' feet.	Christ washes Judas's feet, which represents a greater *fineza* than washing the other disciples' feet.	Vieira's argument is illogical because it argues cause instead of effect. The effect (action) infers the cause (motivation). (The effect proves the cause and makes the cause even more unfathomable.)

APPENDIX B
Vieira's Opinion of Christ's Greatest *Fineza*

After Christ's example, humankind should wash one another's feet (love one another). Christ left humans a debt they could not pay to him, but rather to each other.

References Given as Proof:

1. John 13.14: "If then I being your Lord and Master, have washed your feet; you also ought to wash one another's feet."
2. 1 John 4.11: "My dearest, if God hath so loved us, we also ought to love one another."

3. John 13.34: "A new commandment I give unto you: That you love one another, as I have loved you, that you also love one another."
4. Leviticus 19.18: "Seek not revenge, nor be mindful of the injury of thy citizens. Thou shalt love thy friend as thyself. I am the Lord."
5. Matthew 5.44: "But I say to you, Love your enemies: do good to them that hate you; and pray for them that persecute and calumniate you."
6. John 15.12: "This is my commandment, that you love one another, as I have loved you."
7. Romans 13.8: "Owe no man any thing, but to love one another. For he that loveth his neighbour hath fulfilled the law."
8. John 15.17: "These things I command you, that you love one another."
9. Luke 23.12: "And Herod and Pilate were made friends, that same day: for before they were enemies one to another."
10. John 13.1: "Before the festival day of the pasch, Jesus knowing that his hour was come, that he should pass out of this world to the Father; having loved his own who were in the world, he loved them unto the end."

APPENDIX C
Sor Juana's Refutation of Vieira's Argument on Christ's Greatest *Fineza*

Christ wants humankind's love, but he wants the benefits that result from loving him to go to others.

References Given as Proof:

1. Mark 12.30: "And thou shalt love the Lord thy God with thy whole heart and with thy whole soul and with thy whole mind and with thy whole strength. This is the first commandment."
2. Matthew 10.37 "He that loveth father or mother more than me, is not worthy of me; and he that loveth son or daughter more than me, is not worthy of me."
3. Luke 14.26: "If any man come to me, and hate not his father and mother and wife and children and brethren and sisters, yea and his own life also, he cannot be my disciple."
4. Matthew 18.8: "And if thy hand, or thy foot, scandalize thee, cut it off, and cast it from thee. It is better for thee to go into life maimed or lame, than having two hands or two feet, to be cast into everlasting fire."
5. Matthew 16.24: "Then Jesus said to his disciples: If any man will come after me, let him deny himself, and take up his cross, and follow me."
6. Luke 12.49: "I am come to cast fire on the earth. And what will I, but that it be kindled?"
7. Matthew 10.34–36: "Do not think that I came to send peace upon earth: I came not to send peace, but the sword. For I came to set a man at variance against his father, and the daughter against her mother, and the daughter in law against her mother in law. And a man's enemies shall be they of his own household."

8. Exodus 20.5: "Thou shalt not adore them, nor serve them: I am the Lord thy God, mighty, jealous, visiting the iniquity of the fathers upon the children, unto the third and fourth generation of them that hate me."
9. Ezechiel 16.42 (probable): "And my indignation shall rest in thee; and my jealousy shall depart from thee, and I will cease and be angry no more."
10. Genesis 22.2: "He said to him: Take thy only begotten son Isaac, whom thou lovest, and go into the land of vision; and there thou shalt offer him for an holocaust upon one of the mountains which I will shew thee."
11. John 15.12: "This is my commandment, that you love one another, as I have loved you."
12. John 14.15, 21, 23: "If you love me, keep my commandments" (15). "He that hath my commandments and keepeth them; he it is that loveth me. And he that loveth me shall be loved of my Father; and I will love him and will manifest myself to him" (21). "Jesus answered and said to him: if any one love me, he will keep my word. And my Father will love him and we will come to him and will make our abode with him" (23).
13. 1 John 5.3: "For this is the charity of God: That we keep his commandments. And his commandments are not heavy."
14. John 15.5: "I am the vine: you the branches. He that abideth in me, And I in him, the same beareth much fruit: for without me you can do nothing."
15. John 21.17: "He said to him the third time: Simon, son of John, lovest thou me? He saith to him: yea, Lord, thou knowest that I love thee, He saith to him: Feed my lambs."
16. Psalm 49.14–15: "Offer to God the sacrifice of praise: and pay thy vows to the most High. And call upon me in the day of trouble: I will deliver thee, and thou shalt glorify me."
17. 2 Kings 18.5, 33: "And the king commanded Joab, and Abisai, and Ethai, saying: Save me the boy Absalom. And all the people heard the king giving charge to all the princes concerning Absalom" (5). "The king therefore being much moved, went up to the high chamber over the gate, and wept. And as he went he spoke in this manner: My son Absalom, Absalom my son: would to God that I might die for thee, Absalom my son, my son Absalom" (33).

APPENDIX D

Sor Juana's References of Support for Her Opinion on God's Greatest *fineza*

1. Matthew 13.55–56, 58: "Is not this the carpenter's son? Is not his mother called Mary, and his brethren James, and Joseph, and Simon, and Jude: And his sisters, are they not all with us? Whence therefore hath he all these things?" (55–56). "And he wrought not many miracles there, because of their unbelief" (58).
2. Luke 4.23: "And he said to them: Doubtless you will say to me this similitude: Physician, heal thyself. As great things as we have heard done in Capharnaum, do also here in thy own country."

3. Gregory the Great: "we who have received something more than others in this world may be judged more severely by the world's Creator. When his gifts increase the responsibility of accounting for them also grows greater" (Gregory, *Forty Gospel Homilies* 127).†
4. Matthew 26.24: "The Son of man indeed goeth, as it is written of him. But woe to that man by whom the Son of man shall be betrayed. It were better for him, if that man had not been born."
5. Genesis 6.7: "He said: I will destroy man, whom I have created, from the face of the earth, from man even to beasts, from the creeping thing even to the fowls of the air, for it repenteth me that I have made them."

†Sor Juana's text references homily 9; however, the English translation reorders the first twenty homilies and places number 9 as 18.

The "Mexican" Sor Juana

Stephanie Merrim

The "Mexican" Sor Juana and Feather Headdresses

To ease students into the complexities of grasping the Mexican past, I often turn to Carmen Boullosa's *Llanto: Novelas imposibles* ("In Tears: Impossible Novels"). There we read Boullosa's poignant meditations on Moctezuma, of whom no physical traces remain beyond a feather headdress that he possibly donned once. Boullosa's narrator wonders how to reconstruct Moctezuma, given that we have "no bones, no signs of his thinking, nothing at all" ("Ni huesos, ni señas de cómo era su pensamiento, ni nada de nada" [75]).[1] Yet, since Moctezuma "was a person who lived at a particularly delicate moment in history, a moment of juncture, a crossroads, a battlefront" ("fue una persona y está en un punto histórico especialmente sensible, de entronque, de encrucijada, de campo de batalla" [96]), Boullosa eloquently concludes both that "we cannot possibly understand" and that "we must understand" ("Es impossible que entendamos"; "necesitamos entender" [98]).

We possess vastly more traces of Sor Juana. Still, to understand the nun's relationship to Mexican moments of crossroads and battlefronts holds considerable challenges. Some of the challenges find their emblem in another headdress. "I, the Worst of All," a film that my students invariably view, has the Countess of Paredes giving Sor Juana a gorgeous crown of quetzal feathers, just like Moctezuma's. Sor Juana preens and twirls with it, parading the headdress's, and her own, exultant exoticism. All too similarly, for undergraduates the most appealing texts that impart a sense of Sor Juana's engagement with the sociopolitical realities of New Spain tend to purvey a patent exoticism. I refer to the *ensalada* portions of her religious festivals (2: 14–17, 39–42, 71–74, 82–85, 94–98, 107–10, 138–43, 159–63). Their comic medley of Indian, Afro-Hispanic, European, and Creole voices conveys Sor Juana's consciousness of Mexico's racial and ethnic diversity, but it does so through parody. Although the dissident positions intermittently expressed by the *ensaladas*'s African and Indian speakers cue students into Sor Juana's tendency to make political statements in unexpected places, her parodic renditions of dialects may leave them hungering for a Sor Juana who expresses her sense of Mexico in ways more profound than exoticizing.

Where and how does that Sor Juana come alive? The truth is that her involvement with "Mexican" issues contemporary or historical can appear quite limited. With good reason, gender and personal politics rather than Mexican protonationalist politics of the times seem to prevail in the works of the "Mexican Phoenix." Only her sonnet 206 (1: 310) explicitly deals with the Virgin of Guadalupe, who was a rallying point of the Mexican imaginary community and whose cult swelled in the seventeenth century. Sor Juana also largely eschews the Creole patriotism, or cultural nationalism, launched on a platform of renewed pride in pre-Hispanic Mexican culture that her friend Carlos de Sigüenza y Góngora (1625–1700) and other Creole writers like Augustín de Vetancurt (1620–1700) promoted. Hence, our customary canon for the "Mexican" Sor Juana is rather slim. It generally contains just the *ensaladas* mentioned above, the poem to the Duchess of Aveyro (1: 100–05), and the introductory *loas* to the sacramental dramas (3: 3–21, 97–115, 184–200).

My essay proposes to expand the canon as well as our radar for the Mexican Sor Juana by examining some of her connections to Mexican literary traditions and by attending to the contexts that frame the Mexican texts. In tandem with other scholars (González Echevarría, *Myth*; Higgins), I will call the aggregate of Mexican literary tradition the Mexican archive. Space constraints, of course, make it impossible to do justice here to all of the nun-writer's conceivable relationships with the Mexican archive. Therefore, I have limited my focus to Sor Juana's rich, important engagement with a contingent of Creole and *radicado/a* (Spaniards with deep roots in Mexico) writers and with Creole political issues. Be it the familiar territory of the Mexican Sor Juana or sites that we've barely begun to identify or mine, her texts bound up with these facets of the Mexican archive gain serious Mexican dimensions that transcend exotic headdresses and irreverent parodies.

What follows presents two units of study that involve the foregoing aspects of the Mexican archive and background for their "moment[s] of juncture." Both units may be of value to instructors, whether or not they utilize the suggested readings provided in endnotes. First, however, it befits us to consider the *modus vivendi* of the Mexican archive in Sor Juana's writings.

Sor Juana and the Mexican Archive

To sleuth for Sor Juana's Mexican intertexts is to run up against series of roadblocks. Granted, some of her Mexican sources, like Juan Díaz de Arce in the *Respuesta*, leap out. The major Mexican *sorjuanistas* Alfonso Méndez Plancarte and Octavio Paz note other sources, especially Aztec and religious ones. Nonetheless, I believe that these two star source sleuths, propelled by their own Mexican cultural politics, have exercised a substantial studied blindness toward Sor Juana's cultural politics. Méndez Plancarte and Paz have concentrated massive efforts on unearthing *European* allusions in the nun's work. Paz sees Sor Juana as following a "universalist esthetic" (*Traps* 57–58). To tout her as a world-class writer who thwarted colonial intellectual oppression, both he and Méndez Plancarte punctiliously document how Sor Juana wields the lion's share of Western culture, classical and coeval (see Cohn). Instead of "Mexicanizing" Sor Juana they pointedly Westernize her, with the odd result that the two

Mexican scholars' seemingly exhaustive, definitive scholarship impedes awareness of many of her local sources.

Simple logic tells us that Sor Juana would have been deeply invested in Mexican discourse. From her Creole-dominated convent, she could not have failed to absorb and use Mexican texts, which were readily available and sanctioned. Mexican texts, accepted by her local readership, could legitimate Sor Juana's often audacious writings. Moreover, Dalmacio Rodríguez Hernández posits that Sor Juana participated in a Creole literary group that included Sigüenza y Góngora and Juan de Guevara, a group first consolidated in print by the poet Diego de Ribera in 1668 and that reappeared together in publications for over twenty years (85–88; see Sor Juana's sonnets to Ribera, nos. 202 and 203 [1: 307–08]). Ignacio Osorio Romero establishes that a contingent of Mexican Creoles thrilled to the works of the German Jesuit Athanasius Kircher, so prominent in Sor Juana's writings (*Luz*). In view, then, of Sor Juana's Creole literary connections, together with her own proclivities as a *bricoleuse*, it is almost inevitable that the nun employed Mexican texts as the basis for all kinds of sharp, if hidden, strategizing.

The question of how, concretely, Sor Juana deploys Mexican works raises some vital textual issues. To promote herself as an outstanding luminary, Sor Juana does indeed write in the interstices of Western and Mexican literature, keeping open her mobility between them. Thus, her literary allusions can pack a multiple punch. A pungent example of Sor Juana's multiply inflected images is the eagle, also the prime example of the hybrid, or syncretic, Sor Juana who manipulates Mexican and European cultural capital that Rafael Catalá adduces in the prescient 1987 study from which I have drawn much inspiration. Catalá details at length the multiple valences of the eagle that introduces the "Intermezzo of the Pyramids" in the *Primero sueño* ("First Dream"), and therefore the poem's first epistemological inquiry (1: 343, lines 327–39). Pulsating with resonances, the eagle at once evokes Tenochtitlan and Huitzilopochtli (the foundation of the Aztec city), Jupiter (eagle as bird of divine majesty), Cuauhtémoc, and even Juan Diego (both of whose Nahuatl names relate to the eagle), the Virgin Mary (Rev. 12.14), and more (see Catalá, ch. 4). Each of these references could make sense in and forge new readings of the *Sueño*. Instead of going into them, however, I will extrapolate from the model of the eagle two general points. First, that the same diffuse intertextuality obtains in other of Sor Juana's privileged images, as we will see. And second, or consequently, that in mining Sor Juana's work for resonances of the Mexican archive, we undertake a mission no less risky or enthralling than Boullosa's vis-à-vis Moctezuma.

This said, I'll try to entice you to join the endeavor by offering some "teachable" material. I start with a thesis and an instance of it. Thesis: Sor Juana is at her most overtly Mexican in works for a mass audience, as in her public ceremonies, and/or for Europe. The curious phenomenon may derive from Sor Juana's acuity for self-promotion and self-preservation. She recognizes that the public sphere holds both great advantage and great danger for her; when she writes for Europeans, Sor Juana likes to exploit her cachet as a Mexican *rara avis*. The instance: poem 37, to the Portuguese Duchess of Aveyro, referred to above as forming part of our Mexican Sor Juana canon. When scrutinized through the Mexican archive, the poem yields echoes of late-sixteenth- and early-seventeenth-century Creole complaint not found elsewhere in the nun's oeuvre.

The important second movement of poem 37 segues from the myths of American abundance that foundational Spanish New World texts like those of Columbus and Pietro Martire d' Anghiera had propagated (1: 102–03, lines 81–93) to the very heart of nascent Creole discourse. Sor Juana declares that an insatiable Europe has bled dry the mines of Mexico and that avaricious Spaniards have swarmed into her homeland (1: 103, lines 99–104). Here, significantly, she replays the bitter tirades of the conquerors' first Creole descendants, who, increasingly divested of the Indian labor and territory that they considered to be their birthright, protested their disenfranchisement by the viceregal regime and the rapacity of Spanish newcomers. Sor Juana speaks in total unison, for example, with the Creole Baltasar Dorantes de Carranza's 1604 fevered report on the plight of the conquistadores' descendants, an early Mexican archive unto itself. Even a brief excursion into his anthology-like *Sumaria* (say, from the last paragraph of page 112 to page 114, which includes the wonderfully biting sonnet, "Minas sin plata" ["Mines with no Silver"], likely by the satirist Mateo Rosas de Oquendo) suffices to cement the affiliation with Sor Juana's poem and thereby to place a new spin on a core Mexican text of the nun's repertoire.

Mexican Origins of the Baroque

The climate and period that engendered Dorantes de Carranza's rant do far more than illuminate corners of Sor Juana's poem 37. They open the gateway to a crucial, underexplored aspect of the Mexican Sor Juana: her relationship to Creole writers who, under the sway of the recently arrived Jesuits, broke away from Renaissance literary modes before the Spanish baroque per se entered the colonies. In other words, they lead us to a Sor Juana who reactivates the Mexican origins of the rebellion against Renaissance aesthetics, which adds another layer to the vexed question of the derivative or innovative nature of the New World baroque that Sor Juana epitomizes.

Paz has much to say in *Sor Juana* about the imprint of Jesuit hermetic syncretism, such as Kircher's, on the nun's writings (see chs. 3, 17, 23, 24). Surely, for reasons political, philosophical, and literary, Sor Juana employed the characteristically baroque Jesuit protocols of weaving together all manner of knowledge—local and foreign, secular and religious—when she crafted essential texts like the *Sueño* and the *Respuesta*. Yet the intellectual influence of the Jesuits on Sor Juana, or, of course, on Mexico, by no means ends there.

Jorge Alberto Manrique's indispensable work brings into focus the period that registered the Jesuits' arrival; transformed Mexico; and, I maintain, galvanized Sor Juana ("Manierismo"; *Manierismo*).

Manrique relates the influx of the Jesuits, from 1572 on, to viceregal Mexico's "second project" and "first crisis." By "second project" he means the definitive shift into a postconquest, demilitarized society and from the ascetic founding Franciscans to the worldly Jesuits. The "first crisis" of the viceregal world entailed a dramatic drop in the Indian population, the reassigning of Indian labor from private hands to the state auspices, and the attendant burgeoning of the rancorous Creole class that Dorantes de Carranza represents. Adept at infiltrating local milieux, the Jesuits immediately began to cater to the still-rich (despite their complaints), aimless Creoles, especially by founding schools for their youth. The Jesuits inaugurated the Colegio de San Pedro y San Pablo in 1574 and the boarding school of San Ildefonso in 1588. By 1599 the Jesuit schools had enrolled more than eight hundred students (see Jacobsen).

With the schools came the famed Jesuit curriculum, which wrought its own transformations on the newly minted Creole intelligentsia. The enlightened, humanistic Jesuit curriculum prescribed study of pagan and religious works, classical and contemporary, in Latin and in Spanish. How the program would seed syncretism and prove expedient to Sor Juana now becomes clear. The Jesuits also set up their own printing press to publish textbook versions of the classics. Further, concurrent with the Jesuits' arrival, Mexico City experienced the advent of European mannerist artists, architects, and treatises. According to Manrique, the mannerist sensibility that arose from European crises and deranged Renaissance harmony easily took root in the troubled, transitional climate of New Spain. The intensely iconoclastic mannerism, he argues, struck a chord in the refined, Jesuit-educated, secularized, restless Creole youth. They responded by adopting it. Whence emerged, in Mexico City Creole and *radicado* writers alike, a Mexican mannerism that shared traits of the baroque before that current was heavily imported from Spain. Far in advance of the 1630s, when a full-blown Gongorism manifested itself in Mexican literature, we find a panoply of texts written there that display the love of experimentation, disproportion, excess, the abstruse, and the artificial that align mannerism seamlessly with the baroque. Bernardo de Balbuena's 1604 *Compendio apologético en alabanza de la poesía* ("Apologetic Compendium in Praise of Poetry"), the first New World treatise on poetics, articulates these impulses as it ordains that poetry express the "ordinary and commonplace" "in special and extraordinary ways" (131).

The literary texts that Mexican mannerism spawned constitute the genesis of a colonial Mexican literature. They capture, for the first time, many elements of the local reality. Edgy and extreme, similar to the modern avant-garde, they are not always too abstruse for undergraduates to enjoy. A neat unit of mannerist works related to Sor Juana revolves around the pastoral. The three texts recommended below establish a specifically Mexican pastoral tradition that weighs, among other texts, on Sor Juana's *auto sacramental* ("sacramental drama") written for performance in Madrid, *El divino Narciso* (*The Divine Narcissus* [3: 21–97]).

"Bucólica: descripción de la laguna de Méjico" ("Bucolic: Description of Mexico City's Lagoon"), by the *radicado* Eugenio de Salazar y Alarcón, from the end of the sixteenth century: one of the first poems in Spanish on Mexico City, it literally floods the city with the pastoral.[2] Unequivocally colonialist, wildly allegorical, the bizarre text dramatizes Neptune conquering Tenochtitlan atop a mother-of-pearl whale. Neptune then ensures the idyllic nature of the city by installing tribute structures for Indian labor and cedes the pastoral kingdom to the viceroy and vicereine. Its pastoral and mannerist cast, together with Neptune, link the poem to Sor Juana.

Chapter 6 of Balbuena's *La grandeza mexicana* ("Grandeur of Mexico" [1604]): the widely anthologized pastoral chapter, available in English translation by Samuel Beckett, inaugurates various literary techniques customarily associated with the baroque. A constant touchstone for Creole discourse, Balbuena's "Immortal Spring" resonates into the exquisite natural abundance with which Sor Juana's Eco tempts Narciso and into Sigüenza y Góngora's Guadalupan *Primavera indiana* ("Indian Spring").

Francisco Bramón, *Los sirgueros de la Virgen sin original pecado* ("Heralds of the Virgin Free from Original Sin" [1620]): the first novel published in colonial Mexico, *Sirgueros* is a religious pastoral novel dedicated to the festival of the Immaculate Conception so dear to the Jesuits and a text that exemplifies their educational influence. The Marian *Sirgueros* will probably interest only specialized students. However, its first twenty-three pages alone, in the excerpted modern edition, evince such unmistakable links to Sor Juana as opening references to Ovid and Narcissus and to Persephone, Arethusa, Diana, and Aurora, female characters in the *Sueño*; valorized, erudite female figures (might the text have been directed to female festival patrons?); hyperliterary characters and verbal artifice; references to the local university and cathedral; and primordially, supreme exaltation of Mary, troped through a fountain associated with Narcissus. The novel later culminates in a "tocotín," or Aztec dance, of Mexican rejoicing akin to the final portion in Nahuatl of Sor Juana's *Ensaladilla* 224 (2: 14–17).

The potent alliances between these pastoral texts and *El divino Narciso*, which go unnoted by Méndez Plancarte, transfigure our understanding of the text. They reveal that the sacramental drama traffics extensively in the Mexican archive and that the play thus possesses untold conjunctions with its conspicuously Mexican *loa*. It may be no coincidence that both texts saw print together in 1692, the bicentennial of Columbus's "discovery." Conjointly, they deliver a stunning retrospective of Hispanic Mexico—directly of the Mexican Conquest (the *loa*) and tacitly of viceregal culture (the *auto sacramental*).

Sor Juana and the Virgin of Guadalupe

Approaching *El divino Narciso* from a Mexican perspective additionally calls attention to the Devil-Eco, dark-skinned like the Virgin of Guadalupe. (Remember that the play's fallen angel Eco still bears some resemblance to Christ!) Sor Juana's scant overt devotion to the Virgin of Guadalupe has puzzled scholars. After all, beyond the popularity of the beloved icon, the Jesuits sponsored Guadalupe, and the nun's confessor was a Jesuit; Sor Juana's first patron, Viceroy Marquis de Mancera, championed the cult; Sor Juana's order, the Hieronymites, maintained the shrine of Guadalupe in Spain; and Archbishop Francisco Aguiar y Seijas placed Guadalupe on his coat of arms. The fraught politics surrounding the Virgin of Guadalupe gave Sor Juana ample motivation either to reject or to embrace her. Hedging her bets, the nun-writer charts a third and sinuous course. She chooses diffuse rather than outright reference to Guadalupe, similar to the dynamics of the eagle.

The Mexican archive plays a determining role in that indirect course. Perhaps the Guadalupean poem by the Jesuit Francisco Castro, to whom Sor Juana dedicates her sonnet 206, somehow molded her work, but Castro's tortuous *Octava maravilla* ("Eighth Marvel," excerpted in Méndez Plancarte, *Segundo siglo* 225–53) defies deciphering. Indeed, the nun-writer seems to mock Castro's unintelligibility in her unusually cryptic sonnet. The Jesuit Miguel Sánchez's watershed 1648 Guadalupean treatise, on the other hand, provides an indisputable and accessible key (I quote from Demarest and Taylor's excerpted English translation) to Sor Juana's contrivances.

Once chaplain to Sor Juana's convent, Sánchez put Guadalupe on the global Catholic map. His text, the first published study of Guadalupe in Spanish and the most influential of its times, inserts the Mexican apparition into biblical tradition. Sánchez syncretically weds the apparition to legions of Old and New Testament scriptures, since, as he states, every aspect of the miracle has "some aura of prophecy" (Demarest and Taylor 74).[3] Above all, Sánchez identifies Guadalupe with the woman of Patmos in the prophetic Revelation: "a woman clothed with the sun, and the moon under her feet, and upon her head a crown of twelve stars" (Rev. 12.1), who crushed the devil as dragon and serpent (12.9–17) and who took flight with the "wings of a great eagle" (12.14). Much as this wonder had long been linked to Mary (Brading, *Phoenix* 25), for Sánchez the iconography of Guadalupe unequivocally binds the Mexican figure both to Mary and to the woman of Revelation.

Sánchez's exegesis of Guadalupe held dramatic implications. It universalized the Mexican Guadalupe, endowing a formerly local cult with enormous significance. It rendered the Mexicans a chosen people under special protection of

Mary, catalyzing Mexican patriotism of then and now. Finally, given Sánchez's characterization of Guadalupe as a "sacred *criolla*" (Brading, *First America* 357), it mobilized Creole devotion. That Guadalupean writings and worship greatly took off after 1648, some 120 years after the apparition, therefore comes as less of a surprise.

Readers familiar with Sor Juana's Mariolatry will already have discerned the traces of Sánchez's treatise in her representations of the Virgin Mary. Sor Juana's devotion to Mary is legend, and the malleability of Mary in the nun's hands is no less so. The exculpatory Mary can be anything that Sor Juana needs or wants her to be, even to the detriment of doctrine (1: 449). And what Sor Juana most frequently wants Mary to be is the prototype of the Virgin of Guadalupe filtered through the woman of Revelation.[4] As several scholars have noted (Bénassy-Berling, *Humanisme* 209–11; Kirk, *Sor Juana* 53–57; Tavard 94–98), from her earliest compositions and in reams of subsequent texts, Sor Juana imbues Mary with the attributes of Guadalupe: Mary crushing the dragon and serpent; Mary as eagle or bird; dark-skinned Mary (coalescing with the "black but beautiful" woman of the Song of Songs, as in *El divino Narciso*); Mary dressed in moon, sun, and stars; Mary adorned with Guadalupe's signature roses (for the Mexican Mary, see especially poems 256, 281, 282 [2: 67–69, 105–10] and the prose exercise 406, *Ejercicios devotos* [4: 475–507]). Almost half of Sor Juana's works on the Virgin Mary invoke the Virgin of Guadalupe's characteristics. Sor Juana's refracting of Guadalupe into her attributes and replacing of those features elsewhere endow the conventionally baroque roses so common in the nun's works with a special aura. Sánchez wrote of the Guadalupean roses: "each flower, burgeoning in that mountain, was saying Mary" (Demarest and Taylor 82; Sánchez 189). Accordingly, everything from the roses that unite Sor Juana's two idealized self-figurations—Mary and Saint Catherine, Rose of Alexandria—to the magnificent meditation on the rose in the *Sueño* may carry Guadalupe in their wake. We see that a wave of allusion stretches out from Mary as Guadalupe to influence variegated works, "Mexicanizing" them.

For his part, Sánchez rejoices in every new incarnation of Mary, saying: "there is always miracle when She is to be reborn and . . . each of her miraculous Images is the foreshadowing of another miracle" (qtd. in Demarest and Taylor 64; Sánchez 178). Sánchez's words may have authorized Sor Juana not only to refigure the Virgin Mary extensively but also to reincarnate Mexican (and European) literary traditions continually. It follows from Sánchez that each audacious literary rebirth of the Mexican archive that Sor Juana effects would constitute not a transgression but a miracle. And although, as Boullosa might say, we cannot possibly understand Sor Juana's "Mexicanness" definitively, I believe that we have much to gain from trying to understand her involvement with the Mexican archive and attendant contexts, since the risky venture can yield the pleasure of uncovering previously hidden "miracles."

NOTES

[1]Translations from Boullosa are my own.

[2]Salazar y Alarcón's "Bucólica" appears in full in Gallardo's *Ensayo de una biblioteca española de libros raros y curiosos,* volume 4, and in a useful excerpted version in Méndez Plancarte, *Poetas novohispanos. Primer siglo (1521–1621)* 69–76.

[3]An even more excerpted English translation than their hard-to-obtain edition is contained in Sousa, Poole, and Lockhart, *The Story of Guadalupe: Luis Laso de la Vega's Huei tlamahuiçoltica of 1649* 131–45.

[4]Works by Sor Juana that endow the Virgin Mary with characteristics of the Virgin of Guadalupe include from the *Obras completas*, volume 1, at least poems 138 and 139 (267–70). From volume 2, see poems 222 (10–12); 224, 225, 226 (14–20); 229, 230, 231, 232 (22–28); 251 (60–62); 253 (63–65); 256, 257 (67–71); 268 (86–87); 270 (88–90); 272–73 (91–94); 280, 281, 282 (104–10); 306 (152–53); 310 (157–58). From volume 3, see the prose exercise 406 (475–507). (I have skipped the *villancicos* [carols] attributable to Sor Juana.) Interestingly, the ceremonies to Mary of this nature generally took place in Mexico City. The 1691 festival written for Oaxaca contains the poems associating Saint Catherine of Alexandria with the rose 313 (2: 164–66); 315, 316 (2: 167–70); 320, 321 (2: 177–79).

Colonial No More: Reading Sor Juana from a Transatlantic Perspective

Yolanda Martínez–San Miguel

In *The Black Atlantic*, Paul Gilroy proposed that the reconstitution of the Atlantic as a significant political and economic unit is crucial to understanding the colonial/imperial networks in which race and ethnic identities were conceived in the Euro-American context of modernity. Recent scholarship produced in the United States and Latin America advocates a "global" framework for studying early modern texts in the Americas from a transatlantic and early modern perspective (Klor de Alva; Adorno; H. Bennett). One positive result of this disciplinary renewal is its move toward comparative studies of the Hispanic, Anglo, and French colonial experiences and its connection between colonial productions and their metropolitan counterparts (Seed; Young; Pagden; Fuchs). Some of these new disciplinary paradigms also suggest that reconstituting the Europe-Africa-America network will help us understand the structure of the colonial world order without imposing contemporary national configurations of geography and culture (Gilroy; H. Bennett; Mignolo, *Local Histories*). In studying the Americas, there is also an increasing interest in the comparative study of early "Ibero-Anglo American discursive productions" (Bauer; Spengemann). One danger of these new approaches is that the consistent displacement of the use of the notion of "colonialism" to refer to the cultural productions of the sixteenth through the eighteenth century in Latin America lessens the significance of the political context in recent scholarship about this period. Another consequence of early modern and transatlantic studies is the reestablishment of the study of literary influences to explain the cultural productions of the Americas. These rearticulations of the field of studies are simultaneously complex (Rabasa) and paradoxical (Ashcroft, Griffiths, and Tiffin, *Empire;* Merrim, "Hemispheric").

The question I would like to explore in this essay is how we can benefit from the broadening of debates and critical perspectives that are offered by the transatlantic study of the early colonial Americas without erasing some of the crucial differences that inform the specific historical and cultural processes defining the diverse geopolitical regions of the New World (Kubayanda; Mignolo, *Local Histories*). To answer this question I propose a pedagogical intervention that will focus on the teaching of Sor Juana at the undergraduate level. My objective is to incorporate recent disciplinary paradigm shifts into a close reading of the ways in which an imperial/colonial, transatlantic perspective could be both enriching and limiting to an understanding of the ambivalent discourse of a colonial subject.

Baroque Readings

One of the best ways to introduce Sor Juana in undergraduate courses is through her redondillas "Hombres necios" ("Foolish men") and her sonnets. We begin by reading "Hombres necios" as an argument against patriarchal double standards and as an introduction to formal aspects of Spanish baroque poetry. Antithesis, paradox, and chiasmus are used in the poem to perform the "arte de ingenio" ("art of wit") so crucial in Spanish *conceptismo* (see Hunt, this volume). Students enjoy the decodification of this poem because its main subject is current and controversial. Most anthologies of Hispanic literature also include a selection of Sor Juana's philosophical poems, such as sonnets 145 and 147. I frame class discussion of these poems with selections from the following secondary texts: a definition of carpe diem from *The New Princeton Encyclopedia of Poetry and Poetics* (Preminger et al.); José Antonio Maravall's (*Cultura del Barroco* 23–51) and Walter Benjamin's (*Origen* 168–75) definitions of a baroque culture in Europe; John Beverley's reflection on the relation between modernity and the baroque, and his denomination of the artistic discourse of the period as a "literature of the imperial age" (14); and Judith Butler's definition of cultural intelligibility in her book *Gender Trouble* or Dalia Judovitz's study of "baroque embodiments" in her book *The Culture of the Body*. I usually read in class a short passage from one of these critical texts, and we use it as a point of departure to frame our exercises of literary and cultural analysis on that particular day.

I focus on Sor Juana's continuation and transformation of the topic of carpe diem by identifying her points of contact with Garcilaso de la Vega and Luis de Góngora (see Rabin, this volume) and her addition of a colonial or feminine perspective to the treatment of this well-known literary trope.[1] We first discuss the different notion of originality in the seventeenth century. Sor Juana is then seen as a participant in a baroque notion of "literary mimicry" conceived as "a virtuoso performance in its own right" (Luciani, *Self-Fashioning* 20). In the Americas, however, *imitatio* has to be conceived within a political and cultural milieu that valued the preservation and competitive resignification of artistic motifs as proof of the intellectual and social equality between Europeans and Creoles. From this perspective, Sor Juana's performance of carpe diem is an active appropriation of literary tropes within a Euro-American imperial network, not a simple example of passive literary influences or colonial assimilation.

We also analyze the feminist and epistemological inflections of the topic of carpe diem in Sor Juana's poetry.[2] We study the differences in the objectification of the feminine subject in Garcilaso de la Vega's sonnet 23, "En tanto que de rosa y azucena" ("While the colors of roses and lilies"); Góngora's sonnet 166, "Mientras por competir por tu cabello" ("While to compete with your hair" [*Sonetos*]); and Sor Juana's sonnet 145. We also compare Góngora's sonnets with the active perspective assumed by Sor Juana's lyric voice in sonnet 145, "Este, que ves, engaño colorido" ("This object which you see—a painted snare"), by looking at the artificial and static representation of feminine beauty in a portrait. Sor Juana displaces the baroque tropes of "apariencia y engaño" ("appearance and deceit") to focus instead on the redefinition of a concept of feminine beauty that includes intelligence as one of the crucial attributes of the beloved lady. Here I usually include other examples of her poetry, such as her *romance* 43 and 48 (1: 123–26, 136–39) and her *villancicos* to Saint Catherine, numbers 316, 317, and 322 (2: 169–72, 179–81), or I discuss her use of pedagogic/intellectual language to describe feminine beauty in her sonnets 147, 145, and 148 (1: 277–79; Martínez–San Miguel 51–69). In some courses I also focus on her performance of gender in *Empeños de una casa* ("House of Trials"), and I have included a selection of plays by María de Zayas y Sotomayor and Ana Caro Mallén in which the interplay of domestic and public spaces with female agency promotes engaging class discussions. The analysis of the intersection of gender and colonialism is a useful theoretical framework from which to promote a class discussion on how Sor Juana participates in and transforms the aesthetic episteme of the early modern Hispanic world without referring yet to her American colonial condition.

Barroco de Indias ("American Baroque")

Once we have conceived the baroque as an overarching social, epistemic, and aesthetic system of the early modern period, we focus on how Sor Juana incorporated the New World in her works. We situate Sor Juana's work in a broader context, by taking into consideration how Góngora, Francisco de Quevedo, Lope de Vega, Juan Ruiz de Alarcón, and Miguel de Cervantes referred to Muslims, Jews, *moriscas/os* (Christianized Muslims), *conversas/os* (Jewish converts), Africans, *indianas/os* (Creoles), and the Americas in their dramatic, lyric, and narrative pieces. Depending on the level of the course, I can include selections from some of the following texts: "Zambambú, morenica del Congo" ("Zambambú, Dear Black Woman from Congo"), from Góngora's "En la Fiesta del Santísimo Sacramento" ("In the Festivity of the Most Holy Sacrament"); Quevedo's "Boda de negros" ("Black People's Wedding"); Lope de Vega's play "El Nuevo Mundo descubierto por Cristóbal Colón" ("The New World Discovered by Christopher Columbus"); "La verdad sospechosa" ("The Truth Can't Be Trusted"), by Ruiz de Alarcón; and Cervantes's "El rufián dichoso" ("The Lucky Cur"). I assign articles and book chapters by Leslie Wilson, Cyril Jones, Mabel Moraña (*Viaje*), and Georgina Sabat de Rivers (*Busca*) on the representation of racial and ethnic minorities in Sor Juana's works. Diana de Armas Wilson's *Cervantes, the Novel, and the New World* is an excellent study of the representation of the Americas in Cervantes's works. Finally, John Lipski's study of

African and European contact from a linguistic and historical perspective, *A History of Afro-Hispanic Language*, includes a detailed list of representations of African voices in Spanish and American texts from the sixteenth century to the present.

We frame class discussions with a redefinition of the baroque by using excerpted readings on the following topics: a definition of "Barroco de Indias" following Mariano Picón Salas ("Barroco" 121–50), Moraña (*Viaje* 25–61), Leonardo Acosta (11–34), Irlemar Chiampi (17–41), and Janice Theodoro (139–50); a reconsideration of such notions as "Indias Occidentales" and "indiana/o" using the definitions included in the *Diccionario de autoridades* ("Dictionary of Authorities") and Sebastián de Covarrubias y Horozco's *Tesoro de la lengua castellana* ("Treasure of the Castilian Language"); Michel Foucault's (*Power/Knowledge* 97) and Donna Haraway's reflections on the intersection of context or location and the production of knowledge through their definition of subjugated, or situated, knowledges; and a working definition of criollo ("Creole") discourse using Kathleen Ross's, Antony Higgins's, and Angel Rama's work.

We first address Sor Juana's formal depiction of indigenous subjectivities in her *loa* to the *Divino Narciso* ("The Divine Narcissus"), an *auto sacramental* ("theological drama") written with the explicit intention of being performed in Madrid. The *loa*, following the conventions of the genre, is a brief allegorical representation of the conquest of America that serves as an introduction to the *auto* (see Alker, this volume, for a summary of the *loa*). In class we discuss the opposing gestures of the *loa* as representative of an ambiguous Creole discourse. On the one hand, Sor Juana idealizes indigenous cultures, and Aztec heterogeneity is replaced with an image of an indigenous culture that is already monotheistic. On the other hand, the American subjects are represented as intellectual and rational beings, and evangelization is criticized as an irrational and destructive imposition that displaced indigenous spirituality. Human sacrifices, conceived in imperial European discourse as a proof of indigenous inferiority, are redefined in the play as a parallel ritual to the Catholic Eucharist. Finally, all the characters of the play are subsumed under two key principles of indigenous and oral cultures: practical conceptualization of abstract knowledge (Ong 42–43) and reciprocity, an important narrative motif in Amerindian accounts that explains why the European conquest failed since the early phase of cultural contact (Cummins; Lienhard 208–34; Harrison 52–53). Instead of celebrating Catholic religion, the Spanish and the American couple end up legitimizing Aztec religiosity through syncretism.[3] Sor Juana performs her "Barroco de Indias" precisely in the tensions represented in the play and in the novelty of legitimizing indigenous religiosity for a metropolitan audience

The *villancicos* ("carols") allow us to analyze the representation of ethnic minorities in a collection of texts written for performance in church. In this case Sor Juana includes indigenous and African voices, along with other European ethnic minorities, appropriating Catholic knowledge for a popular audience. As the name of the genre itself suggests—*villancico* is a diminutive version of *villano*, or *aldeano* ("villager")—the text opens its discursive space to the representation of the popular voices of a Catholic community (Méndez Plancarte, "Estudio" xi). One of the main differences between the *villancicos* and the *autos sacramentales* is that in the *villancicos* Sor Juana explores and attempts to re-create the different dialectical appropriations of the Spanish language, and in some cases she even includes words in the native languages of the diverse populations coexisting in the American and imperial Hispanic world. This diversity of languages and dialects contrasts with the apparent homogeneity of religious ideas represented in the *villancicos*.

In discussing a selection of the *ensaladas*, that is, the sections of a *villancico* in which the genre allows for a mixture of diverse colloquial discourses and voices, I usually read the "Villancico a la Asunción" ("Carol to the Assumption" [1676]), because it depicts a couple of African slaves talking about the significance of the Virgin Mary in their daily lives. The "Villancico a San José" ("Carol to Saint Joseph" [1690]), devoted to Saint Joseph's life and meaning in Christian beliefs, includes a competition among a Spaniard, an Indian, and an African to define the most important role played by Saint Joseph according to each speaker's definition of Catholicism. Using Haraway's notion of "situated knowledges" (188), we read this competition of guessing riddles as a juxtaposition of different worldviews and social experiences that transforms the way religion is understood and appropriated. We also analyze the representation of dialects and languages and the redefinition of Christianity as a common ideology that allows for the symbolic reunion of a heterogeneous and complex viceregal society. We conclude our discussion of the "Barroco de Indias" by comparing the ways in which Sor Juana represents indigenous and African voices in her *loas* and *villancicos*, or in her texts written to be performed in the metropolis versus her texts produced to be read or performed in New Spain. The tension between the colonial and the imperial as hermeneutical networks is one of the most productive motifs of Sor Juana's works. The question we explore next is what happens when these two dimensions of Sor Juana's writing are represented in the same text.

Colonial No More: Transatlantic Short-Circuits

I usually conclude my discussion of Sor Juana's work by proposing a close reading of her last poem, "¿Cúando, Númenes divinos . . . ?," to reflect on the possibilities and limits of a Euro-American or transatlantic study of an American colonial discourse (1: 158–61). We review the late-seventeenth-century context in which this poem was written, specifically Sor Juana's final years, which were characterized by a consistent and often too-public debate over her role as an artist, intellectual, and theological authority. Recent scholarship suggests that Sor Juana's intervention in theological debates through her *Carta atenagórica* produced tense relations with the ecclesiastical bureaucracy in New Spain (Trabulse, *Años*; Bijuesca and Brescia; Glantz, *Comparación*). Her public response to the admonition of the bishop of Puebla in the *Respuesta a sor Filotea* ("Answer to Sister Philothea" [1691]) made it even more evident that her location as a colonial religious woman with intellectual and artistic interests was culturally and socially unintelligible in the context of New Spain.

The enormous success of her published works during the last years of her life allowed her to become more visible and to have access to metropolitan readings of her writings. Among the best-known examples of the reception of her work in Spain are precisely the introductory texts and remarks by various religious and courtly admirers that were included at the beginning of the *Segundo volumen* ("Second Volume"), published in Seville in 1692. In her essay "El elogio más calificado" ("The Best Qualified Praise"), Margo Glantz reads these texts as a well-orchestrated defense of Sor Juana that questions the censorship of her writing and secular works after the publication of the *Carta atenagórica*.

Sor Juana's last poem, found unfinished, is a response to the readings of her works by European admirers:

¿Cuándo, Númenes divinos,
dulcísimos Cisnes, cuándo
merecieron mis descuidos
ocupar vuestros cuidados?
¿De dónde a mí tanto elogio?
¿De dónde a mí encomio tanto?
¿Tanto pudo la distancia
añadir a mi retrato?
. . . .
No soy yo la que pensáis,
sino es que allá me habéis dado
otro sér en vuestras plumas
y otro aliento en vuestros labios,
y diversa de mí misma
entre vuestras plumas ando,
no como soy, sino como
quisisteis imaginarlo. (1: 158–59)

When, oh divine Inspirations, sweetest Swans, when did my careless writings deserve your attention? Whence has all this praise come to me? Whence such tribute? Was distance so able to enhance my image? . . . I am not who you think; your pens have given me a different being, and your lips have given me a different spirit; I go among your pens, different from myself, not as I am but as you wished to imagine me. (Luciani, *Literary Self-Fashioning* 140)

Margarita Zamora's reading of the colonial subjectivity of this poem in her essay entitled "América y el arte de la memoria" ("America and the Art of Memory") is a good point of departure for class discussion. Although the poem can be read as a classic example of the rhetoric of humility and false modesty, we focus on the representation of Europe as a distant place that distorts the original image of the colonial subject and produces instead a "retrato" ("portrait") in which the lyric speaker is unable to recognize herself. I use four brief theoretical passages to stimulate class discussion: Homi Bhabha's critical reflection in *The Location of Culture* on the ideological function of stereotypes in a colonial context; the subaltern's reappropriation of these stereotypes by using what Gayatri Spivak terms "strategic essentialism" (*Other Worlds* 205); Aníbal Quijano's notion of the "coloniality of power," to trace the continuity of certain colonial structures and modes of thought in Creole discourse; and Walter Mignolo's proposal of the "locus of enunciation" as a crucial and productive category for the analysis of cultural productions and our critical interventions (*Local Histories* 114–16).

A close reading of the first two stanzas of the poem allows us to notice that the lyric voice is asking her metropolitan readers *in what context*—when and from where is their distorting reading produced—and not *why* the transatlantic hermeneutic network is applicable to her writing. So we also explore how the displacement of "¿por qué?" (a question of origins) by "¿cúando?" (a question of temporality and register) signifies in a postcolonial reading of Sor Juana's work. Therefore, Sor Juana is not questioning the transatlantic reading of her works per se; she is intrigued by a representational system that promotes an "epistemological failing" (Luciani, *Literary Self-Fashioning* 144).

The second part of the poem traces two of the most crucial differentiating elements of Sor Juana's subjectivity: her condition as a self-taught woman and her cultural hybridity as a colonial subject. In this section of the poem Sor Juana includes an ironic reappropriation of indigenous culture to define the unreadability of her poetry:

> ¿Qué mágicas infusiones
> de los Indios herbolarios
> de mi Patria, entre mis letras
> el hechizo derramaron?
> . . . .
> La imagen de vuestra idea
> es la que habéis alabado;
> y siendo vuestra, es bien digna
> de vuestros mismo aplausos.
> Celebrad ese, de vuestra
> propia aprehensión, simulacro,
> para que en vosotros mismos
> se vuelva a quedar el lauro. (1: 156–61)

> What magical infusions did Indian herbalists of my homeland pour to enchant my lines?[4] The image of your own idea is what you have praised, and since it is yours, it is indeed worthy of your applause. Celebrate that simulacrum of your own creation, so that the laurel will remain with you.
> (Luciani, *Literary Self-Fashioning* 142)

Three details are significant to my teaching of this passage. First, throughout the poem, the lyric voice establishes an opposition between a "there" and "here" that resists the idea of a transparent cultural continuity between New Spain and Europe. Second, perhaps as a gesture of "strategic essentialism" (Spivak, *Other Worlds* 205), the indigenous magical "infusions" are represented here as a parodic exoticization of American otherness to stress the cultural differences that intervene in any exercise of cultural interpretation and exchange. In another essay, Electa Arenal and I have proposed that the indigenous magical infusions implicitly refer to the ambivalence of a Creole subjectivity vis-à-vis American indigeneity. The indigenous abstract intervention refers here to an alternative system of knowledge production, yet the poem proposes a productive juxtaposition, not a complete identification, between the native populations and the Creole perspective in the Americas. But if we go beyond the rhetorical strategy of including indigenous culture to signal an irreducible otherness that constitutes a Creole discourse, we find that in this poem Sor Juana is also questioning the transatlantic horizon of reception as a functioning hermeneutical context.

Therefore, the poem resists its transatlantic reading by focusing on the meanings and referents that are lost in the cultural and literary reappropriations of the American context by the audience overseas. Instead of becoming the ideal mediator/translator between American and European cultures, the (Creole) lyric voice proposes a closure in the hermeneutical networks existing between the colonies and their metropolitan counterparts. In this sense, European eulogists have created a false image of the colonial subject that is a reflection of their own (imperial) conceptions, and, as such, the greatness of their depiction reflects a tribute to themselves and not to the "real" American subject behind the "obscuros borrones" ("drafts and scratches" [1: 161; my trans.]). At the same time, however, in Sor Juana's incorporation of the indigenous presence, the lyric voice creates again an abstract category that is completely deprived of political and social agency. I follow Ross's conception of seventeenth-century Creole discourse as a "literature [that] shows a constant wavering of language from dominant to subordinate positions, resulting in subversions of European models even when those models are consciously being imitated" (7), and Higgins's contention that in the eighteenth century we find a mature Creole discourse that is more differential and subversive than European models. It is precisely in this "wavering" tension produced in a transatlantic hermeneutical network that we can locate the specificity of a maturing colonial/Creole discourse. Closure and dependency, rejection and imitation become crucial aspects in the horizon of signification of Sor Juana's work. We conclude our analysis of Sor

Juana's writing by reflecting on our own hermeneutical approaches to literary works and by questioning our own invested readings of colonial and contemporary cultural productions.

Reviewing the multiple dimensions of Sor Juana's performance of the Euro-American baroque goes beyond the readings that locate her as a passive or subversive performer of metropolitan discourses. Transatlantic or early modern approaches should not imply a depolitization or dehistorization of colonial works. By incorporating *coloniality* as an integral part of our conceptualization of modernity and imperialism (Quijano; Mignolo, *Local Histories*), we are able to focus on the multiple poetics and discourses that interact and collide in Sor Juana's work. My pedagogical intervention proposes a refocusing of the early modern period by considering the peripheral position of the colonial Americas in the cultural, epistemological, and political milieu of the second half of the seventeenth century (Mignolo, *Local Histories*; Poblete; Kubayanda). By using Sor Juana's own works as concrete examples of the theoretical debates proposed in the passages used to promote class discussions throughout the semester, we incorporate the recent disciplinary paradigm shifts into a close reading of the ways in which an imperial/colonial, transatlantic perspective could be both enriching and limiting to an understanding of the ambivalent discourse of a colonial subject. We also question the artificial divide between literature and literary theory, since we allow Sor Juana to provide us with a thought-provoking critique of cultural interpretation while remaining "diversa de sí misma" ("different from herself") in her own writing.

NOTES

[1]Quevedo's sonnets—such as "Amante agradecido a las lisonjas mentirosas de un sueño" and "Venganza de la edad en hermosura presumida" (*Poesía original*)—can also be included in class discussions, specially to focus on the intersection of "conceptismo" and carpe diem.

[2]Among the most useful studies proposing feminist readings of Sor Juana's works are Merrim's anthology, *Feminist Perspectives on Sor Juana Inés de la Cruz*; Sabat de Rivers's *En busca de sor Juana; Untold Sisters*, by Arenal and Schlau, and Arenal and Powell's bilingual *The Answer / La respuesta*.

[3]On the intersection of indigenous and European discursive modes in colonial texts, see Brokaw and Mazzotti. Díaz Balsera has analyzed the use of Jesuit syncretism to trace the incorporation of Christian and Nahuatl beliefs in the religious practices depicted in the *loa*.

[4]The first line of the translation is from an unpublished translation by Electa Arenal and Amanda Powell. The rest is Luciani's.

Across the Atlantic: Sor Juana, *La respuesta*, and the Hispanic Women's Canon

Lisa Vollendorf

Since Sor Juana Inés de la Cruz rose to fame in the noble and artistic circles of seventeenth-century Mexico, she has been hailed as one of Latin America's finest authors. Her contemporaries granted her patronage coveted by the finest artists of the day and called her "fénix de México, décima musa, poetisa americana" ("phoenix of Mexico, the tenth muse, American poetess" [*Fama* frontispiece].[1] More recently, many of Latin America's preeminent thinkers have taken up the pen to extol, decipher, and psychoanalyze her life and works. The Chilean poet Gabriela Mistral returned again and again to considerations of Mexico's wise nun; the Mexican novelist Carlos Fuentes dubbed her Latin America's first great poet (Paz 1); and the Mexican poet Octavio Paz, in his biography of Sor Juana, devoted six hundred pages to her case, which he termed unique.

Paz's and others' insistence on Sor Juana's unparalleled uniqueness brings us to the crux of a problem that has led many students and scholars to misunderstand Sor Juana's place in history. Indisputably, Sor Juana Inés de la Cruz was an erudite, incisive, engaged thinker. Yet she was not the only woman in the Hispanic world who wrote during the seventeenth century. Historical and literary studies from 1985 through today have shown that hundreds of other religious and secular Hispanic women wrote during and even before the age of Sor Juana (Arenal and Powell; Arenal and Schlau; Merrim, *Early Modem*; McKnight; Myers, *Neither Saints*; and Vollendorf). Recent advances in knowledge about Hispanic women's literary history suggest that Sor Juana shared many characteristics with other female writers. In combination with new discoveries about women in colonial Spanish America and early modern Europe, the similarities between Sor Juana and her American and European sisters demand that we situate her work in the context of other women writers to fully understand her political as well as aesthetic importance.

Like other women who wrote in the long seventeenth century (1580–1700), Sor Juana fought to defend women's intellect. Critical of a cultural system that excluded women from the benefits of education and other mechanisms of social inclusion, she and other writers depicted women as having moral, emotional, and intellectual prowess. Sor Juana and her seventeenth-century literary sisters participated in a political project that not only engaged the centuries-old debate on the worth of women (known as the *querelle des femmes*) but also transcended the simplistic pro- and antiwoman rhetoric of the debate. They refused flat, uncomplicated representations of gender relations and exposed the systematic subordination of women in their culture. On both sides of the Atlantic, women writers revealed the hypocrisy in a cultural system that failed to include women.[2]

By positioning Sor Juana as one of many erudite women who challenged the status quo, we can better understand the broader intellectual and cultural contexts in which she and her literary sisters lived and wrote. Scholars have long acknowledged Sor Juana's indebtedness to European tradition and New World thought. Gender, however, needs to be factored into this contextualization. Despite of the cultural and geographic distance that separated Europe and the New World, in both places women were relegated to subordinate roles by science (which viewed them as flawed males), Christian theology (which demanded their subjection to men), and even humanists (who partially supported female education yet demanded obedience of women). Spain's imposition of its religion, government, and social structure in the Americas only partially explains the emphasis on women's subordination in the New World, where indigenous cultures favored male power and rule.

Given the similar gender politics on both continents, we should not be surprised by the many commonalities in writing strategies and ideological messages in early modern European and colonial Spanish American women's writing. While Sor Juana lambasted "hombres necios" ("foolish men") for accusing women of dishonorable behavior (1: 228; Arenal and Powell 157), dozens of other women on both sides of the Atlantic declared men unfair and unjust.[3] Such similarities can be used to frame a dialogue about a female literary tradition that began to flourish in the late 1500s. Thanks to the emphasis on monastic reform and convent foundations embraced during the Council of Trent (1545–63), the second half of the sixteenth century saw a marked rise in the foundations of new convents. This, in turn, contributed to a significant rise in women's literacy, as convents attracted educated women of the upper classes and also emphasized education as an important part of female monastic culture.

At the same time that women's literacy was rising within convent walls, the change was afoot in a society shifting toward mercantilism and transatlantic trade and expansion. The modern book market emerged, and books in the vernacular (rather than in Latin) were produced for an ever-growing literary trade. The printing press, invented in 1453 and introduced to New Spain in 1539, revolutionized the reproduction of texts and, consequently, paved the way for a mass market of readers. While it is true that most of the population remained illiterate and did not have the financial or educational resources to form part of that growing market, it also is true that women formed part of that market in increasing numbers. Research on women's reading culture demonstrates that female literacy rose during the period. Literacy statistics are nearly impossible to measure, but Pedro Cátedra and Anastasio Rojo argue convincingly that we must take into account that reading was taught separately from writing. Thus, literacy rates based simply on the ability to sign one's name do not accurately reflect the ability to read (Cátedra and Rojo 39–44). Nonetheless, inventories of women's libraries suggest that aristocratic women owned, whether or not they read, religious texts (including devotional and prayer books), fiction (for example, Boccaccio and the anonymous *Amadís de Gaula*), philosophy (such as Aristotle), and recipe books (Cátedra and Rojo 289–93).

The policies of the crown in the early modern era also affected women's relation to knowledge and to the public sphere. The expulsions of Jews (1492) and Muslims from Spain (1502) profoundly affected the large minority populations, as thousands were forced to make the choice to flee or convert to Catholicism. The public sphere became off limits for Jewish and Muslim religious practice. Many Muslim men went into hiding; others were arrested and pressed into service as galley slaves. Thus women of Jewish and Muslim descent took over roles as the keepers of religion, teaching prayers and traditions to their children even in the face of inquisitorial scrutiny.[4] Broadly speaking, the entire population felt the effects of nation building. When men began leaving for the Americas in high numbers, Spain saw an increase in female business owners, female influence in politics and aristocratic culture, and women's participation in legal disputes.[5] These data suggest that women played a larger role in the public and private spheres than ever before imagined.

The rise of literary and convent cultures coincided with the popularization of Teresa of Avila's works throughout Spain. By 1580, women's literary activities had increased; and the date signals the start of the first boom in early modern and colonial women's writing.[6] Beginning in the late sixteenth century, as Teresa of Ávila's writings became popular, her work became known to a broad public. This period marks a shift in the history of women's literacy and literature, since Saint Teresa would not have become so popular if women could not read her texts. In turn, fewer women would have been encouraged to write without her example. The following century saw a significant rise in women's participation in public life and the literary scene. Sor Juana wrote at the end of that period. Her last publication, *La respuesta* (*The Answer*), provides a fitting bookend to the first measurable boom in Hispanic women's writing, which lasted from 1580 to 1700.

Like many of the writers who formed part of the first great movement of Hispanic women's cultural production, Sor Juana was an advocate for intellectual freedom, education, and equality. No text better synthesizes that advocacy project than the *Respuesta*. Written in 1691, it was published in Mexico in 1700, and then in Spain, but only at the instigation of María Luisa Manrique de Lara y Gonzaga, the vicereine who had become Sor Juana's staunch supporter in Mexico. That the *Respuesta* was published in Spain highlights the transatlantic nature of Hispanic culture and, more specifically, of Catholic women's religious culture in the early modern period.

The *Respuesta*, a brilliant defense of Sor Juana's incursions into book learning, positions theology and intellectualism as inclusive, expansive, and interrelated enterprises. Inclusive, because women and men should be included in theological considerations both as learners and as teachers. Expansive, because theology and spirituality cannot be isolated from other branches of learning.

Thus Sor Juana defines the two enterprises as intimately connected: no individual seeking spiritual perfection and theological clarity can succeed without broad knowledge of arts and sciences.

Such connections among gender, learning, and writing are crucial to early modern and colonial women's arguments about equal educational opportunities. Using a tactic found in all the known secular Spanish authors of the 1600s, Sor Juana further legitimizes women's experiences by placing the female experience—in this case her own—at the center of her text. Other Hispanic women who employ this strategy include María de Zayas y Sotomayor (c. 1590–?), the popular Spanish author whose female characters decry that men "nos negáis letras y armas" ("deny us access to pen and sword" [*Novelas* 34; *Enchantments* 175]). With these and other statements, Zayas links women's lack of access to arms and letters to their lack of power in situations of violence and abuse.

Sor Juana, concerned with her male colleagues' criticisms of her devotion to learning and writing, also valorizes the power of education. Lamenting that church authorities sought to prohibit her from studying (Arenal and Powell 73), she argues extensively that spiritual efforts are meaningless unless accompanied by an illumination of the mind. Learning, therefore, is an obligation for those seeking spiritual enlightenment (Arenal and Powell 52–53). The dissertation on education as obligation concludes that the world would be better if women as well as men had opportunities to teach and learn. Where Zayas depicts the deadly consequences of women's exclusion from arms and letters, Sor Juana emphasizes religious women's obligation to cultivate the intellect. Both strategies support an ideology of access and equity.

The similarities between Zayas and Sor Juana lead us to wonder if, despite the prohibition on publication or importation of novels in the New World, the Mexican nun read her Spanish predecessor's texts. We do know that Sor Juana's inclusion of several of her spiritual sisters in the *Respuesta* reveals that she saw herself as belonging to a tradition of religious women writers. In addition to four specific references to Saint Teresa in the *Respuesta,* for instance, she also mentions María de San José Salazar (1548–1603), María de Agreda (1602–65), and María de la Antigua (1566–1617), using the examples of the Spanish nuns to argue for Catholic women's right to write (Arenal and Powell 91). The connections among Sor Juana and her writing sisters suggest that the Mexican nun may have read these and other nuns' texts while living in a Carmelite convent in Mexico City (Arenal and Powell 117). Likewise, Sor Juana's uses the same literary techniques as other religious and secular female writers of the seventeenth century, strategies designed to present women's ideas to male authorities and to the public.

Defending women's intellectual capacities, decrying men's desire to impede learning, and placing female experiences at the center of fictional and nonfictional texts are only three of a number of strategies used by women throughout Latin America and the Old World. Sor Juana mobilized all three techniques, often casting her ideas in self-denigrating prose to emphasize humility while simultaneously asserting her intellectual prowess. Known as the topos of humility and coined a "rhetoric of femininity" by Alison Weber, this technique is evident in Sor Juana's references in the *Respuesta* to writing she describes as "mis borrones" ("drafts and scratches" [4: 440; 39]), "un papelillo" ("a trifling thing" [4: 471; 97]), and "una simple narración de mi inclinación a las letras" ("a simple account of my inclination to letters" [4: 460; 77]). Zayas, too, referred to her writing as "borrones" ("scribbles" [*Novelas* 159]). Another Spanish author, Mariana de Carvajal (1610–?), called her novella collection "un aborto de mi corto ingenio" ("an abortion of my small wit" [5]).

The emphasis on female humility resonated profoundly with Christian femininity, as evidenced by the repeated references to humble behavior in religious autobiographies and biographies known as *vidas*. One such text recounts the life of the religious laywoman (beata) María de Orozco y Luján (1635–1709), who cultivated an aura of spirituality through a humble, albeit humorous, refusal of suitors, reportedly telling them she had four strikes against her: "vieja, fea, enferma y pobre" (qtd. in Barbeito Carneiro 33 ["old, ugly, sick, and poor"]). Orozco's humble actions included sweeping the streets, eating excrement as penitence, and only learning to read and write through a miracle of God (Vollendorf 147–55). Like the sixteenth-century aristocrat Luisa de Carvajal y Mendoza (1566–1614), who wore tattered clothes and waited in food lines with the poor (Cruz 182), Orozco wrote countless letters detailing her quest for spiritual perfection. Similarly, the biography of Catalina de Jesús y San Francisco (1639–77) repeatedly highlighted the subject's struggle to overcome vanity and to aid the poor. While Catalina de Jesús y San Francisco's middle-class relatives criticized her daily hospital visits, arguing that they potentially endangered her family, "none of this could stop the flow of her piety" ("nada de esto podía detener el corriente de sus piedades" [Bernique 183]). These pious depictions of María de Orozco, Luisa de Carvajal, and Catalina de Jesús are only a handful of hundreds of examples of idealized Catholic femininity that permeated Hispanic culture and writing.

Sor Juana and her seventeenth-century cohort played off of that model of submissive femininity by using rhetoric that suggested they were extraordinarily humble, unschooled, and dim. In doing so, the women explicitly acknowledged and manipulated dominant beliefs that held them to be inferior. In a twist of rhetorical irony, women employed the humility topos as a means to legitimize their writing. Adding a rhetoric of obligation to their humble self-presentations, Sor Juana, Zayas, and Mariana de Carvajal all referred to their lack of education and worth, concluding that they were blameless for any errors or offenses in their texts. The rhetoric of obligation is double-edged with religious women, who almost universally claimed, as did Saint Teresa and Sor Juana, to write out of obedience and obligation. This rhetoric takes on a defiant tone in the *Respuesta:* "Y, a la verdad, yo nunca he escrito sino violentada y forzada y sólo por dar gusto a otros" ("And truth to tell, I have never written save when pressed and forced and solely to give pleasure to others" [4: 444;

46–47]). Secular women use a variation on this rhetoric: Zayas tells her readers that they are obligated to read her texts because she is a woman (*Novelas* 161), and Carvajal presents herself as a widow whom readers should pity (5).

To justify the defense of female education and intellect, female writers on both sides of the Atlantic commonly integrated catalogs of famous women into their texts. Following the tradition of prowoman writers such as Christine de Pizan, female authors of prose fiction and nonfiction frequently included lists of exemplary women to bolster their arguments. Zayas incorporated such catalogs, as did María de Guevara, the Countess of Escalante (d. 1683), who devoted an entire chapter to brave women in *Desengaños de la Corte* ("Disenchantments at Court" [1664]). Similarly, Juana Inés de la Cruz refers to many historical and mythological figures in the *Respuesta*. By citing women noted for their learning, bravery, patience, and countless other virtues, she puts her learning on display and validates that erudition with examples of well-regarded women. Sor Juana's diverse list includes philosophers, goddesses, mothers, poets, and mathematicians. The wisdom and success of these women are used to fortify Sor Juana's argument that Saint Paul's famous dictum ("Let women keep silent in the churches") was meant only to ban women from "la publicidad de los púlpitos" ("public speech at the pulpit" [Arenal and Powell 89–91]). This argument is crucial for the *Respuesta*, in which Sor Juana argues against those who would silence and control what she casts as her spiritual obligation to learn. Indeed, she uses the argumentation about Paul's prohibition to bolster her attack on "Sor Filotea" and other men who wanted to control her intellectual activities. She boldly phrases the struggle for intellectual freedom in a question to her detractors: Why must others forbid me from writing if the Holy Mother Church does not? (4: 468; 91).

Despite the defiant tone of the challenge put to male authorities in *La respuesta*, a tone of loneliness and defeat prevails. Sor Juana concludes her exquisite argumentation by announcing that she will retire from writing altogether: "Lo que es por mi defensa, nunca tomaré la pluma" ("I shall never in my own defense take up the pen again" [4: 471; 96–97]). The defeatism of *La respuesta* echoes the tone of many other texts that decried men's control over women. One predecessor with a similar message was the French writer Marie de Gournay (1565–1645). Author of numerous essays and an active participant in the *querelle des femmes*, Gournay lamented women's subordination when she wrote, "Happy are you, reader, if you do not belong to this sex to whom all good things are forbidden" ("Ladies' Grievance" 23). She also bemoaned "men's arrogant belief in their own superiority" ("Equality" 15). Acknowledging the exhausting enterprise facing women, constantly under attack by men, the Italian writer Moderata Fonte (1555–92) constructed an all-female environment in *Il merito delle donne* ("The Worth of Women" [1600]), in which characters celebrate the absence of men and proclaim, "I'd rather die than submit to a man!" (48).

Perhaps the most striking parallels in defiant rhetoric and ideology exist between Zayas and Sor Juana. Lisis, the protagonist in Zayas's novella collection, states that she has taken up the pen and will also take up the sword in women's defense (*Desengaños* 507). And, citing men's abuses of women, Lisis cancels her wedding and withdraws to a convent at the end of *Desengaños amorosos* ("The Disenchantments of Love"). The narrator applauds the decision to live among women as the happiest possible ending, because the protagonist "no se sujetó a ninguno" ("did not subject herself to any man" [*Desengaños* 510–11]). Sor Juana echoes these sentiments by declaring her retirement from the male world of writing. In so doing, she announces a symbolic retirement from the control of men. Readers today are moved by the *Respuesta*'s autobiographical account of her irresistible desire for knowledge and her signed statement renouncing secular studies in 1694.

The similarities between Sor Juana Inés de la Cruz and her European and Latin American predecessors and contemporaries confirm that the nun was not alone in her fight to defend women's intellectual merits and educational rights. On both sides of the Atlantic, in convents and without, a sorority of writers shared her ideology and employed similar strategies to combat misogyny. The extent to which these women knew of one another's existence remains to be explored, but Sor Juana herself gives us clues to her relationship with her transatlantic sisters. She clearly had an awareness of some of their writing, as evidenced by explicit references to several women. She also wrote a text destined for a sorority across the Atlantic: Sor Juana's *Enigmas*, discovered only in 1968, was written for nuns living in a Portuguese convent.

Emerging textual clues and scholarship should encourage teachers and students to work together to place Sor Juana Inés de la Cruz in a transatlantic context of women's intellectual history, feminist history, and baroque literature. By reading her in conjunction with authors who participated in the artistic and scientific innovations of the day, we can recognize Sor Juana as an extraordinary baroque writer. By considering her alongside other women who dared to take up the pen and challenge male dominance, we can appreciate her as a woman who, with countless others on both sides of the Atlantic, fought to dismantle gender inequality.

Like other women who wrote during the boom of 1580–1700, Sor Juana Inés contributed to the foundations of a canon of Hispanic women's writing. For the mere fact of their literacy and their willingness to write, all of the women who participated in the early literary culture of Europe and the Americas were extraordinary. It is up to future students and scholars of Sor Juana to integrate those women's words into discussions about what it meant to write and live in a time in which Sor Juana's infamous "hombres necios" demanded female subservience and silence.

NOTES

[1]All translations are mine unless otherwise indicated.

[2]See Arenal and Schlau; Arenal and Powell; Jordan; Merrim, *Early Modern*; and Wilson and Warnke.

SOR JUANA AS A BAROQUE WRITER: A COLONIAL LATIN AMERICAN WOMAN'S WAYS OF KNOWING

Gendered Ways of Seeing with Sor Juana: "Situating Knowledge" in New Spain

Catherine M. Bryan

A fascinating aspect of Sor Juana's literary works is the often remarkable way in which they seem to project beyond the historical and sociocultural context in which they were produced, to reach into our own contemporary moment and enter into dialogue with issues and problems we are confronting today. Sor Juana studies can engage students who seem to be far removed from the colonial baroque context of New Spain and create conversations that cross time and space. It is almost as if, through her telescopic lens, Sor Juana could see into the future and offer ways of elaborating gendered strategies of resistance, change, and freedom.

Therefore, I believe an important task of teachers of Sor Juana and her works is to create bridges, or points of mediation, between Sor Juana and her new readers in order to facilitate communication (dialogue, analysis, interpretation, critique). To address this challenge, my approach in the classroom and in this chapter arises from an essay written by Electa Arenal in which she calls for a continued study of the "prefigurements of the theoretical modes of twentieth-century feminist scholars, especially literary critics" in the works of Sor Juana ("Where" 125). In responding to that call, I diverge from it somewhat, in that I draw on critics of visual culture as well. A fruitful point of contact between Sor Juana's colonial baroque period and our contemporary moment can be found in a relatively new area of critical analysis: feminism and visual-culture studies. This is a field that we might say was "prefigured" by Sor Juana.

While Sor Juana's contributions to a gendered critique of baroque culture have been well established in previous studies of her work (and continue to be explored), scholars have also begun to examine the visual aspects of Sor Juana's literary production in connection with her interest in optics as a science and with the ocular elements of baroque culture (see Avilés; Bergmann, "Amor"; Luciani, "Emblems"). In her works, Sor Juana includes references to optical instruments newly developed during her historical period, and she poetically questions the reliability of the sense of sight, especially in connection with the image and power.

In her essay "Latin American Visual Cultures," Andrea Noble emphasizes the importance of the image in the colonial project as a site in which differences in language could be mediated and social relationships represented. The image served to transmit the values and ideals of dominant society, presented a model of perception, and offered a way of imagining one's place in colonial society. Noble also highlights the role, or agency, of the viewer of the image as one who engages with it in consent or resistance (155). I suggest that Sor Juana assumes, and proposes that we assume with her, this engaged and resistant stance of the viewer, especially as it is informed by gender: it is a "feminist" stance to which Sor Juana alludes.

In the introduction to *The Feminism and Visual Culture Reader*, the editor, Amelia Jones, describes the intersection of feminism and visual culture: "[F]eminism has long acknowledged that visuality (the conditions of how we see and make meaning of what we see) is one of the key modes by which gender is culturally inscribed in Western culture. Feminism and visual culture, then, deeply inform each other" (1). The two poems that form the center of this essay will be studied at that intersection of "feminism" and "visual culture" and are particularly interesting because they are connected to visual art—portraits of Sor Juana—and to Sor Juana's views about perception and representation, about baroque ways of seeing, knowing, and being. First is the often studied sonnet 145, "Este, que ves, engaño colorido" ("These lying pigments facing you" [1: 277; Trueblood 95]). This poem contains Sor Juana's remarks on a portrait of herself. The second, "Verde embeleso de la vida humana" ("Green allurement of our human life" [1: 280–81; Trueblood 101]), concerns the themes of hope and vision. Before it was published in collected works by Sor Juana, this sonnet was painted directly onto the portrait of Sor Juana by Juan de Miranda.

A useful pedagogical tool in the classroom study of these two sonnets are visual references to portraits of Sor Juana (see Meléndez, in this volume). As a companion to the literary analysis, these baroque visual images allow students to practice visual-culture studies directly and in connection to Sor Juana's literary works.

An interesting point of departure is to compare the feminist theologian Pamela Kirk's description of the Miranda and the Miguel Cabrera portraits (*Sor Juana* 150–55) with that of the intellectual and poet Octavio Paz (*Traps* 272–74). One can begin to have an idea of how highly charged this clash in visuality can be by reading first a brief excerpt from Kirk:

> The Miranda painting . . . clearly portrays Sor Juana as an active, multifaceted personality. We are apparently interrupting her as she stands at her writing pulpit. She has her quill in hand and has just signed her name under the untitled poem which begins, "Verde embeleso. . . ." Two inkwells and letter openers frame the page on the desk. . . . [W]e see three volumes with "Juana Inés de la Cruz" engraved on their spines. . . . The bookshelves behind her contain authors she cited and presumably loved. . . . A glass container with a plant specimen holds a paper with a geometric formula from falling off the shelf. In short, we see, stylized, the "working office" of an intellectual with a wide range of interests, a writer and a poet with ink still wet from her latest creation. (152)

And, second, a section from Paz:

> One hand, at once slender and rounded, is white against the white sleeves of her habit and the whiteness of the paper. In Miranda's painting the hand is holding a quill pen, like a dove lifting a twig to its beak. . . . Her elegant habit falls to her feet without entirely disguising the slender waist. . . . In both portraits the left hand is caressing the beads of an enormous rosary worn as a necklace. The gesture is more courtly than devout. . . . The mouth is sensuous, fleshy, with just the suspicion of down on the upper lip. The nose, straight and "judicious": the flared nostrils accentuate the vague sensuality of that remote face. . . . We see Sor Juana among her books as we would glimpse naked goddesses through a break in the mythological clouds. (*Traps* 272–73)

Their differently nuanced descriptions bring to the forefront the dynamics of the sociocultural (gendered) location of the observer in the process of "reading" the visual work and provide a provocative starting point for opening classroom discussion and for transitioning to the study of Sor Juana's sonnet "Este que ves." In the poem, Sor Juana can be seen to provide her own description of a portrait of herself, from the position of an engaged and resistant viewer.

"Este que ves": Do You See?

Analysis of the sonnet begins by discussing the poetic situation that the title sets up, a poet commenting on her portrait: "Procura desmentir los elogios que a un retrato de la poetisa inscribió la verdad, que llama pasión" ("She disavows the flattery visible in a portrait of herself, which she calls bias" [1: 277; Trueblood 95]). The sonnet's critical allusions to the baroque literary trope of carpe diem and its connection to a painting; the interplay between appearance and reality; and the deceits of artistic artifice are made even more urgent given this poetic situation: it is both a sociocultural critique and a personal-gendered defense, with the added paradoxical twist that the desirable female image is that of a nun.

Luis Avilés studies the title in connection to the opening line, "Este, que ves, engaño colorido," pointing out the problem of absence or lack for the reader who is excluded from the central event represented in the sonnet. First, the reader does not know to which specific portrait the poet refers, and, second, the reader does not know with whom the poet is speaking. Who is the "tú," subject of "ves" (415–16)? While, on the one hand, this represents a commonplace apostrophe, it can also open up an interesting pedagogical strategy.

I have mentioned the ability of many of Sor Juana's works to be specific to their historical moment and to project simultaneously into ours—and that, I think, is one of the potentially fruitful dimensions of her opening "ves." Rather than feel a sense of exclusion, the readers could understand that the poet speaks directly to and with them. The poetic voice thus creates a sense of immediacy and intimacy with the reader, an interlocutor who would look, and attempt to see, as she does. In this way, Sor Juana poetically creates community, inviting her readers to see beyond baroque literary-artistic tropes influenced by the repressive forces of the Counter-Reformation and a colonial patriarchal order. If, as Noble suggests, the image is a contested site for the creation of meanings, and we, as viewers, are included in that contestation process, it would seem that the poetic voice in "Este que ves" seeks to appeal to the agency of the resistant viewer/reader to collaborate in the creation of other meanings and, perhaps, other modes of representation.

Referring to the world of art from the 1500s to 1900, John Berger explains that "new attitudes toward property and exchange" produced "a new way of seeing" that "found its visual expression in the oil painting": "Oil painting did to appearances what capital did to social relations. It reduced everything to the equality of objects. . . . The soul, thanks to the Cartesian system, was saved in a category apart. A painting could speak to the soul—by way of what it referred to, but never by the way it evisaged. Oil painting conveyed a vision of total exteriority" (86–87). These observations regarding perception and the oil painting as embedded in and contributing to socioeconomic processes of the period are interesting on a number of levels for our study of Sor Juana's sonnet/portrait.

On the one hand, as Magali Carrera explains in her study of portraits and *casta* paintings in New Spain, "[A]rtists employed a conventional visual vocabulary of portraiture to represent the . . . status of women" (23) and other members of New Spain society marked by race and class. Through the painted image, members of a heterogeneous colonial community were shown their ideal roles in that community. By way of exterior markings (clothing, jewelery, hairstyle), one's social position was represented for the viewing public. Thus private individuals became public models through the artistic process of the colonial baroque portrait.

At the same time, the predominance of portraiture in the privileged field of the visual during the baroque period (Maravall, *Culture* 257; Schloder 78), created a space that brought into view a central tension of baroque culture, the relation between appearance and reality. A defining aspect of baroque portraiture was the faithful reproduction of the human subject, the notion of "verisimilitude," of "baroque naturalism" (Martin 12), and yet philosophical currents of the period simultaneously questioned how the artistic method would represent or capture the soul, the genius, the true *geist* of the human subject. Light, shading, color could perhaps allude to emotion, as some suggested, but the intellect, the soul? Clearly, in passing from human subject to painted object, something would be lost in the translation. It was at that tension between the modern individual—newly endowed with Cartesian free will, cogito, consciousness as thinking subject and creator of knowledge—and the artistic representation of the individual through baroque visual practices that the emerging modern self confronted previous notions of subjectivity, the Counter-Reformation, and a semifeudal society at a moment of crisis and transition. Perhaps it is Sor Juana who appears at that intersection as the poetic voice of the modern self willing to contest the signs and symbols employed to represent her. As Richard Brilliant sums up, "Portraits exist at the interface between art and social life and the pressure to conform to social norms enters into their composition because both the artist and the subject are enmeshed in the value system of their society" (11).

On the other hand, with the development of the "new science" of optics in the seventeenth century, René Descartes described the phenomenon of color as differently reflected rays of light that bounced off of unevenly graded surfaces and that were then received and refracted within the mechanism of the eye (*Discourse* [Olscamp] 70–74). The new technology of artistic representation, the oil painting, used the smooth and seductive portrayal of color and light. For Sor Juana, though, it displayed a deceit of color ("lying pigments"): it was both pure exteriority and a jumble of uneven light rays reflected, absorbed, and refracted (thus, distorted) in the process of representation. Color lacked the ability to bring forth the interiority of the person: the soul, ideas, genius, for they are without surface, without light rays or color.

How would the baroque mode of portraiture represent Sor Juana's intellect, her soul? Sor Juana understood the masks, costumes, and idealized behavior that the "masters" had in mind for her and women like her. Of all the levels of baroque deceit represented in the sonnet, perhaps that model of behavior was the most serious, the one that must be contested. And the subject of the portrait wrote back.

As Emilie Bergmann observes, the female poet of "Este que ves" "deflects the possessive gaze from her own image and turns a mirror toward the male observer"("Sor Juana" 166). When the mirror is turned toward the male observer (poet, painter, reader, or viewer), as Bergmann suggests, there is a change in relations: suddenly we can see his face, and the possessive male gaze is embodied; his way of seeing and knowing has been situated. This sociocultural move is precisely what Donna Haraway calls for in her chapter "Situated Knowledges":

> I would like to insist on the embodied nature of all vision, and so reclaim the sensory system that has been used to signify a leap out of the marked body and into a conquering gaze from nowhere. This is the gaze that mythically inscribes all marked bodies, that makes the unmarked category claim the power to see and not be seen, to represent while escaping representation. (188)

When we bring into view the sociocultural and political reality in which Sor Juana lived and worked, the move to embodied vision becomes even more imperative. The last words of the sonnet attest to the urgency of the matter: "es cadaver, es polvo, es sombra, es nada" ("a body goes to dust, to shade, to naught" [1: 277; Trueblood 95]). The move to embodied vision, to "situated knowledge," has to do with the historization and social location of the subject and its "way of seeing," in short, its relation to power. This is an imperative that we, as contemporary viewers of images and readers of literature, could take up with Sor Juana. We could allow ourselves to be interpellated by sonnet 145 and enter the process of feminist visual culture studies that she begins. Following her lead in sonnet 145, we would analyze the myriad of images that surround us each day: to see with her and unmask the artifice of baroque deceit; to reveal the distorted rays of the slick design of colorful (contemporary) images; to embody the "conquering" gaze; to be resisting observers.

Hope and (Partial) Vision in "Verde embeleso"

In his introduction of Haraway in *The Visual Culture Reader*, the editor, Nicholas Mirzoeff, makes connections between Haraway's work and that of Descartes:

> Like Descartes, Haraway recognizes that understanding vision is central to what will be accepted as rational method. Unlike him, she overtly acknowledges that vision is always about power and positioning, meaning that any method must be partial in both senses of the term.
> ("Introduction" 598)

Haraway's focus on vision, optics, and the gaze and how they are connected to relations of power seems to be "prefigured" by Sor Juana in sonnet 145 and, as we will see, is problematized further in "Verde embeleso." But, we might ask (as many others have), what was Sor Juana's relation to the new science of optics, and that of Descartes in particular?

One example that Descartes employs to illustrate his explanation of the workings of vision, perception, and light is that of blind people, who, by way of the cane, he suggests, "see with their hands"(*Discourse* [Olscamp] 67). With her sonnet "Verde embeleso," Sor Juana seems to enter into dialogue with Descartes. In the final lines she writes, "tengo en entrambas manos ambos ojos/y solamente lo que toco veo" ("I'll place my eyes right at my fingertips /

and only see what my two hands can feel" [1: 281; Trueblood 101]). Whether Sor Juana had read Descartes or not, she certainly was contemplating and writing about important modern issues related to optics—as science, as vision, as visuality.

Descartes chose the concrete analogy of the blind person navigating the world with the cane in order to help the uninitiated understand how light rays and vision work. He wanted artisans to be able to understand the basics of optics so that they could work on the new instruments of sight (glasses, telescopes, microscopes) with a certain level of understanding and knowledge. Sor Juana, on the other hand, seems to allude to something quite beyond a utilitarian description of vision and light. Instead, I believe, in the poem she suggests a different way of seeing and of knowing, a different way of understanding the world and one's place in it.

Frederick Luciani has analyzed the sonnet "Verde embeleso" in conjunction with images from emblem books of the seventeenth century. Referring to an emblem that shows a "seeing hand," or, a hand with an eye drawn in the middle of it, Luciani reads this association as an "illustration of prudent skepticism"("Emblems" 159). He then connects the poem to a second popular emblem, which represents tinted eyeglasses of self-delusion (160), and asks: "Why is there no middle possibility; that is, why are the only two alternatives the foolish self-delusion of those who see with tinted glasses, and the skepticism of the one who 'sees' only what she can touch and hold?" (161). The solution, he suggests, is a third way of seeing, that of "moral insight," of one who sees "with the lucid eyes of the intellect" (162).

In her discussion of Sor Juana's cautious (possible) incorporation of elements of the "new science" into her work, Stephanie Merrim states, "from the margins outside the institutions of knowledge, Sor Juana nonetheless takes a faintly perceptible but radical scientific stand of her own . . . (she) appears to advocate an empirical attitude toward the acquisition of knowledge . . ." (*Early Modern* 242). In the final lines of "Verde embeleso," Merrim reads that advocacy for empiricism. Citing Francisco López Cámara, she adds that this favoring of empiricism must be blended with the New World "spirit of skepticism" in the reception of Cartesian thought (244). Reading with Luciani and Merrim, what, then, is the hope to which Sor Juana refers in her sonnet? What does it mean to have eyes in one's hands? And what is the green tint of the lenses that some choose to wear?

We can begin to answer those questions by studying the relationships created by the first-person poetic voice: "they" with their green-tinted glasses who see all according to their desire in opposition to the "I" who is more measured in her fortune, holds her eyes in her hands, and sees only what she touches. Both are then mediated by "you," which represents hope itself: green, crazy, vain, decrepit, dynamic, "soul of the world," hope. Hope is a highly charged, overdetermined, exceptionally baroque category as represented in the sonnet, except in the measured way in which it is treated by "I."

What is the careful way of hope that the poetic voice insinuates in the last lines? We could borrow from Merrim the preference for the empirical; from Luciani the preference for moral insight; and from Descartes and López Cámara the colonial preference for skepticism and arrive at a possible answer. Hands that have eyes to see or eyes that are held in hands and can therefore touch could be empirical eyes that see in different ways. They could combine not just seeing and touching but reading (eyes) and writing (hands). This is a vision (and knowledge) that is embodied and connected to the empirical. It is a measured, partial vision that the poetic voice suggests, one that is aware of its social location, in this case marked by gender, and aware of those who would assume the invisible location behind the green-tinted glasses.

To further develop the relation between the invisible location of the green-tinted lenses and partial, embodied vision, Haraway is again useful:

> The eyes have been used to signify a perverse capacity—honed to perfection in the history of science tied to militarism, capitalism, colonialism, and male supremacy—to distance the knowing subject from everybody and everything in the interests of unfettered power. (188)

> The moral is simple: partial perspective promises objective vision. . . . Vision is *always* a question of the power to see—and perhaps of the violence implicit in our visualizing practices. With whose blood were my eyes crafted? (192)

Haraway's last lines, cited above, are powerful, and students may seem perplexed. To formulate an explanation, we return to the green-tinted glasses.

Most students are familiar with the saying, "Looking at the world through rose-colored glasses," which is commonly understood to represent a naive view of the world, in which one sees only goodness and light. A critical interpretation of the "rose-colored glasses" is offered in a popular lyric by John Lennon, "Living is easy with eyes closed. Misunderstanding all you see"(Alan Aldridge 39; Turner 121). In this case, rose-colored glasses become closed eyes, and the unconscious folly ("self-delusion") of that position is critiqued in its irresponsible attitude toward the world. Perhaps this is what Sor Juana sought to represent with her green-tinted lenses. But, in reading "Verde embeleso" with Haraway, another kind of tinted lenses come into view. It is not only an innocent or unconscious (self- or class-protective) outlook that can tint one's view, adjusting all that one sees to green/pink. Couldn't the green tint be a bit more ominous as well, perhaps representing a worldview or way of seeing stained by extreme religious orthodoxy (the Inquisition), a restrictive patriarchal order, or a mercantilist colonial system—all views in which certain social subjects are denied full access to their humanity? When we consider those "hues," it is not a far leap for one to recall the terrible images of Latin American military dictators and their dark glasses.

When we "situate" the vision and knowledge produced through the green-tinted glasses, we can, as Haraway suggests, take into consideration the power and possible violence of "visualizing practices." And, when tinting is understood to be ideology, of course, we realize that none of us sees perfectly clearly. This is the importance of recognizing partial vision, and doing so calls to mind Walter Benjamin's well-known observation, "There is no document of civilization which is not at the same time a document of barbarism" (*Illuminations* 256).

Finally, once again we ask, where does hope lie? Perhaps it could be seen in the "alternative scopic regime" (Jay 11) to which Sor Juana seems to allude—that is, embodied vision and situated knowledges, subjects who are visibly located in society and culture, who are aware of the "blood" on their hands and thus in their eyes. This could be a situated hope, empirically informed by science, knowledge, agency, moral insight, and "New World" skepticism—the partial vision of one who would enter into informed dialogue with power.

I "hope" that by including in the classroom readings and ways of teaching Sor Juana like this one, students not only begin to see with Sor Juana but also allow themselves to see Sor Juana in other ways. Although she was a brilliant intellectual with encyclopedic knowledge, she also had partial perspective and was quite aware of this. She openly stated it, sometimes ironically,[1] sometimes as (in)direct criticism,[2] sometimes (strategically) complying with the trope of "feigned humility."[3] But even in her irony, critique, and compliant humility, Sor Juana marked her space, situated her vision/knowledge and that of others: she poetically let others know that she could see herself, could see them, and sometimes even could see through them.

NOTES

[1]See, e.g., "A las inimitables plumas de Europa" ("To the matchless pens of Europe" [1: 158–61; Trueblood 10]).

[2]See "Respondiendo a un caballero de Perú" ("Replying to a gentleman from Peru" [1: 136–39; Trueblood 26–33]) and "Hombres necios que acusáis" ("Silly, you men—so very adept" [1: 228–29; Trueblood 109]).

[3]*La respuesta a sor Filotea* ("The Reply to Sor Philothea" [4: 440–75; Trueblood 205–43]).

Seventeenth-Century Pansapphism: Comparing "Exceptional Women" of the Americas and Europe

Tamara Harvey

The frontispieces of both Sor Juana Inés de la Cruz's *Segundo volumen* ("Second Volume" [1692]) and *Fama y obras pósthumas* ("Fame and Posthumous Works" [1700]) show a bust of the learned nun that has an angelic herald above it and that is flanked by the figures of Mercury and Athena (*Segundo volumen*) or Europa and America (*Fama y obras*). Beneath her portrait are various emblems of the arts and sciences including a lyre, a mask, two books, a compass, a globe, and a square, iconology that supports the name of "tenth muse" bestowed on her by the title pages of several editions of her poetry, beginning with the first one published during her lifetime, *Inundación Castálida* ("Castalian Overflowing" [1689]) and including *Fama y obras pósthumas*. The name tenth muse pays tribute to the achievements of women intellectuals. An honorific first given to Sappho, by Sor Juana's time this title was used to name women with knowledge in many areas of the arts and sciences and with literary productions in various forms. As signified by the emblems at the bottom of this frontispiece, tenth muse may actually suggest something like the other nine rolled up into one—a helicon unto herself. The title page of *Inundación Castálida* is dominated by lists emphasizing the variety of Sor Juana's poetry in form ("various meters, idioms, and styles"), quality ("elegant, subtle, clear, ingenious, useful"), and aim ("for instruction, recreation, and admiration"). Likewise, the title page of the first collection of Anne Bradstreet's poetry published in England, *The Tenth Muse Lately Sprung up in America* (1650), centers graphically on two lists cataloging the contents of her "compleat discourse and description of the Four Elements, Constitutions, Ages of Man, Seasons of the Year" and listing the four monarchies of which Bradstreet gives "an Exact Epitomie." In the epistle that prefaces a 1659 English edition of Anna Maria van Schurman's *Dissertatio logica*, translated as *The Learned Maid; or, Whether a Maid May Be a Scholar? A Logick Exercise*, Schurman, who was also known as the tenth muse, is described as having "a vast understanding piercing into all things" and "a skillful hand marvelously obedient to that guide, executing and expressing in all materials whatsoever" (A3). Margaret Cavendish, Duchess of Newcastle, was less at the mercy of others to publish and comment on her wide-ranging works, and perhaps as a consequence her title pages were more muted and dignified ("thrice Noble" is the most common indicator of variety repeated across her title pages). However, *The Worlds Olio* (1655), a miscellany treating, as the title suggests, a broad range of scientific, historical, and social topics, has a frontispiece similar to that found in *Segundo volumen*—the engraving shows Cavendish with Athena on her left and Apollo, lyre in hand, on her right. In short, many women were called by the seemingly singular title, the tenth muse.

In most cases the title was linked directly to the encyclopedic quality of these women's writings. This did not mean, however, that they were simply compilers of knowledge. "Encyclopaedia," as a recent translator of Schurman's *Dissertatio logica* notes, refers to "the whole circle of liberal arts," further reinforcing its relevance for characterizations of the tenth muse (Schurman, *Christian* 26). Entries in the *Oxford English Dictionary* would suggest that this was the more common use of the term into the seventeenth century. The transformation of *encyclopaedia* into a name for more static collections of knowledge demonstrates one of the reasons that it is so difficult for modern readers to appreciate fully the dynamic relation among fields of knowledge in early modern texts.

In a period when modern disciplinary boundaries did not hold and the practice of syncretism among cultures and subject areas was an intellectual, artistic, and spiritual norm, it is not surprising that, like their male peers, the women publishing and participating in public discourse at the time would bridge what are now regarded as separate disciplines of knowledge in their research and creative work. And yet contemporaries and modern readers alike were surprised. As Gilles Ménage remarks in his preface to *The History of Women Philosophers* (originally published in 1690 as *Historia Mulierum Philosopharum*):

> So great is the number of women writers that their names alone could fill a large volume. . . . It is therefore astonishing that Didymus, the most learned grammarian of his time, should have written of Theano that she was the only woman who had philosophized, and that Lactantius, the most erudite Church writer, should have said the same thing of Themiste. (Ménage 3)

Repeatedly, learned women are characterized as singular exceptions, even as people like Ménage and Sor Juana, as well as earlier writers like Christine de Pizan, compiled catalogs of notable women that belied this exceptionalism.

There are many helpful discussions of what Stephanie Merrim calls "the Tenth Muse phenomenon" (*Early Modern* xli) that explore the similarities among these women in terms of both what they write and how they are positioned by those who give them this title.[1] Electa Arenal ("This life"), Nina Scott ("Tenth Muse"), and A. Owen Aldridge pioneered a comparative approach to examining Anne Bradstreet and Sor Juana that not only helps us understand these two women writers but also anticipated the field of early trans-American studies that only now, twenty years later, is coming to the fore. More recently, Merrim and Stephanie Jed have expanded this comparative work, Merrim by considering Sor Juana alongside other early modern women (including several tenth muses), and Jed by considering the way *tenth muse* circulated almost as a taxonomic term, rendering Sor Juana and Bradstreet wonders from the New World to be placed in the museums and curiosity cabinets that gained popularity in Europe with the spread of colonialism. Instead of focusing on that name and the meaning of its exceptionalism, however, in this article I discuss how attention to the breadth of intellectual endeavors for which tenth muses were celebrated can be used in the classroom to develop comparisons among early modern women that look beyond their status as exceptions. We might call this "encyclopedic pansapphism" as a way to focus on the dynamic, multidisciplinary character of these women's writing and how that enables us to make connections among literary women throughout Europe and the European colonies.[2]

My aims in having students compare seventeenth-century women writers are threefold. First, I want them to develop a richer, more nuanced knowledge of the women who preceded more familiar modern feminists. Often these women are treated as isolated "prefeminists" who almost magically anticipated later feminist critique when in fact they were among many women who participated in the debates of their day and in doing so inevitably justified their own public voices in ways that challenged the sanctions of church and state against women's public speech. In addition to resisting modern tendencies to treat feminist positions in early modern writing as exceptional, I want my students to recognize that although we find arguments for the humanity and rights of women in these texts that resonate with postenlightenment feminist rhetoric, their intellectual and aesthetic force (and their arguments regarding women) are developed within intellectual frameworks of their time and not ours.

Second, comparative work on women in this period is still an open field, providing students with ample opportunity to develop original research projects. When I asked students to compare two women from or residing in different countries during the seventeenth and early eighteenth centuries for a graduate class on seventeenth-century women I taught in the English department at the University of Southern Mississippi, students developed fascinating original papers, including comparisons of Mary Wortley Montagu's treatment of otherness in her discussion of women in the harem with Mary Rowlandson's treatment of the otherness of Native American women in her captivity narrative, Mary Carleton's with Esther Rodgers's crime narratives, and Sor Juana's feminist arguments with those of Mary Astell and Elizabeth Cary.[3] The challenges of this kind of comparative work also provide an opportunity for students to hone their research skills.

Microfilm and online collections such as Evans Early American Imprints, first series, 1639–1800 and *Early English Books Online* (*EEBO*) are excellent resources for this class. Although they obviously privilege English writers, some key women writers who were translated into English are also included, providing an opportunity to consider transnational circulations of discourses by and about women. Unfortunately, texts by Sor Juana are not included in these collections. Even without easy access to Evans or *EEBO*, there is an increasing number of excellent Web resources with links to digitized primary texts as well as a wealth of secondary information, including the *Sor Juana Inés de la Cruz Project* (www.dartmouth.edu/~sorjuana/), the *Early Americas Digital Archive* (www.mith2.umd.edu/eada), *Other Women's Voices: Translations of*

Women's Writing before 1700 (http://home.infionline.net/~ddisse/index.html), the *Emory Women Writers Resources Project* (http://chaucer.library.emory.edu/wwrp/index.html), *A Celebration of Women Writers* (http://digital.library.upenn.edu/women/), and the *Brown University Women Writers Project* (www.wwp.brown.edu/ [this site requires a library or personal subscription]).

The third aim addresses an increasingly important question in early American studies: how we carry out transatlantic and trans-American comparative work. The comparison of exceptional women can provide a model despite significant personal and cultural differences and no evidence of direct influence. The study of women should be integral to the development of methods for comparative trans-American studies, not a subset of such studies. Comparing women writers in different parts of the Americas and in Europe is an especially useful way to address this issue because women writers used many of the same formal strategies to respond to commonplaces about women while registering distinctive regional and personal differences. Attending to how they bridge areas of learning further provides nuance to our understanding of their use of these strategies and, as I discuss below, sheds light on both positive and negative engagements of colonialist discourses.

Before turning more substantially to the range of knowledge these writers treat, I begin by introducing my students to familiar (and frequently anthologized) defenses of women. In my experience, a fair number of graduate and upper-level undergraduate students have already encountered Sor Juana's *Respuesta a sor Filotea* ("Answer to Sister Filotea") and Bradstreet's "The Prologue" (*Tenth Muse*); other defenses by early modern women are less familiar. Although students and scholars first working with early modern women writers are often surprised to find familiar prowoman arguments in these defenses and may be tempted to assume that these are the statements of an unusually prescient feminist vanguard, in fact any woman whose works are published at this time must in some way justify or defend her public voice or have it justified for her by her editors. Thus, defenses and apologies can be relied on as a productive basis for comparison among women whose works were published during the seventeenth century. Among the variety of conventional tropes, arguments, and rhetorical strategies used in these justifications, we most frequently find a claim that publication was against the will of the writer and that whatever is published is inevitably flawed (male writers also use this humility topos). Nevertheless, we also find frequent arguments that acknowledge the achievements of women and impugn the false logic and social power that limit the recognition of women writers. Indeed, Sor Juana's *Respuesta* is a marvelous compendium of these strategies. Catalogs of learned women, historicist arguments reinterpreting authoritative scriptural and legal texts, and logical arguments uncovering the contradictions in belief systems in which women cannot succeed even if their works are successful are just a few of the strategies marshaled in defense of the intellectual activities of women.

Many defenses are mounted using a breadth of knowledge and variety of rhetorical and logical strategies that echo those that earn women writers the title "muse." For instance, in explaining her compulsion to learn, Sor Juana observes in her *Respuesta* that "[h]ad Aristotle cooked he would have written a great deal more" (Arenal and Powell 75), suggesting that her range of knowledge exceeds his. The catalogs of learned, powerful, and good women that frequently appear in these defenses (again, Sor Juana's *Respuesta* is exemplary [76–79]) also demonstrate an awareness of classical, biblical, and contemporary literature in a manner that uses a common rhetorical trope, responds to similar lists compiled by misogynists, and belies the exceptionalist treatment of learned women. The range of learning and variety of strategies found in these defenses and shorter apologia by women tend to distinguish them from the less varied humility topoi conventionally used by male writers of the period.

Having discussed defenses, we then look more closely at how these women engage the learning of their times. In Sor Juana's most ambitious poem, *Primero sueño* (*First Dream*), she refers to philosophy, medicine, theology, and mythology as she shows us a dreamer striving to attain total, divine knowledge. Areas of knowledge are arranged on at least three levels, almost like a musical score. Classical allusions to human endeavors and hubris contextualize the dreamer's exploration of successive philosophies while an ongoing description of the body as it falls asleep, maintains the processes that feed the dreamer's fancies, and awakens thrums through the poem like a bass line. Different areas of knowledge in Sor Juana's poem are beautifully layered and intellectually complex, characteristics that have earned praise then and now. Although Octavio Paz and others see something modern in the *Primero sueño*'s emphasis on subjectivity and epistemology, the connectedness among subject areas she explores is a product of her time. In the *Respuesta* she encourages the study of many subjects, explaining that they

> help one another, shedding light and opening a path from one to the next, by way of divergences and hidden links—for they were set in place so as to form this universal chain by the wisdom of their great Author. Thus it appears that they correspond each one to another and are united with a wondrous bond and harmonious agreement. (Arenal and Powell 57)

Using *Primero sueño* in a class focused on comparing early modern women writers is helpful because similar writings by Bradstreet, Schurman, Cavendish, and others are frequently dismissed as derivative or eccentric attempts at literary cross-dressing. As Nathaniel Ward says in his commendatory poem at the beginning of Bradstreet's *The Tenth Muse*, "Let man look to't, least women weare the Spurs" (n. pag.). Moreover, by attending to the complexities of these works and worldviews, we shift attention away from considerations of roles and place that are so prevalent in defenses of women and in much scholarship on women writers. For instance, Bradstreet's quaternions are rarely anthologized, unlike her so-called personal poems. Like *Primero sueño*, they treat many fields of knowledge; are largely responsible for Bradstreet's fame as the tenth muse; and imply a syncretism among the four groups, though not so fully developed and integrated as in *Primero sueño*. The quaternions are important works in which, among other things, we find Bradstreet taking on large intellectual questions with implications for her understanding of theories about sexual difference; this comes into clearer focus when taught alongside Sor Juana's poetry rather than the New England texts with which Bradstreet's are conventionally grouped.[4]

Exceptional status is accorded not only to learned and literary women but also to women whose achievements defy categorization in a single role or subject position, like Marie de l'Incarnation—a mother and a nun, a mystic and a pragmatic manager of her brother-in-law's business and of the first Ursuline convent in New France. I argue that focusing on pansapphism also encourages us to see these women not simply as exceeding or multiplying conventional roles but rather as integrating activities and allegiances in more complex ways.

When focusing on the encyclopedic nature of these works, classes can go in many different directions, comparing uses of new science (for instance, medical functionalism or narratives of "new worlds" founded in part on developments in optics, experimental science, and the Copernican revolution), philosophical systems, theology, approaches to history and cultural syncretism, and so forth. These works, their title pages notwithstanding, are not just helpful lists of other people's observations but rather developed intellectual treatments that relate various fields of thought. Ian Maclean has shown that dominant discourses about women, most of them arguing against women's participation in the public sphere, engaged scientific, theological, legal, and ethical thought; in works by women writers of the period we also find an engagement of contemporary topics and debates in all these areas, often with implications for women that are more subtle and theoretical than those evident in the defenses.

Emphasizing pansapphism allows us to locate early modern women more substantially in the debates of their times, to acknowledge that they were exceptional and were treated as exceptions but to move beyond this through a dynamic and comparative consideration of their encyclopedic productions. I also ask students to consider some of the more negative implications of this pansapphism. Women in the Americas like Sor Juana, Bradstreet, and Marie de l'Incarnation combined observations of land and natives with theology, history, and scientific discourses in ways that authorized their voices by figuratively transporting the "new world" back to Europe. In Sor Juana's *loa* to *The Divine Narcissus*, for instance, Religion defends herself for "wanting to transport [the Indies] to Madrid," asking rhetorically, "Is it beyond imagination / that something made in one location / can in another be of use?"(3: 19–20; Peters and Domeier 34–35).[5] Such uses of colonial discourses are not found solely in works by women who lived in the Americas. Cavendish's *The Description of a New World Called the Blazing-World* and Aphra Behn's *Oroonoko* and *The Widow Ranter* are just a few works by English women influenced by the discovery and settlement of the Americas that make use of colonial points of view to gain authorial credibility. While catalogs of notable women belie their treatment as exceptions, catalogs of New World commodities and wonders compiled by women writers of the early modern period also deflect attention from their exceptionalism in ways that are complicit with the acquisitive practices of colonial discourse.

The seventeenth-century women whose writings we know were exceptional, but they were not unique. Their defenses of themselves as writers and of women generally are a good launching point for comparing these women, but examining the ways these women engaged the interconnectedness of different subjects opens up a broad range of associations that enrich our understanding of the Americas and of women in the early modern period. This approach, in addition to expanding our understanding of women's writing, is promising because it can encourage students and teachers alike to develop comparisons between female and male writers that are not grounded solely on the stark contrasts of gender distinctions and patriarchal oppressions but that rather explore any or many of the subjects brought together in these encyclopedic works. By integrating women more fully into all our classes, we may at last be able to move beyond the generational need to recatalog the achievements of notable women.

NOTES

[1]See Merrim's course Web site *The Book of the Tenth Muse* at www.brown.edu/Departments/Comparative_Literature/10th_muse_book/index.html.

[2]In an earlier version of this article, I stressed the *pansophism* (and not a global "sophism") that linked these women, by which I meant the ways in which their works bridged many fields of knowledge. A reader of the manuscript suggested a more felicitous neologism, *pansapphism*, which nicely emphasizes the breadth of knowledge displayed by these women while also highlighting a trend that links intellectual women across national boundaries.

[3]I would like to thank my students for all they taught me that semester: Megan-Marie Bakenhaster, Rowe Carenen, Miranda Freeman, Stephen Fuller, Jeremy Lespi, Kristina Lucenko, Peggy Price, Vincent Roger, Farley Walker, and Shanti Weiland.

[4]See my article " 'Now Sisters . . . Impart Your Usefulness, and Force': Anne Bradstreet's Feminist Functionalism in *The Tenth Muse* (1650)."

[5]I discuss this topic further in " 'My Goods Are True': Tenth Muses in the New World Market."

"Guileful Deception of Sense": Semantic Fields and Sor Juana's Baroque Poetry

Rocío Quispe-Agnoli

The popularization of Sor Juana's works in the graduate and undergraduate curricula of Spanish programs poses distinct challenges in the classroom. Her baroque poetry introduces topics, objects of study, and ideological perspectives that appear simultaneously too far away in time and too conceptually sophisticated for students with limited historical knowledge, critical experience, and fluency in Spanish. In addition, because students often have little or no experience doing research on literature, they may feel daunted by the expectation that they should produce original observations, analysis, or comments about texts written more than three hundred years ago. It is not initially clear to students confronting literary texts for the first time that the ability to read, understand, analyze, and comment is the product of time and familiarity. Instructors should intervene with the following objectives in mind: to empower students with self-confidence, to make students aware of how verbal structures with dynamic potential of multiple meanings—at both the denotative and connotative levels—can help them develop their thought, to give students the stylistic tools for refining their insights, and to free students from the hegemony of established critics.

For the past five years I have taught Sor Juana's baroque poetry to Spanish-speaking and English-speaking students on diverse university levels. As an instructor, my pedagogical approach addresses the linguistic context of the literary text, specifically the semantic fields of key words and concepts of the baroque, including such techniques as pairing bilingual versions of this poetry; using selected short readings to offer concise information on the historical, social, cultural, and ideological perspectives implied in the seventeenth-century European baroque; and utilizing seventeenth- and twenty-first-century references in order to collect information on various levels of meaning and their transformation throughout time. With this linguistic base, teacher and students are able to focus on analyzing complete poetic texts in class and organizing students' ideas on topics and structural devices of the baroque, thus helping them appreciate and genuinely enjoy baroque poetry. In the process students can become aware of Spanish as a language in continuous transformation through the study of semantic fields of key concepts, themes, and motifs in baroque poetry produced in Spanish America, also known as "Barroco de Indias."

In this essay I present the organization of semantic fields as a specific strategy for teaching Sor Juana's poems. The term *semantic field*, also known as *conceptual* or *notional field*, comes from lexicological analysis. It refers to a set of lexical utterances that share features in terms of their meaning and underlying semantic structures (Greimas and Courtés 49). Through the organization of these fields of meaning, students discover the range of poetic speech acts—acts characterized by baroque verbal devices and images. I understand poetic speech acts within the linguistic theory of speech acts (Austin; Searle). A speech act is an act that a speaker performs when making an utterance with any particular intention. This intention is understood as illocutionary force (for example: suggestion, command, promise). I bring this notion to the literary text where the poet/speaker performs a speech act by means of the poem and produces an effect in the reader. Understanding poetic speech acts and their illocutionary force facilitates the students' comprehension of the semantic fields in the poem.

To prepare the ground for analysis of these semantic fields, it is necessary to take some initial pedagogical steps, appropriate to the linguistic and literary competence of the students. To "warm up" before textual analysis, I use the following preparatory analysis: a review of the choice and use of bilingual editions and of the awareness of different possibilities for translating the poetic texts, a discussion of the need for some literary and historical competence about the main features of Spanish baroque, and training in the use of a variety of reference works.

Despite the academic expectation of teaching advanced undergraduate and graduate courses on Spanish literature entirely in Spanish, I have always used bilingual editions to approach Sor Juana's poetry. This choice has proved especially useful for those advanced undergraduate majors who are not fluent in Spanish or who are unfamiliar with literary Spanish. At the undergraduate level, I initially chose Alan Trueblood's bilingual edition *A Sor Juana Anthology*, since Octavio Paz praised its lyricism (x).

I do not disagree with Trueblood's effort to transmit Sor Juana's poetic endeavors. The "creative" aspect of this translation, however, does not always help the reader fully understand the sophisticated verbal games of baroque poetry. Nina Scott's bilingual anthology of early modern women writers of Spanish America is extremely useful, especially in undergraduate classes. I prefer her translations to Trueblood's because I find that they preserve the baroque texture and syntax of Sor Juana's poetic creativity. For example, the first quatrain of Sor Juana's sonnet 145:

> Este, que ves, engaño colorido
> que del arte ostentando los primores,
> con falsos silogismos de colores
> es *cauteloso engaño del sentido*. (1: 277; my emphasis)

In this poem, Sor Juana argues against her flatterers. However, this text also plays with the popular baroque questioning of the false appearances of images and the correspondence between semantic dualisms such as interior/exterior and true-real essence/false deception-appearance.

Spanish models. They help students locate the baroque with respect to repressive Counter-Reformation and inquisitional censorship. Despite, or because of, these repressive practices, the baroque develops extreme verbal ornateness while it questions the falsehood of external images and privileges the shadows between light and darkness (chiaroscuro). Trueblood reads Sor Juana's poetry through the influence of the most baroque of Spanish poets, Luis de Góngora. Among a variety of topics and devices, Trueblood comments on Greco-Roman mythology, commonplaces of philosophy and Ptolemaic cosmology, and rarities of natural history, accompanied by a rich and highly symbolic imagery: precious metals and stones; splendid fabrics; rare fragrances; the rose and other flowers; and exotic colorful birds such as the peacock, the phoenix, and the nightingale (11).

The second issue deals with using reference works to help students situate the semantic fields of the key words, terms, and concepts in Sor Juana's poetry. My own research and teaching experience leads me to conclude that knowing the semantic fields of the key terms in the seventeenth century is crucial to understanding the writings of any author who is not contemporary to the reader. In advanced graduate courses I encourage students to use the edition of Sor Juana's works by Alfonso Méndez Plancarte, whose footnotes are very helpful for identifying the seventeenth-century meanings and sources of key terms. In addition, I require students to refer to sources that enable them to trace seventeenth-century connotations of terms that are not obvious to the twenty-first-century reader, such as Joan de Corominas's *Diccionario crítico-etimológico* ("Critical-Etymological Dictionary"), the *Diccionario de autoridades* ("Dictionary of Authorities"), and Sebastián de Covarrubias y Horozco's *Tesoro de la lengua castellana o española* ("Treasures of the Castilian and Spanish Language"). Since we are working with a symbolic literary language with highly connotative signs, it is indispensable to review reference works such as Covarrubias y Horozco's *Emblemas morales* ("Moral Emblems"), which includes medieval and Renaissance bestiaries, and the twentieth-century writer J. Eduardo Cirlot's *Diccionario de símbolos* (*A Dictionary of Symbols*). Finally, Julio Casares's *Diccionario ideológico de la lengua española* ("Ideological Dictionary of the Spanish Language") is unique in that it orders the entries, with all their potential and contextual meanings, not only in the manner of any dictionary but also in groups of semantic fields for key terms.

With careful consideration of bilingual editions, variations of meaning in translation, and competence regarding the baroque, the teacher may use translations to explain the notion of semantic field. For example, in the stanza used to comment on different translations above, one can observe that *engaño* ("deception") and *falso* ("false") share the semantic feature of misleading appearance (they are not what they seem). In this sense, *silogismo* ("syllogism") produces the association with false reasoning, and, added to *colores* ("colors"), suggests the false appearance that exterior objects produce to the sense of sight. Hence the poetic voice advises paying attention to this well-constructed (*cauteloso* ["guileful"]) image in order to avoid the trap of false external appearances.

To further illustrate the use of semantic fields in analyzing Sor Juana's baroque poetry, I use examples from a poem addressing the author's self and the topic of fame. I choose this theme because it helps reveal the search for identity of the human being and artist in Sor Juana, which is a popular approach among students. In addition, *romance* 48 (1: 136–39) has a highly satirical tone, which demonstrates Sor Juana's effective use of irony. Once understood with the aid of the teacher, this *romance* becomes one of the favorites of students.

The three concepts of fame, praise, and modesty are intrinsically related and appear regularly in Sor Juana's poems of self. *Romances* 48, 49, 50, and 51 reveal Sor Juana's consciousness of her fame as a poet and her response to the public admiration of her literary achievements. These texts establish both intra- and intertextual literary rapports, since they also constitute speech acts. Drawing on the most effective stylistic devices of the baroque, Sor Juana replies to both criticism and praise of her poetic wit by structuring her poems as part of a literary web. Within this web, the poet reflects on the nature of false impressions that set up a misleading conception of fame.

We can observe this in *romance* 48, titled in the *Obras completas* "Respondiendo a un caballero del Perú, que le envió unos barros diciéndole que se volviese hombre" ("Replying to a gentleman from Peru who had sent her some [verses], telling her she should become a man" [1: 136–39; Trueblood 24]). For *romance* 48, I use Trueblood's translation in class (26–33) because this poem is not included in Nina Scott's anthology. However, the bracketed terms are my own translations, different from Trueblood's and closer to the original text. For example, in this case Trueblood translates "barros" as "small clay vessels." My translation, "verses," matches the seventeenth-century meaning of "barros." Another important observation in teaching the poems is that their published titles were not necessarily Sor Juana's. Rather, this task was performed by the original seventeenth-century editor of *Inundación Castálida* ("Castalian Outpouring").

In this poem Sor Juana uses a satirical voice that returns criticism disguised as flattery-praise back onto the Peruvian gentleman who is also a poet. Since his main premise amounts to censorship of Sor Juana's writing because she is a woman, the nun mock praises the male poet and casts herself and all classical artistic sources of inspiration as inferior to the "excellences" of the gentleman's art. This poem displays the recurring use of three semantic fields: Greek mythological figures who symbolize the arts, images of femininity sketching a definition of *woman*, and the extensive use of speech acts at all textual levels. In the last field, we observe how the Peruvian gentleman (whom Sor Juana addresses as "tú" ["you"]) criticizes Sor Juana and how the poetic "yo" ("I" or "self"), identified with the author, replies to this criticism. In addition, she uses figures from classical mythology to ironically undermine what initially appears to be praise.

In the first semantic field that I mention, Sor Juana makes extensive use of mythological figures such as the Muses, the nine goddesses of arts; Apollo, god of poetry and leader of the Muses; Pegasus, the winged horse that carries the gods through the skies; and Helicon and Aganippe, springs in Mount Helion, considered sacred to the Muses and emblematic of poetic inspiration (Trueblood 27). All these mythological references are associated with classical literature, a privileged source for the Renaissance and baroque periods. With these authorizing images, the Mexican nun introduces the concept of fame, but she distorts the serious tone through the comic technique of unexpected speech acts attributed to traditional classical figures. When Sor Juana replies with exaggerated praise to the flattery of a gentleman who considers himself a poet, she uses a speech act (praise) as a medium for another speech act (replying to flattery). In her display of speech acts, Sor Juana uses irony by imagining Apollo and the Muses rendered speechless before the excellence of the gentleman's poetic skills. The instructor can have students compare the verbs I have italicized in the Spanish excerpt with the words and phrases I have italicized in the translation:

> Señor: para *responderos*
> todas las Musas *se eximen*,
> sin que haya, ni aun de limosna,
> una que ahora me *dicte*;
> y siendo las nueve Hermanas
> madres del donaire y *chiste*
> no hay, *oyendo* vuestros versos,
> una que *chiste ni miste*.
> Apolo *absorto* se queda
> tan elevado de *oírle*
> que para aguijar el Carro
> es menester que le *griten*.
> (1: 136; my emphasis)

> Sir, in *reply* to your note,
> No help at all is at hand.
> No Muse *dictates a word*,
> None is disposed to be bland.
> No, not one of those nine
> Mothers of wit, jest and *joke*,
> *dares respond* to your verse
> with even the *feeblest croak*.
> Apollo himself is *struck dumb*.
> See how *he stops* in his tracks.
> (Trueblood 27; my emphasis)

At this point, the instructor should address the meaning of the speechlessness of Apollo, the Muses, and Pegasus. The obvious answer will be the poor quality of the gentleman's poems that Sor Juana is mimicking in hers. The next question posed to the students is, Why does Sor Juana respond with irony to this apparent praise to her creative ability? The title gives the student the clue to this question: "telling her she should become a man." This is the moment to investigate another semantic field related to issues of female characteristics in general and then applied to the Mexican poet. We find the elements for this semantic field in lines 85 to 108, which also start with the reference to the gentleman's main speech act: the advice that a woman should become a man. Sor Juana immediately relates this advice to male violence against women by means of Tarquin, Lucretia's legendary rapist:

> Y en el consejo que dais,
> yo os prometo recibirle
> y hacerme fuerza, aunque juzgo
> que no hay fuerzas que me entarquinen. (1: 138)

> Regarding the *advice you proffer,*
> I'll take it as part of the bargain
> And *do myself violence*, although
> No violence can make me a *Tarquin.*
> (Trueblood 31; my emphasis)

In the next lines, the Mexican nun turns her female condition into a neutral entity, using one of her favorite self-fashioning images: an unmarried virgin, not socially a woman: "sólo a las casadas dicen / *úxor*, o mujer, y que / es común de dos lo Virgen" ("A virgin has no sex at all— / or indeed she has both, being unwed" [1: 138; Trueblood 31; my emphasis]). In other words, her fame as a poet is not related to her gendered condition, since she has no explicit gender: she is either neutral or has both male and female genders within herself.

In addition, the poet uses the topic of fame that produces praises. Sor Juana herself is famous because she is a renowned author in her own time, but her gender and religious status as a nun impede such a public acknowledgment and therefore her acceptance of praises. Taking her problems with fame as a point of departure, the poet answers this gentleman by reflecting on the reasons for his fame: he has been exiled from Lima because he exceeded all his peers in poetic endeavors. In Sor Juana's poetic reasoning, this exceeding makes the Peruvian gentleman so famous that he arouses envy:

> El a que todos se aventaja,
> fuerza es que a todos incite
> a envidia, pues él lucir
> a todos juntos impide. (1: 139)

> Envy pursues the superior
> Perforce. They're always dismayed
> When people charge their brilliance
> Puts everyone else in the shade.
> (Trueblood 33)

This poem is clearly related to *Primero sueño* ("First Dream"), in which Sor Juana defines the soul as a nongendered, neutral entity who seeks the paths to knowledge. The final speech act of *Primero sueño* is ambiguous: is it authentic praise or ironic critique? In addition, it is not clear to what extent Sor Juana's poetic self is reflected in the Muses, the exemplary unmarried virgin, or the artist who suffers the consequences of public fame: she implies that envy forces her into different kinds of exile within her own spaces.

Finally, as the instructor of a text located in the past, I expect that the students perceive the relevance of baroque poetry. I disagree with the received wisdom that baroque poetry, like other older literary texts, constitutes a challenging experience for twenty-first-century undergraduate and graduate students. Once more, teaching is a key element in inspiring students' passion about texts that they had considered especially foreign.

Sor Juana's *Dream*: In Search of a Scientific Vision

Elias L. Rivers

Sor Juana's major poem, *Primero sueño* or "First Dream," "thus entitled and composed by Mother Juana Inés de la Cruz in imitation of Góngora," is not easy to read in a literal sense, let alone to understand fully in its personal and historical context. The following pages, with translations and paraphrases, constitute an attempt, first of all, to help with the problem of understanding the text as a whole literally; they will also try to explore the special meaning that the poem had in terms of Sor Juana's own life.

The modern reader of Spanish, even if well trained in Renaissance and baroque poetry, often has to struggle with the original text of the *Sueño*, no matter how carefully edited and punctuated. And translations of the poem are never adequate to the thought and the poetic impact of the original. The length of the sentences, their parentheses and other syntactic complexities, as well as the circumlocutions and mythological allusions, make decipherment of the text, whether in Spanish or in English, a laborious process that reflects, and is reflected by, the difficulty of the subject matter. Sor Juana's imitation of Luis de Góngora's *Soledad primera* ("First Solitude"), acknowledged in the title, is a matter primarily of versification and syntax. The verse form is known as the *silva*, which uses the basic Spanish classical lines (either eleven or seven syllables long, corresponding to the iambic pentameter or trimeter in English) irregularly combined and rhymed in an order that does not repeat itself in stanzaic form. The normal word order of phrases is frequently inverted; clauses are enclosed within a meandering syntax of prolonged subordination. Sor Juana's run-on versification contains sentences that are even longer than Góngora's, often over twenty lines long; the reader must learn to keep numerous phrases and clauses in suspense until the sentence as a whole finally reaches closure. Even at a second or third reading it is a struggle to repeat this complex linguistic process.

At the same time, the protagonist of Sor Juana's poem is quite unlike Góngora's passive traveling observer of the local countryside; her protagonist is an active intellect that soars and struggles to understand the whole world in a self-conscious, rational way. If we read her subsequently written prose *Respuesta* (*Answer*) to "Sor Filotea" (the pseudonym chosen by the bishop of Puebla), we discover details indicating Sor Juana's peculiarly modern scientific curiosity. In this autobiographical document Sor Juana comments on her keen personal desire to understand common phenomena of the natural world, which she was able to observe wherever she was in her cloistered convent. In the kitchen she noticed that eggs reacted differently to hot oil and to sugar syrup; she wittily comments that if Aristotle had done any cooking, he would have had much more to write about. In the patio she observed the complex patterns made by children's spinning tops and tried to see these spiraling patterns more clearly by spreading flour on the pavement before the tops were set spinning. In the rooms she could see the spatial illusions of geometric perspective: the farther away the beams, ceilings, and walls were, the smaller they seemed; she thus anticipated an eventual vanishing point at the top of a pyramid. The awareness of such empirical evidence was a major factor in the sixteenth- and seventeenth-century advances in science. But her own theoretical frames of reference were the traditional ones, deriving from antiquity and the Middle Ages: Platonic, Aristotelian, Ptolemaic, scholastic. She was apparently unaware of the revolutionary heliocentric hypothesis of Copernicus and others. At the same time, she was aware of some of the recent technological inventions, such as the primitive optical projector known as the magic lantern, invented by Athanasius Kircher, a German Jesuit polymath who was one of her favorite authors. And, as we have just seen, she certainly believed in personal observation, experimentation, and analysis. Like many other modern minds of her period, she tried to integrate new empirical data into the traditional written authorities.

Sor Juana's *Sueño* imitates certain aspects of a real dream, a sequence of subjective experiences that takes place during sleep, which the dreamer may try to remember and recount later on. But, in this case, the narrative is from the beginning a carefully constructed poetic composition designed to represent at its center an epistemological struggle to understand the whole of reality in rational terms. The reader's difficulties seem to reflect those of the dream's protagonist, a disembodied human intelligence seeking to comprehend the entire world, from stars to flowers. The poem as a whole, unlike a real dream, is a well-organized sequence of clearly delimited parts. It begins with a prologue, which is a description of nightfall, and ends with an epilogue, the return of sunlight the next morning. The following is a brief schematic outline:

Prologue: nightfall, and the world of nature goes to sleep
- Human soul's intellectual dream
- Human beings go to sleep
- The soul's attempt at Neoplatonic intuition: failure
- The soul's Aristotelian analysis: partial success, then failure
- Human beings begin to wake up

Epilogue: daylight returns, and I awake

In the prologue, first of all, the earth casts shadows upward, in the geometric form of pyramids and obelisks; from the sublunar domain the shadows reach the moon, but not the planets, and even less the stars, which are far above and inaccessible, unchangeable. Within our glimmering hemisphere's growing darkness and silence, only night birds' voices are heard as the screech owl drinks oil from temple lamps; the following lines, in English translation, give us an idea of Sor Juana's gongoristic style (lines 25–38):

Con tardo vuelo y canto, del oído
mal, y aun peor del ánimo admitido,
la avergonzada Nictimene acecha
de las sagradas puertas los resquicios,
o de las claraboyas eminentes
los huecos más propicios
que capaz a su intento le abren brecha,
y sacrílega llega a los lucientes
faroles sacros de perenne llama
que extingue, si no infama,
en licor claro la materia crasa
consumiendo, que el árbol de Minerva
de su fruto, de prensas agravado,
congojoso sudó y rindió forzado. (1: 336)

With slow flight and song, by the ear
Scarcely accepted and even less by the mind,
Shameful Nyctimene [the screech owl] spies
Through the chinks in the sacred doors
Or into the lofty skylights'
Most propitious hollows,
Opening a breach sufficient for her purpose,
And sacrilegiously she reaches
The gleaming sacred lamps of perennial flame,
Which she extinguishes, if not desecrates,
By consuming the fatty matter in the clear liquid
Which Minerva's tree [the olive], from its fruit,
Weighed down by presses, in anguish
Sweated out and yielded to force.[1]

Bats too flit about noiselessly. In the sea, fish, normally silent, are doubly silent at night. Land animals also go to sleep: deer, birds, even the eagle, who, as the vigilant monarch of his feathered kingdom, holds a pebble in his claw to serve as an alarm clock in case he dozes off. There are animals of this sort, natural or mythological, but human beings are barely approached at the end of this musical prelude, which ends in a sudden shift from long sentences to short ones, a coda of four complete sentences in four lines (147–50):

El sueño todo, en fin, lo poseía;
todo, en fin, el silencio lo ocupaba:
aun el ladrón dormía;
aun el amante no se desvelaba. (1: 339)

Sleep, finally, possessed everything.
Everything, finally, was occupied by silence.
Even the thief was sleeping.
Even the lover was not awake.

The dream itself occupies the central section of the poem. It begins near midnight, when tired human bodies, whatever their social class, grow drowsy. Each person's soul, in sleep, is partly separated from its body, which it continues nevertheless to provide with the minimal warmth of life; the heart beats, and the lungs breathe more slowly; the external senses do not respond to stimuli, and the tongue is silent. The stomach, like a blacksmith's forge, continues to nourish the rest of the body. It distills the four Aristotelian humors into vapors that it sends to the brain; there the faculty of fantasy, feeding on images stored in the memory, transforms, both concretely and abstractly, and combines them in new ways, showing them then to the soul. The soul, or understanding, free now from the body and its sense perceptions, soars in intellectual flight and contemplates the heavenly bodies, like the eagle that tries to climb through space and make its nest on the sun (lines 292–305):

La cual, en tanto, toda convertida
a su inmaterial sér y esencia bella,
aquella contemplaba,
participada de alto Sér, centella
que con similitud en sí gozaba;
y juzgándose casi dividida
de aquella que impedida
siempre la tiene, corporal cadena,
que grosera embaraza y torpe impide
el vuelo intelectual con que ya mide
la cuantidad inmensa de la Esfera,
y el curso considera
regular, con que giran desiguales
los cuerpos celestiales. . . . (1: 342–43)

The Soul, meanwhile, completely reduced
To its lovely immaterial essence,
Contemplates the divine spark that it shares
With God Himself,
Delighting in their mutual resemblance;
And finding itself almost separated
From that physiological chain that always
Impedes it, the gross and clumsy chain that blocks
Its intellectual flight, which is already measuring
The immense extent of the sphere,

It considers the regular course
With which the different celestial bodies
Revolve. . . .

The soul's upward flight is like that of the Egyptian pyramids, seen by Homer as symbols of the soul seeking to rise to God, who is the central point and circumference of all. But the Pyramids, like the Tower of Babel, cannot rise as high as the human understanding, which can imagine embracing all of Creation. Even so, overwhelmed by the many details, the intuitive understanding fails like Icarus and cannot comprehend even the basic elements of the world.

Like eyes that, dazzled by an excess of light, recover their sight by administering to themselves small doses of darkness, or like a wind-driven ship that furls its sails and undergoes repairs, so the understanding, overcome by the disordered deluge of data, makes a new attempt to concentrate its attention; it sets out again more gradually, observing single objects one by one and organizing them according to the ten Aristotelian categories, rising step-by-step, from mineral to vegetable to animal and finally to the human being, the summit of Creation, capable of embracing God himself in the Incarnation. But at other times the understanding does not dare try to grasp reality as a whole because it realizes it cannot comprehend even the simplest aspects of the world: the underground courses of water, for example, or a flower's fragrances and ivory and purple shades. If the understanding cannot cope with such relatively humble matters, how can it attempt to comprehend the whole amazing universe? And yet, once again, sometimes, it takes heart from the daring example of Phaeton, the son of Apollo the sun, who attempted to drive his father's chariot across the sky, even if he was struck down by his father's bolt of lightening; the news of this famous punishment, when spread abroad, incites not so much fear of authority as an increased desire to imitate such daring deeds. But at this point the body's nutritive functions begin to slow down, and the fantastic mental images of the dream begin to fade away.

The epilogue returns to a mythological world in which the sun drives the night away: first the planet Venus appears, followed by Aurora, and then birds begin to sing, recruiting rays of sunlight to battle against the shadows of night, who finally flees to the other hemisphere, where it reestablishes its reign (lines 967–75):

mientras nuestro Hemisferio la dorada
ilustraba del Sol madeja hermosa,
que con luz judicïosa,
de orden distributivo, repartiendo
a las cosas visibles sus colores
iba, y restituyendo
entera a los sentidos exteriores
su operación, quedando a luz más cierta
el Mundo iluminado, y yo despierta.
(1: 359)

Meanwhile, this hemisphere is made bright
by the golden skein
of the Sun's lovely light
that with judicious order slowly
distributes colors to visible objects
and restores full power
to the physical senses,
leaving the world illuminated
by a truer light, and me awake.

These last two words of the poem, "me awake" ("yo despierta"), suddenly take us to another level: with them Sor Juana presents herself to us openly, for the first time, not as a generic human mind but as a first-person protagonist with a woman's subjectivity, reflected in the feminine ending of the word "despierta." No longer solely the neutral narrator and explainer of the poem, her first person at this point reveals her to be the female dreamer, her body and her soul finally reunited. This conclusion seems to suggest that she, Sor Juana, may now continue her scientific speculations in the real light of day, or perhaps later on in another dream poem.

Having rapidly surveyed the central narrative of the *Sueño*, we find it difficult to place Sor Juana's major, and highly original, poem in the history of seventeenth-century Hispanic poetry, for it is unique in fundamental ways. The dominant theme of Spanish lyric poetry had always been the courtly love of a self-subordinating male poet who addresses a glorious, inaccessible, and omnipotent lady. This poetic situation lent itself to many different complications and gendered variations that we do find in other poetry by Sor Juana. But in the *Sueño* we find no trace of this tradition of love poetry. There was also a related tradition of Spanish Renaissance poetry that described the natural world in a pastoral or mythological landscape; in the *Sueño* we have seen passages close to this tradition. Aristotelian physiology and psychology, however, belonged to natural philosophy, what we now call science, and were normally the subject not of poems but of prose treatises written by male clerics and university professors. The one great antecedent in classical Latin for a poem about science, Lucretius's *De rerum natura* ("On the Nature of Things"), was too materialistic and Epicurean for moralistic poets, whether pagan or Christian, to consider imitating. In sum, we find no earlier poem in Spanish that expresses the poet's yearning desire to see the whole of reality in an orderly and rational way set forth in a philosophic or scientific vision.

In our own day, most of the recent discoveries and theories of time and space, of subatomic particles, and of cells and genomes are so far removed from common human experience that we modern readers find it hard to associate the aesthetic beauty of poetry with an all-embracing scientific vision; for us, more than for the sensibility of the seventeenth century, mathematical science is the antithesis of verbal poetry. For Sor Juana it was still possible to dream of grasping, with her intellect and imagination, the whole of reality. But what she and her reader feel most deeply at the end of her poem is the sad failure of the human mind to accomplish this grandiose mission.

From an autobiographical point of view, a suggestive aspect of this ambitious poem is the poet's association of scientific exploration with the transgression of authoritarian rules. Had she perhaps heard of Galileo's problems with the Inquisition? She knew that many of her clerical superiors considered it inappropriate for a nun to read and write about secular matters. For more than two hundred lines (617–826) she has her protagonist ("mi entendimiento" ["my understanding"]) vacillate between feelings of failure and of daring: at first, there is confidence in the power of the human mind that is created by God; afterward despair, caused by an inability to understand the simplest phenomena of nature; and finally an admiring inclination to make yet another attempt, provoked by Phaeton's public punishment (lines 781–95):

> Otras—más esforzado—,
> demasiada acusaba cobardía
> el lauro antes ceder, que en la lid dura
> haber siquiera entrado;
> y al ejemplar osado
> del claro joven la atención volvía
> —auriga altivo del ardiente carro—,
> y el, si infeliz, bizarro
> alto impulso, el espíritu encendía:
> donde el ánimo halla
> —más que el temor ejemplos de escarmiento—
> abiertas sendas al atrevimiento,
> que una ya vez trilladas, no hay castigo
> que intento baste a remover segundo
> (segunda ambición, digo). (1: 355)

> At other times, more bravely,
> it [the mind] accused of excessive cowardice
> the surrender of the laurel before even
> entering into battle,
> and turned its attention
> to the daring example of the famous youth,
> the proud driver of the blazing chariot,
> whose attractive, if unfortunate,
> bravery aroused one's spirit
> and, rather than to fear of punishment,
> opened the way to daring,
> and, this way once trod, no discouragement
> can keep one from trying again,
> (from being ambitious, I mean).

The poet goes on to analyze, in a somewhat Machiavellian way, the disadvantages of public punishment, which, instead of discouraging misbehavior, may actually encourage someone to follow a daring example. This passage thus seems to reflect an ambiguous defiance of authority. The author, according to this passage, does not question the rules themselves or the punishment of those who break the rules; she does question, however, the wisdom of allowing punishment to be publicized.

Although a devout Catholic believer, Sor Juana's vocation to live as a cloistered nun, as she clearly explains in her *Answer*, was in no sense mystical: she wanted to avoid the life of a married woman and to devote herself to the life of the mind, reading and writing. But she found that in practice this was not easy for her as a woman, subordinated to the church's long misogynistic tradition and to the men in Mexico who tried to restrict her intellectual freedom. From the beginning she had shown signs of insubordination. It was unusual to move, as she did early in her life, from one religious order to another. A major indication of her unwillingness to submit to authority is her letter of 1682 written to her confessor, Antonio Núñez; apparently he had reprehended her for writing poetry and for studying and had in addition criticized her outside the confessional for such activities. Her letter is painstakingly courteous, but she objects strongly to his public reprehensions and declares that she will find another confessor. Later on, in her revealing *Answer* to the bishop of Puebla, who had also reprimanded her publicly, Sor Juana was to declare that the *Dream* was the only thing that she had ever written of her own volition. It was, then, a poem of special importance to her, and hence is so also to us, her twenty-first-century readers.

NOTE

[1]All translations are my own.

Spectacles of Power and Figures of Knowledge in Sor Juana's *Allegorical Neptune*

Verónica Grossi

The *Neptuno alegórico, Océano de Colores, Simulacro Político* . . . ("Allegorical Neptune, Ocean of Colors, Political Simulacrum . . ." [printed c. 1680 and republished in 1689]) is both a description of and an interpretive guide to the triumphal arch conceived by Sor Juana Inés de la Cruz and built by the chapter of the cathedral of Mexico City to welcome the twenty-eighth Mexican viceroy, Tomás Antonio de la Cerda y Aragón, Count of Paredes and Marquis of la Laguna and his wife, María Luisa Manrique de Lara y Gonzaga, Countess of Paredes and Marquise of la Laguna, on 30 November 1680.

As was customary in New Spain, the chapter of the cathedral and the city council of Mexico City commissioned two of the most reputable local writers, Sor Juana Inés de la Cruz and Carlos de Sigüenza y Góngora, to conceptualize and write detailed descriptions of two triumphal arches representing the ideal qualities of the viceroy. That is, Sor Juana and Sigüenza were not only to devise the arches—their architecture, allegories, paintings, inscriptions and verses—but also, after the festival, to write the literary descriptions of the monuments.[1] Sor Juana's arch, in which mythological figures from antiquity served as emblems of the viceroy and his wife, was built in front of the west door of the cathedral, while Sigüenza y Góngora's, with an autochthonous allegory based on the exemplary virtues of the Aztec emperors, was constructed at Santo Domingo Square (Toussaint 20–21, 52–53).

Sor Juana's *Allegorical Neptune*, like other arches of the period, contains a dedication to the incoming viceroy, an "argument about the allegorical edifice," and a "succinct explication of the arch." In the dedication, Sor Juana explains to the viceroy the use since antiquity of symbols, or hieroglyphs, to represent superior ideas or abstract concepts. In the argument, an extensive treatise, she expounds on the meaning of her allegory and, alluding to a number of classical and early modern authorities, discusses her choice of the figure of Neptune to represent the viceroy. She also provides a detailed description of the physical dimensions and components of the arch, as well as an explanation of the eight canvases that represent the feats and virtues of the god Neptune and of the six hieroglyphs that symbolize the innumerable excellences of the viceroy, located at the four bases and two intercolumniations (the clear spaces between the columns of a series) of the pedestals. At the end of each description, there is a brief poem (Sabat de Rivers, Introduction 67–68).

The "Explication of the Arch," a 298-line poem printed in advance and distributed the day of the festival, was recited during the ceremony by an actor standing before the arch to explain its symbols and allegories to the viceroy and his escort as well as to the city's population. It was also published at the end of a more detailed description in prose, titled *Allegorical Neptune*, which included a dedication and an argument. This encomiastic poem recapitulates the description and allegorical guide contained in the forementioned parts. The sonnet that closes the "Explication" invites the viceroy to pass through the arch and enter the cathedral (Paz, *Traps* 157; Sabat de Rivers, Introduction 67–69; Toussaint 11–12).

Sor Juana's arch was displayed before the new viceroy and other members of the court and church, as well as the wider, multiethnic population of Mexico City. Whereas the "Explication" was first heard during the reception festivities for the viceroy by a heterogeneous, massive audience, the printed *Neptune*, with its three parts, circulated among members of the clergy and the nobility, *letrados*, or lettered persons, who could read and decipher—at least in part—its conceits and allegories.

The ephemeral monument, the leaflets that circulated during the festival, and the book published shortly afterward all display Sor Juana's name as an author before a wide public. She had already gained artistic recognition in her local milieu, especially as a result of the commissioned composition of her *villancicos* ("popular carols"), but the design and publication of the *Neptune* brought her international visibility. However, the publication of a nun's writings was not an accepted practice in those days, and public fame was mostly a male domain. For these reasons, she received a severe reprimand from her confessor, Antonio Núñez de Miranda, a figure of high authority among the ruling class of New Spain (see her *Autodefensa* [Tapia Méndez]).

In an informal, private letter (1681 or 1682), Sor Juana responded boldly to Núñez de Miranda's injunctions against her intellectual and literary activities, in particular, her composition of the arch. In the epistle, she states with irony that the *Neptune*, among her "published writings that have so scandalized the world, and so edified the good" (Paz, *Traps* 497), was commissioned by high ecclesiastical authorities—higher than Núñez himself—such as the archbishop. She takes the opportunity to assert her prerogative to "learning and knowledge" (499) and dismisses Núñez as her confessor since God "has made many keys to Heaven and has not confined Himself to a single criterion" (502). Thus, Sor Juana's triumphal arch also marks the beginning of the wave of ecclesiastical persecution against her literary and intellectual endeavors (Arenal, "Enigmas" 89–90 and "Sor Juana's Arch" 175, 183; Grossi, "Claves" 227). This institutionalized censorship would culminate in her rhetorical masterpiece titled *Respuesta a sor Filotea de la Cruz* ("The Answer"), dated 1 March 1691, in which the Mexican nun defends with unsurpassed eloquence women's universal right to create, think, learn, and interpret.

The Reception of the Neptune

Sor Juana's *Allegorical Neptune*, because it includes verse and prose interconnected to painting, emblematic figures, sculpture, architecture, dance, and theater, as well as to the spoken and printed words, is one of her most hermetic pieces. Challenging to teach in the classroom, its conceptual language, intricate network of symbols, erudite allusions, quotes in Latin, different intended audiences, and formal and semantic complexity have also discouraged both a wide readership and many scholars. Although the *Neptune* brought Sor Juana international recognition in her own time, it has been labeled, across the centuries, as a composition that has no literary value and that is too occasional, in bad taste, unpleasant, and excessively obscure (Maza, *Mitología* 109).

Against this trend, some critics, such as Electa Arenal, María Dolores Bravo Arriaga, José Pascual Buxó, Octavio Paz, and Georgina Sabat de Rivers, have undertaken the ambitious project of providing basic interpretive tools for the *Neptune* while restoring it to prominence within the corpus of the nun's writings.[2] Sabat de Rivers, for instance, studies it within the larger historical landscape of the European and Mexican baroque festival, which had the conservative function of creating a sense of harmony and unity in a highly heterogeneous, stratified society. In this way, the popular, public festival, which combined secular and religious motifs, was an instrument of social control.

Arenal examines various aspects of Sor Juana's arch from a feminist perspective ("Emblema," "Enigmas," "Sor Juana's Arch") and, with Vincent Martin, is editing an annotated and illustrated edition. Bravo Arriaga re-creates the context of the seventeenth-century Mexican festival based on primary sources ("Festejos"; "Signos"). Pascual Buxó develops a comparative iconological analysis ("Francisco"; "Función"). Paz situates the *Neptune* within an emblematic vision of the universe, "a fabric of reflections, echoes and correspondences" (*Traps* 163), as well as within the genealogy of the European entrance and triumph. He traces the *Neptune*'s philosophical traditions, such as Neoplatonic hermeticism, and classical mythographic sources, both primary and secondary, Eastern and Western.

Understanding the Neptune *in the Classroom*

The main approaches for teaching the *Neptune* are:

contextual: introducing the cultural codes that were in vogue in colonial New Spain

comparatist: relating the *Neptune* to other Mexican arches (for these primary sources, see Pascual Buxó, *Arco* and *Impresos*)

intertextual: noting how some of *Neptune*'s symbols and allegories are present in some of the author's other works

interartistic: showing the interplay of the different arts in the *Neptune*'s complex semiotics and semantics (for artistic manifestations in New Spain see Cuadriello, *Juegos*)

performative: reenacting the centrality of the human voice, vision, and body in both the representation and the interpretation of the arch interdisciplinary: approaching the *Neptune* from a variety of academic disciplines to appreciate its formal and cultural hybridity

An important step in teaching the *Neptune* is to acknowledge that we are approaching it from our historical perspective, through our ideological biases and ways of seeing. Understanding Sor Juana's arch involves both historical restitution as well as an act of appropriation or ideological projection. This allegorical composition is kept alive through our own interested readings. A balanced approach combines a respect for the text's insuperable difference and distance and a conscious and even bold initiative to construct unprecedented meanings from and for our own lives.

Furthermore, a historical contextualization allows the instructor to approach Sor Juana's arch not as an obscure oddity, but rather as a representative cultural artifact of seventeenth-century New Spain, characterized by the centrality of the allegorical trope, use of mythological and emblematic language, competition and interrelation of the arts, and by other cultural conditions: didacticism, eclecticism, hermeticism, hybridity (*mestizaje*), and syncretism.

Teaching the *Neptune* also leads to encounters with other widespread phenomena, such as the sociopolitical function of art; dependency of imperial rule on public spectacles or festivities; concept of the urban space as a cultural text and a theatrical stage; intense cultural exchanges between New Spain and Europe; as well as the cosmopolitan character of life in Mexico City, an "enormous emporium [. . .] where all the paths of the world converged" (Rubial García, *Plaza* 22; my trans.).

Finally, the *Neptune* can educate us about the strict ecclesiastical control of nuns' literary and intellectual activities and how Sor Juana was able to maneuver within these sociocultural strictures to encode through allegory a transgressive model for action: a woman's search for knowledge through writing. This powerful message, expressed eloquently in the *Neptune* and other works by Sor Juana, has reverberated through the centuries to our time.

The Epistemological and Political Dimensions of the Arch

The *Neptune*'s allegorical figures point to the connections among artistic creation, interpretation, and learning. The process of deciphering the different components of the arch becomes a cognitive venture, in which different actors, spectators, and readers have an active role. Furthermore, the interpretive guide or explication that forms part of the texts in prose and verse presents a hermeneutical model that is also an epistemology.

Sor Juana's arch includes concepts, symbols, and allegories centered on the positive value of feminine knowledge, a recurrent theme in her writings (Arenal, "Enigma" 87–92, "Arch" 173–94, "Emblema"; Grossi, "Fiesta" 665; Kirk, "God" 31–32; Paz, *Traps* 169–79; Sabat de Rivers, Introduction 70 and "*Nep-*

tuno" 260). Thus, the *Neptune* is a key to understanding the network of intertextual allusions found in Sor Juana's works that configure an original allegorical system. One can thus affirm that the arch inaugurates Sor Juana's literary career, her lifelong artistic and intellectual project. It marks her triumphal entrance into the male domain of public fame. Through publication, her works have been made available to an ever-growing international readership (Grossi, "Claves" 226–27 and *Sigilosos*)

Sor Juana manipulates and revises mythological and emblematic sources to compose a "mirror of princes" that presents wisdom as the "most important virtue for the monarch" (Kirk, "God" 30–31). In this way, she distances herself from the counterreformist contents, moral and propagandistic in character, of the allegorical genre in New Spain (Osorio Romero, "Género" 175).

Neptune, conflated with Harpocrates, the Egyptian divinity of silence, is the son of Isis, a goddess of wisdom and a poet (Paz, *Traps* 159–62). Thus in Sor Juana's arch, Harpocrates, as an emblem of silence, is associated with feminine knowledge rather than with the political and military virtues of prudence, secrecy, and dissimulation that are standard in the emblematic literature of the period (Pedraza 44; for an example see Andrea Alciati's emblem 11 at www.mun.ca/alciato; see also *Book of Emblems*).

In the seventh canvas of the arch, feminine wisdom, personified in the figure of Minerva, competes with and vanquishes the bellicose political power of Neptune. Furthermore, Minerva produces the green olive, a symbol of peace and a fruit, which when pressed "becomes oil, the precious liquor that serves as sunlight for the person who studies at night," such as Sor Juana (my trans.; see Arenal, "Emblema," for this connection and Grossi, *Sigilosos*, for a prose rendering of the "Explication").[3] The association among learning, a nocturnal, solitary activity; the emblem of silence; and feminine mythological figures such as Minerva is also present in Sor Juana's *Dream* (see for instance 1: 336; Trueblood 172).

Allegory, as the trope that structures or weaves the verbal and physical fabric of the piece, consists of a dynamics of tension between composing and glossing; encoding and decoding; writing and reading; acting, feeling, and seeing. Through allegory the reader/spectator is able to construct and reconstruct a multiplicity of meanings or "truths" that are historically and culturally bound. The double nature of the allegorical trope, which hides and at the same time illustrates meanings, allows Sor Juana to establish these subversive symbolic associations with the act of knowing.

In the *Neptune*, knowledge is articulated through an interdependent dynamics between body and intellect, voice and silence, painting and writing, acting and imagining, reciting and reading. The contemporary reader can also appreciate a series of translations and competitions among the visual languages and the spoken, written, and printed words.

By incorporating pedagogical exercises in the classroom such as short theatrical skits centered on body and voice, on pantomime or creative visualization, as well as those that focus on research, textual analyses, and discussions that involve speaking, reading, and writing, one can re-create some of the cultural codes and discourses that come together in this piece. Variegated cultural traditions converge in the *Neptune*, such as the baroque rhetoric that privileges the aural and visual modes of communication and that is aimed at creating a strong impression on the senses of spectators and the modern prevalence of the silent reception of the printed text (Egido, "Poética" 70–71).

The *Neptune* exemplifies what Paul Julian Smith terms the baroque "rhetoric of presence," a symbolic appropriation of vision, body, and voice through language. Writing competes with painting in material vividness and splendor. In one of her sonnets, Sor Juana writes, "Este, que ves, engaño colorido, / que del arte ostentando los primores, / con falsos silogismos de colores / es cauteloso engaño del sentido" ("These lying pigments facing you, / with every charm brush can supply / set up false premises of color / to lead astray the unwary eye" [1: 277; Trueblood 95]). Yet in another, feminine fantasy can capture, apprehend, "grasp" the image or emblematic body of her beloved one, hitherto an unattainable—perpetually abstract and distant—object of desire in patriarchal courtly discourse:

> Mas blasonar no puedes, satisfecho,
> de que triunfa de mí tu tiranía:
> que aunque dejas burlado el lazo estrecho
> que tu forma fantástica ceñía,
> poco importa burlar brazos y pecho
> si te labra prisión mi fantasía. (1: 288)

> Even so, you shan't boast, self-satisfied,
> that your tyranny has triumphed over me,
> evade as you will arms opening wide,
> all but encircling your phantasmal form:
> in vain shall you elude my fruitless clasp,
> for fantasy holds you captive in its grasp.
> (Trueblood 81)

The truths embodied in the arch, product of a woman's imagination and reason, have a higher ontological status than sociohistorical doctrines, laws, and institutions of power. As a symbolic mode of representation centered on the sensuous materiality of the sign, allegory is the centerpiece of the semiotics of this work. By resignifying poetic allegory as an instrument of feminine knowledge, Sor Juana's arch brings the body back to writing, thought, and representation. The material body of allegory is the source or sustenance of theory (*theory* in the Greek sense of spectacle, of viewing and contemplating something at a distance). The body, subordinate in the Western phallogocentric metaphysical tradition to abstract thought is in fact, as Luce Irigaray explains, its unacknowledged or erased foundation (74–75). Janet Kauffman also reminds us that language is always bodily and material: there is no signification without bodies and their dispositions in space (Hollywood 504–05).

The central function of the body in Sor Juana's arch becomes more evident when we consider that the festival, as a whole, was an emblem or an allegory that "incarnated" itself before the eyes and ears of the spectators:

> "The political ceremony was a true fiesta, by which I mean a collective act wherein symbols were embodied and made palpable. It was the return of society to its origins, to the pact that had founded it; a pact expressed vertically in the bond that joined the lord with his vassals, and horizontally in the original wholeness to which the parts of the social body were being restored." (Paz, *Traps* 141)

The verbal simulacrum, product of the imagination, aspires to become more memorable than the architecture of the ephemeral monument, composed of "wood, cloth and plaster" (Paz, *Traps* 156). To do so, the material space of language encompasses all the other arts. As Aurora Egido explains:

> The word erects art within its limits and perpetuates it beyond its temporary existence. This becomes even more evident with the potential for multiplication of printed editions. The illustrated book synthesizes the continuity of images and texts. Emblematics also corroborates the sisterhood between painting and literature. ("Página" 185–86; my trans.)

Allusions to the physical, aural, and visual dimensions of the arch and its components seek to reconnect the reader to voice and body, essential for the production and reception of the concrete object of wood, paper, and paint. Thus, reciting and performing the *Neptune*, in particular the explication in verse, instead of just reading it in silence, restores its theatrical, interartistic dimensions. Acting can also reconnect us to other works by Sor Juana that present a fundamental performative dimension, such as her popular carols, sacred plays, secular theater, and some of her poems. Sor Juana's interest in the epistemological interconnections between body and mind is also fully developed in her long metaphysical poem "First Dream" (*Primero sueño*), where the cognitive act consists of a series of translations among physical perceptions, visual re-creations, and mental interpretations in which both imagination and intellectual understanding participate. Angeles Romero's performance, *Sueño*, a useful tool for instructors, reenacts the connection among body, voice, and words in Sor Juana's texts.

Thus the interconnectedness between body and intellect makes artistic representation possible. In fact, emblematic allegory, the centerpiece of the arch's epistemological dimension, is composed of body and idea. As Arenal reminds us, "[f]ollowing emblem books, a fundamental model for triumphal arches, each of the fourteen paintings [of Sor Juana's *Neptune*] was tripartite: it had a Latin motto ("the soul"), a pictorial image ("the body"), and a *subscriptio* in verse epigram, sonnet, *octava* or *redondilla*" ("Sor Juana's Arch" 179). This oscillating dynamics between body and idea does not privilege abstract thought over the materiality of voice, vision, body, and even handwriting (*borrones*, or scribblings, which are the product of a hand). Rather, it brings them together in the conflicted, ever changing space of embodied idea, allegory, meaning, knowledge.

Through its conventional intermediary role, Sor Juana's arch may have exerted an influence on society. The second and fifth canvases of the arch take on the important role of voicing the demands of the population and current authorities to the new viceroy, such as completing the project of the drainage of the valley of Mexico to protect the city from its periodic flooding and finishing the construction of the cathedral. The new governor, whose last name was Laguna, meaning lagoon—let us remember that México-Tenochtitlan was erected on a lagoon—is represented in the classical figure of Neptune, in the hope that he, like the Roman deity, would "control the waters that were menacing the capital" (Rubial García, *Plaza* 13). The fifth canvas, a revision of the classical myth of Neptune recounted by Baltasar de Vitoria, encodes another request, with an unprecedented focus on learning: that the viceroy would become a patron of the arts and letters, represented in the figure of the learned centaurs (Paz, *Traps* 521n1).

The epistemological dimension of the arch also connects us to questions of both power and gender, insofar as the system of allegorical analogies sets into motion a series of translations or associations revolving around the question of authority and authorship. Even though the arch's didactic, propagandistic function is meant to exemplify the governor's ideal qualities and authorize his new rule, the semantics of Sor Juana's symbolic network converge in the exaltation of the verbal and physical monument, of feminine wisdom, and of Sor Juana's superior power as a creator and imitator (Grossi, "Figuras" 189).

Her allegorical representation, composed of figures of speech and visual emblems, aspires to capture eternal, immutable entities through visible hieroglyphs, or symbols. This ambitious epistemological enterprise, authorized by the cultures of antiquity, particularly that of Egypt, supersedes the formulaic, occasional encomium of a new viceroy or the idealized portrait of a mundane political figure. There is never a perfect analogical correspondence between Sor Juana's allegories and the ideal virtues of the new prince that form part of the Neoplatonic realm of transcendental ideas. As a result, the creative process of imitation moves to the center stage of the ephemeral monument and its description.

The allegorical imitation of the ideal model is essential for embodying before the eyes of the enthralled spectators—for making tangible and therefore real—the imperial hegemony of the Spanish monarchy, otherwise a distant abstraction (Mínguez 63). As Victor Mínguez suggests, imperial power was concretely supported by artistic, public spectacles (63). Thus, Sor Juana's allegories aid the push by the new political ruler to consolidate power. The persuasive splendor of Sor Juana's *figmenta* ("fictions"), as well as her breathtaking spectacle of erudition, displaces the absolute authority of the viceroy (Grossi, "Figuras" 189).

The *Neptune* is a work of the imagination, a product of the intellectual and artistic ingenuity of the author. Through her symbolic edifice, composed of "mentales pórfidos" ("imaginary sculptures in jasper" [*Inundación* 447]), Sor Juana makes a public display of her superior intelligence and capacity to emulate the classics. In this way, she carves a place for herself in the long, for the most part undocumented, lineage of exceptional women thinkers and creators.

In our society, as in the baroque era, the borders between the virtual and the real have become disquietingly blurred. Yet, even in the age of global markets and massive commodification of culture, the indivisible dynamic of creating and interpreting, feeling, seeing, acting, and analyzing with our bodies and our minds, as Sor Juana's *Allegorical Neptune* exemplifies, can open new horizons for critical learning, resistance, and innovation.

NOTES

[1]The paintings were done on canvases mounted on the arch. For a visual re-creation of Sor Juana's arch, see Sabat de Rivers, *Busca* 261; Aguiar's drawing in Glantz, *Saberes* 100–01; and López Poza 266.

[2]On this piece, see Arenal, "Emblema," "Enigmas," and "Sor Juana's Arch"; Arenal and Martin; A. Boyer; Bravo Arriaga, "Búsqueda"; Checa Cremades; González García; Grossi, "Figuras," "Fiesta," and *Sigilosos*; J. Jones; Kirk, "God"; Kügelgen; López Poza; Merkl; Pascual Buxó, "Cervantes" and "Función"; Paz, *Trampas* and *Traps*; Sabat de Rivers, Introduction and "*Neptuno*"; Salceda; and Toussaint.

[3]The original passage of Sor Juana's explication in verse is "apenas hiere [a la "Gran Madre" Tierra], cuando pululante, / aunque siempre de paz, siempre triunfante, / verde produce oliva que adornada / de pacíficas señas, y agravada / en su fruto de aquel licor precioso / que es Apolo nocturno al estudioso, / al belígero opone bruto armado, / que al toque del tridente fue crïado" (Sabat de Rivers, *Inundación* 444, lines 231–38).

CONVENTIONAL GENRES, SUBVERSIVE GESTURES

Sor Juana in Text and in Performance: Confronting Meaning

Catherine Boyle

This essay suggests ways of approaching a main challenge of a baroque event such as *Los empeños de una casa* ("House of Desires"). It aims to provide students with a method of reading that unlocks a series of meanings and performance possibilities, a method through which they are invited to engage in close analysis of key dramatic moments. Its starting point is that this is a joyous text that begs performance; its core lesson is that if we trust the text and allow ourselves to be guided by it at all stages, it will yield enormous wealth in our understanding of the spectacle, Sor Juana, and the spaces they occupy. So, here, I follow the principle that guides performance: that we must confront problems of meaning and create and re-create the internal coherence of structures of meaning on stage. To that end, I do not separate text and performance but treat the text as performance. I propose all Sor Juana's writing as different aspects of a performance of complex being. In that sense she is quintessentially baroque.

The opening scenes of Sor Juana's play, as all hapless first readers of it know, deposit us in the midst of uncertainty, an experience both baroque and modern. What is interesting is how we can trust this uncertainty to teach us about the possibilities of analysis and performance. This essay will suggest approaches in three key areas: performance, space, and the structures of meaning; translation and the transmission of the meaning; the performance of uncertainty and the unraveling of meaning.

Performance, Space, and the Structures of Meaning

As we study a work such as this baroque event, it is important to keep in mind that theater is process: during this process a series of social, historical, political, intellectual, and creative spaces are negotiated to create the production. At the moment of performance five central elements are represented: the author, text, director, actor, and audience. The presence of the actor, audience, and text may be obvious; that the director's presence can be felt is also perhaps uncontroversial, particularly with respect to performances in which the audience is familiar with the director's previous work. It is also useful to separate out text and author because what actors, directors, scholars, critics, and students work from is the text. Yet strong awareness of the presence of the author may color our approach, which obviously occurs with Shakespeare, for example. The presence of the text in performance is not the same thing as the presence of the author; we will explore how Sor Juana uses this distinction to perform herself through her text.

By following the model outlined above, I invite students to use the complexities of the play to reveal its dynamics and identify its essential intellectual coherence, its dramatic backbone. In this sense, the performance is analogous to the space occupied by the baroque body, the self, which is "never autonomous, but, rather, a space defined by multiple and conflicting discourses of sex, religion, politics and power" (Robbins 119). The projection of self is refracted through these elements vying with one another in personal or public spaces.

As we seek to understand *Los empeños de una casa*, we can enter into its space by recognizing an initial reality: that this is not a *play* as we might understand the term, it is a baroque *festejo* ("celebration"), that is, a series of performance pieces written for a public festival. The three acts that form the play are part of a larger scheme of events, "which would begin with a dramatic praise or *loa*, followed by humorous interludes or *sainetes* between the acts, and with original songs composed for the festival, and with a masque or *sarao* to conclude the spectacle" (Schmidhuber 43). I guide students to Guillermo Schmidhuber de la Mora's treatment of *Los empeños de una casa* for an excellent full study of the *festejo* and its context, including the following elements relating to the social, political, cultural, and creative spaces *Los empeños* occupies: it was a courtly piece, performed in the presence of the new archbishop, Francisco Aguiar y Seijas, in a noble house for the viceregal couple (who were the important patrons of the arts and protectors of Sor Juana, Tomás Antonio de la Cerda y Aragón and María Luisa Manrique de Lara y Gonzaga, the Count and Countess of Paredes) as a celebration of their firstborn. The two centers of power—the court and church—were, then, present, and the audience was composed of the social and intellectual elite. Schmidhuber, significantly, tells us:

> The theological subtleties, the allusions to important persons and events of the time, and the mythological allegories were mere private games

> between the dramatist and some members of the audience, because if it is certain that the baroque works were theatre productions for only one day—a Corpus Christi or another feast day—it is also certain that the dramatist knew, one by one, her audience's opinions and that the rest of their thoughts also were not strange to her. (42)

Sor Juana knows the members of her public and relishes the opportunity to prove from her physical distance in the convent that she is an intellectual match and superior to them. She writes accordingly, exhibiting her wit, her ingenuity, and the scope of her knowledge in a fantastically well-constructed set of allusions, historic references, and social and cultural critique (see, for example, the satire of Fortune and Merit in the *loa* (4: 7–8, lines 100–46). In true baroque style, she makes herself known to her audience—she makes her private being public by performing herself for them. It is a game in which she takes gleeful delight. Two aspects of this performance of self are salient: the intellectual and the autobiographical.

Los empeños de una casa is a sumptuous and closely controlled display, and the student of the piece should be alert to how Sor Juana manages the performance. Note how its integrity is built on establishing and then echoing a core set of concepts, recognizable in terms of the structures of meaning and comportment of the audience. The first *loa* sets these out, as Fortune, Diligence, Merit, and Chance compete to determine "¿Cúal es de las dichas mayor?" ("Which is the greatest joy of all?" [4: 30]).[1] The allegorical battle introduces the repertoire of the play: the human virtues of Merit and Diligence in competition with Fortune and Chance are the keys to one of the internal battles of the characters in the house—the two lovers Leonor and Carlos struggle to use their inner virtues to guide them to love and happiness. The question finds a perfect echo in the second act, where Sor Juana delivers the entire play in one song that asks: "¿Cuál es la pena más grave / que en las penas del amor cabe?" ("Which is the greatest of all love's sorrows?" [4: 91]), a song to which all the characters respond in turn, allowing a full panoply of possibilities of the pains of love, from the courtly sublime to the profanities of the servants Celia and Castaño (4: 91–93).

The first *sainete*, inserted between the first and second acts, subverts the codes of love by pitting Love, Respect, Deference, Courtesy, and Hope against one another to win the prize of disdain: yet none does, for "aun los mismos desprecios / son imposibles" ("For even disdain itself is impossible" [4: 74]), "and a shadow of female disdain is cast over these feelings" (Schmidhuber 111). The *loa* and the first *sainete* alert us, as modern readers, to key tensions in the play between apparently fixed values and the autonomy of the characters, who are always caught in the gap between the free expression of love on the one hand and honor on the other, a gap suggestive of a state of uncertain flux around the values of love and honor.

Now look at the second *sainete* and the *sarao* that closes the event: they perform functions relating to theatricality and the Creole intellectual. The second *sainete* has two members of the audience heckle the work and seek to silence the author (whom Sor Juana mischievously names as another intellectual of the time), finally threatening him with the garrote unless he is silent or copies line by line what he has written. This being the worst of all fates, he begs to die, ("se hunde a silbos" ["drowned by whistles"; 4: 122]). Dramatically, this *sainete* destroys the fourth wall, the barrier between stage and audience that Sor Juana tests throughout by having characters talk in asides to the audience more often than to other characters (see, for example, 4: 53–59, act 1, lines 801–945, and consider also the roles of Celia and Castaño, who collude shamelessly with the audience). This *sainete* also forcefully completes the presence of Sor Juana at the center of the *festejo*. For it is her play whose merit, length, plot, and mixed race (*mestizaje*) are being commented on. And it is she who faces silencing for her secular activities, of which playwriting was perhaps the most reprehensible, and for thus being obviously sinful in the context of her religious vows. And if we return to the first *sainete* we find an interesting connection. The final lines were added to announce the presence of the new archbishop (an extreme misogynist who loathed the theater), which makes Sor Juana's performance of her self and of her potential silencing all the more transgressive of the cloistered space assigned to her as a nun.

The final *sarao* completes this intertextual weaving, presenting members of four nationalities—Spaniards, Africans, Italians, and Mexicans—in yet another type of game, with Love and Obligation fighting for consideration by the viceroys and their son. Again the spectator is part of a dizzy game of riddles, oppositions, counterpoint, and tension, now between the old world and the new, the power of the crown and a Mexican identity that has not forgone the cultural belief systems of the past (4: 180–81, lines 158–201). And at the end is the customary expression of humility before the court, which, in Sor Juana's lexicon, becomes an ironic veil pulled over her intellectual superiority (4: 183–84, lines 270–301). Thus her presence in the play—as the foremost mind of her generation, performing her presence for her adoring public—is complete.

Students are now asked to explore the second aspect of the performance of self, the autobiographic. The most obvious autobiographical "presence" is, of course, in Leonor's soliloquy in the first act (4: 36–43, lines 259–546). The ways in which it relates to Sor Juana's life have been amply studied. The second obvious allusion is in the third act where Leonor vows to Celia that she will cloister herself in a cell, where she will face the stars of her destiny (4: 128, lines 81–94). For want of biographical detail of this crucial period in her life, readers have pounced on these teasing comments, as Sor Juana—always aware of her audience—surely knew they would. It is a mistake, however, to privilege them as autobiographical information; we must relate to them, rather, as dramatic speeches, with dramatic functions, and in that sense they play two principal roles.

They perform visibility—they are a crucial part of the writing of her self into the play, into visibility beyond the convent. They are, furthermore, a conscious part of her game with the members of her audience, who cannot fail to recognize a form of self-portrait by the most famous woman of the period, who has, by coincidence, "hidden" herself in a convent cell and who is guided, it seems, by stars and destiny rather than divine influence. And yet she destabilizes this self-portrait by simultaneously alerting us to the fact that she is not "sepultada" ("buried") in a convent cell; through the *festejo* she is, in fact, "in dialogue" with the viceregal couple, addressing the new archbishop, displaying her awareness of courtly games and eroticism, and lampooning the creaky codes of honor. By very virtue of the *festejo*, and particularly of the second *sainete*, she is performing—celebrating—her self on stage and, moreover, drawing her attention to the trials of her presence and "fame," which, of course, she will eloquently expose and explore in her *Respuesta de la Poetisa a sor Filotea* ("The Answer") eight years later.

These speeches play another, equally significant, role. They are the first-person unveiling of a stock female character of the Golden Age: the beautiful, aloof, and learned woman who will not be loved and yet who can only be tamed by love. By the simple fact of writing, Sor Juana subverts this type, for she was not tamed by love. The dramatic role of Leonor's first monologue, then, is to create a picture of the codes that we are being taught to recognize, of decorum and excess, merit and diligence, fortune and chance, honor and disgrace, absence, jealousy, and the trials of love. The force of these battling entities is what the performance has to translate to the stage.

Translation and the Transmission of Meaning

Translation is the closest form of reading. It forces us to confront meaning and take risks with it, and, as in performance, decisions have to be made, interpretations reached. A couple of elements exemplify this process. What, for example, are we to make of the translation of the title, *Los empeños de una casa*, and what does that tell us about the play? The answer is, almost too much, for the title signals many aspects of the the play's space and meaning. *Empeños* means trials, intent, perseverance. It can also mean pawns in both of the English senses of the word, to pawn for money and to be a pawn in a power game. Like many of the words and concepts we deal with in Sor Juana, the word is a part of an extraordinary fragmenting of meaning. The question we have to consider as students, readers, and translators is how we re-create this multisignifying process—the emphasis being here on process, not fixed meaning, for the language, as we have suggested, performs flux. The answer is, partly, that we translate by dramatizing the different elements of the word. That is to say that Sor Juana plays on the meanings of *empeños* throughout the play, and each character is tested in ways that relate to these meanings. The title signals how each character is driven by specific desires, the fulfillment of which is thwarted at each turn and for which they have to battle. The sense of the original Spanish-language title persists in the play as a dramatic action. In theater, signifying is shared by many elements of the spectacle, and we use text, movement, gesture to build meaning as completely as possible in the course of each performance.

The English title used in the Royal Shakespeare Company (RSC) production, *House of Desires*, seeks to express the dramatic backbone of the play; that is, it seeks to express the desires of each character in a group enclosed for a period of time in a house. In translating the title, we needed to convey that it locates the dramatic motor of the play. If *empeños* leads us to the plight of the characters, then the word *house* here is also multisignifying. *Empeños* may be easier to translate, but *casa* frames the notion of the space: intimate, domestic, the domain of the female—until big brother comes home, that is. It establishes a field of gendered meaning that Sor Juana will explore ruthlessly, as a space of female confinement, particularly in terms of locks, keys, enclosure.

Nancy Meckler, the director of the RSC production, used a simple and effective device to engage with this idea of the trials of desire in a conventlike setting. This consisted of a twofold question that is worth posing to the classroom: what is each character's desire, and what is impeding each character from attaining it? That is, what is the nature of each one's trial? Working through this problem reveals the dramatic motor for each scene and serves another dramatic function: it forces the actor-student to create a type of internal memory for each character, which creates a collective—and necessary—internal memory for the play. This is important in a process of reading and rehearsal where much of the plot is confused for so long. Furthermore, by confronting the knot at the center of each desire or trial, the contemporary reader-actor is forced to confront the workings of honor and the ways in which honor is decoded by Sor Juana. The games the characters play entrap them, and they become pawns in a noble house; they are not merely suffering the trials of a noble house. As Jeremy Robbins tells us, there is little autonomy in this world (118), only the hand that moves its inhabitants, and Sor Juana—as she shows us—has stepped out of this entrapping space to play at being that hand.

Yet as all translators know, and as Umberto Eco so eloquently demonstrates with his subtitle in *Mouse or Rat?*, translation is a process of negotiation. Translation for the stage is a multifaceted and often fragmented process. It involves negotiating the act of linguistic translation and cultural transmission alongside, for example, the material possibilities or restrictions of the production; the venue itself; the projected audience; or the interpretations of the director, actor, and designer. In deciding on a translation there is loss and gain, always and inevitably. What was lost in the process of the RSC production was this translator's dream and desire to see the complete *festejo* performed. It was lost because of the perceived physical impossibility of the performance in the context of a modern theater experience. What this means is that the range of meanings and the potential resonance of the *festejo*—its complex intertextuality—are reduced; the connections and interlocking languages that make up its brilliance are lost. Lost too is the sense of a complete piece of work into which is written as one element what we now generally look on as a three-act (or two-act in the RSC production) play. In this context, the range of allegorical meanings is compromised, and the subversive elements of the play on which these meanings are founded and interwoven are left without their broader context. The backbone of the play then becomes the symbolic field of the images in the three acts of the play. Yet, in practice, these acts may also be sacrificed because of this perceived impossibility in the modern context of translating to the stage the complete theatrical event, the complete performance of self and context. The text of the play is left largely unsupported by the contextualizing *loas*, *sainetes*, and *sarao*, becoming vulnerable, too capable of being performed above all as farce. In this modern context, the "play" *Los empeños de una casa* becomes a discrete unit, and it is that unit that is read for its performability and linguistic and cultural resonance. And while we may maintain the joyous excess of Sor Juana's writing, we risk losing sight of the intellectual brilliance that allows this profoundly baroque excess its fully controlled expression.

The Performance of Uncertainty and Unraveling Meaning

Imagine a space that is shaped in the first instance by silence, by a distant locking and unlocking of doors, by sounds that can be heard and identified—a stable, known space. Then imagine that it fills up with barely recognizable sounds, unidentified movements, the muted articulation of ideas and desires or emotions that have not been expressed openly before. And imagine that these must finally be silenced and controlled in order for equilibrium to be established and the space to be known again. That is the space of *Los empeños de una casa*.

Sor Juana signals from the start of the play that this is a gendered space. Unusually, the beginning of the play is a space filled with women, plotting, seeking to take control of their destinies, of the spaces they occupy. When the male voice is heard it is a shock, an intrusion (4: 33, 4: 44–47, act 1, lines 181–93, 573–660), but it quickly takes command. Later, when female voices reappear, they are again a surprise. The sexes meet only to engage in the conventional battles of love and disdain, into which the entities in the *sainetes* initiate the audience and for which they create an ironic counterpoint. For this is, by and large, a segregated space, in which the characters are trapped by the idiocies of codes created by men.

Octavio Paz calls *Los empeños de una casa* a drama of "empty perfection," adding that it would be useless to seek any transgression in it (*Traps* 326). I call it the dramatization of an insight into emptiness. For, as we work with the language we find that it begins to disintegrate; unravel the baroque syntax and we find that it turns endlessly on recognizable examples of honor, absence, jealousy, and love, with endlessly inventive new ways of saying the same thing. That is, the concept of honor is, essentially, empty of meaning, cynically based on appearance alone. The play's choreography moves around that central empty concept. Paz warns us not to look for transgression in the play. I would say that students of the piece should keep their eyes fixed on how Sor Juana perfects the baroque form of the *festejo* in order to dazzle the audience with the form's perfection while inserting into the play a performance of honor as farce. We cannot avoid hearing the "Sátira filosófica" ("Philosophical Satire") as a template for *Los empeños de una casa*; as a description of that empty space that yawns beyond the games, the circular entrapment of those first lines cannot be bettered: "Hombres necios que acusáis / a la mujer sin razón, / sin ver que sois la ocasión / de lo mismo que culpáis" ("Misguided men, who will chastise / a woman when no blame is due, / oblivious that it is you / who prompted what you criticize [1: 228; Peden, *Poems* 149]). Indeed, Don Carlos is given words akin to those in Sor Juana's most famous poem as he battles to maintain equilibrium and discretion in the house, against the better judgment of his manservant Castaño (4: 76–77, act 2, lines 33–100).

The manner of the search for honor is a materialization of the absurdity of the concept: the men battle to know what it is, yet adhere blindly to its power. Sanity and madness are defined in relation to the state of their honor (4: 158, act 3, lines 879–84). And the men masquerade from behind the language that masks the emptiness of the concept. The concept of honor merely serves as a type of common language that hides the emptiness beyond. And the characters scurry around in that space between private (and often scandalous) desire and public honor, or, more specifically, reputation. If honor—as we see it represented in so many of these plays—defines male identity, resides in the woman, and is guarded in the quintessentially female space of the home, the characters are trapped in a world in disintegration. And what becomes subversive about Sor Juana is that she does not seem to care!

Honor is the motor for the externalization of the private self in the public space, and without a true understanding of how this process operates honor begins to disintegrate. Sor Juana performs this most vividly in the character of Don Juan. Throughout the play he struggles to understand his position: like Don Carlos, he has been given reason to doubt his lover's constancy but cannot prove it fully and so cannot take revenge. For, as he "reasons," if he takes revenge wrongly, he will defile his honor and hers; but if he does not take revenge and has, in fact, been wronged, he will also have defiled his honor. In his gloriously incoherent speech in the third act—which is a prime example of the complexities of unraveling language (4: 130–31, act 3, lines 143–80)—he tries in vain to make sense of the codes of honor and to work out how to apply them consistently to his own situation. But he cannot control the lofty register he tries out, and he does not have the intellect to engage in a difficult discourse of oppositions about the subtleties of preserving a balance in honor. His reasoning becomes less and less coherent until he is immobilized—he can only wait to be governed once again by pure instinct, by revenge. In a wider discourse where reason is male and instinct is female, he is feminized.

Moreover, Don Carlos, the epitome of manly perfection, is also immobilized: he has seen "his Leonor" and is honor-bound to remain in the house until he has rescued her (4: 99–100, act 2, lines 583–637). And yet Don Carlos is somehow beyond mere manhood in his understanding and self-knowledge as he struggles valiantly against the evidence of his senses in this seemingly delusional game of love, intensified in the character of Don Juan. But if we think of Don Carlos as a further projection of Sor Juana, something else happens. Leonor's portrait of Don Carlos is, in reality, a glory of irony: oppositions and contradictions are heaped one on the other to create the vision of a perfectly balanced being. If Sor Juana paints herself in Leonor, in Don Carlos she paints a perfection that can, in the cultural structures of the time, only reside happily and freely in a man. But coursing through this portraiture is the ideal that gender ceases, as in *Primero sueño*, to matter and define. For if perfect love is to be found in *Los empeños de una casa*, it is found in the mirroring of equal souls.

Thus gender is destabilized: Castaño dresses as a woman and becomes the object of passionate adoration (4: 135–45, act 3, lines 286–580). Don Juan is feminized in his inability to reason; Don Carlos, through his perfection, is beyond gender; Leonor is "manly" in her love of learning and her autonomy of action. The play is fantastically uncontainable—and fantastically camp, in Susan Sontag's formulation of camp as "Being-as-Playing-a-Role" (109). Life is reflected as theater, and *Los empeños* is a hall of mirrors in which each reflection refracts, each image is fragmented, each certainty is demolished. For Sor Juana projects from the stage the uncertainty, the potential emptiness, that really lies beyond the blustering about honor. And she materializes that uncertainty and emptiness through the mad confusion of a farce that seems to be reeling out of control. The space has been the scene of a type of choreography of endlessly futile steps, a space from which Sor Juana has physically absented and liberated herself only to project onto it a hilarious and devastating image of its own disintegration. And her presence as something other than a woman.

NOTES

In writing this essay I draw from the experience of working as academic consultant and then translator of *Los empeños de una casa* for the Spanish Golden Age Season by the Royal Shakespeare Company in Stratford-upon-Avon in 2004. It is written in full acknowledgment of all I learned from the director, Nancy Meckler; the RSC dramaturge, Paul Sirett; the designer Katrina Lindsay; and the company.

[1]Translations are from the performance text used by the Royal Shakespeare Company production; see Boyle, *House of Desires*.

Sor Juana's *Loas*: Hybridity in a Historical Context

Gwendolyn Alker

> When we read Sor Juana, we must recognize the silence surrounding her words. . . . Sor Juana's words are written in the presence of a prohibition. . . . Through [the author's voice] speaks that other voice: the condemned voice, the true voice.
>
> —Octavio Paz

A challenge in teaching performance is that the object of study continually disappears. Often a teacher has only the text with which to lead students toward understanding what the performance might have been. Reading and teaching dramatic texts, therefore, must be viewed as a process of active rediscovery. Students of such texts can be recast as cocreators of a theatrical event because theater is, at its very core, an exercise in collaboration. The *loas* of Sor Juana Inés de la Cruz offer a valuable site for such endeavors. They provide succinct, accessible points of entry into her dramatic work; in addition, engagement with them as performance texts leads to a discovery of multiple voices. Hidden in these plays are not only the subversive elements of Sor Juana's own voice but also an indigenous perspective foregrounded through her characters, thematic content, and play structure. In this essay, I aim to share my own experiences and insights in teaching two such *loas*, those that accompany *El divino Narciso* ("The Divine Narcissus") and *El cetro de José* ("Joseph's Staff"), and to demonstrate how an active reimagining of these plays from page to performance can introduce students to the hybrid intricacies of Mexican culture and performance in the late seventeenth century.

First, with any pedagogical endeavor, it is essential to define the key terms involved. The *loa*, literally translated as a "hymn of praise," is a short one-act play that often introduced a larger work that followed. The two *loas* that I teach are composed as introductory vignettes to the larger *autos sacramentales*. The *auto*, a particularly Spanish form of drama, is often, but not exclusively, a metaphoric retelling of the miracle of transubstantiation and the Eucharist. While the *loa* can be read as a discrete play, it should not be bracketed as an independent creation. Indeed, one of the joys of teaching the *loas* is the intuitive way in which both the form and the content of these plays allow a teacher to immediately introduce the idea of the interstitial. An intriguing question to pose is whether this liminal status of the *loa* gave Sor Juana a fitting arena to introduce her more rebellious themes.

A second key term, and the idea that grounds this reading, is the notion of *hybridity*. Hybridity, while certainly connected to genetic interbreeding, is used to signify "diverse intercultural mixtures" in myriad cultural forms

(García Canclini 11). This wide-ranging term can include subcategories such as syncretism (religious mixing) and *mestizaje* (racial mixing). Hybridity is now a familiar concept because of the work of authors such as Stuart Hall, Homi Bhabha, and Franz Fanon, whose work arose in the field of postcolonial studies. Similarly, the rise of new historicism in literature departments encouraged subversive readings of historical and literary texts with an eye toward detecting cultural mixing and rediscovering voices that may have been hidden behind canonical narratives.[1] Latin American scholars such as Néstor García Canclini also encourage resistant readings but give a more complex understanding of the historical implications of cultural hybridity than the terms *postcolonial* or *new historicism* would imply. In *Hybrid Cultures*, García Canclini discusses a particularly Latin American notion of hybridity. He questions if the movement toward modernity in the late twentieth century stands in opposition to a culture that has always mixed past and present in the contemporary moment. For García Canclini it is imperative that we approach such complexities by acknowledging the temporal mixing that also invades this term. Thus, when discussing foundational Latin American authors such as Sor Juana, one has the responsibility of applying this term to plays with hybrid content and in a manner that acknowledges the temporal complexities of Latin American hybridity. In teaching the work of Sor Juana, it is a question not so much of reading subversively—in other words, against authorial intent—as of teaching a student to expect subversive hybridity in the text.

I teach Sor Juana's work in an undergraduate class on Latin American theater to a diverse mixture of students training in the theater and other fields in the humanities. I use the *loa* to *El divino Narciso* in a section of the course entitled The Drama in Conquest, where students are asked to think about the role that liturgical theater had in the conquest and conversion of the indigenous peoples of Central America and to consider spectacle and performativity as effective companions to the Spaniards' more widely regarded technologies of war.[2] Positioning these *loas* toward the beginning of a historically teleological syllabus allows me to introduce the ideas of hybridity early on in the semester. I introduce the idea of cultural mixing through the work of Sor Juana and others even before these terms are defined in later readings of the contemporary playwrights and theorists García Canclini and Robert Stam. I have found that such circumlocution allows for a deeper and richer understanding of such key ideas by the end of the semester. This has been one of the most rewarding aspects of teaching her work: students have been surprised and enlightened to find hybridity so centrally expressed in an early modern text. Being introduced to these ideas early on in the semester, they are able to realize retrospectively that she has set the stage for many of the central themes of twentieth-century Latin American dramatic literature. Since my current class includes students with limited Spanish skills, I use the *loa* to *El divino Narciso*, which is available in a good English translation and is also the more intriguing of the two works.[3] While I have used the *loa* to *El cetro de José* in differing contexts to discuss themes of hybridity, it is currently unavailable in English. I find, however, that it is not necessary to read both texts to engender a fruitful conversation.

Both *loas* enact the syncretic similarities between Aztec festivals and Catholic rituals of baptism and communion. These similarities greatly disturbed early Spanish clergy in the New World. Sor Juana entered into fraught theological terrain with her discussion of these comparisons.[4] The *loa* to *El divino Narciso* begins with the Aztec characters Occident and America, who celebrate the festival of the "great God of the Seeds" (3). Here, Sor Juana refers to the annual Aztec festival of Teocualo, wherein grains and seeds would be mixed with the blood of sacrificed children and shaped into a representation of the god Huitzilopochtli; this figure would then be riddled with arrows and subsequently eaten. Such festivals had been banned by the government of New Spain in the First Conference of Mexico of 1555. Thus, if these *loas* were indeed performed, this would have been one of the few legally condoned theatrical representations of such spectacles on the public stage.

Before encountering Sor Juana, my students have already read selections from the excellent text *Aztecs: An Introduction* by Inga Clendinnen, which asks them to rethink the retributive acts of human sacrifice in the context of Aztec daily life. This reading allows them to see the fundamentally differing way that the Aztec people, or Mexica as Clendinnen calls them, dealt with systems of signification and symbolism, an element that will become important in our reading of the *loa* to *El divino Narciso*. It also asks that they shift their moral perspective to question their own judgments of such outwardly reprehensible acts. I have also recently paired the *loa* to *El divino Narciso* with Max Harris's excellent article "Disguised Reconciliations: Indigenous Voices in Early Franciscan Missionary Drama in Mexico." In this essay, Harris argues for the existence of "hidden transcripts of indigenous opinion and even appropriation" in the accounts of the Spanish witnesses to early liturgical drama in the sixteenth century (13). Placing his essay alongside the *loas* allows me to introduce the question of how a voice might be detached from a specific authorial body in a theatrical context. From here, it is a logical step to ask how an indigenous voice can be housed in the Creole body of Sor Juana. Theater necessitates that the author hand her voice over to the character to be embodied and interpreted by the actor.

It is particularly interesting to ask students how they would perform the characters of Occident and America. I recommend having them read specific passages out loud as a way of internalizing the quality and flow of each character's language. While no indigenous performers would have been allowed on such a publicly sanctioned stage, would the European or Creole actor consciously connect to and manifest native desires and experiences? To a certain extent, this is a tongue-in-cheek question. Contemporary actors trained in the Stanislavsky method are more likely to presuppose an emotional affinity with their characters, but actors in the seventeenth century would have had no such training. Instead, acting technique in the early modern period would have been primarily oratorical. Actors would have used a highly codified system of gesture and facial expression instead of relying on interior psychological motivation. Nonetheless, such questions raise awareness of the theatrical doubling of voice and emotion. Using the medium of theater allowed Sor Juana to more effectively compare and contrast two voices: her own and that of an embodied Aztec character.

Before beginning any discussion of the *loas*, I contextualize the dialogue between two historical guideposts by first giving students background about the indigenous festivals as detailed above, and then offering a biographical sketch of Sor Juana's life that emphasizes the ambiguous aspects of her personal history. The combination can be suggestive for students' thinking about the hybrid qualities of her work. For example, I discuss the possibility that she may have been born in 1648 (or 1651) as an illegitimate "daughter of the Church" or that the identity of Sor Juana's father plagued her ability to claim clear bloodlines in an age when *limpieza de sangre* ("purity of blood") held important cultural and political ramifications. Even the very question of what we should call the author allows for a suitably fragmented entry into a discussion of her identity.

Students must be made to understand that this prolific writer traveled at the boundary of socially acceptable behavior for a woman of her era. On the one hand, Sor Juana forged alliances with key figures such as the vicereines Marquise Leonor Carreto and María Luisa Manrique de Lara y Gonzaga, who inspired Sor Juana's poetry and encouraged the nun to compose the *El divino Narciso*. On the other hand, she challenged regulatory figures such as her confessor Antonio Núñez de Miranda and the more troubling archbishop Francisco Aguiar y Seijas.

Additionally, and perhaps most important for the reading at hand, Sor Juana can be introduced as a nun who had a deeply conflicted relation with her personal religious views and with the institution of the church. Certain biographical facts, such as her entry into the order of the Carmelites and her rapid departure and subsequent shift to the more lenient order of Hieronymites could be mentioned, as could the circumstance surrounding the publication of her *Carta atenagórica* ("Athenagoric Letter") and her subsequent *Respuesta a sor Filotea de la Cruz* ("Answer to Sister Filotea de la Cruz"). Finally, the abandonment of her expansive library and the murky circumstances surrounding her rededication of faith in 1694 and her death soon thereafter in 1695 provide fertile terrain for introducing the depth of her personal complexity. Students faced with the contradictions and uncertainties of her life will be more open and enthusiastic about unveiling the complexities in her writing.

To conclude, I offer a brief reading of the *loa* to *The Divine Narcissus* to share some insights into the hybrid nature of this text that have surfaced in class discussion of the *loa*'s literary and performative qualities. Students often begin discussion by noting that the character names Occident and America provide an important point of entry into an otherwise complicated text. It is interesting to note that Occident is described as "Indio galán, con corona" ("a gallant-looking Aztec, wearing a crown"), and his female partner, America, as "India bizarra: con mantas y cupiles" (3: 3) ("an Aztec woman of poised self-possession . . . dressed in the *mantas* and *huipiles*" [3: 3; 3]).[5] These two characters enter first and monopolize the stage, freely celebrating their festival of the "God of seeds" for the entire scene before the entry of their European counterparts, Zeal and Religion, at the beginning of scene two. It is significant to note that these later characters are given no such glorified descriptions, merely entering as "*Dama Española*" ("a Spanish lady") and a "*Capitán General*, armado" ("Captain General in armor" [3: 6; 7]). Such descriptions suggest a much larger and grander stage presence, more theatrical costumes, and stronger emotional cues for the actors playing Occident and America.

I have also encountered interesting moments in my students' analyses of the characters of Zeal and Religion. *Zeal* is the translator's choice for the Spanish word "Celo" of Sor Juana's original text. *Celo*, as some bilingual students have noted, translates to zeal or fervor yet also contains the more negative connotations of jealousy. Indeed, when one reads closely, Sor Juana has made this character the least appealing of the four main figures. At the beginning of scene two, as Zeal enters with Religion, she cautions him not to continue ignoring heathen idolatry. Zeal immediately shifts from apparent inaction, and he and America confront the native couple, who, in turn, sense only insanity from these newcomers and continue with their festivities. In the passages that follow, Sor Juana bestows the gift of forceful and poetic language on her Aztec characters. America states, "Bárbaro, loco, que ciego, / con razones no entendidas, / quieres turbar el sosiego / que en serena paz tranquila / gozamos" ("Madman, blind, and barbarous, / with mystifying messages / you try to mar our calm and peace, / destroying the tranquility / that we enjoy [3: 9; 15]). While one might assume that it is these characters who would be cast as villains, here Sor Juana situates them as the rightful first inhabitants of this land. The conversation escalates, and, by the beginning of scene three, Occident states, "Ya es preciso que me rinda / tu valor, no tu razón" ("[he] must bow to your aggression, but not before your arguments" [3: 11; 17]). Zeal is overwhelmed by this show of spiritual steadfastness (a quality that he himself lacks) and becomes enraged and overly belligerent. On the verge of killing the two Aztecs, he must be stopped by the more pacific hand of Religion. Scenes four and five follow, in which the character of Religion explains the mysteries of the Eucharist. The female figure of Religion is given the greatest agency in these later scenes. Yet by the end of this *loa*, the two female characters of Religion and America seem to merge; both claim responsibility for the writing of the play. Thus they connect through authorial agency and are clearly linked as two halves of their shared author.

Attention to the theatrical use of repetition also leads to some interesting conclusions. While ostensibly the plot of this play moves from the Aztec characters celebrating the festival of Teocualo to their eagerness to see the mysteries of the Eucharist explained to them in the ensuing *auto*, in the *loa* itself the Aztec festival is staged with gleeful excess. Occident and America verbally enact their celebration, invoking "the great God of the Seeds!" no less than thirteen times in this short, five-hundred-line *loa*. This phrase is also uttered, curiously, as the final lines of the play, "¡Dichoso el día / que conocí al gran Dios de las Semillas!" ("Blest be the day / when I could see / and worship the / great God of Seeds [3: 36; 37]). The *loa* signals the transition to the *auto* with the indigenous characters' excitement surrounding their imminent ability to witness and participate in the sacrament of communion. Yet semantically Sor Juana has given a linguistic victory to the Aztec god. For it is his original nomenclature that is used in reference to the imminent *auto sacramental* and the internal celebration of the Eucharist therein.

Furthermore, this final line is interesting in the light of its recasting of the literal audience as the figurative audience of the play. References in the penultimate lines of the text suggest that this *loa* was performed in Madrid, probably for the Corpus Christi festivals of 1689 or 1690. There is no record of this *loa* being performed in New Spain. While the *loa* ostensibly introduces the *auto* by showing the figurative audience's desire to see the mystery of the Eucharist unveiled, the literal audience is metaphorically turned into an indigenous one in order to embody such desire. In other words, the audience is led to see the similarities of the two rituals through the eyes of the Aztec characters. In a masterful bait and switch, Sor Juana has turned her Spanish, and probably royal, audience into a metaphorical indigenous one, waiting to see the *auto* as their own expression of the "God of Seeds."

Octavio Paz cites Sor Juana as one of the earliest playwrights to consciously influence audience response. In her second *sainete*, she "foreshadows a technique of modern theater: within her fiction Sor Juana introduced a criticism of that fiction," effectively breaking the "conventions separating stage from spectator" (*Traps* 328–29). Sor Juana seems to have been intimately aware of the audience-performer relationship, the possibilities of eradicating the fourth wall, and the possibilities of manipulation in the genre of theater.

At its deepest, most philosophical level, the *loa* grapples with the difference between physical reality and mimesis. The theological debate between the Aztecs and their European counterparts in scene four hinges on the discussion of how the Christian "true god" may be made physically present to these potential converts. Indeed, this is the key layer of difference between the festival of Teocualo, in which a figure of the god is fashioned out of sacrificial blood and then ingested, and the Catholic communion, in which the blood and body of Christ are ritually transferred into a cleansed object through the process of transubstantiation. It becomes clear that mere words will not suffice in the conversion experience. The Aztec couple must see the way in which the Christian God will be made present to them through the celebration of the Eucharist. Religion's final monologue in this scene speaks to these differences:

> Que en una idea
> metafórica, vestida
> de retóricos colores,
> representable a tu vista,

te la mostraré; que ya
conozco que tú te inclinas
a objectos visibles, más
que a lo que la Fe te avisa
por el oído. (3: 30)

I shall make for you a metaphor,
a concept clothed in rhetoric
so colorful that what I show
to you, your eyes will clearly see;
for now I know that you require
objects of sight instead of words,
by which faith whispers in your ears
too deaf to hear. (31)

This, then, is the ultimate rationale for the staging of the *auto* and its Eucharist: this production will be the grandest metaphor of them all. It will move beyond language to the florid details of apparently baroque imagery. Yet Sor Juana's language is also slightly ambiguous, as if the ensuing *auto* will be almost swaddled away from the clarity of truth. Such questions of seeing, metaphor, and the reality of representation are at the heart of theatrical expression. Yet within the confines of this logic, and in the heart of this *loa*, it is the theatricality of the Aztec characters and their god Huitzilopochtli that is celebrated most profoundly and effectively. As theater, a medium that asks that we focus on seeing and the power of enactment, this short vignette stages the desires, rituals, and humanity of the people who are ostensibly converted by play's end.

NOTES

[1]While the birth of postcolonial studies can be traced back to the earlier writings of Chinua Achebe, Franz Fanon, and others, the field rapidly developed in the late 1970s and 1980s with the publication of Edward Said's *Orientalism*, a plethora of articles by Homi Bhabha such as "Of Mimicry and Men: The Ambivalence of Colonial Discourse" and "The Other Question . . . Homi Bhabha Reconsiders the Stereotype and Colonial Discourse," and Gayatri Spivak's essay "Can the Subaltern Speak?" By the mid-1990s, Routledge published *The Post-colonial Studies Reader* (Ashcroft, Griffiths, and Tiffin), suggesting the saturation and maturity of the field. The rise of new historicism can be seen most prominently in the publications by Stephen Greenblatt, Jonathan Dollimore, and Alan Sinfield in the later 1970s and 1980s. Notable texts are Greenblatt's *Renaissance Self-fashioning* and "Learning to Curse: Aspects of Linguistic Colonialism in the Sixteenth Century."

[2]The fullest discussion of this topic comes in Tzvetan Todorov's *The Conquest of America*.

[3]See the translation by Patricia Peters and Renée Domeier. This edition is recommended for theater scholars, since the translators attempt to pay special attention to the

"dramatic language" of the piece for a contemporary audience (xxviiii). This translation is also reprinted in the fourth edition of the *Wadsworth Anthology of Drama*, edited by William B. Worthen.

[4]For more on this topic, see Paz, *Traps* 348–50.

[5]Translations are from Peters and Domeier's edition of *Divine Narcissus*.

The House of Trials and the Trials of Master's-Level Research

Kathryn Joy McKnight

The cross-dressing Castaño in Sor Juana's *Los empeños de una casa* provides an amusing and rich subject with which master's students can learn the research methods of literary and cultural studies. The challenge I assume in teaching research methods is how to train students to articulate a viable and original research question within a clear theoretical framework and to develop a bibliography that will help them answer that research question. In most incarnations research-methods courses place heavy emphasis on locating and citing resources and organizing a paper and somewhat less often on reading critical theory—and then not always as an activity integrated into the design of the research project. When I teach the course, I ask students to consider that all critical readings emerge from a conceptual framework, which generally includes a notion of what literature is and what it does. The more consciously students work to mold their own conceptual framework, and the more familiar they become with various theories of meaning making, the better critics they will become.

This format is largely a result of my first experience teaching a graduate seminar in colonial literature. With some coaching, students overcame the hurdle of identifying a viable research topic for the term paper, only to find another, less obvious, one: few students had a clear concept of what it meant to design an original inquiry into a textual problem. Several students went straight to the *MLA International Bibliography* to find what scholars had to say about their topic and proceeded to construct a pastiche of these ideas in an argument lacking original analysis. Others saw the research task as one of finding sources to support their thesis.

So I have designed an approach in which students build a theoretical framework from which they develop an inquiry into a textual problem. To do so, we move along a single thread in the historical development of critical theory, starting with Aristotle and arriving at a feminist version of cultural studies, which we apply to Sor Juana's *House of Trials*. We read a few theoretical texts that allow students to build a "tool kit," which contains, among others, the concepts of discourse, discursive practices, literary and social conventions, hegemonic practices, and counterhegemonic discourses. These concepts inform significant twentieth-century developments in Latin American cultural theory, and they allow me to bring the discussion back throughout the semester to the idea that language, literature, and critical thought are historically constructed. At the end, I encourage students to explore other areas of theory, but I believe that they achieve a greater ability to comprehend and apply theory when we limit our focus to a small number of critical concepts.

In conducting class, I try to focus as much on how students learn and develop intellectually as on what I want to teach. I believe that students need a carefully sequenced or scaffolded approach that starts with reading then progresses to hearing ideas explained and articulating those ideas, consulting models, applying new knowledge, receiving feedback and finally to working back through the cycle again—this time with a stronger grasp of the concepts, thought processes, and methods. I strive to make the classroom a space in which student talk dominates, believing that to own an idea one must be able to explain it. I do give minilectures, but I also provide a great deal of my input—instructions, summaries, lists of resources, sample outlines, annotated bibliographies, and abstracts—in a supplemental text I have compiled.

The Sor Juana research project occupies weeks three through eight of the course and involves articulating theory-based research questions appropriate for a term paper and compiling a bibliography that provides a starting point for answering the questions. I have chosen Sor Juana's *Los empeños de una casa* ("The House of Trials" or "House of Desires") for this project for a variety of reasons. As a scholar of colonial literature who has studied women writers and textual constructions of gender, I choose to center the course on a cultural studies approach with a feminist focus. *Los empeños* provides a shared text around which students design a preliminary research bibliography before carrying to completion their independent projects. Sharing a single text enables us to discuss cogently the strengths and weaknesses of each student's research design. The play is both brief—thus quickly read—and sufficiently challenging, complex, and distanced from students' general experience with literature that it motivates a wealth of research questions. As a seventeenth-century comedia, the play provides a fitting text for the application of Aristotle's *Poetics* and Lope de Vega's *Arte nuevo de hacer comedias* ("The New Art of Writing Plays in This Age"), two works I believe students of Hispanic literature should read. Aristotle and Lope also allow students to discuss theory as historically constructed. Students compare Aristotle with Lope's seventeenth-century reading of him; compose a hypothetical reading of Sor Juana through Lope's eyes; and, finally, contrast this reading with Sandra Messinger Cypess's feminist–cultural studies critique of the *gracioso* ("clown") Castaño's cross-dressing. Last but not least, I have chosen *Los empeños* because students have fun with it.

Before tackling the research process, we discuss the discipline, asking the following questions: What is literature? What is theory? And what is the task of literary criticism? Our first conversations draw on the experiences students bring with them to the master's program. We then read Herbert Lindenberger's foreword to the *MLA Style Manual* and the first two chapters of Jonathan Culler's *Literary Theory: A Very Short Introduction*. Culler unsettles the students' prior concepts of literature by positing that, despite some historical consensus on literary qualities, none of these qualities distinguishes literature definitively from other discourses (35). He suggests that we maintain a tension between these definitions of literature and the question, "what is involved in treating things *as* literature in our culture?" (22). Lindenberger illustrates the history of this treatment in a lively review of how critics have conceived of both their task and their public. I suggest with Culler that reading theory will help us see the historicity of both the object of our study—literature—and our disciplinary methods, because theory critiques common sense and shows us that what we see as "natural" is historically constructed (Culler 14–15).

Students spend the next week and a half remembering and honing their skills in formal analysis as a foundation for working with theory. They read Culler's chapters "Language, Meaning, and Interpretation" and "Rhetoric, Poetics, Poetry," and René Wellek and Austin Warren's "Image, Metaphor, Symbol, Myth." Culler helps students "denaturalize" these traditional analytical techniques they have already studied, some of them since high school, and to see them as a specific historical development. Students present orally a close reading of a poem and hand in a written explication. Later, they will both contrast this formal approach to Raymond Williams's cultural materialism as well as find the continuity between formalism and Williams's view of convention as a "mode of junction" between the literary and the social (179).

At the end of the third week, we begin the Sor Juana research project, which has five major objectives: to gain a clearer understanding of the effect of theory on critical reading, to examine a critical analysis of the play as a model for posing theory-based questions, to develop original research questions that apply theory to a reading of the play, to identify secondary sources that will help answer the research questions, and to become skilled at MLA citation style.

We begin by reading Aristotle's *Poetics*. I assign students the task of thinking about and taking notes on the following questions: What does Aristotle do in this treatise? (We consider both descriptive and prescriptive aspects of his theory.) What are the sources from which he works? (In other words, how did he develop his poetics?) What does Aristotle see as poetry's function, and how poetry should be experienced? What are the principal elements that Aristotle identifies in his definition of mimesis, tragedy, and the epic? Does any of this sound familiar? Where and how have the students learned it?

Next we read Lope's *Arte nuevo de hacer comedias*, and I ask students to list the principal elements of Lope's new comedia, identify the ideas Lope takes from the *Poetics*, and note where his theory of theater differs from Aristotle's. Lope's burlesque characterization of his readers and his references to his own theatrical success help students historicize his dramatic theory. *El arte nuevo* is a very difficult read, and so I include in my supplemental packet a brief summary and outline and have students read William T. Brewster's English prose translation (Vega, *New Art*).

For their first reading of *Los empeños*, I assign each of the various topics of the *Arte nuevo* to a particular student. The topics include the thematic choices a playwright makes, unity of action in the dramatic structure, word play, the art of deceiving with the truth, the matching of verse type to dramatic situation, and the matching of language to character type (plain speech for servants, gravity for kings, modesty for fathers, passionate language for the leading man, respectfully restrained passion for the lady). Students prepare a brief statement that assesses *Los empeños* through Lope's eyes by studying Sor Juana's use of their topics. They find that Sor Juana works ingeniously with Lope's precepts.

After seeing the play as Lope might have, we make the historical leap to cultural studies and feminism, reading Cypess's article "Los géneros re/velados en *Los empeños de una casa* de sor Juana Inés de la Cruz" ("Genders Revealed and Veiled in *The House of Trials*"), in which she examines the transvestism that Castaño, the *gracioso* manservant, performs. Cypess argues that it is Castaño in his performance of this scene, and not the beautiful and intelligent Doña Leonor, whose voice is most allied with that of Sor Juana. Though Sor Juana veils her meanings in baroque ambiguity, Cypess sees her as using Castaño to give, "una lectura femenina de un hombre que lee a la mujer" ("a feminine reading of a man who reads woman" [178; my trans.]). In this hilarious scene, Sor Juana deconstructs the image of women that the theater and Catholic patriarchal society of her times construct. As Castaño puts on Leonor's clothing to escape confinement, he addresses the women in the audience, his words revealing that it is men who create the female image with which they fall in love:

> Es cierto que estoy hermosa.
> ¡Dios me guarde, que estoy bella!
> Cualquier cosa me está bien,
> porque el molde es rara pieza.
> Quiero acabar de aliñarme,
> que aún no estoy dama perfecta.
> Los guantes: aquesto sí,
> porque las manos no vean
> . . . .
> ¡Válgame Dios! cuánto encubre
> esta telilla de seda,
> . . . .
> Un trasunto el abanillo
> es de mi garbo y belleza
> . . . .
> Ya estoy armado, y ¿quién duda
> que en el punto que me vean
> me sigan cuatro mil lindos
> de aquestos que galantean
> a salga lo que saliere,
> y que a bulto se amartelan,
> *no de la belleza que es,*
> *sino de la que ellos piensan*?
> (4: 137–38; my emphasis)

I really am beautiful.
Good God, but I'm gorgeous.
I'm of such a fine mould
everything looks a treat on me.
Now for the final touches,
I'm not quite the perfect lady yet.
Gloves, definitely,
to hide my hands
. . . .
Good grief, how well
this silk cloth conceals!
. . . .
This fan is the image
of my grace and beauty
. . . .
Well, I'm ready. And what's the bet
that four thousand of those idiots
that chase anything that walks
will fall over each other to get at me;
not with the beauty that I am,
but with the beauty they think I am.
(Boyle, *House* 86–87)

Cypess concludes that through Castaño, Sor Juana deconstructs both theatrical and societal images of women, as she questions gendered social relationships both on and off the stage.

Cypess's article is brief, clear, well-organized, and provocative, and it illustrates wonderfully two theoretical concepts that I ask students to use in developing their research questions: hegemonic discourse and literary and social convention. As they read Cypess, students think about what she sees that Lope does not, and they conjecture about what makes possible the differences. Their answers bring out how literary theory and scholarly method connect to historical changes in gendered social relationships and the way societies think about them.

The reading of Cypess has a second purpose, which is to encourage and enable students to read critical articles as models of scholarly method. The second part of their assignment is to articulate in writing the primary question Cypess answers in her article and to list five other questions that Cypess must answer before she can answer her primary question. Even at the master's level, students too often mistake a statement of topic or process for a thesis. If they learn to pose research questions, then, by answering those questions, they are more likely to state a position by which they can control their argument.

While students successfully articulate questions that Cypess answers, they find it more difficult to distinguish a primary question from the supporting questions. I suggest to students that a critic's primary question is often about what the text means or does, but that, in order to answer this question, the critic must first research the various contexts with which the text engages in its meaning making. After we compile on an overhead transparency the questions that Cypess articulates, I present my own version of her primary question: How does Sor Juana use the character of the *gracioso* and the theatrical convention of transvestism to question the gender codes that her society and its theater construct? There are many secondary or supporting research questions implied by this primary question, including the following: How did aristocratic men and women dress in seventeenth-century Spain and New Spain? What were the meanings ascribed to these gendered practices? How was the convention of transvestism used in Golden Age theater, and what meanings did its deployment produce?

A significant methodological difference between a hypothetical Lope reading and Cypess's critique of *Los empeños* emerges from these questions. In applying Lope's primarily formal precepts, we can do much of the analysis of Sor Juana's play without additional research. To answer the questions Cypess raises, we must engage other disciplines. I ask students to look through Cypess's footnotes and to list the disciplines from which her research draws. They find she consults criticism of Spanish classical theatrical conventions, scholarship on Sor Juana's writing, history of Western theater, feminist theories of gender construction, and social histories of Spain and New Spain.

After discussing Cypess, we take a step back to become conversant in a few of the theoretical concepts that inform her work. We return to Culler for his discussion of "literature and cultural studies" (42–54) and to prepare the way for the more difficult engagement with Williams. To ease the students into reading Williams, I explain the chapters on "culture" and "literature," which illustrate Culler's point that theory deconstructs what appears natural and true. Over the next two classes, pairs of students present Williams's definitions of base and superstructure, determination, hegemony, structures of feeling, conventions, and genres. They also hand in paragraph-long definitions of four terms they might like to use in their research projects.

In discussing Williams, I ask students to articulate how Cypess's analysis of Castaño engages with the concepts of hegemony and convention. For Williams, hegemony is the organization of "the whole lived social process" according to "dominant meanings and values" (109). Members of a society perceive this organization as reality rather than as a historically particular set of meanings and values that they are called on to accept as their own. He posits that hegemony is not monolithic or static but rather that it manifests a constant, complex, and dynamic process, which allows resistance and thus must also be constantly renewed (112). Williams explains "convention" as "the mode of junction of social position and literary practice" (179). He lays out a social theory of literature that can "show the real grounds of the inclusions and exclusions, the styles and the ways of seeing, that specific conventions embody and ratify" (173). Some students are able to explain that Cypess looks at Castaño in terms of the junction between literary (theatrical) and social conventions when she sees Sor Juana engaging critically with the literary conventions of the *gracioso*, staged cross-dressing, and societal images of women. In deconstructing the female image onstage, Sor Juana presents a counterhegemonic discourse on the social conventions of female image making, courtship, and marriage.

Students bring to the next class meeting a set of research questions that apply *Marxism and Literature* to *Los empeños*. I recommend that they find a second junction in the play between theatrical and social conventions. I also encourage them to think about what the play does with that convention in relation to the hegemonic values of seventeenth-century Spain and New Spain. The following are the question sets that two students have presented:

> Student 1: Does *Los empeños* question or reinforce class relationships between the lady and her female servant? How do contemporary works treat these relationships? What are the theatrical conventions for representing social class and for distinguishing between a lady and her female servant? How are these social situations represented in nontheatrical discourses? What is the meaning of the relative social position of the two characters that is constructed by the parallel marriages that close the play?
>
> Student 2: In this play, Castaño is presented as a Mexican servant, in opposition to the other characters that are Spanish. Besides, the play is set in Toledo. Considering these facts, what is the meaning produced by having a minority character in the context of the play? What are the social conventions that Castaño follows and that distinguish him from the majority, and how do these conventions help to construct the idea of otherness? What literary and theatrical conventions does Castaño follow? How is otherness (based on colonial birth and colonized status) treated more generally in dramatic pieces written in Spain and Mexico? How is otherness treated in dramatic pieces not written in Spanish?

To reinforce the methods of a cultural studies approach, I have students work together to identify the various disciplines they will need to consult to answer their questions. We review the types of sources Cypess consults in her argument. Then we use an overhead transparency to brainstorm the types of sources that may answer the questions posed by a couple of the students. This step is key, as many of our master's students tend to know about and use the *MLA International Bibliography* but do not know how to find relevant sources in history, anthropology, sociology, linguistics, or in other disciplines that literary scholars today find essential in working with texts.

We spend the next two class periods in a computer classroom in the library with the reference librarian whose field of expertise is Latin American studies. The librarian walks students through the use of general reference materials (encyclopedias, dictionaries, literary histories, bibliographies) and databases, including not only the *MLA International Bibliography* but also the *Hispanic American Periodical Index*, the *Handbook of Latin American Studies*, and *Historical Abstracts*. I work with her ahead of time to outline the Sor Juana project, and she tailors her presentations to the project. It is important to time this introduction to library and database research right when students will immediately use and retain the information.

To ensure that students create a bibliography that supports a cultural studies reading of *Los empeños*, I make specific requirements of the types of sources students must include. They must find literary criticism on *Los empeños*; literary criticism or theory regarding the conventions of Golden Age theater; secondary sources from at least one other discipline, for example social history or feminist theory; and books, journal articles, and works of reference. Students are to organize their bibliography in separate sections dedicated to each research question, including at least three sources per question.

I require students to follow MLA style rigorously in their Sor Juana bibliography. At this point, we take time for students to polish their use of MLA citation style. They read carefully several sections as well as the table of contents of the documentation chapter of the *MLA Style Manual* and skim the remainder of the chapter (Gibaldi). They then correct an error-riddled bibliography for homework, and we go over the corrections in class.

The final step in the Sor Juana project is a class discussion based on five-minute presentations in which students outline the research questions they have posed and the types of sources they have found. I ask them to bring to our attention any databases we did not look into as a class and any exciting discoveries (especially interesting and helpful sources or techniques) they have found along the way. I also give students generous feedback on their bibliographies, which will help them improve their techniques as they develop their individual research projects.

Completion of the Sor Juana bibliographic project brings us to midterm break. The remainder of the course is dedicated to finishing out the cultural studies thread. We read Michel Foucault's *History of Sexuality* and then move to Latin American literary criticism that draws on cultural materialist and post-structuralist theories. We read sections of Antonio Cornejo Polar's *Escribir en el aire* ("Writing in the Air"), in which the author develops a literary history of the Andean region centered on the textual problem of sociocultural heterogeneity. We read one final literary text—a narrative, Clarice Lispector's *A hora da estrela* (*Hour of the Star*)—and carry out a similar comparison of critical approaches, examining the novel with formal analysis and then with a cultural studies approach generated by questions students raise using both Williams and Foucault. Throughout this second half of the semester, students develop a second research project using the same methodology as the first. This time they produce an annotated bibliography, an outline, and a paper abstract. I strongly encourage students to use this assignment to develop their research paper for another class.

While all students find this a difficult class, I receive positive feedback from them later in their program, even from some of those students who struggle the most. They comment that this class has enabled them in subsequent courses to formulate their research according to research questions, identify an appropriate theoretical framework, and repeatedly question where they want to go with the research in ways that help them delineate a narrow but productive area of inquiry. Several have mentioned using the concept of the convention to guide subsequent research projects. They find useful the intersection the course creates among primary texts and critical theories, particularly the reading of primary texts through different theoretical lenses. They appreciate the practice of defining critical terms and examining and making transparent the opaque assumptions hidden in the structure of texts. They especially appreciate the applied nature of the course, including discussing their particular projects in class during its various stages. One student commented that she did not understand theory when we read it at the beginning of the semester but that the theoretical concepts made sense after she applied them in analyzing a literary text.

In today's academic world, in which most graduate students tend to specialize in contemporary literary and cultural topics, the required research-methods class provides a wonderful opportunity to take students off the beaten track and introduce them to one of Sor Juana's less anthologized works. While many texts provide rich possibilities for a research-methods course, I find Sor Juana's *Los empeños* works especially well. To understand and work with the broad textual concept of conventions and to see how conventions are embedded in hegemonic discourses and how authors creatively manipulate these conventions are ways of thinking that support inquiry in many literary and cultural areas. Sor Juana's theater provides the perfect grounds for this inquiry, since Sor Juana plays with the ambiguities of the baroque, allowing herself to be read as both conventional and subversive to protect her own space of expression.

NOTE

I would like to express my deep appreciation to the students in my Research and Critical Methodology class the three years I have taught it at the University of New Mexico, whose feedback has been essential to the evolution of the project described in this article. I especially thank those former students who responded to my plea and wrote very thoughtful reflections on the project, which inform this article. Student quotations used with permission.

Sor Juana's Petrarchan Poetics

Lisa Rabin

Sor Juana Inés de la Cruz and her baroque Petrarchan poetry is a cornerstone in my courses in Spanish American literature at George Mason University in Fairfax, Virginia. Our undergraduate Spanish classes in the Department of Modern and Classical Languages at George Mason are composed of a mixture of students educated in Spanish-speaking countries, heritage speakers of Spanish who may have little formal training in the language, and nonnative learners. My encounters with these students have led me to a greater awareness of the ideologies involved in teaching literature as representative of a "privileged" or "elite" variety of Spanish and of teaching a particular body of texts as a national tradition. A primary goal in my courses is to teach students how to assess these ideologies as they learn how Hispanic texts both construct and challenge national paradigms of language, culture, and identity.

My approach is philological, poststructural, and feminist. I teach Sor Juana in my literature courses in Spanish at the undergraduate and graduate level and also in courses in Spanish American literature in translation. My teaching centers on how Sor Juana as a woman, colonial poet, and nun both reifies and transforms early modern elite forms of poetry in Spanish. I show students the uniqueness of Sor Juana as a colonial woman poet and nun writing Petrarchan poetry, helping them place her at the crossroads of Old and New World literatures as they learn about her originality within the European male paradigm of Petrarchism.

Class 1: Introduction

I begin with the story of how Petrarch was inspired to codify his vernacular language of Tuscan through the writing of lyric verse on a beautiful female love object. Nancy Vickers makes the argument that the Petrarchan lyric voice, and indeed the entire Petrarchan manner as it evolved in western Europe and the Americas, depends on the objectification of its lover (95). Perhaps the most popularly known Petrarchan trope is that of the *blason*, or the metaphorical description of the lady as a series of parts. We read Petrarch's poems from the *Rime sparse*: number 90, "Erano i capei d'oro / a l'aura sparsi" ("Her golden hair was loosed to the breeze" [193; 192]), and number 192, "Stiamo, Amor, a veder la Gloria nostra" ("Let us stay, Love, to see our glory" [339; 338]), which identify Petrarch's muse, Laura, by her "golden" locks, seductive eyes, angelic voice, and celestial walk.

Petrarch's "rime sparse" or "scattered rhyme" are the fragments of Laura, who remains unavailable to him in her entirety (Vickers 96). Yet Petrarch's failings in love are paradoxically his prize. The crown of laurel that Petrarch so coveted—and which he was eventually awarded in Rome—is punned in his collection as "Laura" herself (Vickers 107; Rigolot; Cottino-Jones). Petrarch's aesthetic goals thus dovetailed with his political ones. In the *Rime sparse* Petrarch fashioned a written standard of poetry in Tuscan that could compete with the Latin classics he and his generation so admired (Menocal, *Shards* 178–79). Through this standard, Petrarch became, as María Rosa Menocal writes in *Writing in Dante's Cult of Truth*, "the most vitally imitated poet in the history of poetry" (173–74).

A history of the popularity of the Petrarchan *blason* in early modern European lyric can be shown to students through references to the 1536 French collection *Blasons anatomiques du corps femenin* ("Anatomical Blason of the Female Body"), in which each *blason* is dedicated to a specific part of the female body, and to the work of sixteenth-century English poets like Philip Sidney, who in his lyric sequence *Astrophil and Stella* praises the lady for her beauty as well as her virtue (Greene 94–95): "That inward sunne in thine eyes shineth so" ("Poem 71," line 8).

In Spain, Garcilaso de la Vega's "Soneto X" calls his muse Elisa's golden locks "dulces prendas" ("sweet gifts" [*Poesías* 46; my trans.]). Francisco de Quevedo, in "Afectos varios de su corazón fluctuando en las ondas de los cabellos de Lisi" ("Several reactions of his heart, bobbing on the waves of Lisi's hair" [*Poesía varia* 242; Ingber]), makes a baroque conceit of his muse Lisi's hair as a snare for the lover, invoking the fates of the mythical characters Leander, Icarus, Midas, and Tantalus. And Sor Juana's colonial baroque *blason* of Lísida, the poetic persona of her court patron the vicereine María Luisa Manrique de Lara y Gonzaga, Countess of Paredes, describes the beloved with an eccentric range of figures, calling her patron's hair a "dédalo" ("labyrinth" [1: 172; Trueblood 49]) of golden knots, her waist a "Bósforo de estrechez" ("a straitened Bosphorus" [1: 173; Trueblood 51]), and her stature a "plátano" ("banana plant" [1: 173; Trueblood 51]). Transcending the visual fragments, Sor Juana adds that Lísida exudes a "bálsamo de fragantes aromas" ("a balm of aromatic fragrances" [1: 173; Trueblood 51]).

This range of examples shows how widely Petrarchan poetry became the privileged mode of writing lyric verse in Europe and the Americas in the early modern period. In the Spanish lyric, although Petrarch's styles and themes had already been present in Castilian verse, the poets Juan Boscán and Garcilaso initiated a vogue for writing Petrarchan verse during the heady years of Charles V, who aspired to Spain's becoming not only the most powerful empire in the world but also the most cultured, in part by imitating Italian forms of knowledge. Petrarchan poetry helped promote Castilian as the privileged or elite form of Spanish and thus became a vehicle for the consolidation of Spanish language and culture at home and abroad (González Echevarría, "Colonial Lyric"; Navarrete).

In a far-flung empire, the use of the Italian hendecasyllabic line became "the hallmark of all aspiring serious poets" in the sixteenth century (González Echevarría, "Colonial Lyric" 191). Toward the end of the sixteenth century, literary communities had been formed in Lima and Mexico City and the publication of Italianate, as well as traditional verse written in Castilian, proliferated (198–203). Sor Juana's Petrarchan verse was indeed part of the Italian vogue, although it departed from earlier imitations of peninsular Petrarchan poetry in its ingenuity and peculiarity, as did that of other poets of the colonial baroque, most notably Bernardo de Balbuena in Mexico and Juan del Valle de Caviedes and Juan de Espinosa Medrano, el Lunarejo, in Peru (197–220). Sor Juana's *blason* of Lísida, in its cornucopia of figures from Europe and the empire, is exemplary of the colonial baroque.

Class 2: Sor Juana, Public Poet and Intellectual

In the next class I show students the frontispiece to *Fama y obras pósthumas* (*Fame and Posthumous Works* [Madrid, 1700]), the first edition of volume 3, the final volume of Sor Juana's work, which included the first publication of her autobiographical letter *La respuesta* (www.ub.uni-bielefeld.de/diglib/delacruz/fama). The frontispiece portrays Sor Juana as encircled by laurel, the quintessential sign of Petrarch. The book invites Sor Juana's readers to "discover a courageous woman / at the farthest extremes of the earth" ("Mulierem forte(m) q(u)is inveniet / Procul et de ultimis finib(us)"; my trans.). Sor Juana is pictured here as a hero of the empire, a beacon of eloquence and civilization in remote domains. The Spanish editors of the *Fama* construct Sor Juana's Petrarchan poetry as a badge of colonial honor. There is compelling evidence that Sor Juana felt similarly. Poem 80, "Seguidillas," written to another of her viceregal patrons, the Countess of Galve (called "Elvira"), constitutes a *blason* describing Elvira's parts as a series of heroic male figures beginning with Ulysses, Julius Caesar, and Hannibal from classical myth and history and continuing into the recent American past with Christopher Columbus, Hernán Cortés, and Francisco Pizarro. Elvira's forehead is "Un Colón . . . por dilatada, porque es quien su Imperio / más adelanta" ("Like Columbus's reach in its expanse, Because it is she who most extends his Empire" [1: 208; my trans.]). The vicereine's body, like that of her predecessor the Countess of Paredes in the *Romance decasílabo* ("Ten-Syllable Ballad"), is political, extending Spain's sphere of military influence (Franco; Burgess Noudehou). Similarly, the author of the vicereine's "beauty," or Sor Juana the poet, would extend Spain's linguistic reach. The colonial poet seems to be depicting herself as heroic, a poet conquering new territory with her powers of eloquence.

From another angle, the frontispiece to the *Fama* can also be seen as proclaiming Sor Juana's courage as an individual. I point out to students that the collection included Sor Juana's poetry alongside a text in which she openly contests the church's censure of her work. In the *Respuesta* she writes to her interlocutor "Sor Filotea," or Manuel Fernández de Santa Cruz, the bishop of Puebla, that she knows that his admonitions to dedicate herself to sacred matters focus on her profane verse: "Bien conozco que no cae sobre ella [la *Carta atenagórica*] vuestra cuerdísima advertencia, sino sobre lo mucho que habréis visto de asuntos humanos que he escrito" ("I recognize full well that your most prudent warning touches not on the letter, but on the many writings of mine on humane matters that you have seen" [4: 443; Arenal and Powell 44–45]). Electa Arenal and Amanda Powell point out that in Sor Juana's love poetry she "displayed depths of emotion and erotic desire associated for us with intimate relationships," dedicating her most personal love poems to the vicereines who were her patrons, the Countess of Paredes and, earlier, Leonor Carreto, the Marquise of Mancera (see Powell's essay, this volume). These were expressions that surely outraged her church superiors.

Later in the *Respuesta* Sor Juana says that her secular poetry has brought her nothing but trouble:

> Pues por la—en mí dos veces infeliz—habilidad de hacer versos, aunque fuesen sagrados, ¿qué pesadumbres no me han dado o cuáles no me han dejado de dar? Cierto, señora mía, que algunas veces me pongo a considerar que el que se señala—o le señala Dios, que es quien sólo lo puede hacer—es recibido como enemigo comun, porque parece a algunos que usurpa los aplausos que ellos merecen o que hace estanque de las admiraciones a que aspiraban, y así le persiguen. (4: 452–53)
>
> Well, as for this aptitude at composing verses—which is doubly unfortunate, in my case, even should they be sacred verses—what unpleasantness have they not caused me, and indeed do they not still cause? Truly, my Lady, at times I ponder how it is that a person who achieves high significance—or rather, who is granted significance by God, for He alone can do this—is received as the common enemy. For that person seems to others to usurp the applause they deserve or to draw off and dam up the admiration to which they had aspired, and so they persecute the person. (Arenal and Powell 63)

Sor Juana's poetry has led to fame, for which "algunos" ("others," or "some men")—Sor Juana is clearly alluding here to individuals in the church hierarchy—are envious. Is this the "fama" to which the frontispiece refers in portraying Sor Juana's bravery? She was persecuted, as not only a nun writing love poetry but also a female public intellectual.

Students can consider here Sor Juana's frustration with, and her solitude in, this position. I direct students to her protest poems: number 92, "Hombres necios" ("You foolish and unreasoning men" [1: 228; Arenal and Powell 157]); sonnet 146, "¿En perseguirme, Mundo, ¿qué interesas?" ("World, why do you pursue me?" [1: 277; my trans.]); and ballad 49, "¡Válgate Apolo por hombre!"

("Defend yourself, Apollo-as-man!" [1: 143; my trans.]); the section of the *Respuesta* that defends her need for solitude among her peers (Arenal and Powell 58); and the long philosophical poem *Primero sueño* ("First Dream") as Sor Juana's vision of her intellectual liberation from objectification (Bergmann, "Sor Juana" 159–60).

In these texts, Sor Juana argues that her status as an object of adulation and as a target of censure conspires to distract her from writing and to detract from her image as a poet and intellectual. I tell students of Sor Juana's appellation in her own time as the "Mexican Phoenix" and show them the series of portraits painted of Sor Juana before and after her death (see Tapia Méndez, "Planos"; also see Meléndez, this volume). We consider Sor Juana's response to being constantly paraded for political purposes, to being codified even in her own time as a beautiful nun writing elite poetry in remote New Spain. I draw on Frederick Luciani's research on Sor Juana's creation of a writerly self in her work to serve "both self-promotive and self-protective functions" (*Literary Self-Fashioning* 16). Here, it is useful to have students consider the struggles of female public figures and intellectuals in our contemporary period and how they compare with Sor Juana's situation. Students engage well with the example of Hillary Clinton's having to "refashion" her public image during her tenure in the White House. Some of my students have compared Clinton's figure with that of Oprah Winfrey, remarking that Winfrey has had less trouble "being herself" in the public eye.

Class 3: Sor Juana's Petrarchan Poetry

We then do close readings of Sor Juana's Petrarchan *blasons*, which are a rich source for understanding—and sometimes disentangling—her dilemma with fame and objectification. We begin with poem 214, the comic *ovillejos*, "El pintar de Lisarda la belleza" ("To paint Lisarda's beauty" [1: 320–30; Luciani, *Literary Self-Fashioning* 33]). Working in groups, students can discover Sor Juana's inversion of the Petrarchan *blason* through in-class exercises identifying Sor Juana's use of *cultismos*, or arcane Latinate vocabulary, and her *conceptos*, or poetic conceits. Native and heritage speakers may be able to supplement dictionaries from the period, including Sebastián de Covarrubias y Horozco (*Tesoro*) and *Diccionario de autoridades* ("Dictionary of Authorities") to decipher Sor Juana's complex plays of conceptual wit.

Luciani's exegesis of this poem in his 1986 article "El amor" and in the chapter "Self-Inscription" in *Literary Self-Fashioning* (26–47) are crucial to understanding this poem. I urge students to narrow in on Sor Juana's lampooning of the Petrarchan *blason:* the lady's hair is a "calva lisa" ("smooth bald spot" [1: 324; my trans.]); her hands are made of flesh and bone, not ivory or silver (1: 328); her unappetizing mouth is "de cecina" ("dried beef" [1: 326; my trans.]). These parodic metaphors of the lady's beauty compose a *contre-*

blason that challenges the traditional verbal portrait and its ideological foundation in masculine objectification (Luciani, *Literary Self-Fashioning* 44). Students can easily see that Sor Juana uses the convention of baroque *desengaño* ("disillusionment"), drolly commenting on the distance between the poetic ideal in poetry and a real woman "de carne y hueso" ("of flesh and bone" [1: 328; my trans.]).[1]

The colonial poet reiterates this process of inversion in her critique of the objectification of beauty in the much-anthologized sonnet 145 "Este, que ves, engaño colorido" ("This object which you see—a painted snare" [1: 277; Arenal and Powell 153]), which resonates with Luis de Góngora's equally famous sonnet "Mientras por competir con tu cabello" ("While trying with your tresses to compete" [*Obras* 447; Ingber]).[3] Góngora's wit is misogynistic at its core, allegorizing the exhaustion of Petrarchan convention as the bodily decay of Góngora's rejecting muse: "oro, lilio, clavel, crystal luciente, / se vuelva, mas tú y ello juntamente / en tierra, en humo, en polo, en sombra, en nada" ("gold, carnation, lily, crystal luminous, not just to silver or limp violets will turn, but you and all of it as well to earth, smoke, dust, to gloom, to nothingness" [*Obras* 447; Ingber]).

Sor Juana's sonnet, however, is an address not to her muse but to her own portrait. She admonishes the viewer—that is, the reader of her poem—not to be fooled by the portrait's "falsos silogismos de colores" ("clever arguments of tone and hue" [1: 277; Arenal and Powell 153]). The beautiful portrait is a sham, a "cauteloso engaño del sentido" ("a cunning trap to snare your sense" [1: 277; Arenal and Powell 153]). It cannot protect the subject from old age or forgetfulness ("la vejez y del olvido" 'oblivion and old age' [1: 277; Arenal and Powell 153]).

Like the *ovillejos*, sonnet 145, "Este, que ves, engaño colorido" points to Sor Juana's consistent refusal to be "appropriated" by the male gaze or artist (Kantaris 7). Yet there is something in addition to Sor Juana's critique of male objectification in these two poems. The key word is "olvido," which can also be read as "oblivion," or the condition of being forgotten or unknown. Petrarchan tropes are worn-out, purged of their meaning (Luciani, "El amor" 23). How will Sor Juana make a name for herself in a "siglo desdichado y desvalido" ("Oh unfortunate and destitute age" [1: 321; Luciani, *Literary Self-Fashioning* 34]), where, as she laments in the *ovillejos*, "no hay voz, equívoco ni frase / Que por común no pase / Y digan los censores: *¿Eso? ¡Ya lo pensaron los mayores!*" ("there is no word, pun or phrase, that isn't a commonplace and of which the critics won't say 'Oh, that? The great ones already thought of it!' " [1: 321; Luciani, *Self-Fashioning* 34]). Poems 145 and 214 showcase Sor Juana's melding of a sense of her own precarious status with a sense of the precarious status of highly codified poetic language in her time.

Indeed, the wearing thin of lyric originality seems to push Sor Juana's imagination in these poems toward what Roberto González Echevarría calls "the desire for something new whose nature is not yet clear" ("Colonial Lyric" 228).

This point is crucial in classes that consider the relation of colonial texts to the development of Spanish American literature. If Sor Juana laments the impossibility of expression in the Petrarchan mode, can she be considered the source of a modern voice?

In the *Romance decasílabo* (poem 61), Lísida's cheeks are so beautiful they are "Cátedras de abril" ("April's lecture halls"), able to impart lessons to "mayo . . . / métodos a jasmines nevados, / fórmula rubicunda a las rosas" ("May: recipes for making jasmine snowy, formulas for redness in the rose" [1: 172; Trueblood 49]). The poem suggests that Sor Juana's beloved—that is, her *blason*, her own legacy in Petrarchism—may in fact instruct other poets on how to "color roses red," or how to write. Earlier in the *Romance decasílabo* Sor Juana calls Lísida's eyes, "Lámparas . . . febeas / . . . / "pólvora que, a las almas que llega, / Tórridas, abrasadas transforma" ("Lamps of Phoebus [that are] gunpowder turning every soul they strike into a flaming Torrid Zone" [1: 172; Trueblood 49]). The lady's eyes are lightning that acts on her viewers like gunpowder, a powerful image in the American context. Ullrich Langer points out that in early modern poetry, gunpowder often came to substitute for the classical reference of lightning, suggesting a violent challenge to the classical register of tropes (97). Lísida's transformation of "souls," or readers, with the "pólvora" of her eyes allegorizes Sor Juana's sense of how worn-out Petrarchan convention might be radicalized by colonial baroque images, a range of which proliferate in her poem. In the *blason* of Lísida, Sor Juana calls attention to a new form of poetic description not bound by stereotype but transformed by her metaphoric vision.

I now ask students to consider how Sor Juana, as not only a woman but also a poet of the New World, has a unique view of literary representation. I point out that her New World vision may have some of its valence in spatial or geographic metaphors, which is suggested not only by the setting and drama of Sor Juana's *Primero sueño* but also by the *blasons* of her vicereines in poems 61, *Romance decasílabo*, and 80, "Seguidillas" (see Franco). Roland Greene reminds us that the *Rime sparse*, set in the landscape of Avignon where Petrarch watched his lady Laura walk, is a geographic setting as well as a temporal narrative (195). González Echevarría describes Latin American writers in general as working within a "strategic marginality" ("BdeORridaGES" 231), one that, according to Greene, obliges Latin American poets to pay closer attention to space and geography (196). Both of Sor Juana's *blasons* turn on a melding of strange yet recognizable geographies, from Lísida's lecture halls and River Bosphorus to Elvira's map of ancient and colonial territories. Sor Juana's belatedness with Petrarchan tradition may very well constitute her agency, her ability to represent her colonial baroque vision of the New World as a new space for poetry.

As a point of comparison, students can consider geographic spaces in colonial Latin American narrative texts, like those in Cabeza de Vaca's itinerary in *Naufragios* ("Castaways"), Garcilaso de la Vega's architectural images of the Inca empire in *Comentarios reales* ("Royal Commentaries"), and Rodríguez

Freyle's Colombian landscape in *El carnero* ("The Trash Bin"). These texts are distinguished by their distance from peninsular rhetorical models and their critical stance on conquest and colonization. By encouraging students to discover the coupling of American geographies with moral satire in Sor Juana and these texts, instructors can creatively inspire student thinking on the features of an incipient Latin American writerly identity, one that will reassert itself in students' studies of Romantic and modern Latin American literature.

NOTES

[1]See Luciani, "El ovillejo" 17–18 and *Literary Self-Fashioning* 40.

[2]Also see Sabat de Rivers, "Sor Juana y su retratos"; Luciani, "Anamorphosis"; Clamurro.

Sor Juana; or, The Traps of Translation

Daniel P. Hunt

After almost thirty years I can still recall how impatient a reader of Sor Juana I was the first time around. Like many advanced undergraduates who had spent time abroad, I imagined my command of Spanish was as good as it ought to be. So when our professor, a gentle old man who had forgotten more than most people ever learn, gave us a handful of Sor Juana's sonnets in mimeograph, it was easy to dismiss the confusion raised by that blue wall of bewildering signifiers. Didn't the title "de la Cruz" make her a mystic after all? If so, weren't we then supposed to be mystified? Not wanting to let on, I pretended in class to understand what she was saying, all divine roses or burning desire or whatever. It was enough to gratify the professor that some of us were actually doing the reading and could help him find his glasses so he could induct us into the holy fellowship of syllabification, as if it held the key to all mythologies. And yet, as an obsessive reader since childhood, I remember being haunted by my failure to disentangle those hendecasyllables. It wasn't until years later, after studying John Donne in a doctoral seminar in English, that I came to realize how important it is to slow down and puzzle things out according to syntax. Only then could I return to make an honest attempt at Sor Juana, to discover that she was not the mystic I had once imagined.

I relate this experience because I suspect that most of our advanced undergraduate students in Spanish, even native speakers, feel a similar bewilderment at their first brush with Sor Juana. The suspicion is confirmed to varying degrees whenever I ask them to paraphrase or translate a given passage. To try to contain the habit of mind that sates itself on a glance, about a decade ago I began to develop collaborative exercises and translation games as a way of getting students to slow down and explore in depth a limited set of lines in class. Once induced to attend to details of syntax and style in a setting that sparks their interest, students can usually achieve a more accurate and satisfying gloss of Sor Juana's poetry. Consequently, they are generally more inclined and better prepared to negotiate the tricky turns of her tropes and conceits.

A primary aim of these exercises is to help students capture the spirit of play that permeates Sor Juana's lyrics. I hope that some of them learn to enjoy the intellectual challenge of finding their way through her labyrinths. Experience teaches that students left to their own devices more often than not rush ahead to arrive at fanciful interpretations of a poem based on faulty readings of its syntax, leaping to judgment before they have a clear view of the traps that lie ahead. I believe they ought to see the grain before they begin to read against it. So I usually start by asking students in class to try translating a quatrain from Spanish to English on their own. Alternatively, they may be asked to disentangle the prose sentence hidden in a quatrain by transposing the main clause and its dependents into standard subject-verb-object order, without changing the vocabulary of the original except to introduce subject pronouns or subordinators where these are implied. Native speakers in particular benefit from this latter approach. Since every class brings different reading abilities to the table, I have found it is a good idea to check students' skill levels before going on. Moreover, this gives me a chance to identify the better readers, so that they can be distributed evenly among groups.

For example, I ask students in class to translate this clause from "Si los riesgos" on a sheet of paper: "Si del fogoso bruto ponderara / la furia desbocada en la carrera / el jinete prudente" (1: 279). Most students predictably try to make "fogoso bruto" or "furia desbocada" the subject, oblivious to the trap until they fail to make sense of the rest of the clause. Before correcting them, I ask them in a *PowerPoint* demonstration to consider a parallel translation in modern Spanish, as follows:

> How would you translate this sentence: "Del hombre que vino ayer habló mi amigo"? Like this: "The man who came yesterday spoke to my friend"? Or like this: "My friend spoke about the man who came yesterday"? Clearly, you would choose the second translation. How do you know that the first is wrong, the second right? You intuit that "hombre" is in a prepositional phrase marked by "de" and therefore cannot be the subject, so you look for other cues. The other noun, "mi amigo," stands alone, and it also matches the verb. Now return to Sor Juana and apply the same strategy. What's the subject of the verb "ponderera"? Because this is poetry, you might be tempted to ignore what you already know about prepositions and guess "bruto." But guessing this way will blind you to what she is really saying. As in the example we just considered, look for a noun that stands alone and can logically be the subject of "ponderar." You might try "furia desbocada," unbridled fury, which stands alone, but, since fury is an emotion rather than a person, it is unlikely to do much pondering. All that remains is the prudent rider, waiting at the end of the clause, who can indeed ponder the unbridled fury of his runaway horse. Just so, by pondering and rearranging the words, you can make sense of the sentence. The language of Sor Juana, and of poetry in general, is condensed, precise, and demanding. "Poetic license" belongs to the writer, not to the reader.

Once students come to understand that the grammar underlying sentence formation is generally the same for prose and poetry but that the surface order of poetry is frequently inverted, interrupted, or juxtaposed in surprising ways, they are more likely to take the time to untangle the syntax and discover the logical idea residing beneath the surface. They also learn that if they fail to make the essential connections among subjects and their verbs, subordinators and their referents, they will consistently misread Sor Juana.

After students have practiced translating lines into English or transposing them into modern Spanish, we reverse the logic. I give small groups a quatrain or tercet translated into English, together with its scansion rules for Spanish, and challenge them to try and "reinvent" the original Spanish. Everyone can translate the same stanza, or each group can tackle a different part of a longer poem to reconstruct a whole sonnet, for example. For this Borgesian exercise, it can be useful to reveal the last word or words of key lines in Spanish as well, or an entire line, depending on how much time can be allotted, and let students fill in the missing parts. The results are invariably amusing, and the students learn a good deal about the difficulty of applying the rules of rhyme and meter along the way. What is more, they come to appreciate just how efficiently Sor Juana uses language, how much information she can pack into the "sonnet's scanty plot of ground," or into her redondillas or *romances*, when they compare their efforts with the original verses.[1]

This exercise also lends itself well to introducing the topic of comparative translation, since it requires the class to look closely at one published version. When given a second translation of the same poem, students are ready to examine how different translators struggle to achieve similar effects in English using other means, how they can be forced to sacrifice meaning or feeling to remain faithful to the original. In turn, providing such parallax views of a particular poem will not only help students deepen their awareness of polysemy in that poem; it can also help build their ability to read baroque poetry in Spanish independently, since common vocabulary and idiomatic structures are reinforced through repetition.

Another game that students enjoy is one in which small groups are given the first line from one of Sor Juana's redondillas or quatrains in the original Spanish and asked to compose the remaining lines of the stanza according to the rules of scansion and the central conceit of the original poem. Each group can work with the same first line, or each can be assigned a different stanza. Where the first option lends itself to a more concrete analysis of form, the second enables a broader look at content. A competitive edge can be added by awarding a first place for speed and another for wit. This exercise works particularly well with "Hombres necios," and it generally helps if students have already read the poem before class so they are familiar with the paradox of the double standard. Once they have completed their stanzas, usually within twenty minutes or so, each group shares its version with the entire class. The lines are scanned for accuracy and evaluated for integrity in conveying the conceit, and they often yield surprisingly good poems. As a formalistic exercise, collaborative composition enables students to learn scansion quickly and effectively by practicing it, especially since they usually correct one another's syllabification and end rhymes as they work. But the real payoff comes when students open their texts and compare their efforts, as good as these often are, with Sor Juana's original verses. Once students have more or less surmounted the initial obstacle of squeezing a big idea into thirty-two syllables, they are in a much better position to be astonished by her gift for suspending solid matter in air, as in "la que peca por la paga / o el que paga por pecar" (1: 228–29). They can then return to the poetry with a better sense of what they should be seeing and feeling as they grapple with the more difficult challenge of identifying and interpreting conceits.

Here I begin by reviewing the general concept of metaphor and by taking the conceit as a particular, thorny case. The definition given by Alan S. Trueblood in the introduction to *A Sor Juana Anthology* serves as a good model:

> Wit expressed in conceit, wordplay which startles and diverts by unexpected couplings of terms usually far apart or belonging to different orders of phenomena, is the fundamental figure of thought. Paradox, antithesis, hyperbole, and periphrasis are constant props. Patterns of scholastic logic, parallelisms, inversions, plain or incremental repetitions, are favorite ways of disposing conceits syntactically. Governing all is a rhetorical tendency that highly prizes ingenuity in unraveling variant expressions of an unvarying conceit. Sor Juana's dexterity in manipulating this poetic idiom was the amazement of her contemporaries. (11)

Once students feel relatively conversant with the contours of the abstraction, it is important that they learn to identify conceits in a relatively transparent example, such as "Hombres necios." This will happen more readily if they have already worked closely with the poem in either of the translation exercises outlined above.

For native speakers of English, I have also found it rewarding in class to look at John Donne's "A Valediction Forbidding Mourning." Donne seems to pose a degree of conceptual and aesthetic difficulty in English similar to that of Sor Juana for readers in Spanish. Some students are enlightened when they discover in Donne that the barrier is not entirely linguistic but conceptual; others are encouraged when they grasp for the first time, without mediation through a second language, what Trueblood means by "wordplay which startles and diverts."

Another useful analogue for conveying the curves of emotion that radiate from the play of repetition, juxtaposition, and inversion in this poetry is baroque music. Sometimes we listen to and discuss Johann Sebastian Bach, Antonio Vivaldi, or George Frideric Handel or selections from the Spanish American baroque performed by choral ensembles like Chanticleer or Coro Exaudi de Cuba. Not only does this music dramatize the forms and feelings of the poetry, if left to play softly in the background it can also help ease the stress of the next undertaking.

After this overview, we move on to the more elaborate or opaque conceits found in many of the court and convent lyrics and sonnets. Over the last decade or so I have come to rely on an informal, admittedly often idiosyncratic, technique for teaching tropes in Sor Juana using color-coded *PowerPoint* demonstrations. Invoking a right-brain response seems to aid in the process of disentangling surface complexities, which in turn can clear the way for a better view of the central conceit. In the body of the poem itself, I highlight various tropes, images, or relations using different colors, fonts, and arrows as a way of tracing their iterations and transformations across an entire poem. One slide, for instance, illustrates how Sor Juana deploys verbs in interesting patterns, and another how she juxtaposes tropes across synonyms and antonyms to dispose a conceit.

For example, with "Rosa divina" we first read straight through the poem aloud, stopping only to gloss new vocabulary, and then emerge to face the central mystery of the conceit: "con que con docta muerte y necia vida / viviendo engañas y muriendo enseñas" (1: 278). We consider how a rose might deceive by living and teach by dying, and what the apparently absurd phrases "learned death" and "dumb life" could possibly mean. Then I project a series of color-coded slides of the poem, each of which traces a discrete pattern of logic or allusion that can be brought to bear on these paradoxes. For instance, red might be used to highlight nouns and adjectives that allude to biological nature and its presumed origin in divine creation, whereas blue can draw attention to contrasting words that suggest culture, including artifacts and institutions created by human hands and minds. In the following example, italics designate nature while underlining indicates culture:

Rosa divina que en gentil cultura
eres, con tu *fragante* sutileza,
magisterio *purpúreo* en la belleza,
enseñanza *nevada* a la hermosura.

Amago de la humana arquitectura,
ejemplo de la vana gentileza,
en cuyo ser unió *naturaleza*
la cuna alegre y triste sepultura.

¡Cuán altiva en tu pompa, presumida
soberbia, el riesgo de morir desdeñas,
y luego desmayada y *encogida*

de tu *caduco* ser das *mustias* señas,
con que con docta *muerte* y necia *vida*
viviendo engañas y muriendo enseñas! (1: 278)

Projecting such a scheme in color allows the viewer to see at a glance how allusions to nature and culture initially appear to be more or less evenly balanced in the first quatrain. The color contrast also underscores an initial tension in the poem between natural sensory perception ("fragante," "purpúreo," "nevada," etc.) and culturally mediated forms of knowing ("sutileza," "magisterio," "enseñanza," and so on). Soon the crux of the problem seems to coalesce around models and monuments of culture in the second quatrain, only to spill over into accusatory personifications of arrogance and recklessness in the sestet, where Petrarchan convention would stipulate a resolution. Finally, nature returns in allusions to the perennial life cycle of the rose as these ideas resolve in the verbs of the final conceit. Of course, it should be noted that this construction of a binary opposition nature/culture, like other schemes presented here, is to some degree an arbitrary and reductive intrusion on the poem, one that begs to be deconstructed. Far from foreclosing such discussion, what I intend with these models is to provide a convenient place for students to start.

To continue, a following slide reveals a similar pattern in the dichotomy teaching/lying across the same lines. And in another, active and static verbs are separated by color, so the reader is forced to note that virtually the entire octave orbits around the copula "eres." Thus the weight of suspended signification is released late in the second quatrain with the verb "unió," where nature unites cradle and grave. Here Sor Juana poses the key riddle of the conceit. This initial scarcity of verbs, unusual in Sor Juana, contrasts vividly with their full florescence in the sestet, where the answer is all verbs and adverbs, "viviendo engañas y muriendo enseñas" ("by living you deceive, by dying you teach"; my trans.).

In *PowerPoint*, color or fonts may be combined with other features to help students visualize more complex relations, as in the following case of paired oxymorons, crossed in chiasmus:

> Rosa divina que en ***gentil*** *cultura*
> . . . Amago de la humana arquitectura,
> ejemplo de la *vana* ***gentileza***

In this example, boldface type highlights each oxymoron. Italics point to an ambiguous and surprising contrast between *gentil/gentileza*, whose shared root makes them appear to be synonyms, even while they reverberate as antonyms across the chiasmus of the underlined opposites *vana/cultura*. Because students using modern Spanish will find it counterintuitive to suppose that *gentil* can be opposed to *cultura* and *gentileza*, this illustration offers a good opening for teaching the archaic connotations of *gentil* as "airoso" or "gallardo," with consequent parallels to *vana* when the trait is taken to extremes.

As students begin to feel more at ease with such intricacies, similar patterns in the paradox of the central conceit are rendered visible. Again, colors, fonts, or lines highlight tropes. In the following illustration, underlined terms inform the senses, while those in italics distort or block them. External lines draw attention as well, either to the chiasmus:

> viviendo *engañas* y *muriendo* enseñas!

or to the paired contraries:

viviendo *engañas* y *muriendo* enseñas!

Likewise, these relations of similarity and difference can be extended vertically to reveal how Sor Juana binds one allusion to another. Each term in the conceit traces a path backward through the poem. For instance, continuing with the pattern already established, italics show nature and the senses in demise or decay. In *PowerPoint*, arrows work well to traverse the entire space of the poem, and these features can be animated so that each idea appears in its turn:

¡Cuán altiva en tu pompa, presumida
soberbia, el riesgo de *morir* desdeñas,
y luego *desmayada* y *encogida*
de tu *caduco* ser das *mustias* señas,
con que con docta *muerte* y necia vida
viviendo engañas y ***muriendo*** enseñas!

Naturally, such devices can be applied to any term and extended in any direction throughout the poem, either exhaustively to dramatize baroque profusion or selectively to isolate an interesting string.

Once the parts have been extricated using such devices, the whole poem is then reconstructed to show how the conceit works holistically. In this final step, previously introduced colors or fonts come into play against a new sign. As before, in the underlined passages the rose appears to instruct or animate, whereas in italics it works to deceive or disappoint. In the end, these competing motifs merge into the dense wordplay of the final lines, highlighted in boldface:

Rosa divina que en gentil cultura
eres, con tu *fragante sutileza*,
magisterio purpúreo en la belleza,
enseñanza nevada a la hermosura.

Amago de la humana arquitectura,
ejemplo de la vana gentileza,
en cuyo ser unió naturaleza
la cuna alegre y *triste sepultura*.

¡Cuán altiva en tu pompa, presumida
soberbia, el riesgo de morir desdeñas,
y *luego desmayada* y *encogida*

de tu caduco ser das mustias señas,
con que con **docta muerte y necia vida**
viviendo engañas y muriendo enseñas!

After so many iterations of the same lines viewed from different angles, students generally find it easier to capture the unvarying conceit behind the apparent contradictions. The living rose deceives because its beauty is transitory; like all living things, it is destined to wither and die. And yet only by dying does it teach this simple, powerful lesson of Renaissance Platonism, presaging John Keats: "Beauty is truth, truth beauty."[2] Sor Juana's conceit is at once physical and metaphysical, and its logic rigorous, unfolding with "almost mathematical effects of symmetry and congruity" (Trueblood 11).

I always hope, after working through these presentations, that students are encouraged to slow down, untangle the syntax, and savor the particulars of this and other poems, whether they work in collaborative groups or read alone. Naturally, the interpretation of any metaphor is open to debate in the final analysis, and each time I teach these poems I revise my own views. It is important to warn students away from the trap of reducing the inherent multivalence of metaphor to any univocal, authorized reading. So while I still would not presume to know how seriously Sor Juana may have taken the mystical rose of heaven as a Neoplatonic reality, I also would not want to discourage a good student from going down that path. Even so, no interpretation based on an erroneous reading of the syntax can survive for long. This approach at least gives students some firm ground on which to stand initially as they develop their own interpretative skills. And in the end, I hope it opens a window through which they come to experience the beauty and complexity of Sor Juana's art directly, rather than strain to see through a glass of middling Spanish, darkly.

NOTES

[1]The phrase is from William Wordsworth's sonnet "Nuns Fret Not at Their Convent's Narrow Room" (1807), line 1 (Noyes 332).

[2]The quotation is from John Keats, "Ode on a Grecian Urn" (1819), line 49 (Noyes 1194).

The Answer to Sor Filotea: A Rhetorical Approach

Rosa Perelmuter

At first glance *La respuesta a sor Filotea* (*The Answer*), Sor Juana's acclaimed 1691 reply to a letter penned by Manuel Fernández de Santa Cruz, bishop of Puebla, using the pseudonym of Sor Filotea de la Cruz, might seem a bit awkward to read and especially to teach. The printed version runs about thirty-five pages, or 1,438 lines, in the Spanish edition and thirty-three pages, or 1,397 lines, in the English translation and is full of digressions, many citations (some of them in Latin), long and rambling sentences, and complex arguments. Yet it remains one of Sor Juana's most popular texts, most recently because of what has been perceived as its feminist content and throughout the centuries because it is one of the few places where we find what may be considered autobiographical information about the celebrated Mexican nun. One way to make this fascinating document more accessible to students (at both the undergraduate and graduate level) is to introduce them to the letter's rhetorical structure, to reveal that beneath its apparent lack of organization and perceived spontaneity lies a formal organization whose outstanding feature is precisely its ability to conceal itself.

Why Sor Juana might have wanted to conceal or minimize the appearance of a deliberate scheme or order to her letter might be best explained if we consider the circumstances under which she penned the *Answer*. The bishop's letter to Sor Juana, which he sent about three months before she replied and which he enclosed with his published version of her *Carta atenagórica*, asks her, not as the bishop of Puebla, but as another nun, Sor Filotea de la Cruz, to curb her excessive interest in profane letters and spend more time devoted to the study of the Bible and divine letters in general. As this essay will argue, Sor Juana does not seem to take kindly to the bishop's admonition (we shall have occasion to remark on the presence of irony in her letter), nor is she happy with his having published her *Carta atenagórica* (a rather hyperbolic title of his own confection), a publication that many believe cost her dearly and may have led to her eventual withdrawal from the literary scene. To avoid making matters worse, Sor Juana will mount her defense against the bishop's charges, but will do so under the guise of friendship, using a tone that she describes as "[de] casera familiaridad" ("[of] household familiarity" [4: 474; Arenal and Powell 103]). She pretends to respond to her religious sister with a familiar letter (this was a popular genre during her time; see Todd, esp. 21–22, and Thompson's chapter "Familiar Letters" in *Literary Bypaths*) yet skillfully argues her case (in the legal sense) before her judge and jury. Reading the text attentively, while keeping in mind rhetorical principles, students will perceive that it is carefully crafted yet dissembled. The use of the two models—of the forensic oration and the familiar letter—makes Sor Juana's letter effective and particularly engaging.[1]

During Sor Juana's time, rhetoric was a recognized, indispensable science and was studied in all disciplines. A self-taught scholar, Sor Juana most likely became well versed in rhetorical theory and practice through the study of Latin, since many of the lessons in the grammar books included long passages from the most famous practitioners of rhetoric.[2] Indeed, the first paragraph of the *Answer* concludes with a quotation from a Latin translation of Quintilian's massive and highly influential treatise, the *Institutio oratoria*, and she cites him once again toward the end of the letter (4: 468; Arenal and Powell 91). Of the three types of oratory (forensic, or judicial, which is concerned with accusation and defense in the courts; deliberative, which deals with the recommendation of a course of action in deliberative assemblies; and epideictic, which is concerned with praise and blame), Sor Juana relies most often on the first type, forensic oration, which suggests that she was defending herself against accusations of punishable offenses. The *Answer* generally follows the Ciceronian division into four parts (*De partitione oratoria* 4, part 1; 33–51, part 2): the exordium, or introduction (4: 440–45; Arenal and Powell 39–49); the narration, or statement of facts, which includes the *divisio*, a forecast of the main points (4: 445–60; Arenal and Powell 49–77); the proof (which contains both the affirmative proof and the refutation of contrary opinions [4: 460–74; Arenal and Powell 77–103]); and, finally, the peroration or conclusion (4: 474–75; Arenal and Powell 103–05). Dividing the letter into these four sections gives the reader a key to understanding Sor Juana's purpose and direction. The instructor too can profit from introducing the letter's rhetorical structure in the classroom, since doing so establishes Sor Juana as an educated woman of her day and also helps make this long letter more manageable for students. By dividing the letter in this fashion, students can better visualize its organization—Sor Juana's possible reasons for the selection of specific topics and rhetorical figures, for choosing to expand or abbreviate a given section, and for deciding to be more or less formal in executing a section's presentation.

According to classical rhetorical rules, the function of the introductory section is to render the listener attentive, benevolent, and docile (Cicero, *De inventione*, bk. 1, ch. 16, par. 21). Doubtless aware of the importance of the opening paragraphs, Sor Juana draws on a repertoire of formulas of proven efficacy, standard topics of the exordium. These collections of topoi, or commonplaces, were a resource for an orator or writer in search of the idea or formula that best suited the situation. Here, Sor Juana employs many topics of "affected modesty." Since it was understood that the speaker's submissiveness and humility would put the audience in a favorable state of mind, Sor Juana begins by apologizing for her delay in answering Sor Filotea's letter, blaming it on, in her words, "mi poca salud y mi justo temor" ("my scant health and a rightful fear"[4: 440; Arenal and Powell 39]). This type of excuse, by which the speaker alludes to his or her feebleness and inadequate preparation, derives from judicial oratory; Quintilian mentions it in his *Institutio oratoria* (bk. 4, ch. 1, par. 8) as a formula intended to win the judge's favor. The popular formula soon passed to other genres; Ernst Robert Curtius has traced it to a great number of writers (83).

Throughout the exordium (and, in fact, throughout the letter, since the modesty topos is not limited to the exordium), Sor Juana continues to present herself as a humble and respectful subject. She does this in two ways. On the one hand, Sor Juana praises the listener's character or ethos, as in the passage where—in a hyperbolic display that betrays the underlying irony—she employs a series of superlatives to characterize Sor Filotea's letter: "vuestra doctísima, discretísima, santísima y amorosísima carta" ("immensely learned, prudent, devout, and loving letter" [4: 440; Arenal and Powell 39]). On the other, she diminishes her own worth, using what Curtius terms "formulas of self-disparagement" (84), as for example when she insists that she is inept and insignificant and uses derogatory expressions such as "mi torpe pluma" and "mis borrones" ("my dull pen [and] my drafts and scratches" [4: 440; Arenal and Powell 39]), as well as when she calls herself "una pobre monja, la más mínima criatura del mundo y la más indigna de ocupar vuestra atención" ("a poor nun, the slightest creature on earth and the least worthy of drawing your attention" [4: 441; Arenal and Powell 41]). In her letter, then, the declarations of humility (*humilitas*) figure alongside her protestations of incapacity (*mediocritas*), but with such insistence that, using the rhetorical figure called prolepsis or anticipation, she tries to forestall the reader's skepticism by claiming that "[n]o es afectada modestia, Señora, sino ingenua verdad de toda mi alma" ("It is not false humility, my Lady, but the candid truth of my very soul" [4: 441; Arenal and Powell 41]).

Sor Juana proceeds in a manner similar to that of Cicero in his exordium to the *Oratoria*: she explains that replying to the bishop's letter is beyond her powers (4: 441; Arenal and Powell 41–43) and that it would thus be best to keep silent. She finally agrees to proceed only because of her addressee's merit and largesse (4: 442; Arenal and Powell 43). Further on, in the proof, Sor Juana returns to this point, reminding her interlocutor that she decided to respond, but only to please Sor Filotea: "Y protesto que sólo lo hago por obedeceros; con tanto recelo, que me debéis más en tomar la pluma con este temor, que me debiérades si os remitiera más perfectas obras" ("Yet I protest that I do so only to obey you; and with such misgiving that you owe me more for taking up my pen with all this fear than you would owe me were I to present you with the most perfect works" [4: 464; Arenal and Powell 83]). This popular excuse, called the "obedience topic," often accompanies the modesty formula (Curtius 85). As Sor Juana prepares to move on to the narration, she thanks her addressee profusely (again, the intensity of her words betrays the irony that lies beneath) for granting her—and here she does recur to legal terminology—"benévola licencia para hablar y proponer en vuestra venerable presencia" ("kind license to speak and to plead my case in your venerable presence" [4: 442; Arenal and Powell 45]).

Next, also in keeping with the method prescribed by Cicero, who suggests that the exordium should contain the exposition or part of the exposition of the facts, Sor Juana introduces and begins her defense of the accusations leveled at her by Sor Filotea. Given that in this case judge and prosecutor are one and the same, Sor Juana proceeds with caution. She appears to be repentant and humble, telling her interlocutor, "recibo en mi alma vuestra santísima amonestación de aplicar el estudio a Libros Sagrados, que aunque viene en traje de consejo, tendrá para mí sustancia de precepto" ("I declare that I receive in my very soul your most holy admonition to apply my study to Holy Scripture; for although it arrives in the guise of counsel, it shall have for me the weight of law" [4: 443; Arenal and Powell 45]). But, again, the vehemence with which Sor Juana expresses herself points to the irony that lurks behind her words. The passage is full of rhetorical questions and the insistent use of the relative and interrogative pronouns *quien* and *qué* (*who* and *what* [4: 442; Arenal and Powell 43]). This is followed by the repetition of the personal pronoun *vuestro*, which appears eight times in the space of twelve lines (4: 442–43), and the reappearance of superlatives (this time *santísima* and *cuerdísima* [4: 443]).

The lengthy defense that follows confirms the underlying irony in Sor Juana's declarations of repentance and humility. Here, the Mexican nun first justifies not devoting herself to sacred letters on the grounds that studying sacred letters is forbidden by her sex; her age; and, above all, tradition (4: 443; Arenal and Powell 45), and then maintains that she ought not to be censured for her inclination to learning both because it is a natural, God-given impulse (4: 444; Arenal and Powell 47) and because she has only written to please others and "no sólo sin complacencia, sino con positiva repugnancia" ("not only without taking satisfaction but with downright aversion" [4: 444; Arenal and Powell 47]). On this last point, a recurrence of the obedience topic, we would do well to recall Curtius's words: "Innumerable medieval authors assert that they write by command. Histories of literature accept this as gospel truth. Yet it is usually a mere topos" (85). Before ending her exordium, Sor Juana makes an appeal to the reader's sympathy (pathos) by recounting the accusations and difficulties she has experienced during her life, and then whets her correspondent's appetite by promising to tell her "things never heard before," a topic that Curtius identifies as a common introductory formula (85–86): "Si yo pudiera pagaros algo de lo que os debo, Señora mía, creo que sólo os pagara con contaros esto, pues no ha salido de mi boca jamás, excepto para quien debió salir" ("If I could repay any part of my debt to you, my Lady, I believe I might do so merely by informing you of this, for these words have never left my mouth save to that one to whom they must be said" [4: 445; Arenal and Powell 49]). With these words Sor Juana is able to proceed to the narration of the facts, confident that she has achieved *docilitas*, that her addressee is eager and willing to hear her.

The narration is clearly demarcated, beginning with "Prosiguiendo en la narración de mi inclinación" ("To go on with the narration of this inclination of mine" [4: 445; Arenal and Powell 49]), and ending with the clear expression of the narrator's intention to stop in order not to bore her reader (the so-called fastidium topos, a much used modesty topic that is meant to promote good will by showing concern for the interlocutor): "las dejo por no cansaros, pues basta lo dicho para que vuestra discreción y trascendencia penetre y se entere perfectamente en todo mi natural y del principio, medios y estado de mis estudios" ("I leave them out in order not to weary you. I have said enough for your judgment and your surpassing eminence to comprehend my nature with clarity and full understanding, together with the beginnings, the methods, and the present state of my studies" [4: 460; Arenal and Powell 77]). And, as if this were not enough to mark the end of her narration, Sor Juana repeats in the next paragraph, where the *divisio* (the exposition of the argument that she is about to prove) is introduced, that "esto no ha sido más de una simple narración de mi inclinación a las letras" ("this has been no more than a simple account of my inclination to letters" [4: 460; Arenal and Powell 77]).

This insistence on underscoring the limits of her narration points to the importance that Sor Juana ascribes to that section of her letter. After all, it is here that she explains why she has studied and how dearly she has paid, and her addressee must keep these arguments well in mind before hearing her proof. The strategy that Sor Juana follows is twofold: first she makes an appeal to ethos, a mode of persuasion by which one tries to gain the judge's favor by stressing the subject's good deeds and character. In this, she follows Aristotle's suggestion in his *Rhetoric*, where he observes that it behooves the orator to narrate anything that will show his virtue (bk. 3, ch. 16, par. 5). Second, she makes an appeal to pathos, the rhetorical appeal to the emotions, by describing in her letter the many tribulations that her literary inclination has caused her and the gossip and persecutions she has had to endure. In this Sor Juana appears to be following Cicero, who prescribes dwelling on the misfortunes that have befallen the orator to gain the benevolence of the audience (*De inventione*, bk. 1, ch. 16, par. 22). When teaching Sor Juana's letter, however, if time is an issue or if the students' interests or strengths require it, instructors may wish to forgo the discussion of Sor Juana's classical models. In more advanced classes it has been my experience that students appreciate learning about the Mexican nun's literary formation, and they also appreciate becoming acquainted with well-known and influential authors of antiquity.

The beginning of the proof, necessarily the most rigorous and formal part of her defense, is marked—as noted earlier—by the *divisio*, the projection of the principal points to be addressed. But here, as in the rest of the proof, we observe that the discussion is handled subtly, by keeping the judicial tone to a minimum. This is reasonable indeed, since Sor Juana's intent is to appease (or pretend to appease) an interlocutor who wants her to be more submissive and compliant and less focused on scientific and secular learning. She thus avoids emphasizing the legal or scholastic terms and frames her arguments indirectly, as in the following articulation of the *divisio*: "Si éstos, Señora, fueran méritos (como los veo por tales celebrar en los hombres), no lo hubieran sido en mí, porque obro necesariamente. Si son culpa, por la misma razón creo que no la he tenido" ("If studies, my Lady, be merits [for indeed I see them extolled as such in men], in me they are no such thing: I study because I must. If they be a failing, I believe for the same reason that the fault is none of mine" [4: 460; Arenal and Powell 77]). Sor Juana couches the passage in a rather plaintive, humble tone, underscoring her addressee's feminine identity ("Señora" ["my Lady"]) while also insisting on her own innocence.

Sor Juana argues that she is not guilty for two reasons: first, because the writing and studying of profane subjects of which she is accused are not crimes (further pointing out that, if anything, they are virtues, since they are viewed thusly in men); and second, because her inclination (to learning) is a God-given gift over which she has no control. The appeal to the judge that follows (the judicial formula called *permissio*, whereby the orator places the case in the hands of the judge) marks a change to a more official tone: "y así remito la decisión a ese soberano talento, sometiéndome luego a lo que sentenciare, sin contradicción ni repugnancia" ("And so I entrust the decision to your supreme skill and straightway submit to whatever sentence you may pass, posing no objection or reluctance" [4: 460; Arenal and Powell 77]). In a passage from the *Rhetorica ad Herennium* (bk. 4, chap. 29, par. 39), a text often attributed to Cicero that Sor Juana may have had in mind, this formula is prescribed as a strategy to arouse the sympathy, or pathos, of the audience. Here it also serves as a smooth transition to the proof.

In this key section the Mexican nun argues in favor of women's right to study and write freely and employs two different kinds of proof: inductive proof (through example, as when she furnishes a catalog of learned women who were praised and respected in antiquity or when she enumerates those women who, in her own time, stand out for their discretion) and deductive proof (through enthymeme, an incomplete syllogism; see Aristotle, *Rhetoric* [bk. 2, ch. 24]). Sor Juana moves from the universal (the rights of women) to the particular (a consideration of her own case). She proves that writing the *Carta atenagórica* was not a crime, that writing poetry is not criminal, and that her being a woman does not make writing poetry a crime. After this long and necessarily formal section, where she again uses legal terminology, Sor Juana sets out to mitigate the impression that she has in fact just delivered an impassioned defense, and she devotes the rest of the proof to this goal. She maintains (thus contradicting what she has written so far) that, given her "natural aversion" ("aversión natural") to this type of thing, she will never take up the pen to defend herself and that, furthermore, she does not even feel assailed (4: 471–72; Arenal and Powell 97, 99). Returning to the humble tone that she conveyed in the exordium, Sor Juana tells Sor Filotea that her wish is to remain silent and that her duty as a Catholic is to be tolerant. With this return to the modesty of the introduction, she begins to prepare her interlocutor for the conclusion. But before embarking on the peroration, Sor Juana once again makes an appeal to ethos, underscoring the favorable aspects of her character by referring to such things as her generosity and her indifference to fame.

This final technique aims to generate in the reader the sympathy necessary for her to begin the concluding statements. In place of the usual recapitulation of the facts of the case, which would have required too formal a tone, Sor Juana devotes the conclusion to strengthening her bonds with her reader and follows the indications of Quintilian in his *Institutio oratoria*, where he explains that at times it is better to try to convince the judge by an appeal to the emotions than by going over the facts (bk. 4, par. 6; bk. 6, ch. 1, par. 23). Toward the end of the letter, Sor Juana adopts an informal, even playful attitude, as in the wordplay we observe in the following passage: "y si os pareciere incongruo el *Vos* que yo he usado por parecerme que para la reverencia que os debo es muy poca reverencia la *Reverencia*, mudadlo en el que os pareciere decente a lo que vos merecéis" ("and if you think unsuitable the familiar terms I have employed—because it seems to me that given all the reverence I owe you, 'Your Reverence' is very little reverence indeed—please alter it to whatever you think suitable" (4: 474–75; Arenal and Powell 103). Having bridged the distance between judge and accused, Sor Juana is able to end her letter with a note of familiarity.

The preceding observations on the structure of the *Answer* establish, I believe, Sor Juana's acquaintance with rhetorical precepts and the skill with which she employed certain devices to compose her letter. Still, that we can observe this structure neither proves nor disproves the spontaneity or sincerity of her words. The disposition of Sor Juana's text could well have been the result of an intuitive, unconscious process. Let me venture to say that in Sor Juana's case, given her erudition, her literary production, and the historical moment in which she wrote, it is likely that rhetoric in general and the forensic oration in particular supplied her with a way to set forth her position and defend it cogently yet diplomatically. A forensic oration dressed in familiar letter clothing—not a bad way to address a bishop disguised as a nun, wouldn't you say?

NOTES

[1]For a more thorough discussion of rhetoric in Sor Juana's time and her application of these principles to her *Respuesta*, see Perelmuter, *Límites*, chapters 1 and 2.

[2]The rhetoricians most often cited by Sor Juana, in her *Answer* and elsewhere, coincide with those Ignacio Osorio Romero judges most prevalent in colonial Mexico: "[T]he cornerstone is Aristotle because all the other rhetors learned from him; next is Quintilian, because he found a way to organize his teachings; and, as a mixture of both, [we have] Cicero, in whom are found not only the doctrine but also the best practice" ("el pilar básico es Aristóteles porque de él bebieron todos los retóricos; a su lado se encuentran Quintiliano, porque supo organizar su enseñanza y, como compendio de ambos, Cicerón, en quien se encuentra no sólo la doctrina sino también la mejor práctica"; *Conquistar* 205; my trans.).

Sor Juana Inés de la Cruz: Three Hundred Years of Controversy and Counting

Nina M. Scott

Teaching about the tangled personal and ecclesiastical politics of Sor Juana's final years can be a real challenge in the undergraduate classroom, especially since ours is a diverse, secular age and many students have little background in either Catholicism or convent life. Add to this the convoluted and coded manner in which many documents were written, and the challenge is even greater. The last twenty years have seen a number of good translations of Sor Juana's key works, but engaging students with these issues is not easy. I have taught Sor Juana in undergraduate survey courses and in translation, to students with limited background and knowledge of Spanish, as well as on the graduate level. One way I have found to make her accessible and interesting to the undergraduate is to concentrate on the heated controversies that always surrounded her, both during her lifetime and more recently among contemporary scholars who have unearthed and examined new information on Sor Juana's final years. At the end of this essay I list the key players and a timetable of events to facilitate understanding of this charged period.

It is no secret that Sor Juana ruffled feathers in her time. That she was a gifted poet, beautiful, intelligent, and already famous when she chose the veil irremediably altered the way she would live her life in the Hieronymite convent where she spent her adult years. Despite the assumption that nuns were to become "dead to the world" when they chose the religious life, she maintained her ties to the viceregal court and continued to write a great deal of secular poetry. Her ecclesiastical supervisors criticized her for the worldliness of her pen: exquisite love sonnets, but also some very bawdy variations thereof (1: 284–87); "Hombres necios"("Foolish Men"), satiric verses decrying the double standard of the sexes (1: 228); a swipe at the dubious paternity of a critic who had alluded to her illegitimacy (1: 230); and the romantic comedy *Los empeños de una casa* (*House of Desires*), in which a male servant cross-dresses as a woman (4: 3–184). It was her bad luck that this play was performed just when the new archbishop of Mexico, Francisco de Aguiar y Seijas, came to assume his post (in 1683). Sor Juana worked some compliments to the new prelate into the introduction of this play but did not know that Aguiar thought all theater immoral. Furthermore, that one of his nuns dared to write plays made him her enemy from the start.

When she turned to theology, because women were not allowed to engage in interpretation of scripture, especially not in public, she was also criticized. In 1690 she had taken the famous Portuguese Jesuit Antonio Vieira to task for constructing what to her was an illogical example of speculative theology (see Wray, this volume). Sor Juana critiqued his published sermon, and this critique was subsequently published—without her knowledge or consent, she claimed—by Manuel Fernández de Santa Cruz, bishop of the city of Puebla, a cleric who greatly admired her. When the bishop sent her the publication, which he entitled the *Carta atenagórica* ("Letter Worthy of Athena") (4: 412–39), he also sent the nun an open letter censuring her worldly ways and advising her to pay more attention to the word of God and less to "las rateras noticias del mundo" ("the petty affairs of the world" [4: 696; my trans.]). The bishop signed the letter "Sister Filotea," as though the reproof came from a sister nun instead of a male bishop, but everyone was aware of the writer's true identity. Again the archbishop was incensed: what gave a nun the right to dispute a venerated preacher, especially of the Jesuit order, and to engage in public exegesis? Perhaps he had not noticed Sor Juana's surreptitious interpretation of many religious topics in the *villancicos* ("carols") she wrote for religious festivals.

A third aspect of her writing that caused offense was her persistent defense of women and their right to an intellectual life. This argument is emphatically presented in her last cycle of *villancicos,* written in 1691 in honor of Saint Catherine of Alexandria (2: 163–81), a legendary martyr whose intellectual and rhetorical skills confounded kings and made her the patron saint of nuns as well as philosophers. In the same year Sor Juana, stung by the bishop of Puebla's censure of her, composed her famous *Respuesta a sor Filotea* (4: 440–75), a personal, impassioned, and detailed defense of a woman's right to use her God-given intellect.

As the *Respuesta* affirms, Sor Juana's last years were difficult. The viceroy, the Marquis of la Laguna, and his wife, the Countess of Paredes, who had been Sor Juana's patrons, friends, and protectors since 1680, were recalled to Spain in 1688. Sor Juana was thus left alone to face the wrath of not only the archbishop but also her former confessor, the powerful Jesuit Antonio Núñez de Miranda. The countess had been able to publish the first volume of Sor Juana's writings in Madrid and was influential in bringing out a second volume in 1692, perhaps a mixed blessing, since it contained the *Carta atenagórica* and elicited a polemical reaction to her critique all over again.

At the beginning of 1694 Sor Juana signed a number of documents renewing her vows, lamenting her sins, and calling herself "la peor del mundo" ("the worst in the world" [4: 523; my trans.]). Two of these she signed in her own blood, a common act among nuns of her time. Sor Juana died of a virulent and unknown disease in April 1695, two months after the death of her confessor.

The third volume of her works, *Fama y obras pósthumas* (*Fame and Posthumous Works*), was published in Spain in 1700, edited by a Mexican cleric, Juan Ignacio de Castorena y Ursúa. It contained the first biography of the nun, written by a Spanish Jesuit, Diego Calleja (Maza, *Sor Juana* 139–53). In 1702 another Jesuit, Juan de Oviedo, published a biography of Sor Juana's confessor, Núñez de Miranda, and included a chapter devoted to the strained relations between the nun and her spiritual father (Maza 278–82). These are the first biographies of Sor Juana. They present the nun as a far different person from the rebellious and skilled rhetorician of the *Respuesta*. Calleja and Oviedo both described a woman who had seen the error of her ways, renounced the vanity of worldly fame, voluntarily sold her magnificent library to give the proceeds to the poor, and embraced humility and ultimate silence. Sor Juana disciplined her body so severely that she had to be restrained, said Oviedo (Maza 281), whereas Calleja related that she died a virtuous death after nursing her sister nuns (Maza 152–53). The problem with this hagiographic portrait is that it ran against the grain of all that she had stood for before, leaving scholars with a seemingly insoluble puzzle and many conflicting theories, ranging from a genuine conversion and transformation into a "model nun" (Lavrin, "Unlike" 80) to playing possum until times became more favorable again.

Several discoveries of new materials relating to the nun's life—as well as reevaluations of previous finds—have made Sor Juana scholarship particularly exciting in recent years. I have never found it hard to transmit this excitement to students. It is primarily a question of examining documents and asking students how they change what we assumed before. Archival research is often similar to a detective's quest for evidence, and students can certainly become involved in following this process of evaluating the clues found in documents. For example, in 1980 Aureliano Tapia Méndez discovered in the archdiocesan archives of Monterrey, Mexico, a contemporary copy of a letter written in 1681 by Sor Juana to Núñez, dismissing him as her confessor. Tapia Méndez called me shortly before the 1986 Latin American Studies Association meeting in Boston, for which I had assembled a distinguished panel of Sor Juana scholars: Georgina Sabat de Rivers, Marie-Cécile Bénassy-Berling, Electa Arenal, and Rosa Perelmuter. He told me of his find and asked for time to introduce it during my panel, which I gladly gave him. His discovery was a bombshell, because the "Monterrey Letter" turned out to be a preliminary and more strident version of the *Respuesta*. It indicated the degree of safety and protection that the viceroys afforded Sor Juana during these years, since she dared to tell her former confessor that she resented his public criticism of her; that he had no direct jurisdiction over her body, mind, or soul; and that she would appreciate his not thinking about her at all. I translated this letter as soon as I could, since I felt it was a very important contribution to the primary sources of her life ("If"). For example, scholars had always assumed that Núñez had organized the considerable dowry Sor Juana needed to join her convent, but this letter reveals that she got the money herself from a wealthy relative. The find substantially shifted scholars' perception of the power relationship between them.

The three-hundredth anniversary of Sor Juana's death was celebrated in 1995 in Mexico with two important conferences: one in April, the month of her death, in Toluca and another in November, the month she was born, at the university that now occupies her former convent. The historian Elías Trabulse from the Colegio de México, a prestigious graduate institution, has long been known as one of the most dedicated and accomplished of archival researchers in Mexico. A rumor began to circulate at the conference that he had an important new find to share; as a result the conference hall was packed when he rose to speak. Trabulse did not disappoint: he unveiled a highly coded letter in prose and poetry, written in 1691, one month before Sor Juana wrote the *Respuesta*, signed by one "Seraphina de Christo," who belonged to the same convent as Sor Juana. It defended Sor Juana against the attacks of a "blind soldier," which Trabulse felt was a reference to Núñez: Jesuits are known as soldiers of Christ, and the confessor's eyesight was practically gone by that date. In the letter Serafina referred directly to the *Carta atenagórica* and, coupling that with the allusions to the "blind soldier," led Trabulse to surmise that Sor Juana's criticism of Vieira was in fact a veiled attack on her former confessor. Furthermore, Trabulse had checked the names of nuns living in the Hieronymite convent in 1691, and there was no one with the name of Serafina. Finally, he showed the audience a comparison of Sor Juana's and Serafina's signatures, which appeared to be remarkably similar, leading him to conclude that Sor Juana had written the letter herself. I certainly was convinced. It was an incredibly exciting discovery, especially if one had the good fortune to be present when it was initially announced. The letter, if indeed authored by Sor Juana, would change our perceptions of the guarded language of the *Respuesta*. I remember going home to share this information with my graduate seminar and welcomed the palpable excitement of my students at being among the first to know of Serafina.

In November Trabulse had more treasures to share. First, he had found proof of a secret inquisitorial trial that the archbishop brought against the nun in 1693. When she was found guilty, the archbishop then had the right to confiscate her library and her personal property, which he did (Trabulse, "Silencio" 146). But Trabulse had more to tell: for the last nine years of her life Sor Juana had been the convent accountant, a heavy burden on her time, since the convent had many possessions and expenses, but one that she never renounced, not even when she was hounded by the archbishop and Núñez at the end of her life. Customarily, another accountant from the archbishop's staff, Mateo Ortiz de Torres, reviewed her books annually and signed off on them. Trabulse revealed that Sor Juana had made some substantial investments with a rich banker without the permission of the archbishop ("Mayordomo" 26–27); even more startlingly, she did this in 1692 and 1693, the years of greatest persecution, and with Ortiz's knowledge. Her investments, in Trabulse's opinion, showed that far from capitulating, she was looking toward the future. Both findings thus significantly undermined the conversion narratives by Calleja and Oviedo.

At the same conference another discovery was unveiled, one for which scholars had been searching for years: the inventory of Sor Juana's cell on her death. The historian Teresa Castelló de Yturbide had come into possession of this inventory, which was copied from the convent archives in 1842 or 1843 at the behest of Justo Gómez, Count of la Cortina, an important official who was interested in possibly acquiring some of the objects that had belonged to Sor Juana (Trabulse, *Muerte* 57). The inventory was highly significant, since many religious archives were destroyed in the 1860s, when religious institutions were closed and their property expropriated. Documents that were not destroyed at that time disappeared during the revolution (1910–20), so the survival of this copy seemed miraculous. The most important objects listed in Sor Juana's cell were "un estante con ciento ochenta volúmenes de obras selectas [y] quince legajos de escritos, versos místicos y mundanos" ("a bookcase with one hundred eighty volumes of selected works [and] fifteen bundles of writings, mystic and secular poetry" [Castelló 177; my trans.]). Here, then, was another indication that Sor Juana had not been silenced before her death.

These three finds caused a seismic shift in Sor Juana scholarship, especially as they demanded revision of her final years. I recall sitting in the audience with goose bumps on my arms and tears in my eyes: finally, proof positive that Sor Juana had never given in to the pressures of the Mexican clerics who were hounding her. Many scholars immediately began to distribute Trabulse's and Castelló's findings, and Trabulse himself published a series of articles and short books on the subject. There were, however, two problems with what he wrote: the hypothesis that Sor Juana and Serafina might be one and the same quickly became accepted as fact; and there was, overall, an unsettling lack of footnotes and sources. Naturally, scholars noticed this problem but did not say much about it, since so many of us loved what Trabulse had to say. His 1998 essay "El silencio final de Sor Juana" ("Sor Juana's Ultimate Silence") neatly tied up all manner of loose ends, particularly because it explained how the archbishop was able to recast Sor Juana's biography in the hagiographic mode that had bothered many *sorjuanistas* for three hundred years. This article, however, also lacked documentation of sources. Trabulse began to make amends for this problem with the publication in 2000 of *La muerte de Sor Juana*, which has many substantive footnotes, but he still has not revealed his sources for the secret trial against the nun. Despite the bibliographic vacuum, Trabulse's theories have been incorporated into many recent studies on Sor Juana. This is not to say that his conclusions are either wrong or implausible—indeed, I hope they are not—but until we have documented proof we must be very careful in what we teach our students. Marie-Cécile Bénassy-Berling, who has analyzed these scholarly controversies in depth, hopes for more discoveries but in the meantime counsels a healthy dose of doubt ("Actualidad" 286).

Back to Serafina. In 1998 a serious controversy erupted when Antonio Alatorre, Trabulse's colleague at the Colegio de México and a superb Sor Juana scholar, published, with Martha Lilia Tenorio, *Serafina y Sor Juana*, which openly challenged Trabulse's theories on this topic. By consulting a handwriting expert, they debunked the similarities in the signatures. They also stated that the lack of elegance and overblown rhetoric of Serafina's text, as well as her clumsy theology, ran counter to Sor Juana's usual style (88), an observation that another critic had also made (Pascual Buxó, *Sor Juana* 118). Alatorre and Tenorio, whose text is very well documented, were quick to attack Trabulse for not revealing his sources (116). Alatorre has a reputation for irascibility and did little to hide his disdain for his colleague's work, classifying it as "una novela por entregas" ("a serial novel" [113; my trans.]), full of unsubstantiated conjectures. However, Alatorre and Tenorio are often guilty of the same offenses, and their work features abundant hypotheses and speculations in such phrases as "quien escribió esta carta bien puede haber sido" ("the person who wrote this letter may well have been" [117; my trans.]), or "según pensamos, Calleja no hizo sino repetir lo que Oviedo le habrá contado" ("according to what we think, Calleja only repeated what Oviedo must have told him" [118; my trans.]). In their opinion Serafina was actually Castorena y Ursúa, the editor of Sor Juana's posthumous works. To be fair, Alatorre and Tenorio themselves recognize that because of the lack of documentation of Sor Juana's last years, "[n]o queda más remedio que echarse a imaginar, cada cual por su lado" ("there is no alternative than to begin to imagine, each one in his own way" [127; my trans.]), which is what so many scholars have done and will probably continue to do.

Serafina's letter was roundly questioned, but we still had the inventory to prove that Sor Juana kept on writing until the day she died. Or did we? The historian Nuria Salazar Simarro raised some serious questions about the authenticity of the inventory in a study she published in 2001. First of all, the Count of la Cortina, for whom the existence of such an inventory would have been fortuitous, especially if he actually had acquired some of her possessions, had a rather shady reputation as an art collector (208). Salazar Simarro, who had examined seventy similar inventories of nuns' cells, was also struck by two other points: the use of the word "pupitre" ("desk") appears neither in the other inventories she examined nor in the 1732 *Diccionario de autoridades* she consulted; and the reference to a "catre de tijera" ("scissor-legged cot") is also unique to Sor Juana's inventory. All other inventories listed beds and the wood from which they were made. Salazar Simarro, an expert on the material culture of the convents, articulated considerable skepticism about the inventory. Clearly, it is in the details of archival research that theories are made and broken.

One last document, the authenticity of which has occasioned no controversy, is the collection of poems that Sor Juana apparently wrote around 1693, the *Enigmas ofrecidos a la Casa del Placer* ("Enigmas Offered to the House of Pleasure"). Despite the somewhat racy title, these poems were intended for aristocratic nuns in a Lisbon convent. They are in essence rhymed puzzles that must be deciphered to find their solution. Sabat de Rivers and Alatorre have both written on the intriguing circumstances surrounding the composition of these poems. Apparently the Portuguese nuns heard of Sor Juana from the Countess of Paredes, who, with her relative the Duchess of Aveyro, urged them to ask Sor Juana for these poems, a good example of the solidarity between noblewomen and educated nuns (Sabat de Rivers, *Busca* 219). There is a printed title page dated 1695 (Alatorre, *Enigmas* 71), several introductory poems, including one by the countess to her "Amiga" (Alatorre, *Enigmas* 83–85), and the

Enigmas themselves. These poems were discovered in manuscript form in Spain in 1968 but somehow overlooked by scholars until recently. The *Fama y obras póstumas* (1700) does not include them, which Trabulse plausibly conjectured was because the archbishop blocked their publication. Had they been published, they too would have undermined Calleja and Oviedo, who stated that in her last years Sor Juana had renounced writing and worldly pursuits. Whatever the circumstances, the *Enigmas* showed that Sor Juana was indeed continuing to write in 1692–93 (Sabat de Rivers, *Busca* 220). In the *Fama,* Juan Ignacio Castorena y Ursúa included one other poem, *romance* 51 (1: 158–61), which he said was found in incomplete form in Sor Juana's cell after she died. It includes the famous lines: "y diversa de mí misma / entre vuestras plumas ando, no como soy, sino como / quisisteis imaginarlo" ("I go among your pens, different from myself, not as I am but as you wished to imagine me" [1: 159; Luciani, *Literary Self-Fashioning* 140]). These lines could well be Sor Juana's message to the world.

The ever-elusive nun thus remains a mystery and a bone of contention to the end, as much in her own age as ours. But she stirs our passions still. As one of my undergraduates said of her, "Sor Juana rocks!"

Sor Juana's Principal Contemporaries

The Marquesses of la Laguna. Viceroys of Mexico from 1680 to 1686. Returned to Spain in 1688. María Luisa, the Countess of Paredes, was Sor Juana's patroness and close friend. She oversaw the publication of the first two volumes of Sor Juana's works.

Francisco de Aguiar y Seijas. Archbishop of Mexico and a powerful adversary.

Antonio Núñez de Miranda. Jesuit. Sor Juana's confessor and spiritual father. She dismissed him in 1681 but recalled him in 1693.

Manuel Fernández de Santa Cruz. Bishop of Puebla de los Angeles and the "Sor Filotea" who sent Sor Juana a letter of censure along with the published *Carta atenagórica*.

Antonio Vieira. Portuguese Jesuit, known as a famous preacher and theologian. He and Sor Juana never met, but she wrote a critique of one of his sermons, the *Carta atenagórica.*

Juan Ignacio de Castorena y Ursúa. Mexican cleric. Editor of the 1700 *Fama*, in which Sor Juana's last writings were published posthumously.

Diego Calleja. Spanish Jesuit and Sor Juana's first biographer.

Juan de Oviedo. Mexican Colombian Jesuit. Núñez's biographer.

Chronology for the Years 1680–1702

1680 Arrival of the Marquesses of La Laguna as viceroys of Mexico
1681 (1682?) Sor Juana dismisses Núñez as her confessor

1683 Sor Juana writes the play *Los empeños de una casa*. Aguiar y Seijas, the new archbishop of Mexico, arrives in Mexico City
1688 Departure of the viceroys
1689 Publication of volume 1 of Sor Juana's works in Madrid.
1690 (Nov.) Publication by the bishop of Puebla of the *Carta atenagórica* and the "Carta de Sor Filotea"
1691 (Feb.) Letter by Serafina de Cristo
(March) *Respuesta a sor Filotea*
Villancicos to Saint Catherine of Alexandria
1692 Publication of volume 2 of Sor Juana's works in Seville
1693 According to Elías Trabulse, Sor Juana is subjected to a secret inquisitorial trial
Sor Juana writes the *Enigmas ofrecidos a la Casa del Placer*.
1694 Secret trial ends, according to Trabulse
(Feb.–Mar.) Sor Juana signs several documents of abjuration, some in her own blood
1695 (Feb.) Death of Núñez
(17 Apr.) Sor Juana's death
1698 Death of Archbishop Aguiar y Seijas.
1699 Death of Manuel Fernández de Santa Cruz, the bishop of Puebla (Sor Filotea)
1700 In Madrid, Castorena y Ursúa publishes the *Fama y obras póstumas*, the third volume of Sor Juana's works, which contains the *Respuesta a sor Filotea* and the biography by Calleja
1702 Oviedo publishes his biography of Núñez

The Final Silence of Sor Juana: The Abysmal Remove of Her Closing Night

Geoff Guevara-Geer

> Now the sirens have a still more fatal weapon than their song, namely their silence . . . someone might possibly have escaped from their singing; but from their silence never.
>
> —Franz Kafka

> When we read Sor Juana, we must recognize the silence surrounding her words.
>
> —Octavio Paz

> . . . one absence multiplies infinite presences.
>
> —Sor Juana Inés de la Cruz

Even from afar—from a distance of more than three centuries and a vast cultural remove—Sor Juana Inés de la Cruz is an intriguing figure for scholars and students alike. A difficult writer who lived in a world determinedly detached from modernity, Sor Juana still manages to draw in new readers generally unfamiliar with the tradition of New Spain and the baroque canon that frame her works. A consummate poet, Sor Juana proves herself able to do poetic justice to the widest variety of verse forms with Golden Age virtuosity. More controversially—and more intriguingly to those new to her work—she dared to speculate, with feminist prescience, on women's issues from a convent in seventeenth-century New Spain and, even more dangerously, to engage in theological sparring with the ecclesiastical hierarchy. And there the trail goes cold: whether by censure or abdication, her intellectual and literary production dwindles to next to nothing for the last two years of her life: only some poems, such as those contained in *Enigmas*, are extant. As Sor Juana recedes into the far distance of her own withdrawal, her pages run the double risk—for today's readers—of becoming the martyr's testimony or the cautionary tale.

In what follows, I would like to treat Sor Juana's silence not as a heroically delimited dead end but as an invitation that permeated her work and animated the desire for knowledge that so impassioned her. I hope to draw reachable, teachable conclusions while respecting the irreducible otherness of Sor Juana's withdrawal, a withdrawal that can be seen as a projection of certain features of her work. To state my paradox most bluntly: I hope to respect her distance so that we might read her work more closely. In this approach, her *Primero sueño* ("First Dream"), *Carta atenagórica* ("Missive Worthy of Athena"), and *Respuesta a Sor Filotea* ("Answer to Sor Filotea") will be of critical importance.

Although it may seem puzzling to read silence as a quality that enables the reader to read Sor Juana better, I hope to establish precisely this, not only for the scholar but also for the teacher and, ultimately, for the student. While the New Spanish nun cannot be reasonably fashioned into an uppity writer who contested patriarchal empire with overt resistance, the openings she daringly cleared for herself in her writing are both seductive and admirable in ways that students can appreciate. In bringing this to the classroom, it will be necessary to understand and articulate the polemics and dialogues from which Sor Juana withdrew. Such devices as prosody and mythical allusion, although vibrantly alive in Sor Juana's work, are not enough to sensitize students to Sor Juana's contribution. Silence, like a departed ship, responds to the currents around it and, in turn, leaves a wake behind. The slipstream of Sor Juana, students should be told, moves on and through any substantial anthology of Spanish American literature. Hers has become a submerged and subtle tow, but her draw can be felt and shared. It is clear that she has made her mark, but to appreciate the traces of her unfinished project—to contextualize her mark—we must venture beyond the clear and into the unsaid.

That silence can be meaningful may not be immediately obvious, but Sor Juana's silence has been particularly productive for critics. Most notably, Octavio Paz and Stephanie Merrim—certainly two of the most dedicated and astute readers of Sor Juana—read her silent remove in very different ways, and my contention here is that more remains to be said about Sor Juana's saying nothing.

Paz, in his landmark work *Sor Juana; or, The Traps of Faith* sees a sort of Mexicanness avant la lettre in Sor Juana's departure from writing. Although Merrim criticizes Paz for this cultural approach, his notion of Mexican cultural continuity pushes him to great lengths in reconstructing Sor Juana's culture. Paz's book is, in fact and interpretation, prodigiously grounded in her world. He dedicates hundreds of pages to the explications of her cloistered colonial surroundings and, never a facile determinist, is attentive to Sor Juana's detachment in those surroundings. Still, at certain moments, Paz reads her obstacles as already emblematic of a decidedly Mexican sense of oppression. We read, for example, that "[i]t is scarcely necessary to point out the similarities between Sor Juana's personal situations and the obstacles we Mexicans have experienced during the process of modernization" (476), a conspicuous omission in a book of nearly 550 pages. It is this sense of legacy, and even identification—reverentially offered and lovingly pursued—that has Paz describe his book as "a Mexican's reading of the work of a nun of seventeenth-century New Spain" (7). Paz is dedicated to refashioning the culture of Sor Juana that silenced her or, as he puts it more poetically, to transforming her from "a great writer into a mute penitent" (488). In doing so, he reads—with lament—her literary remove, a real-life remove to the convent and within the convent that became, finally, a remove from literature. It is this final move—from sisterly solitude to her ultimate silence—that clearly "seduces" Paz (2). Sor Juana's withdrawal leaves a vacuum that draws him in: "Why did she renounce her lifelong passion for writing and learning? Was that renunciation the result of a conversion or an abdication? This book is an attempt to answer such questions as these" (2). Far from a baroque *horror vacui*, Paz's hugely influential book, offered as a resuscitation of Sor Juana, was clearly animated, not despite but because of Sor Juana's silence.

Merrim points out in an essay that is both explicitly indebted to Paz and critical of lapses in his book that "Octavio Paz once again rehearses the notions of 'Mexican masks' and the alternation between solitude and communion familiar to readers of his other essays" ("Toward" 16). Clearly taken by Sor Juana, but not taken with what she will come to call Paz's "national pride" (*Early Modern* 51), Merrim will also endeavor to bring Sor Juana from solitude into community. However, Merrim's solidarity with Sor Juana is based on gender, not culture. Although she also approaches Sor Juana's literary silence attentively, the community she offers is feminist. Thus, for Merrim, Sor Juana's silence—her lifelong seclusion, her predilection for solitary speculation, and her final disappearance from the page—is not eccentric and particular to Sor Juana, nor is it a manifestation of a particularly Mexican silence; it is the lot of the woman writer in the seventeenth century. In *Early Modern Women's Writing and Sor Juana Inés de la Cruz*, Merrim explicitly resists "Octavio Paz's interpretation of Sor Juana's solitude as 'characteristically Mexican' " (xxiii) and asserts that her retreat into "book-lined cells . . . renders her very isolation from her female contemporaries central and emblematic rather than ex-centric" (xxiii).

In short, Sor Juana's silence admits at least two readings: she was silent as a *Mexicana*, for Paz, and silenced as an early modern woman writer, for Merrim. In both cases, Sor Juana is to be taken from her solitude—a solitude that she clearly treasured, complaining as she did of "the noise of a community [that] interfere[s] with the tranquil stillness of my books" (Trueblood 212). She is also to be resuscitated among communities of readers.

What is needed to understand Sor Juana at her remove is an approach to her solitude that does not feed back into community, into Paz's anticipated Mexico or Merrim's "de facto sorority" (*Early Modern* xxiii). Such a pedagogical maneuver is particularly difficult and requires, it seems to me, deft metaphors. This is because students, though often prepared to imagine a matrix of virtual reality, are often prone to plug it into an underground community immediately. Such a receptive community was terribly elusive for Sor Juana, especially as the viceregal currents shifted to capsize her. The space Sor Juana opened for herself is better understood as a literary remove than a social embrace of her work.

Maurice Blanchot offers such an alternative solitude and a different silence—not of a silence that belongs to Sor Juana but a silence to which Sor Juana's writing belongs. In his book *The Space of Literature*—for which, tellingly, his translator Ann Smock considered proposing the title "The Remove of Literature" (11)—Blanchot makes of silence not just an end but an inchoately productive beginning. In this Blanchot seems to agree with Michel Foucault's negative affirmation: "Because this [type of] emptiness is not a lack, it does not prescribe a gap to fill. It is nothing more, nothing less, than a space where it is finally possible once again to think" (qtd. in Baker 19). Although written in 1955, before Paz's and Merrim's mature treatments of Sor Juana, Blanchot's notion of solitude comprehends Paz's silence as an existential withdrawal and Merrim's notion of personal isolation. *The Space of Literature* opens with a chapter titled "The Solitude of the Work" (21), a solitude that is as enabling as it is limiting, since it makes the work come into being while sanctioning off that sphere of being, even for—and especially for—the writer:

> He whose life depends upon the work, either because he is a writer or because he is a reader, belongs to the solitude of that which expresses nothing except the word *being*: the word which language shelters by hiding it, or causes to appear when language itself disappears into the silent void of the work. (Blanchot 22)

Although counterintuitive, Blanchot introduces two ideas worth keeping here, one needy of revision. The first, already introduced, is that the writer belongs to solitude, not incidentally but necessarily: it is the condition of writing. The second is that the being of writing—of literary space—is a realm unto itself, a realm that one can only enter by renouncing other, worldlier citizenships. The idea that requires tweaking—an idea here rendered in the English "he" and gendered in the original French—is that literary space is essentially masculine. Although Blanchot's infelicitous pronouns would exclude Sor Juana, I see no reason why his literary space must be seen as exclusively gendered. In fact, Blanchot is quite clear that this "essential solitude" of the literary work "excludes the complacent isolation of individualism" (21), an identity dispersion that might well blur, without erasing, such attributes as gender. This transcendence could well dovetail with Sor Juana's often-repeated claims of a certain gender neutrality, as when she writes, in *romance* 19 "pues sabes tú que las almas / distancia ignoran y sexo" ("for the soul, as you well know, ignores distance and gender" [1: 57; my trans.]). Without collapsing Sor Juana's Neoplatonic gender neutrality of the soul with Blanchot's (presciently) poststructuralist notion of writing, it is clear that Sor Juana longed for the freedom and, yes, even the solitude of the written page. As she divulges in her account in the *Respuesta* (*The Answer*) of a desire to cross-dress (Trueblood 211)—a simulation fashioned to help her gain entrance to the university and its libraries—Sor Juana was willing to misrepresent her gender socially to enter into the textual realm of ideas.

I must confess to taking certain liberties with Blanchot. It is clear from the start that the solitude he "intend[s] to invoke" is not the "artist's solitude" (21) but rather the solitude of the work, which maintains a certain distance even from its flesh-and-blood writer. To invoke Sor Juana's biographical obstacles on the way to her desk, though clearly and hugely decisive, is meant only as that, as an obstacle on the way to the promising remove of literary space, even if this promise is not personal.

Sor Juana's inscription into literary space will happen, then, in her texts. Primary among these is the *Primero sueño* ("First Dream"), a work that she owns more fully than others, perhaps precisely because she belongs to it. She writes in the *Respuesta* that "I have never written anything of my own volition, but always at the request, and to the specifications, of others. So much so that the only thing I can remember writing for my own pleasure is a trifle called *The Dream*" (Trueblood 239). "First Dream," which she claims only through this trifling humility topic, projects itself into that inner sanctum of literary space that Blanchot calls "the *other* night" (163), a nocturnal time that corresponds—in its inalienable otherness—to literary space and that will neither be domesticated by diurnal concerns nor be known, even by the most penetrating insight. Blanchot writes, in a section tellingly titled "The Dream," of this other night's lure. It is as if he were reflecting on Sor Juana's poetic transgression of being a woman writing away from the world: "People who sleep badly always appear more or less guilty. What do they do? They make night present" (265). This night described by Blanchot, this *other* night that resists worldly presence and establishes its own only fleetingly, is what Sor Juana claims for herself in "First Dream"; it is what Merrim gestures toward describing when she writes, "the *Sueño*'s space creates its own time outside time" (*Early Modern* 236), although even this formulation is perhaps too quickly recuperated in her project in a larger, more grounded "landscape." Paradoxically, even impossibly, Sor Juana claims this other night as her own and immediately discovers that it is not to be possessed. In the language of the first stanza of "First Dream," read through Alan S. Trueblood's translation, the night that tries to move heavenward must turn back before the "splendid lights" of the stars and renounce that "shadowy war / which the dreadful moving shade / was waging in gaseous blackness" (171). More prosaically, that other understanding, that very poetic understanding that seeks to know and to expand its knowledge throughout the cosmos, is halted immediately—"stopped short" (171), already in the tenth line—but it is not extinguished. The trials of that understanding, utterly speculative and obscurely veiled through symbols that reroute us through so many poetic traditions, are the only matter of "First Dream." This speculative poem is—in a literal mise en abyme of Sor Juana's work—a truncated attempt at total knowledge that explicitly fails, leaving the reader fading traces of possible projected paths.

Clearly, sharing Sor Juana's "First Dream" in the classroom will require a special pedagogical effort. Even in these pages, where I may expect a certain patience from the informed reader, I have streamlined arguments and retreated to straightforward translations of "First Dream." Although primary in understanding Sor Juana, actually reading "First Dream" should, perhaps, only be a prerequisite for graduate students. For undergraduates, the plot of the intellectual voyage of the soul may be presented as introductory material—the synopsis of an ellipsis, so to speak. Teachers can convey that crucial citations, like those above, are the steps with which Sor Juana takes her leave. She thus establishes herself outside the establishment and sheds those trappings of worldly presence where, for example, authors smile at readers from book jackets. Bringing students to the understanding that Sor Juana's is a *poetic* knowledge and that "First Dream" is, as stated above, a literal mise en abyme of Sor Juana's knowledge, may necessitate, ironically, a prosaic treatment. "First Dream" is Sor Juana at her most abysmally silent, and uninitiated students may need to be told that before wading into other texts.

In this initial standstill, where the soul is paralyzed in its quest for total knowledge, "First Dream" is like Stephane Mallarmé's poem "Igitur" as read by Blanchot in *Literary Space*: it is the beginning of an other understanding that is underway only once the time of day is stopped and the space of the world is held at bay. Literary space, the time of the other night, is the anteroom of Sor Juana's understanding, and the reader is not granted entry—one can only glimpse Sor Juana's withdrawal. Blanchot's remarks on Mallarmé fit the experience of reading "First Dream": critique can only produce "remarks on language [that] tend to acknowledge the word's ability to make things absent, to evoke them in this absence, and then to remain faithful to this value of absence, realizing it completely in a supreme and silent disappearance" (109). Sor Juana has withdrawn in "First Dream" and will not be made present.

Such a "supreme and silent disappearance" is tragically explicit at one other point in Sor Juana's career: in the damning theological remark in her "athenagoric missive" about divine withdrawal from creation. While evaluating God's benefactions toward humanity Sor Juana concludes that, given his generous nature, "más le cuesta a Dios el no hacernos beneficios que no el hacérnoslos y, por consiguiente, mayor fineza es el suspenderlos que el ejecutarlos" ("it is more difficult for God to withhold his benefactions than to give them freely such that it is a greater benefaction to withhold benefactions than to grant them" [4: 436; my trans.]). This apparently innocuous remark, a culmination of the obtuse and syllogistic prose of many pages, amounts to saying that God's benevolence is most manifest when withdrawn. Here, shrewdly and dangerously, the nun writes to her clerical audience (the bishop of Puebla) that evidence of absence is the most convincing argument for presence. Even theologically, in another detour through textual citation, Sor Juana resists the metaphysics of presence and keeps a distance, both ontologically and epistemologically, from God: his being must be another kind of being, knowledge of him another kind of knowledge. The God Sor Juana argues for is a withdrawn God, just as she is the disappearing author of the literary project that best encapsulates her career, "First Dream." In both cases, dissemination issues into apparent absence: the work thematizes its own failure and dissolution. It is the appearance of the frustrated, awakened soul at the end of "First Dream," the mundane soul that rejoins humanity goaded by its body and daily concerns, that marks the end of the poetic generally, and this poem in particular. It is the appearance of Sor Juana, the seventeenth-century nun of New Spain, at the expense of Sor Juana, the consummate poet consumed by poetry. It is this simultaneous appearance and disappearance, this flip-flop of presence and absence, that I hoped to introduce by reintroducing Sor Juana's divine dismissal from my epigraph, "one absence multiplies infinite presences" ("una ausencia multiplica múltiples presencias" [4: 415; my trans.]), taken from her *Carta atenagórica.*

This impenetrable otherness, this abysmal withdrawal, is more than Paz endorses when he writes, in the foreword of *The Traps of Faith* (also in my epigraph), "When we read Sor Juana, we must recognize the silence surrounding her words" (6). Paz recognizes that "she did not long to be penetrated by divine light," but he goes on to insist, "she wanted, with the light of reason, to penetrate the opaque mysteries of all things" (477). My contention here is that this "light of reason" is limited and that Sor Juana knew this, opting, as she did, for the impossible freedom of "First Dream," a sort of sleep of reason that would deliver her beyond the monsters of censure and inquisition to an inquiry without end. Without falling into the traps that would make "an edifying example of her fall" one may—perhaps cheekily—ultimately read Sor Juana's transgressive night as able to withstand her unconvincing final "conversion," which Paz rightly puts in scare quotes (*Traps* 488). To read her withdrawal as "not a defeat but a conversion"—or even vice versa—to read her conversion as a defeat—is to give too short shrift to the otherness of her projected position (488). Both accepting her conversion to orthodoxy and condemning it by the light of day dismiss her most impressive gesture as a writer: penning "First Dream" as if it could be extended into the infinity of literary space, as if there could be an other night with a second dream, with a third, and so on—an other life of other nights.

How can this obscure withdrawal to literary space enrich a classroom of students wishing to encounter the Sor Juana so often mightily introduced as victim or idol? The answer, too rarely offered even in classes on poetry, is that an instructor must approach the text reverentially and while respecting the limits of rational reading. This brings me to the most pithy statement of my pedagogical corrective: we must resist teaching both the romantic Sor Juana—the martyred heroine—and the enlightened Sor Juana—the darling of prosody and penetrating insight. To be sure, Sor Juana invites and requires careful, meticulous reading. But her work may well resist that kind of analysis that achieves insight through infiltration, and we would do well to respect this—to concede her a space of remove before rushing to render her a martyr or heroine. Sor Juana's work should be read but not rendered transparent by the light of day. It is better read by her own other night, as in "First Dream." I agree with Paz when he answers his own question, "Was [Sor Juana's] renunciation the result of a conversion or an abdication?" by stating that "the 'conversion' of Sor Juana leaves us nothing, absolutely nothing" (*Traps* 2, 488). The scare quotes would rightly have us question the choice of an articulate poet to become a "mute penitent." Her last "three pious declarations written in prose unworthy of her" are not distant from the world at a literary remove (488); they are absent as erasure in its most trite and banal manifestations, where genius is whitewashed and dissolved

TEACHING SOR JUANA IN THE TWENTY-FIRST CENTURY

Sor Juana's Love Poems Addressed to Women

Amanda Powell

Sor Juana's love poems to women present central but often overlooked or distorted aspects of her work. Their luxuriant language, employing the culturally charged rhetoric of Petrarchan courtship, signals the heightened emotion of erotic love, beyond the homage of what the modern world terms friendship. In a culture uneasy about sexuality in general and about homosexuality and lesbianism in particular, these poems are challenging for teachers to present and for students to encounter. This chapter identifies key strategies of such poems and presents one *romance* ("ballad") in particular as a pedagogical model. My discussion is intended for generalists who teach women writers and want to include more lesbian, historical, or international literature; for queer theorists who aim to treat historical and international writers; and for Hispanists familiar with Sor Juana or her early modern period who wonder how to deal with these homoerotic poems. These love poems to women invite, indeed require, queer readings; that is, the texts propose an alternative to the heterosexual-normative forms that they parody, creating an ironic instability that undermines seemingly immutable patriarchal values and icons. Sor Juana used humor to overturn prejudices and open out beyond heterosexist and misogynist constrictions; these poems are both eye opening and fun.[1]

Sor Juana especially interests women students (consciously feminist or not); lesbian, gay, bisexual, queer, or transgender students; and Latina/o, particularly Chicana/o, students, all of whom find in her a forebear of intellectual and literary renown.[2] Invariably the question arises: are Sor Juana's erotic poems to women "lesbian" texts? (Many students, a priori, either proudly claim or anxiously reject them as such.) When these poems are contextualized in the poet's work and era, they help to clarify the terms of our own cultural times, providing classroom touchstones for reconsidering the origins of our certainties.

Sor Juana addressed to three women more than forty poems that variously emphasize forms of love: devotion, admiration, passion; these constitute some twenty percent of her lyric poetry. The conventional pastoral names Laura, Lysi, Filis, and Elvira represent three aristocratic vicereines: Leonor Carreto, Marquise of Mancera; María Luisa Manrique de Lara y Gonzaga, Countess of Paredes, Marquise of la Laguna; and Elvira de Toledo, Countess of Galve. Sor Juana enjoyed real-life friendship and patronage with each celebrated woman. By contrast, while she wrote love poems with male addressees, none is directed to a stated, extraliterary beloved. Because Sor Juana's extensive personal correspondence is lost, we cannot investigate what took place between the poet and the recipients of these courtship poems: did the texts strengthen the poet's friendships, increase patronage, or elicit steamy embraces? (Such evidentiary information is rarely demanded to establish the heterosexuality of erotic poetry [see Vicinus 59].)

The late twentieth century brought to view a wealth of testimonies of women's and men's passionate homosocial and homosexual relations from the sixteenth to the twentieth centuries. Lillian Faderman placed early modern women's same-sex relations under the rubric "romantic friendship"; her assertion that "most of the female romantic friends that I was studying did not have sexual relationships" is questioned by numerous critics: must relationships be "genital" to be termed sexual, as opposed to friendly (Faderman, *Surpassing* 17, 16)? Again, why are expressions of same-sex passion submitted to a filtering scrutiny not applied to the records of heterosexual alliances? While an important category (especially for the eighteenth- and nineteenth-century contexts that coined and used it), "romantic friendship" is problematic as a catch-all explanation for this discourse. In treating English early modern texts, Laurie Shannon usefully remarks on "the gaping distance between early modern 'homonormative' affects and contemporary heterosexual, erotic normativity" (1). If the love poems by Sor Juana considered here address "friends," then this "friendship" evokes ardent and melting declarations using language figures found elsewhere in the period in avowals of passionate (heterosexual) love.

What then to call Sor Juana's love poems to women, and the sort of love they represent? The term *lesbian,* for instance, connoting modern concepts of identity founded in sexuality, does not perfectly fit modes of the past—or even of the present, as the current critique of identity politics illuminates. However, this observation does not render lesbianism itself anachronistic for the seventeenth century; indeed, sexualized, eroticized, amatory relationships between women remain identifiable across eras and cultures. Social constructionist views have tended to locate the formation of sexual "identities" (under rubrics including for example homosexual, heterosexual, bisexual, or polysexual) in the European and colonial eighteenth or nineteenth century, often eliding the investigation of same-sex desire in earlier periods. This can shut down inquiry both into the erotic power of Sor Juana's poetry and into modes of thought that reinforce patriarchal and heteronormative paradigms (found even in some feminist criticism). As the historian Judith Bennett points out,

> one of our first steps toward understanding the antecedents of modern sexual identities must be to examine how well and how poorly our modern ideas of "lesbians" and "heterosexual women" and "bisexuals" and "queers" work for the past. If we avoid these terms altogether, we will create a pure, inviolable, and irrelevant past: a fetish instead of a history. (14)

No terminology will find utter congruence between past and present. Nevertheless, modern as the concept of "sexuality" may be, it is not—with all its variations—a modern phenomenon.[3]

Caution about anachronism with regard to sexual orientation arises only with the possibility of nonheterosexual readings. (Scholars and teachers do not explain away courtship in Garcilaso or Góngora, Sidney or Shakespeare—except of course in Shakespeare's sonnets, where generations have leaned on the "dark lady" to downplay the "young man." Nor when a male poet addresses a woman do instructors reassure students, "Of course he didn't mean this 'heterosexually'—not as we use the concept 'heterosexual' today.") Whatever their biographical reference points, these poems of Sor Juana are erotic and should be read as such. They are addresses of lyric seduction, and, despite historical shortcomings, the terms *lesbian*, *sapphic*, or *queer* are apt descriptors. Encountering the homoerotic display in the poems, we cannot avoid imagining women romancing women, and it is perverse to pretend that we can.

Unfamiliar with the poetic discourse that Sor Juana uses, undergraduates (like most critics) will read these love poems as idiosyncratic. In fact, sapphic verse was a valued literary fashion in seventeenth-century England, France, Italy, Netherlands, Portugal, and Spain; Sor Juana's production in New Spain by no means stands alone (Dugaw and Powell, "Sapphic Self-Fashioning" and "Feminist Road"). Across languages and poets, this sapphic verse shares characteristics that contextualize Sor Juana's works. From these I have culled three ideas to guide students' reading of these lyrics. First, the poems are seductive: the poet steps into the role of an assertive, if courteous and playful, suitor. Second, they are feminist; in them, unlike the Petrarchan discourse from which they borrow, the female beloved possesses subjectivity and agency. They honor her intelligence as well as her beauty, crediting her quickness to appreciate the parody. Third, through their sexy enlistment of Petrarchan language and a knowing intimacy, they display an ironic campiness or queering—again a term, but not a phenomenon, tied to our times. This parodic move creates a playful shared knowledge in the poems that exposes the arbitrariness of accepted norms and opens up a vibrant, liberatory experience.

Twenty-first-century students usually require supplementary literary, religious, political, and cultural background. The long medievalism of early modern monastic and secular life presents an unfamiliar world. Our sensibility finds it difficult to accept celibacy, for instance, as a viable option rich with affective, sensual, and spiritual experience, rather than as simply a forced fast. Sacred and profane exist differently in the foreign cultural landscape of the early modern world. Many things that twenty-first-century popular culture "knows" to be true are not—for example, that seventeenth-century Catholicism monolithically oppressed women. Many students meet Sor Juana in María Luisa Bemberg's brilliant but distorting film, *Yo, la peor de todas* ("I, the Worst of All"), which usefully portrays material and ritual culture in the convent world but misrepresents the restrictions and freedoms of monastic life and Sor Juana's relation to ecclesiastical and political power, including her vital friendship with the vicereine (see Bergmann, "Abjection").

Sor Juana foregrounds her awareness of her poetic inheritance, both admiringly and parodically showing expertise in the conventions she uses and undoes. Reading one or two predecessor poems that reveal conventions of Petrarchan lyric can help students recognize Sor Juana's echoing, transformative play with the past (see Rabin, this volume). For example, Petrarchan commonplaces thread her *romance* 19 (1: 54–59). The eyes as "suns," the "cult" to the "divine" beloved, and the protestations of purity of intent hearken back to the *canzoniere*, by way of such Spanish poets as Garcilaso de la Vega, Luis de Góngora, and Francisco de Quevedo.

Students are alert to flirtation, the playful coyness of Sor Juana's transgressive overstating of Petrarchan elements. In *romance* 19 the speaker, wanting to win over the beloved, asks permission for her daring incursion: "permite escale tu Alcazar / mi gigante atrevimiento" ("Permit my giant audacity / to scale your towering fortress" [1: 54, lines 13–14]).[4] In the Petrarchan schema, the poet-lover is positioned as suppliant before the "mighty" beloved. With facetious aplomb, Sor Juana occupies her role as wooer. The "blazing" beauty of María Luisa even more hyperbolically overwhelms the poet in the complex *romance* 61 (1: 171–73). In an extraordinary feat, every ten-syllable (*decasílabo*) line begins with an *esdrújulo* (word accented on the third-to-last syllable; my translation imitates with an English dactyl): "Lámina sirva el Cielo al retrato, / Lísida, de tu angélica forma" ("Heavenly should be the canvas to bear the portrait, / Lysida, of your angelic figure and face" [lines 1–2]). Imaginative as well as lexical powers fill such luscious lines as "[c]árceles tu madeja fabrica" ("Prisonhouse fetters are fashioned by your tresses" [line 6]), "Lágrimas del Aurora congela, / búcaro de fragancias, tu boca" ("Lachrymal droplets of Dawn, condensed within this / sweet-scented vessel—your mouth, with its perfumes" [lines 29–30]), or "Tránsito a los jardines de Venus, / órgano de marfil, en canora / música, tu garganta, que en dulces / éxtasis aun al viento aprisiona" ("Transiting to the gardens of Venus, / musical organ of marble, your sculpted throat / captivates even the air, in bewitching / ecstasies of a melody long and low" [lines 37–40]). The sumptuous imagery and dazzling technique arguably outdo the poetic "masters" to whose work Sor Juana repeatedly makes reference, thus raising the value of her praise to the beloved. The homage itself is stunning—the woman may be more so, and must in any case be flattered, moved, and left chuckling at this boldness.

Sor Juana recasts courtship to represent the subjectivity for women that Petrarchism excludes (Bergmann and Middlebrook 145–48). The poems to the vicereines reconfigure the conventional gender hierarchy to establish a beloved "object" who is admired but equal (see Gimbernat). While Sor Juana evokes her beloved's beauty in conventionally superlative Petrarchan bits—hair, eyes, cheeks, mouth, hands (see Vickers)–her addressees are unusually whole subjects. Friends' bodies are cherished in relation to their minds and life circumstances: they receive loving gifts, mentioned in poems that accompany these offerings—for example, a pearl (*romance* 40 [1: 117–19]), an offering of chocolate and embroidered slippers (*romance* 44 [1: 127–28]). Physical absence is mourned with reference to occasions that demand the beloved's attention; for example, in *romance* 18 (1: 52–54), the vicereine meets the demands of "ejercicios espirituales" ("a retreat for spiritual exercises"). The poems present a reciprocal exchange; the interlocutor is more empowered and the speaker less arrogant than those of, say, Garcilaso.

Numerous details in Sor Juana's poems represent the beloved's embodiedness not as a reductive objectification but as one aspect of a vital and attractive autonomy. The breathtaking image of breasts in *romance* 61—"jardines de Vénus" ("gardens of Venus" [1: 172]) refers to the countess's voice and musical artistry, giving the beauty of her "sculpted throat" a complexity usually elided by Petrarchan poets. *Romance* 23 (1: 67–70) recalls María Luisa pregnant, "cuando con dos almas / estabas, aunque no sea / menester estar encinta / para que mil almas tengas" ("when you possessed / two souls—although for you, / it's not necessary to be pregnant, / to have one thousand souls" [lines 7–12]). Sor Juana summons up María Luisa's heterosexual and (as vicereine) publicly reproductive realm and then vaults right over it, conferring a thousand souls on her (not just one more). Flattery leads to an evocation of the vicereine's "antojo o capricho" ("food-cravings or whim" [lines 30–31]); Sor Juana pokes fun yet seeks to forestall such hankerings in the future by sending more walnuts. The sublime and quotidian blend in celebratory yet parodic humor. When Apollo, the powerful deity of poetry and the sun, puts on an apron to make sweetmeats for a woman's beloved woman, established "verities" of gender norms are thrown into question, if not out the window. The honored addressee—or any knowing reader—is saluted for erudition and comic sense.

Though loving and respectful, the poet's homoerotic avowals are rarely earnest. Students quickly see how the hyperbole of such witty tributes tips to humor as we observe cultural commonplaces with amusement; a new subjectivity lets us move from outsider to insider. Comic overstatement ennobles the interlocutor and deflates limiting clichés about women. In *romance* 61, the convention of fresh, rosy cheeks appears in baroque transformation as "cátedras de abril" ("endowed professorships of April"). Springtime itself, by studying hard, may learn beauty from María Luisa:

> Cátedras de Abril, tus mejillas,
> clásicas dan a Mayo, estudiosas:
> métodos a jasmines nevados
> fórmula rubicunda a las rosas. (1: 172, lines 25–28)

> Scholarly cheeks master the lessons of April, and
> studious, serve as classic instruction to May:
> disciplined methods set down for the snowy jasmine;
> rubicund formulas taught to the rose on the spray.

This extended metaphor, with terms from Scholastic philosophy ("métodos," "fórmula"), takes sublime beauty to ridiculous extremes. The combined effect of tribute and humor renders simultaneously a devoted poet and a beloved with her own autonomous life. Women are not reduced to screens for a male poet's projections.

Sor Juana's humor—especially her over-the-top flattery—encloses two women in an intimacy that allows commentary on a masculinist history and its icons. Where Petrarch's "you slay me with a glance" disempowers the female beloved (held mute in the male poet's powers of representation), Sor Juana gives a wink. The comic *ovillejo* (1: 320–30) gives cascading examples for reading or class discussion; in one example, the poet complains that all metaphors have become cliché (citing classic passages in Spanish poetry). Nonetheless, Sor Juana moves through all passages requisite to Petrarchan tradition to portray a woman's beauty. Reaching the forehead (which convention decreed must be ample), and facetiously avoiding worn imagery, she praises its "acreage":

> Tendrá, pues, la tal frente
> una caballería largamente,
> según está de limpia y despejada;
> y si temen por esto verla arada,
> pierdan este recelo,
> que estas caballerías son del Cielo. (lines 189–94)

> Well then, this forehead must
> measure a good acre more or less,
> so broad and clean and well-cleared her brow;
> but if therefore you fear it may be ploughed,
> give that thought no haven;
> this is an acre not of earth, but Heaven.

Such joking relies on reciprocity with the addressee, who by implication has an active presence. Sor Juana's spin on courtly tradition honors the recipient, who with the speaker can claim mastery of and independence from convention and its heterosexual imperatives.

The seductive, sexually ambiguous speaker position of Sor Juana's Petrarchan supplicants draws attention to the lesbian character of the relation. Students can reflect on the implications of an anonymous early editor's alarm, warning us not to read the poems as what they appear to be—passionate, erotic declarations of love by one woman to another:

> Advertencia. O el agradecimiento de favorecida y celebrada, o el conocimiento que tenía de las relevantes prendas que a la Señora Virreina dió el Cielo, o aquel secreto influjo (hasta hoy nadie lo ha podido apurar) de los humores o los Astros, que llaman simpatía, o todo junto, causó en la Poetisa un amor a Su Excelencia con ardor tan puro, como en el contexto de todo el libro irá viendo el lector. (1: 48)
>
> Notice: Either her gratitude at being favored and celebrated, or her knowledge of the outstanding gifts that Heaven bestowed on the Lady Vicereine, or that secret influence (which to this day no one has been able to verify) of the humors or of the Stars, that is known as sympathy—or all these things together—caused the Poet to bear a love for Her Excellency with such a pure ardor as the reader shall see throughout this entire book.

A similarly squeamish headnote before *romance* 19 warns against the obvious implications of the poem: "Puro amor, que ausente y sin deseo de indecencias, puede sentir lo que el más profano" ("Pure love, which in absentia and with no wish for indecencies, can feel all that the most profane love does" [1: 54]). The editor's opposition of pure/profane seeks to emphasize purity but obviously wrestles with the poem's erotic expression.

Nina Scott suggests that the passion expressed in *romance* 19 and other poems of love reflects above all Sor Juana's gratitude for María Luisa's patronage of her poetry (" 'Ser mujer' " 168). While true, this analysis fails to account for the poet's insistence on erotic language, even while she parodies the heterosexual codifications of poetic convention. The opening lines entwine the risk and attainment of "taking" the beloved's stronghold by erotic assault. "Paintbrush" and "pen" transgress in seeking to capture the beloved's ineffable beauty. The poet herself, her passion, and her beloved are praised but joshed for grand but silly derring-do:

> Lo atrevido de un pincel,
> Filis, dió a mi pluma alientos:
> que tan gloriosa desgracia,
> más causa ánimo que miedo.

Logros de errar por tu causa
fue de mi ambición el cebo;
donde es el riesgo appreciable
¿qué tanto valdrá el acierto?
Permite, pues, a mi pluma
segundo arriesgado vuelo,
pues no es el primer delito
que le disculpa el ejemplo. (1: 54, lines 1–14)

Phyllis, my pen is given wings
by a paintbrush and its temerity,
for the artist's dazzling disgrace
inspires not fear, but bravery.
The chance that my errors might do you honor
is a bait to draw my ambition on;
when a great risk looms so substantial,
what value falls to a mere good shot?
Then permit the hazardous undertaking
to a wingéd quill that longs to fly;
if my crime can find excuse
in precedent, it will not be the first time.

Students enjoy learning to follow the hyperbolic burlesque of these images, which construct and then deflate the mock heroic tone. By implication, Sor Juana pokes fun at the "heroic" Petrarchan stance ("daring all" against the lady's coldness)—what is at stake but courtship, with its altogether human risks and rewards? And yet we feel the urgency of this quest.

Romance 19 unfolds not with the verbal portrait we expect (which would entail the reification that Sor Juana rejects) but by entertaining a tricky question: can a woman properly write in this manner to and of another woman? What should prevail at the altars dedicated to "Phyllis" is the soul's "sacrificio puro / de adoración y silencio" ("pure sacrifice of adoration and silence" [1: 55, lines 55–56]). But the assertion of "silence" is undone by this notably talkative poem. Both woman lover and woman beloved step outside "proper" silence to make new expressions possible.

The passionate intensity of this poem, which opts for utterance rather than silence, similarly abandons the abstract, remote disembodiment it at first seems to endorse. Instead, it rushes to enter the purely physical, with an early modern understanding of the physics of irresistible attraction: "como a lo cóncavo el aire, / como a la materia el fuego, / como a su centro las peñas, / como a su fin los intentos" ("like air drawn to what is hollow, / like fire, to feed on matter, / like boulders tumbling to the earth / and intentions, to their goal" [1: 56, lines 97–100]). Here the poem undermines all pretense of disembodiment. Air, fire, and earth (those tumbling boulders) rush where they must; of the four elements composing all matter, only water (which might douse ardor) is missing. Seductive intentions, like forces of physics, are drawn inexorably to their goal as the poem briefly reveals its intent: "bien como todas las cosas / naturales, que el deseo / de conservarse, las une / amante en lazos estrechos . . ." ("indeed, like every natural thing / —all united by the desire / to endure, which ties them tight / in bonds of closest love . . ." [1: 56–57, lines 101–04; ellipses in original]). A provocative ellipsis ends (or resists ending) these lines, suggesting that this silence—what is left unsaid about loving unions within tight bonds—is on the one hand beyond speech, on the other, poetically trite. The next line acknowledges, "¿para qué es cansarse?" ("but why do I go on, why should one wear oneself out?"). We come to the poem's outright declaration: "como a ti, Filis, te quiero" ("just so, Phyllis, do I love you" [1: 57, line 106]).

Students will now be equipped to reread as parody, with a suggestive insistence on "sexiness," *romance* 19's protestations of what the unknown editor termed "pure" love (1: 54). A particular passage is recited by critics including Octavio Paz (*Traps* 218–19) as if they are relieved that this Neoplatonic love is safely of one disembodied soul for another (forgetting, as the early modern period did, the inconvenient "queerness" of Plato): "Ser mujer, ni estar ausente / no es de amarte impedimento; / pues sabes tú, que las almas / distancia ignoran y sexo" ("Your being a woman, your being gone / cannot pose the slightest hindrance / to my love, for you know that our souls / have no gender and know no distance" [1: 57, lines 109–12]).[5] However, close reading demonstrates that the textual context undoes the stanza's apparent message. The poem eschews the disembodied abstract it seems to claim, insisting on the physicality of this love. Students, in the position of knowing addressee, can begin to build the poet's meanings from what Sor Juana suggests, not only what she states flatly. Alert to parodic undermining, we are enjoined to inhabit with poet and addressee the spaces between shifts of declaration and ellipses, over- and understatement, caution and boldness. Through these shifts we enjoy the playful, innovative resonance of the poem.

The Neoplatonic allusion to ungendered and disembodied souls is used by Sor Juana not to dismiss physical love between women but to reject the culture that renders such love "indecent." This love of "souls," limited neither by "sex" (the supposed obstacle of both being female) nor "distance" (including physical separation or difference in social standing), has been declared to inhere in a spiritual plane of the "pure sacrifice" of "silence" mentioned earlier. But why did the poem not end at line 56, with the encomium to "silencio" as the only way to express the poet's love, instead of continuing prolifically for another 132 lines? Because we are not meant to believe in either the unspokenness or nonphysicality of this love. Both are undone by a comic, ironic, undermining wit, in which we share. This strategy of undoing, not doing, or doing exactly the opposite of what is claimed creates funny, erotic, transgressive, queer effects that surprise, upset, and delight.

Sor Juana's love poems to women open up the very topic they appear decorously to shut down: one woman's passionate, sexualized love for another woman. Numerous texts evincing female homoeroticism in the early modern period display these opening-shutting moments, typical of sapphic discourse by suggestion. Such works hold a troubling, or intriguing, power of disruption, even when the framing presentation seems to annul transgression or to assuage the reader's stirred anxiety. In the classroom, some students will overread the lesbian potential of such moments and see as outright declaration what is presented obliquely or embedded in a (perhaps ironic) heterosexual paradigm. Such students can be reminded to take the insistent frame into account. Other students will want to underread and can be urged to look again at how the text demands that we see one woman in love with another, if only for a brief space of time.[6]

What is at stake in teaching these poems? Not least is the visibility of lesbian existence in a past more imaginatively habitable and a present also more livable, for readers who need these traces from other times. Is it enough to teach Sor Juana's protofeminist challenges to her times and our own and to leave aside the thorny matter of sexualities? Cheshire Calhoun notes that "feminist values and goals have worked against representing lesbian difference," a point useful to recall when I observe the paucity of attention to lesbian texts or theory, even in many feminist courses (210).[7] The encounter with similar desires and expressions in earlier periods increases the perceived humanity of lesbian, gay, bisexual, and transgender subjects then and now, which is why this pedagogical effort is strenuously championed from some quarters and rejected from others. We can gain a more accurate view of literature and of the cultures of the past by exploring the lively sapphic discourse that Sor Juana employed, as did women poets internationally. With their homage and send-up, conventionality and innovation, affirmation and subversion, her love poems to women reveal and revel in profound dimensions of her poetic expertise. Omitting them or downplaying their significance leaves us with an anemic, diminished view of her work and of our world.

NOTES

[1]Background reading for this chapter includes Sor Juana's *romance* 19, *romance decasílabo* 61, and *ovillejo* 214. Instructors might also refer to other texts that identify variously male, female, or deliberately ambiguous addressees, including *romances* 5, 6; "*romances epistolares*" 16, 23, 33, 40, 43, 44; *endechas* 81, 83; sonnets 187–89; *lira* 211. These poem numbers refer to Méndez Plancarte and Salceda's *Obras Completas*, volume 1. Resources for Sor Juana's love poems to women in English translation include Faderman (*Chloe plus Olivia*), Larkin and Manrique (*Sor Juana's Love Poems*), and Trueblood (*Sor Juana Anthology*). Resources for women's love poems to women in the period (the Portuguese Sor Violante do Ceu; the English Katherine Philips and Aphra Behn; and others in French, Italian, and Dutch) appear in Dugaw and Powell, "Sapphic Self-Fashioning" 153n2.

[2]Analysis of these complex, contested, and overlapping sites of cultural, ethnic, and

political identity, or positioning, exceeds the scope of this chapter, but they will be felt and heard in classrooms. Moraga and Smith (in a dialogue recorded in 1981 and still not out of date) and Chávez Leyva offer pedagogical cautions and encouragement.

[3]Since Foucault's *History of Sexuality*, literary scholarship has wrestled with conceptualizing same-sex eroticism before the formation of modern sexual identities. Terms proposed for premodern, textual appearances of erotic love between women include "same-sex love and desire among women" (Sautman and Sheingorn); the "silent sin" (Saint-Saëns 20); "female homoeroticism" (Brooten); "lesbian-like" presence (Bennett); "homoerotic desire" (Traub, "Desire" 92); "female intimacy" (Wahl); and "sapphism" (Lanser). See also Bonnet.

[4]All translations are mine.

[5]Scott discusses various critics' responses to these lines and to the passionate expression of *romance* 19 in her eponymous essay "'Ser mujer'" 159–61. The critics she cites include Paz, Juan León Mera, Ludwig Pfandl, Stephanie Merrim, Marie-Cécile Bénassy-Berling, Georgina Sabat de Rivers, Jean Franco, George H. Tavard, and Rosario Castellanos.

[6]These ideas on students' over- and underreading derive from a workshop session, Beyond Female Friendship held on 5 November 2004 at the conference Beyond Colonial Studies: An Inter-American Encounter in Providence, Rhode Island. Thanks especially to Elizabeth Dillon, Yolanda Martínez–San Miguel, and Jodi Schorb for insights on teaching.

[7]For a more optimistic view of the relation between lesbian and feminist theory, and for an excellent Spanish-language source, see Suárez Briones.

Visual Technologies as Pedagogical Artifacts: Teaching Sor Juana in a Virtual World

Mariselle Meléndez

Nicholas Mirzoeff has defined visual technology as "any form of apparatus designed either to be looked at or to embrace natural vision, from oil painting to television and the internet" (*Introduction* 3). Although the word *visual* has become popular in the past decade, thanks in part to the widespread technology of the Internet, visual images have served since early times as powerful instruments of communication, not only for societies that lacked a graphic system of writing but also for those that used writing as the primary mode of communication.[1] Visual images have always constituted compelling acts of expression because of their ability to invoke an immediate reaction as well as to persuade without words. The process of interpreting the visual image endows it with specific meanings. As W. J. T. Mitchell suggests, images "are not stable, static, or permanent" because "they are never perceived in the same way by viewers" (*Iconology* 14). For this reason they function in a classroom as a productive means of generating discussion and expanding ideas about societies and their cultural production.

This article discusses how visual technologies can be used in the classroom as an effective way to teach Sor Juana Inés de la Cruz's writing. In focusing on three specific forms of such technology—portraits, film, and the Internet—my aim is to facilitate an understanding of the Mexican nun's difficult texts through an interactive approach in which visual images operate as the center of discussion. In the case of the Internet, I will offer an overview of how certain global resources make Sor Juana's work more accessible to our undergraduate and graduate students in an academic setting.

Portraying Sor Juana: Respuesta a sor Filotea *and Diego Calleja's* Aprobación

Many critics have contended that students today are so much more visually oriented than previous generations that television and the Internet have almost replaced books as objects of entertainment and learning. My experience, however, has shown that when teaching courses in which any form of visual technology is used, difficulties arise for some students in critically analyzing visual images. The transformation from merely looking at an image to interpreting it is a challenging one because many students, undergraduates and graduates alike, lack the critical skills needed to help transcend what they first see. Gillian Rose's book *Visual Methodologies: An Introduction to the In-*

terpretation of Visual Material is an excellent guide for students. It serves as a valuable introduction to the process of analysis and discussion of visual representations through pictures and the Internet. In my graduate classes on visual culture in colonial Spanish America, I have complemented this book with more theoretical readings such as those by Nicholas Mirzoeff, W. J. T Mitchell, Roland Barthes, Marita Sturken and Lisa Cartwright, Donna Haraway, Serge Gruzinski (*Guerra*, *Images*), Walter Mignolo (*Darker Side*), and John Berger, among others.[2]

Before any discussion of Sor Juana's works in an undergraduate or graduate special-topics course on visual culture in colonial Spanish America, it is important to present the historical and cultural context in which Sor Juana lived. After the instructor assigns initial readings that contextualize seventeenth-century colonial Mexico, at least half of a class period should be devoted to discussion of the salient themes on this topic. As an introductory framework for undergraduate students, I usually assign sources such as *Colonial Latin America* by Mark A. Burkholder and Lyman L. Johnson and Susan M. Socolow's *Women of Colonial Latin America.* For a graduate course, I recommend *La época barroca en el México colonial* by Irving A. Leonard, Josefina Muriel's *Las mujeres de Hispanoamérica*, Octavio Paz's *Sor Juana Inés o las trampas de la fe*, or Kathleen Ann Myers's *Neither Saints nor Sinners: Writing the Lives of Women in Spanish America.* The aforementioned texts help facilitate an understanding of the circumstances from which writings such as the *Answer* emerged. For graduate students, critical studies on Sor Juana can be assigned as secondary readings or part of oral presentations.[3]

Once students are familiar with Sor Juana's world and have read the the *Answer*, we can introduce the portraits of Sor Juana painted during the colonial period as a means of understanding the impact that the letter had in the portrayal of her persona. Along with the *Answer*, it is productive to assign the biography written by Diego Calleja, known as "Approbation" and published in 1700.[4] At this point, students will already have discussed both the content of Sor Juana's text and and some of the most important biographical details introduced by Calleja. Two classes can be devoted to the discussion of the two written texts in juxtaposition, and at least one to discussing the portraits. By introducing the portraits, I mainly hope to generate a discussion on the manner in which Sor Juana's works and life were perceived both during her time and after her death in 1695 and to focus on how specific visual images of her were produced, based on what was said in the two biographical works. An important class discussion at this point would introduce portraiture as a form of representational art, addressing how it was cultivated during Sor Juana's time. An examination of the social, cultural, and political roles that portraiture had during the Renaissance and the baroque periods will enhance understanding of what makes the portraits of Sor Juana so appealing. The goal is to comprehend their symbolic meaning in a tradition that developed from ancient times to the present.[5]

Six interesting portraits were made of Sor Juana between 1692 and 1750. These portraits can be reproduced as part of a class Web page and made accessible to the students at a specific site.[6] Two engraved frontispieces are known as the first portraits of Sor Juana. One accompanied the second volume of Sor Juana's works published in Seville in 1692, and the other was part of her *Fama y Obras Póstumas*, published in 1700. The two most famous portraits were those painted by Juan de Miranda (c. 1713) and Miguel Cabrera (in 1750). In addition, a portrait was painted by Miguel de Herrera in 1732, and another by an anonymous eighteenth-century portraitist.

Before discussing the portraits directly, the instructor should offer some general information regarding the artists responsible for the portraits and any other valuable information with regard to when and why the portraits were commissioned. In an undergraduate class, students may then be divided into six groups, with each group in charge of discussing a different portrait. Some potential questions that could be posed as a guide for analyzing the images include the following:

What aspects does each portrait highlight about the figure of Sor Juana? How does each portrait differ from the others? How do these portraits fit in or deviate from the tradition of Renaissance and baroque portraiture?

What objects surround Sor Juana? What do these objects tell us about Sor Juana's life and personality?

What role does color and physical location of the body play in the picture?

What elements from the *Answer* and Calleja's biography are present in the portraits, and why? What kind of meaning do they acquire in the portraits?

What written texts accompany the portraits and what is their relevance?

What aspects of the baroque can we visualize in the portraits?

How do these portraits compare with other contemporary portraits of nuns or prominent women in Mexico and male artists of the time? Bring examples of these portraits to class.[7]

Finally, discussion can conclude with a reading of Sor Juana's famous sonnet "Este, que ves, engaño colorido" ("This that you gaze on, colorful deceit" [1: 277; 169]) and her poem "El pintar de Lisarda la belleza" ("The act of painting the beauty of Lisarda" [1: 320; my trans.]) as metacritical texts in which Sor Juana offers two distinct views of the dangers involved in any attempt to capture a particular physical state through painting.[8] I emphasize the importance of the act of painting as a reconstruction of a specific image that varies according to who is in charge of reproducing it, and when and why it is reproduced.

Yo, la peor de todas and the Critical Eye

Another apparatus of visual technology that can help the students visualize the manner in which Sor Juana's work and persona have been interpreted throughout the centuries is the acclaimed 1990 film by the Argentinean director María Luisa Bemberg, *Yo, la peor de todas* ("I, the Worst of All"). Discussion of the film as a twentieth-century reconstruction of the colonial nun-writer can occur either in a survey or in a special-topics course, especially after assigning a selection of those of Sor Juana's works that are cited in the film: the *Answer*; *Carta atenagórica* ("Letter Worthy of Athena"); and some of the most famous poems, such as "Détente, sombra de mi bien esquivo" ("Stay, shadow of contentment too short-lived" [1: 287; 183]) or "Hombres necios que acusáis" ("Foolish men, who will chastise" [1: 228; 149–51]). Generally, I allow one week for discussion of the writings and a second week for the discussion of the film.

As with the portraits, sections of Rose's *Visual Methodologies* can provide a theoretical framework for studying the representation of visual images in film, along with Sturken and Cartwright's *Practices of Looking*. Both have been very useful in an undergraduate class I teach on cinematographic renditions of the colonial past. But for graduate students, more sophisticated theoretical readings on cinematography can be assigned, such as *How to Read a Film: The World of Movies, Media, and Multimedia*, by James Monaco, or *Film Theory and Criticism: Introductory Readings*, by Leo Braudy and Marshall Cohen. Again, because these texts do not focus specifically on the colonial period, it is important to provide historical contextualization.

As a point of departure, the film can be considered a text that encodes and constructs specific meanings, always bound by the setting from which it emerged. Questions such as asking what image of Sor Juana the film attempts to construct and to what extent this construction is affected by the beliefs of those who produced and wrote the film can lead to analysis of specific scenes that point to that particular construction. For instance, one of the aspects most emphasized in the film is the lesbian nature of the friendship between Sor Juana and the Countess of Paredes, which speaks to the manner in which the Mexican poet has been interpreted by some twentieth-century readers and critics. Since María Luisa Manrique de Lara y Gonzaga, Countess of Paredes, was Sor Juana's patron and vicereine of Mexico (1680–86), it is important to discuss the tradition of poetry dedicated to powerful patrons and courtly *poemas de alabanza* ("poems of praise" or "adulation") in order to address how Sor Juana understood the concept of friendship. Poems such as "Lysi: a tus manos divinas" ("Lysi: into your hands divine" [1: 260–61; 165]) or "Este retrato que ha hecho" ("This portrait traced by arrogance" [1: 259; 163]) usefully contextualize the friendships Sor Juana had with the countess and with her predecessor as patron and as vicereine, the Marquise of Mancera, Leonor Carreto.

Another aspect of the film worth analyzing is its intertextual nature. The class can examine some of the writings cited verbatim by the protagonist and ask which passages of the poems are quoted and in what context? Other questions emerge: Which characters surround the protagonist when those verses are read? What types of light and music are used? Why are certain poems not included in the dialogue that takes place in the film? What does the absence of those works tell us about the choices made by the director in composing Sor Juana's image of the Mexican nun?[9] How are elements of class, gender, and race introduced in the film, and how do they correspond to the cultural, political, and historical reality of the time?

Discussion may also focus on the act of looking itself, not only the act as performed by the characters of the film but also the viewing habits of the film's audience. After all, as Rose suggests, "film is a powerful means of structuring looking" (101). The instructor may elicit from the students how race, gender, and class both affect the manner in which we look and subsequently interpret what we look at. The class, once it is familiarized with Sor Juana's works, should consider what we see and what we do not see in the film. In a graduate course one way to close discussion is to assign some reviews of the film from Latin America and other parts of the world; doing so points out how varied interpretations of a film may be and suggests reasons for those differences. The compositional language that characterizes the film—including the intrinsic connections that exist between the "moving images," as Rose calls them—and the narrative of the film need to be included in the discussion (48). Monaco's and Rose's guides examine the spatial organization of film, including the screen frame, the role of superimpositions, shot distance, focus, angle, point of view, and sound, to understand the effects that the director wished to produce for the viewer as well as the power relation that such images create.[10] This type of reading also enables students to understand the complex re-creation apparent in the act of adapting to film the life and work of historical figures such as Sor Juana.

An outstanding resource when discussing the film in class is the Web site entitled *Yo, la peor de todas (1990) ("I, the Worst of All").* This site offers a comprehensive corpus of information focusing on aspects related to filmography as well as a synopsis of the film; historical sources; a detailed scene log; excerpts of film reviews; critical comparisons with other films such as *Elizabeth*, *Messenger: The Story of Joan de Arc*, and *Song of Bernadette*; a selected bibliography; a list of and links to other audio resources; scene analyses; sound bites; and an image gallery. This basic material can pave the way for in-depth critical discussions related to the many items of interest offered at the site. For example, based on the information provided, the students can focus on how the film was reviewed in the United States and how it was distributed. They can then compare the reception of the film in some Latin American countries. I emphasize in my courses that when making this type of comparative analysis it is paramount to pay close attention to the location where the film was released, as well as to the particular mass venues where the film reviews were published. In some venues, Sor Juana was not considered sexual enough. In other, more conservative venues, the looks and kiss between the vicereine and Sor Juana seemed too shocking. Sor Juana was seen at times more as an intellectual, at others more as a protofeminist (in many instances an accomplished feminist), and at still others as a sexually suppressed nun.[11]

One fruitful class exercise is to assign different film reviews to students working in groups and to guide students to focus on the media outlets in which the film reviews were published. After reading some of the reviews, they can address questions such as: How does the review published in the *New York Times*, for example, compare or differ from the one published in the *Kansas City Star* or the *San Francisco Examiner* or in journals such as *Sight and Sound*? Does it make any difference who writes the review and when it is written? What kind of persons are these reviewers trying to persuade? Are the reviewers familiar with the original works of Sor Juana?

Deconstructing the process of reconstruction through which the film director transfers Sor Juana to the screen from a different historical context, at a distance of three hundred years, provides insights. In the same manner that Callejas re-created a specific persona of the Mexican poet in his seventeenth-century biography or that Paz produced a more complex image of her in *Sor Juana Inés de la Cruz o las trampas de la fe*, Bemberg articulates a unique representation of Sor Juana, one that appealed to her feminist ideology.[12] The film encapsulates a specific reading of Sor Juana that coincided with the director's perspective on the power struggles that a woman suffered when living in a world dominated by male-centered institutions. Sor Juana epitomized that struggle, which made her an excellent instrument for this type of movie adaptation. Indeed, that power struggle in a society dominated by male ideologies and gender bias still makes Sor Juana a fascinating figure today.

Sor Juana on a Global Scale: The Power of the Internet

The Internet is an instrument of distribution of knowledge that can offer advantages to any course in which Sor Juana is taught. Of course, the Internet does not provide equal access to knowledge, despite being considered in the media as a means of exchanging knowledge on a global scale. The information that circulates on the Internet is also the product of ideological constructions that aim to articulate specific cultural, social, and political projects to persuade certain sectors of the population toward certain beliefs; also, access is as culturally, socially, and politically hierarchized as the forms of knowledge presented.

The Internet does, however, make accessible to instructors and students, in the United States and around the world, documents that otherwise would remain only in libraries. For undergraduate students who usually do not engage in travel for research, the Internet constitutes a wonderful opportunity to become familiar with manuscripts and facsimile editions pertinent to an area of study. There are more than 8,000 sites about Sor Juana available on the Internet. Of course, it would take more than a semester to thoroughly study each site; however, a careful selection of a few can enhance class discussion. Because I usually devote two to four class periods to Sor Juana in a survey course, I generally reserve one of those periods for discussing sites carefully chosen because of their pertinence to the readings assigned that particular day.

If the instructor is ambitious and time is not an issue, assigning a small-group Internet-research project is useful. Each group studies a certain number of sites, collecting basic information about the site's nature, its main themes, and the context in which it was created. Students can then report their findings to the class and discuss each site's limitations and values. A book such as *Web Studies* by David Gauntlett and Ross Horsley can serve as a guide. Finally, students may conclude with their impressions of what they believe to be the general image of Sor Juana conveyed by these Web sites.

Two important sites are helpful in any discussion in which visual representations of Sor Juana, her works, and her world are the main focus of study. The Web site developed by Luis M. Villar and sponsored by the Department of Spanish and Portuguese at Dartmouth College and the government of the state of Mexico, entitled "The Sor Juana Inés de la Cruz Project," provides valuable bibliographic information on Sor Juana. It includes a link to the digitized facsimile text of the third volume of Sor Juana's works, published posthumously in 1700 by Juan Ignacio de Castorena y Ursúa. Students can read the first edition and visually familiarize themselves with an early modern text, which is different from the modern editions that they commonly use. They can study the title page; the engraved frontispiece of Sor Juana inserted at the beginning of the volume; the different *dedicatorias* ("dedications") written to the Catholic queen, Mariana de Neoburg Baviera; the "Approbation" written by Calleja; and the many poems written by male figures at the time in honor of Sor Juana Inés de la Cruz.

Discussion can focus on the process of identity construction that takes place on the preliminary pages that precede Sor Juana's work. Questions might include: What image of Sor Juana do those authors portray, and why and how do they portray that image? Who are the authors? What do they have in common when referring to Sor Juana as a writer and as a nun? Can we detect a national sentiment in the reconstruction of Sor Juana's identity? The questions can be used as a guide to the assigned readings. The instructor can add the link to the syllabus or link it to his or her own class Web site. For this kind of discussion, I find it more productive to allow two class periods to fully understand the impact of Sor Juana's writings on the intellectual world of the late colonial period.[13]

There are other interesting sites in which image, sound, and text combine to illustrate re-creations of Sor Juana's works and other works based on her. Of course, given the nature of the Internet, there are numerous Web sites in which Sor Juana appears as a commodity. An interesting example is the one developed by the Philadelphia Rare Books and Manuscripts Company, in which Sor Juana is advertised as the Anne Bradstreet of the Spanish world (www.prbm.com/

interest/i.htm?msshsp-a-b.shtml~main). Biographical information is included to persuade the public to buy a manuscript signed by Sor Juana dated from 1692, early-eighteenth-century editions of *Poemas de la única poetisa Americana,* or her posthumously published *Fama y obras póstumas*. Because sections of the books themselves are digitally reproduced and appear next to descriptions prepared by the sellers, it is interesting to discuss in class what image of Sor Juana they are trying to sell and what aspects of her life are most marketable in the twentieth-first century. As Emily Hind observes in her article in this volume, Sor Juana's iconic presence on the Internet underlines the process of idealization and concomitant paradoxes that surround contemporary interpretations of Sor Juana's figure and works.

A class that studies the numerous Web sites devoted to the Mexican nun with a sense of responsibility and caution can gain an understanding of how Sor Juana has been and is being interpreted in Latin America, the United States, and other parts of the world. That her image has been globalized through visual technologies underscores how the crossing of frontiers in a virtual world can produce discussions that unmask the processes through which Sor Juana has been construed from colonial times to the present.

A visual approach to Sor Juana, made easier by the diverse visual technologies available to us, is valuable for learning about Sor Juana and her society. These visual images emphasize the various processes of construction of meanings intrinsic to any attempt to capture and understand the Mexican nun, her works, and her world. For Sor Juana herself, such acts were considered perilous, always subject to futile attempts to capture reality. According to her, visual images are always reconstructions of what we would like to see. In her famous poem titled "This that you gaze on, colorful deceit" she observes that in a portrait the visual image captured is always "to the senses cunning counterfeit" ("es cauteloso engaño del sentido") and "an artifice, a sop to vanity" ("es un vano artificio del cuidado") and "a fancy, and, as all may see" ("es un afán caduco y, bien mirado" [169; 1: 277]). It is for this reason that we, as observers and interpreters, should always be aware of such processes of construction by critically examining the multiple meanings that emerge from them.

NOTES

[1]For the context of pre-Columbian America, see Boone and Mignolo. For Western societies, see Berger. For a more theoretical approach on the concept of pictorial image, see W. J. T. Mitchell (*Iconology* and *Picture Theory*).

[2]For particular titles, see Mirzoeff, *Introduction*; W. J. T. Mitchell, *Iconology* and *Picture Theory*; Sturken and Cartwright; Gruzinski, *Guerra*; and Berger. Also, Rose's book offers an extraordinary bibliography that could be very helpful for a graduate seminar.

[3]Critical studies on Sor Juana are numerous; however, some of the most useful approaches include those by Arenal, "Sor Juana"; Bénassy-Berling, *Humanisme*; Bergmann, "Ficciones"; Luciani, *Literary Self-Fashioning*; Martínez–San Miguel;

Merrim, *Feminist Perspectives*; Myers, *Neither Saints*; Perelmuter, *Noche intelectual* and *Límites*; and Sabat de Rivers, *Busca*.

[4]The biography was published as part of the third volume of *Fama y obras póstumas del Fénix de México, décima musa, poetisa Americana, sor Juana Inés de la Cruz*. Its complete title was "Aprobación del reverendísimo Padre Diego Calleja, de la Compañía de Jesús, M.P.S."

[5]For information on the history of portrait painting in Spain and colonial Spanish America, see Ayala Mallory; Benson; Carrera; and Portús; as well as the special issue of *Artes de Mexico* dedicated to portraiture in New Spain edited by Sánchez Lacy. Selections of these books can help contextualize the role of portrait painting in Spain in the early modern period as well as in Spanish America.

[6]The portraits have been reproduced in numerous sources. See Perea for reproductions of the four portraits in oil and general information about what is known about their painters. In a seminar I taught at the University of Illinois titled Visualizing Difference in Colonial Spanish America: From Bodily Representations to the Production of Space, I prepared a class Web page that included most of the portraits of Sor Juana, which also can be enlarged.

[7]See Sánchez Lacy for examples of portraits based on an exhibition on civil portraiture in New Spain at the San Carlos Museum in Mexico, accompanied by critical articles offering valuable information on the topic.

[8]All translations of poems are from Peden's *Sor Juana* unless otherwise indicated.

[9]Answering these questions might constitute a difficult task for students, who can be referred to Bergmann's article, "Abjection and Ambiguity in Bemberg's *Yo, la peor de todas*," which provides a useful guide to the quotations from Sor Juana's poems in the film and their uses, contexts, and effects.

[10]Rose recapitulates the main ideas developed by Monaco. For a detailed discussion on how to read and to analyze a film, see chapters 2 and 3 in Monaco.

[11]For an excellent article on the homoerotic nature of the film based on Bemberg's portrayal of the friendship between Sor Juana and the vicereine, see Bergmann, "Abjection."

[12]Bemberg was one of the founding members of the Argentinean feminist group Unión Feminista Argentina. For more information on Bemberg, see the Web site *Yo, la peor de todas*.

[13]As a critical tool for such discussion, Perelmuter's *Límites* is useful.

Sor Juana, Food, and the Life of the Mind

John A. Ochoa

Studies of baroque architecture and music in colonial New Spain can re-create the physicality of Sor Juana's world and illuminate the baroque linguistic excess of her writing. Here, I outline an approach to teaching the work and material world of Sor Juana through culinary history. The relation between Sor Juana and food resonates on many levels and offers several thematic links to her work. One central idea in both the *Respuesta a sor Filotea* (*The Answer*) and the *Primero sueño* ("First Dream") is the contrast between the mental and the material, the *coincidentia oppositorum* (Paz, *Trampas* 106). This return occurs because an ordinary bodily function disturbs Sor Juana's sleep and calls her back: the process of digestion, described in elaborate gongoristic detail (1: 356–57). Likewise, in the *Respuesta*, Sor Juana tells of having been forbidden to read but finding that she has no need of books to read and learn, since the whole physical world is her open book, as when she discerns in some spilled flour the pattern impressed on it by a children's top or when she speculates about chemical reactions by noting that egg yolks cook differently in oil and heavy syrup: "¿Qué podemos saber las mujeres sino filosofías de la cocina? . . . Si Aristóteles hubiera guisado, mucho más hubiera escrito" ("What is there for us women to know, if not bits of kitchen philosophy? . . . If Aristotle had been a cook, he would have written much more" [4: 459–60; Trueblood 226]). The limits and interrelations between the body and the mind, between the physical and the mental, figure importantly in her work.

Considering physical materiality and its relation to culture raises issues of empirical knowledge and of the physical location of the seat of reason. There is, in Sor Juana as much as in René Descartes (1596–1650), a materialist bottom line: the thought process, and the very definition of the self, always returns to and necessitates a body and its sustenance. The body's material dimension limits boundless thinking, but at the same time it also provides, on the most physical level, the tools of perception and contemplation. To explore this contradiction, a useful reading to share with students is Descartes's *Meditations on First Philosophy*.

If possible, especially in a specialized course where some time can be devoted to this topic, it is fruitful to read the *Meditations* in their entirety along with the *Primero sueño*. A similar narrative arc may be observed in Descartes's text and Sor Juana's poem: both tell a story about an escape from the body through a flight of the mind, about reconsideration of what the self truly is from this rarefied position of disembodiment, and about an ultimate return to the body and to the material world. Both Descartes and Sor Juana raise the possibility of deception and error in the process of self-cognition. In a parallel close reading, the subtle similarities and distinctions that will undoubtedly arise provide good anchors for discussion.

Furthermore, this exposition about systematic exploration of materiality can be linked, in the context of a class lecture, to the rise of the scientific method and empiricism during the same period. Good background for such a lecture is a compelling set of related studies by Lorraine Daston and Peter Galison, who explore the history of scientific "objectivity," especially the way in which the binary opposition of objective/subjective has been variously associated with other, previous oppositions from the early Renaissance: truth versus untruth (Daston and Galison, "Objectivity"), practice versus precept (Daston "Image"), partiality versus impartiality (Daston and Galison, "Baconian Facts").

The classroom discussion can then be guided back to an important element of maintaining the physical body, food. The role of food can broaden the discussion in a number of productive ways, by addressing the kitchen as empirical laboratory; the social and economic worth of "women's work" like crafts and specialized foods; and the convent as the place of manufacture of such foods. A good introduction to the handcrafts (and the economics) of conventual labor is Martínez del Río Redo and Castelló Yturbide's *Delicias de antaño: Historia y recetas de los conventos mexicanos* ("Delights of Yesteryear: History and Recipes of Mexican Convents"). This large-folio, coffee table book is sumptuously illustrated; it explores the production of crafts in Mexican convents from the conquest to the present, with a heavy emphasis on foods. Individual convents, under two geographic groupings, organize the chapters: metropolitan and provincial. There are brief histories of the foundation of each convent and anecdotes of interest concerning notable or representative nuns, as well as some references to whatever specialties the particular cloister was known for—not all were culinary. There are some other crafts represented, such as featherwork, beadwork, needlepoint, and artificial flower making, many accompanied with beautiful photographs. The only drawback to Martínez and Castelló's appealing book is that no sources or dates are given for the sample recipes. It is unclear if the recipes are from the colonial period and specifically from a given convent or if they are simply typical, modern-day recipes that may be similar. With the help of this text, classroom dialogue can be guided to a reflection on the material resources necessary to support the rarefied life of learning and contemplation, Virginia Woolf's "room of one's own."

Classroom Implementation: Main Sources

Addressing culinary history in a discussion of the materiality in Sor Juana's work offers several engaging classroom opportunities. There is a solid didactic purpose to producing a *torta de almendra de Santa Inés* (Lavín, *Dulces hábitos* 71), a period wedding cake, or even an entire meal from historical sources. When we try to stay true to the methods and ingredients of a seventeenth-century Mexican convent, the item produced can become an exacting period piece, one obtained through careful historical research that adds a worldly dimension to bookish concepts, a process dear to the Mexican nun. Besides, when we research the cookbooks of the Convent of San Jerónimo and the standard Spanish cookbooks from the period and then bake or cook our findings, we put on the table for discussion not only this feast but also several themes from Sor Juana's work: ownership of press, defiance in the face of institutional constraints, baroque flights of fancy pulled off with whatever resources are at hand, and the appropriateness of costuming oneself in someone else's garb and methods.

On a purely practical level we can mine a useful bibliography, especially recent illustrated cookbooks containing updated recipes taken from conventual archives, including some from the Convent of San Jerónimo, Sor Juana's home. These resources, especially when coupled with readings from Sor Juana's work, offer useful library exercises as well as a fun laboratory workshop. Again, we can supplement fruitfully the themes of empirical knowledge and of the mind-body split with selections from other writers of the period like Descartes, Francis Bacon, and Athanasius Kircher, as well as with some readings in culinary history and theory. The centerpiece of this bibliography is the *Libro de cocina* ("Cookery Book"), an edition of Sor Juana's (supposed) personal cookbook. As the anonymous introduction to this slight volume freely admits, there is some doubt whether this is truly Sor Juana's personal collection. Although it is signed by Sor Juana and contains some verses, the extant manuscript is an eighteenth-century copy and may represent a collective work. The original is lost. Virtually all the recipes in this cookbook have been modernized in volume 4 of the nicely illustrated series Cocina virreinal novohispana ("Viceregal New Spanish Cookery"), a recipe collection consisting of four slim volumes, some with compelling introductions but little in the way of scholarly apparatus. The Cocina virreinal series is probably best used as a practical resource for actually producing these recipes (all are in metric measures and may need some readjustments).

The first volume in the series, *Dulces hábitos*, by Mónica Lavín, treats conventual sweets and pastries. It contains a recipe for a "marquesote" or "mamón," a common type of starch cake, which in her cookbook Sor Juana assumes as a basic ingredient for many of her desserts but never describes (another version for it appears in Martínez del Río Redo and Castelló Yturbide 96). Volume 2, by Rosalva Loreto López and Benítez Muro, presents main dishes from the convents. Volume 3, by Yuri de Gortari Krauss and Edmundo Escamilla Solís, is titled *Guisos y golosos del barroco* ("Dishes and Sweets of the Baroque"), which is relevant to our subject. The introduction briefly alludes to baroque excess, to the joining of dissimilars—what Octavio Paz elsewhere calls the *coincidentia oppositorum* of the baroque (*Trampas* 106)—and to the baroque as a style that allowed *mestizaje* to occur within its effusive impulses. This introduction then suggests parallels with the food of the period, with American and Spanish ingredients producing a baroque, culinary *mestizaje*. This is a compelling argument, if perhaps anachronistic (it is most likely influenced by the twentieth-century notion of the neobaroque as articulated by thinkers like José Lezama Lima). The lack of documentation, however, places some of its claims in doubt and makes it somewhat difficult to recommend to students as a solid source of information. It is, again, best used as a source of recipes, especially the already mentioned volume 4, *Sor Juana en la cocina* ("Sor Juana in the Kitchen"), by Lavín, which contains the modernized recipes of her *Libro de cocina*.

Cocina mexicana a través de los siglos ("Mexican Cookery across Centuries") is perhaps a more solid resource, at least on a scholarly level. This is an illustrated collection on Mexican culinary history edited by Fernán González de la Vara and coordinated by the well-respected Mexican historian Enrique Krauze. The most useful volumes for our purposes are volume 3, *Mestizaje culinario* ("Culinary Mestizaje"), which includes a fairly detailed treatment of native and European foods and ingredients, and volume 4, *La Nueva España* ("New Spain"), featuring sections on medicinal foods, food distribution, and conventual and hacienda cookery. This collection offers a slightly more detailed alternative to Paco Ignacio Taibo's and Salvador Novo's briefer but well-written sections on essentially the same topic (detailed below).

A final note regarding secondary sources: a good resource for brief and accessible works are the published proceedings from recent conferences on Sor Juana. Most conferences devoted to the Mexican nun have had at least one paper devoted to the topic of food. Guadalupe Pérez San Vicente's "Sor Juana y su libro de cocina" ("Sor Juana and Her Cookbook") explains some of the technical terms used in Sor Juana's recipes. The edited volume where this article is found contains other usefully brief pieces on various aspects of Sor Juana's work, life, and times, including conventual life, the *Primero sueño* and visual art, and Sor Juana and music. Likewise Asunción Lavrin's "Vida conventual: Rasgos históricos" ("Convent Life: Historical Characteristics"), in Sara Poot-Herrera's *Sor Juana y su mundo*, is a good overview of the cultural and economic conditions of conventual life during the period and is quite accessible to undergraduates. This edited collection is another good resource on various aspects of Sor Juana: it contains interesting articles on art and architecture as well as on literary forms. A volume developed from a conference in 2003 on the topic of food and literature (Poot-Herrera, *Gustos*) features a number of papers on Sor Juana and on the colonial period. Notable is one by Rosa Perelmuter, "La bella" ("The Beautiful One"), which collects many of the references to food throughout the nun's work, and María Águeda Méndez's "La comida en el claustro novohispano" ("Food in the New Spanish Cloister"), which discusses the everyday routines of conventual life including cooking, eating, and fasting.

Classroom Implementation: Curriculum

Here I offer four specific suggestions for incorporating the theme of cooking into a coherent syllabus. The first three pertain to typical, lower-division course offerings in a Spanish or Hispanic studies department. The fourth is for an interdisciplinary course specifically on food and Mexican culture. Such a course can be offered in a number of departmental contexts including but not limited to Latin American studies, American studies, history, general humanities, or cultural studies.

On a practical note, it is somewhat difficult, but not impossible, to explore this topic in a course taught in English. While most of Sor Juana's primary literary works are available in English translation, most of the primary and secondary sources about food detailed here exist only in Spanish. The advantage is that many of these texts, but especially the recipes, are fairly brief and could be easily handled by students with minimal competency in Spanish and a good dictionary. Depending on the type of course in which this material is taught and the typical profile of the students the course might attract, it could be possible to assemble small teams that include at least one student with a reading knowledge of Spanish.

A Three-Layered Approach within Standard Spanish Department Curricula

To incorporate the topic of food into the core-course selection of requirements for the Hispanic studies major, I suggest employing a progressive, three-part model with each step appropriate first to a large undergraduate survey class, then to a specialized upper-division undergraduate class, and finally to a small seminar; thus, the courses developed become increasingly specialized.

The first part of this incorporation, suitable to a large introductory survey course, assumes the context of a fairly ambitious chronology typical to such courses, which usually covers most of the colonial period and often extends to the present. This means that not much time can be devoted to any single author or period and presupposes only a brief introduction to Sor Juana, usually by way of some very short anthology selections. A good strategy here is to pair the readings with a visual presentation of art from the period, as well as with illustrations of the various foods and handcrafts from some of the sources listed below—and perhaps from some of the recipes. If at all possible, it is interesting to share with the students an actual example of one of these crafts, such as a piece of handiwork like embroidery, waxwork, artificial flower making (still available from some of the convents in Mexico), or a dish made from one of the recipes.

For a smaller, upper-division course on colonial literature, where more time can be devoted to the subject, I would deepen this process by including other relevant primary readings (on or by Descartes, Kircher, or Sigüenza y Góngora). Sometimes at this level—but more often at the next level that corresponds to a small, specialized seminar—a good exercise is to ask students to embark on a guided library-research project. This can involve any of several aspects of material culture, including period cookery, the history of nutrition, and the economics of food in colonial New Spain.

A specific suggestion for such a project: instructors, after assigning readings about American food products, can ask students to track down authoritative Spanish cookbooks from the period. One of the most authoritative texts on cookery, if not the easiest to find, is Francisco Martínez Montiño's *Arte de cocina, pasteleria, vizcocheria y conserveria* ("Art of Cooking, Baking, Bun-making, and Preserving" [1611]). Originally from the late sixteenth century, it was first published in Madrid, reprinted at least twenty times during the seventeenth century, and distributed widely throughout the Spanish empire. It offers a good source with which to compare some of the Mexican conventual recipes, but its most recent editions are from the eighteenth century, available only in major United States research libraries.

Other resources include Diego Granado's *Libro del arte de cocina* ("Book on the Art of Cookery" [1599])—available in a 1971 reprint—and Roberto de Nola's *Libro de cozina* ("Cookery Book" [1525]), originally printed in Toledo; it is available in a 1969 reprint. Have students look for similar ingredients, methods, or recipes in the conventual cookbooks of the period and these Spanish authorities; ask them to address the similarities and differences: how did discovery and colonization change the nutritional and economic landscape, and for which social classes? Did the Mexican nuns develop, adapt, or remain faithful to their European origins? If there are innovations, such as incorporation of these American ingredients, how does this reflect a new reality? How subtly or overtly were these ingredients used, and was there a limit to how much "nativization" was acceptable?

To bring this library project into the class discussion of literary texts, the appearance of "American" touches in the development of food could be compared with some of Sor Juana's references to indigenous culture, as in the *loa* to the *Divino Narciso* ("Divine Narcissus") or some of the scatterings of Nahuatl language in her shorter poetry. Paco Ignacio Taibo's or Salvador Novo's chapters on American ingredients or volumes 3 and 4 of González de la Vara on "culinary *mestizaje*" are readable, basic introductions, which are useful at this stage. Novo was an important poet of the *contemporáneos* generation of the 1920s and 1930s, and his book *Cocina mexicana, o historia gastronómica de la cuidad de México* ("Mexican Cooking, or a Gastronomic History of Mexico City") offers an impressionistic series of vignettes in the style of Ricardo Palma's *Tradiciones peruanas* ("Peruvian Traditions") or Artemio de Valle-Arizpe's various works on Mexico. Novo's work mixes personal impressions and erudition with selections from various primary sources ranging from Bernal Díaz del Castillo's *True History of the Conquest of New Spain* and Bernardino de Sahagún's *General History of the Things of New Spain, Florentine Codex* to printed menus from famous events and newspaper illustrations. Most relevant to Sor Juana are the short chapters on the "virreinato" ("viceroyalty") with headings on hunger, Mexican dowries, the contribution of Mexican ingredients, such as chocolate and tomatoes, to the world; "especie de especies" ("the matter of spices"); tea and coffee; and the "motín de Indios" ("Indian uprisings"), the late-seventeenth-century food riots that disillusioned Carlos de Sigüenza y Góngora. It is, needless to say, very well written.

Taibo's *Encuentro de dos fogones* ("Meeting of Two Hearths") is a two-volume work by a well-known Mexican writer and journalist, and it is mostly impressionistic. Although it is not scholarly in the strictest sense, since there is very little in the way of critical apparatus, it does draw from a fairly impressive array of period sources. The sections on pre-Columbian and colonial food are brief, engagingly written, and offer a good way of presenting to undergraduates the basic history of the introduction of some important American food products—chiles, corn, chocolate—to the world stage.

Of course an entertaining exercise, practicable only in a small class or senior-level seminar, is to make a meal based on the students' library discoveries. Small groups can each be responsible for different dishes or courses. Sometimes, though, depending on the typical student-housing situation, access to kitchens may be a problem. The conventual recipes from the period tend heavily toward sweets and desserts (which reflects the nuns' market niche and offers a point worth discussing) and may result in a very sweet meal. The instructor can steer the conversation over dinner toward reflection on how learning about this food, preparing it, and tasting it have changed the students' understanding of the literary texts and the time and place they represent. Perhaps this dinner could be held in conjunction with a showing of María Luisa Bemberg's biopic *Yo, la peor de todas* ("I, The Worst of All").

I should note that I developed this three-tiered approach with another, pragmatic purpose in mind: it is a good marketing tool. It attracts students from the lower-division courses into more specialized offerings and encourages students into the major or minor. If students are interested enough in the topics of food and culinary history, and they realize that they will feature more prominently in the progressive course of their studies, this approach could entice them to continue.

A Course on Food and Mexican Culture

Finally I offer a proposal for a specialized, cross-disciplinary course, with some variation of the title Writers, Food, and the Formation of Mexican Culture and Identity. There is an abundance of material as well as a wide range of time periods and disciplinary approaches—economic, historical, anthropological, political, cultural—that one could use to build a fascinating syllabus on this topic. I suggest organizing such a course by concentrating on three or four important intellectual figures (one of them being Sor Juana), each of whom had a special relation with food, and then using this relation to explore the specific historical periods through cuisine. Other figures could include Artemio de Valle-Arizpe,

Alfonso Reyes, Carlos Monsiváis, and Taibo. This course presupposes a cultural studies approach, since we will consider food itself as a form of cultural production; an important corollary would be to look at economic, as well as political, history in relation to food.

The syllabus uses the historian Jeffrey Pilcher's *Que vivan los tamales* ("Long Live Tamales") as an organizing text and could incorporate many aspects of economic history and anthropology as well. In particular, such a syllabus could feature changing social values and habits as they were reflected in eating habits: for instance, the nativization of European crops and livestock during the colonial period, the obsession of the elites with French culture during the nineteenth and early twentieth centuries, how the "rediscovery" of indigenous ingredients and cuisines was a part of a nationalistic project—and how Sor Juana's twentieth-century "rediscovery" was related to this nationalistic project. Although Pilcher's readable and well-researched book concentrates more on the nineteenth and twentieth centuries, it offers a widely applicable and synthetic reading of the class implications of food habits that could extend to a reading of the colonial period. Pilcher makes the point that only very recently have the Mexican ruling classes, who have always favored European modes, openly embraced Indian ingredients as authentic national products welcome into high culture. Before this acceptance, since the conquest, incorporations of local and indigenous goods and habits were often muted or surreptitious. In terms of Sor Juana and the topic of food, Pilcher's first chapter, "People of the Corn," and the second one, "The Conquest of Wheat: Culinary Encounters in the Colonial Period," give a succinct, well-documented introduction to some of the larger historical forces surrounding food during the period.

Possible Pitfalls and Benefits

In my experience, the exercise of "performing" food, if not kept rigorous, can result in two main distractions. The first is that, although excitement and energy are always welcome things in a classroom, the exercise can become a kitchen experiment in which the texts, ideas, and historical awareness become secondary to the act of cooking. This risk needs to be counterbalanced by carefully making it clear to the students that the exercise is being carried out in the context of the readings. Furthermore, the instructor should take every opportunity to establish and deepen the connections between the texts and the physical process and to expect the students to articulate, and share, some of these connections.

The second, perhaps rarer but more serious distraction, is that the exercise can fall uncomfortably close to the fantasy, dress-up world of Renaissance fairs and historical reenactments, with all the distortions and inaccuracies these can have. Many of those elaborate pastimes tend to develop a stylized universe of anachronistic playacting for their own and bear only passing resemblance to the time and place that inspired them. If the instructor detects that the course is trending in this direction, a good way to redirect it is by addressing the problem in a conceptual way that is relevant to the work of Sor Juana: is dress-up escapism a legitimate part of intellectual pursuits? When is an invented world too overwhelming, too hermetic—and too distant from the material world that allows it to exist?

In general, however, the topic of food and culinary history offers an appealing way of broadening and enriching a strictly literary approach. In Sor Juana's work, the implications of food and cooking are not just hard to ignore, they offer a particularly resonant perspective on her thought, life, and world, as well as a unique classroom opportunity. Food is a vital part of her aesthetics and worldview on a very basic level. It is a fairly simple task to search for, and find, references to food, digestion, and "women's work" in her writings, but it is a more challenging matter to explore the deeper metaphoric and political resonances of these references. The students engaged in this exercise will benefit greatly from this exploration, especially if they are not spoon-fed the interconnections but are instead allowed to discover and develop them on their own.

Musical Settings of Sor Juana's Works and Music in Works of Sor Juana

Mario A. Ortiz

The close relationship between Sor Juana and music has been highlighted in biographical and critical studies on the poet since the publication of her first biography, the "Aprobación," written by Diego Calleja in the third volume of Sor Juana's works, *Fama y obras póstumas* (Madrid, 1700). In *Vida de Sor Juana* Calleja refers explicitly to Sor Juana's collection of musical instruments (38) and to her musical treatise (27–28). These two references illustrate two general areas of interest among literary critics and musicologists with regard to Sor Juana and music: musical practice and theory. Did Sor Juana play any of the musical instruments that Calleja tells us she owned? Did she compose music? What specific musical activities did Sor Juana perform in the convent? Unfortunately, the existing documentation does not allow us to offer any definitive answers to these important questions. On music theory, however, we do have existing proof of Sor Juana's sophisticated theoretical training: her own literary works. This essay will address some approaches in teaching Sor Juana and music with regard to these two general areas of practice and theory.

As a starting point for any discussion of musico-literary analysis in the classroom, it is necessary to define and contextualize with the students the types of relations and critical approaches that exist between music and literature. Steven Paul Scher's article "Literature and Music" provides an insightful typology of the relations between these two arts. Scher divides musico-literary studies into three general areas: literature in music, music and literature, and music in literature. By literature in music, Scher means exclusively instrumental music based on a literary text, without the use of a singing or reciting voice. Music and literature refers in general terms to works in which the "literary text and musical composition are inextricably bound" (226), that is, vocal musical forms (songs) or musico-dramatic forms (opera and musical theater). The third of Scher's categories, music in literature, is the broadest of the three, and Scher limits his discussion to three subcategories: word music, musical structures and techniques, and verbal music. Word music is, Scher writes, the "type of poetic practice that aims primarily at imitation in words of the acoustic quality of music" (230). Scher's second subcategory deals with the use in literature of musical structures (theme and variation, sonata form, etc.) and techniques (counterpoint, leitmotif, etc. [231–34]). Finally, Scher defines verbal music as "any literary presentation (whether in poetry or prose) of existing or fictitious musical compositions: any poetic texture which has a piece of music as its 'theme' " (234). To these three subcategories, I would add one more, which is more strictly related to the focus of my essay: the use of musical imagery in a literary text, whether to create a musical rhetorical figure or to expound on aesthetic ideas about music.

This essay, based on this musico-literary typology, concentrates on approaches to teaching musical settings of Sor Juana's works (a prime example of Scher's music and literature category) and Sor Juana's use of musical imagery (my added subcategory to Scher's music in literature type), which pervades her literary production. These two general areas of study correspond to the practical and theoretical considerations introduced earlier in this essay.

Musical Settings of Sor Juana's Works

Composers have been setting Sor Juana's works to music during her lifetime right up to the present. She wrote texts that were specifically intended to be sung, such as her entire corpus of *villancicos* (feast-day songs). The musical compositions accompanying these poems were the responsibility of the chapelmasters of the cathedrals for which Sor Juana wrote the poetic texts. Robert Stevenson's studies "Sor Juana Inés de la Cruz's Musical Rapports" and "Sor Juana's Mexico City Musical Coadjutors" deal in detail with the collaborations between the poet and the chapelmasters who set her *villancicos* to music. Unfortunately, none of these original compositions has survived. We do have, nonetheless, extant examples of musical settings by other composers who continued throughout the colonial period to use Sor Juana's texts after her death. In "Sor Juana Inés de la Cruz y los maestros de capilla catedralicios," Aurelio Tello has compiled a valuable catalog of colonial musical settings of Sor Juana's works; this inventory is by no means conclusive, since more compositions have surfaced since the publication of Tello's research and even more will undoubtedly continue to appear. In addition to colonial chapelmasters, we can turn to modern composers, for whom Sor Juana's texts, *villancicos*, and other genres become a rich source of musical inspiration. I will provide specific teaching examples from both colonial and modern composers.

Before introducing musical settings to my students, I try to define with them the "text" that we will study. The "text" of a vocal composition, in its broadest sense, encompasses not only the poetic and musical texts as separate entities but also the interwoven relation between the two, as well as the larger context to which the text belongs (when the composition is part of a larger work). By isolating these components of the text under study, students display more confidence as they proceed with their analysis from the most tangible aspect (the poetic text) to the more abstract concept of aesthetic unity (the work in relation to a larger text).

An important resource for teaching Sor Juana's *villancicos* set in the colonial period is the recording *Le phénix du Mexique: Villancicos de sor Juana Inès de la Cruz mis en musique à Chuquisaca au XVIII*[e] *siècle* ("The Phoenix of Mexico: Villancicos by Sor Juana Inés de la Cruz Set to Music in Chuquisaca in the Eighteenth Century"). The collection consists of sixteen compositions from Chuquisaca (formerly La Plata, and today Sucre, Bolivia). Although they are settings of Sor Juana's *villancicos*, "they weren't just simple reproductions of 'sisterjuanesque' works but correspond well and truly to Chuquisaca's artists' interpretation of the texts, according to their own perception and in adapting them as they felt the[m] necessary" (G. Garrido 34). The flexibility of the period in approaching a particular poetic text resulted in the creation of unique and new texts, in the broad sense. The examination of textual variations provides ample opportunities for stimulating classroom discussions.

One of the *villancicos* in this recording that I have found to be successful in the classroom is "Oíd el concierto" ("Listen to the Concert"), set to music by Manuel de Mesa (c. 1725–1773). The text is a variant of *villancico* 220, "Silencio, atención" ("Silence, attention" [3: 7–8]), in which Sor Juana praises the divine qualities of the Virgin Mary's singing. The entire text is based on complex musical imagery that illustrates Sor Juana's cognizance of highly specialized contemporary music theory. An examination of the eighteenth-century text reveals, however, that the poem was shortened from fourteen to six *coplas* ("stanzas"), simplified in its use of musical imagery, and adapted to reflect its new geographic context.

The musical setting of this particular *villancico* is accessible to students of all levels. The festive musical character closely corresponds to the celebratory theme of the poetic text. In examining the relation between music and poetry, students are able to observe rather obvious musical techniques that illustrate or paint the text (to refer to the early modern practice known as word painting). For example, in the setting of the introduction of the *villancico*, which is completely different from the original version, the festive character of the music changes abruptly from a fast to a slow tempo and from a contrapuntal to a homophonic texture when the text refers to the "dulce melodía" ("sweet melody") to which we are invited to listen. This *villancico*, as well as others in the collection, provides numerous opportunities for analyzing easy-to-grasp musical representations of the poetic text.

Another aspect that I stress in the classroom is the larger context of these *villancicos*. The *villancico* was one of the most popular musico-poetic genres in Spain and the New World during the early modern period. Written primarily for religious celebrations during the seventeenth century, *villancicos* drew heavily on popular poetic imagery and languages, which in turn were reflected by the dancelike quality of the musical settings. Their formal structure consisted of a refrain (*estribillo*) and an indefinite number of stanzas in octosyllables and assonant rhyme. These works were not conceived as independent texts; rather, they were primarily written in cycles of eight or nine compositions to be performed during matins, one of the most elaborate liturgical structures in the seventeenth century. All the surviving colonial musical settings of Sor Juana's *villancicos* are isolated pieces from different cycles; in other words, there is not a single cycle for which we have a complete musical setting. Thus, we are prevented from studying the musical unity of the larger text. However, we can still study the poetic unity of an entire cycle.

In addition to studying the cycle unity of eight or nine *villancicos*, we should also consider the even larger text to which they belonged: the liturgical service of matins. Matins were divided into three liturgical units known as nocturns. Each of these nocturns included three lessons (readings from the Bible or from the writings of the fathers of the church), three psalms, and three responsories (usually long and elaborate chants). Right after each responsory, a *villancico* would be sung, except when the ninth responsory was substituted for the Te Deum, which explains why there could be eight or nine *villancicos* in each cycle. Moreover, the entire set of nocturns was preceded and followed by additional prayers and hymns. For special festivities, most of the ceremony was recited or sung using Gregorian chant or traditional Latin polyphony, resulting in a lengthy ceremony. The *villancicos* had a festive and popular character and used vernacular languages, which provided significant dramatic relief to the overall solemn pace of matins—so much so that on more than one occasion authors advocated the prohibition of *villancicos*, since they were turning the church into an auditorium for secular *comedias* ("secular theater" [Cerone 196]). Although we cannot re-create for our students the complete musico-liturgical unity of a service of matins, they can experience the sharp contrast of listening to a *villancico* right after having listened to a couple of minutes of Gregorian chant.

Funesta, a collection of six arias for soprano and chamber orchestra by the Mexican composer Marcela Rodríguez, exemplifies a modern musical setting of Sor Juana's works (mainly her secular ones) that has produced successful results in the classroom. In addition to the general musico-literary considerations, this setting allows me to address issues of modern reception and representation of Sor Juana. The texts are mainly fragments of Sor Juana's poems; only the second aria is a complete setting of sonnet 164, "Esta tarde, mi bien, cuando te hablaba" ("This afternoon, my love, while I spoke to you" [1: 287]). Rodríguez employs a musical language rich in dissonance and highly inventive in its treatment of the instrumental accompaniment. Having a complete work allows us to discuss the larger musico-poetic text. Students are asked to examine the unity of the texts selected by the composer, as well as the musical unity of the entire work.

The last aria of the set, "Funesta," has consistently been a favorite among my students. The text consists of only three lines: "Piramidal, funesta, / de la tierra, nacida sombra / yo, la peor de todas" ("Pyramidal, funereal, / shadow born of the earth / I, the worst of all").[1] Although the text is short, Rodríguez creates a five-minute musical composition in which there is an elaborate interplay between the vocal and instrumental parts. The result is a powerful dramatic tension that is emphasized by the continuous repetition of "yo, la peor de todas" and set to imaginative musical variations. For teaching this collection, I have created a simple exercise in which I divide each aria into specific segments based on textual or musical events. For the aria "Funesta," for instance, the division consists of the following: instrumental opening (0:00–0:35); "piramidal, funesta, / de la tierra, nacida sombra" (0:36–1:14); "yo, la peor de todas" (1:15–1:41); instrumental interlude (1:42–2:21); "piramidal, funesta, / de la tierra, nacida sombra" (2:22–2:50); "yo, la peor de todas" (2:51–3:09); and instrumental/vocalization (singing on a vowel without text) of "yo, la peor de todas"(3:10–5:00). Students are then asked to take note of how the text and music interact in each of these segments. Usually, they go beyond the mere description of events and react above all to the dramatic effect of the settings.

Music in Sor Juana's Works

"Yo no estudio para escribir, ni menos para enseñar" ("I do not study in order to write, nor far less in order to teach" [4: 444; 47]), wrote Sor Juana in her *Respuesta a sor Filotea* (*The Answer*). In the classroom, far from taking this statement literally, we discuss the strategies used by Sor Juana for teaching through her writings. *Loa* 384, "Encomiástico poema a los años de la Excma. Sra. Condesa de Galve" ("Encomiastic Poem on the Birthday of Her Excellency, the Countess of Galve" [3: 462–82]), clearly illustrates not only Sor Juana's musical imagery, both its use of musical metaphors and its sophisticated exposition of music theory, but also Sor Juana's role as a music teacher. In this sense, this section of my essay might well be titled "approaches to teaching Sor Juana's teaching music."

This *loa* is particularly interesting because it is written for allegorical musical characters. Music herself is the main character and is accompanied by the six musical notes of the traditional hexachord (a six-note scale used since the Middle Ages): named Vt (modern do), Re, Mi, Fa, Sol, and La. The basic plot of the play is rather simple. Music appears first. After a monologue in which she announces the task at hand—to celebrate the birthday and beauty of the countess (the vicereine Elvira de Toledo)—she introduces each of the musical notes one by one. As they are introduced, they have the opportunity to talk about themselves and their specific function in music harmony. After this introduction, Music delivers a long and elaborate dissertation about musical aesthetics. After the musical lesson (we are already beyond the first half of the play), the musical notes show cards with the letters of their names (Vt carries a *V* and a *T*, Re an *R* and an *E*, and so on), with which they begin the laudatory poetic games in honor of the vicereine.

In addition to its explicit goal of celebrating the vicereine's birthday, the play's underlying objective is to offer the audience a sophisticated lesson of musical aesthetics. Sor Juana probably disguises this "music treatise" with the mask of a birthday celebration because during her time women were discouraged from studying music theory—and, even more, from teaching it. The character Music thus becomes the vehicle through which Sor Juana expounds on her musical knowledge. Ironically, we know little today about Sor Juana's practical musical activities, generally encouraged in women, and much more about her incursions into the forbidden area of music theory.

Let us examine the essence of Sor Juana's musical lesson. Music announces that the task of celebrating Elvira's beauty corresponds to music, since it is the art best suited for such endeavors: "nada representa / a la Belleza mejor / que la Música" ("nothing represents / Beauty better / than Music" [3: 470]). But first it is necessary to understand what beauty is. To answer this aesthetic question, Sor Juana provides a fundamental premise. To know what beauty is, she says, we must first understand the intrinsic correspondence between harmony and beauty: "solamente quiero que / se mire la conveniencia / que hay de Armonía a Hermosura" ("I only want / to show the correspondence / between Harmony and Beauty" [3: 468]). Given this basic principle, we must begin by examining how Sor Juana defines harmony.

The *loa* begins when the curtain is still down and "a voice sings inside," which we soon identify as Music's voice, or the voice of Sor Juana, the music teacher:

> Si en proporciones de partes
> sólo consiste lo hermoso
> que no entienden los oídos
> y que lo escuchan los ojos. (3: 463)
>
> If beauty consists only of
> the proportions of the parts,
> that the ears do not understand,
> and the eyes hear it.

Two ideas are introduced in these verses: first, the relation between beauty and proportion and, second, the limitation of the senses in perceiving beauty.

The first of these propositions, the relation between beauty and proportions, is another way of saying "la conveniencia / que hay de Armonía a Hermosura" (3: 468). Sor Juana uses harmony here in its practical sense of music and in its philosophical Pythagorean sense of universal order. The art of music, as a reflection of this universal order, partakes of harmony's mathematical organizational principles. This philosophical definition of music corresponds to Sor Juana's definition of beauty in the *loa*:

> No es otra cosa lo Hermoso
> que una proporción que ordena
> bien unas partes con otras. (3: 469)
>
> Beauty is nothing else but
> a proportion that arranges
> well some parts with others.

In these lines Sor Juana paraphrases the "universal definition of music" given by Pietro Cerone in his music treatise *El melopeo y maestro* ("The Perfect Musician and Teacher"), which was Sor Juana's main source for her study of music theory. Cerone writes: "La música otra cosa no es que una consonante harmonía de tantas y diversas cosas proporcionadas" ("Music is nothing else but a consonant harmony of many and diverse proportioned things" [204]). Moreover, this correspondence of beauty and proportion echoes recognizable Neoplatonic concepts. For example, we find it in León Hebreo's *Diálogos de amor* ("Dialogues of Love"), which circulated widely through the Spanish translation of Garcilaso de la Vega: "La hermosura parece que es la proporción de las partes al todo y la conmensuración del todo a las partes" ("Beauty seems to be the proportion of the parts to the whole and the commensuration of the whole to the parts" [273]).

The character Music further explains the second idea introduced in the opening verses of the *loa*, the role of the senses in the aesthetic experience. She claims that harmony and beauty are one and the same thing, but they are directed to different senses: "la Armonía a los oídos / y a los ojos la Belleza" ("Harmony to the ears, and beauty to the eyes" [3: 468]). The relation between hearing and seeing that Sor Juana establishes, particularly in terms of the confusion that she introduces, "que no entienden los oídos / y que lo escuchan los ojos" ("that the ears do not understand / and the eyes hear it" [3: 463]), is elaborated by Music when she defines the role of the senses in the perception of beauty:

Limitados los sentidos
juzgan mensuras diversas
en los objetos sensibles;
y así dan la diferencia
entre lo que ven o escuchan,
lo que gustan o que tientan. (3: 468–69)

Limited the senses,
they judge different measures
in the sensible objects;
and thus they differentiate
between what they see or hear,
between what they taste or they touch.

Then, we may ask, if the senses are by definition so limited, who is the central judge of the aesthetic experience? Music replies:

Mas el alma, allá en abstracto,
conoce con evidencia
que es una proporción misma,
aunque distinta parezca,
aquella que al gusto halaga
o que al tacto lisonjea,
la que divierte a los ojos
o la que al oído suena. (3: 469)

But the soul, in abstract operation,
knows with certitude
that it is the same proportion,
although it may seem different,
that which pleases the taste
or gratifies the touch,
that which entertains the eyes
or sounds to the ear.

The soul then becomes the central judge of the aesthetic experience and is the only organ capable of transcending the sensorial perceptions of beauty. Therefore, understanding beauty is, according to Sor Juana, an intellectual pursuit; music, through its mathematical and proportional organization, is the best vehicle to express it.

Through this exposition of clearly Neoplatonic foundations, Sor Juana succeeds in fulfilling the two goals of the *loa*: to celebrate the vicereine's birthday and teach a valuable lesson on musical aesthetics. Although the tasks may seem unrelated, the music lesson is the real gift that Sor Juana offers to Elvira. The imaginative and charming game with the cards in the second part of the *loa* is just a diversion, one that only superficially illustrates the concept of musical proportions applied to letters. That is, the letters naming the notes are not in themselves aesthetically significant; only when they are arranged or well proportioned do they express beauty. Thus, while Sor Juana entertains the audience's senses with the visual signs of the cards and the aural dimension of the music that must have accompanied the *loa*, the true aesthetic object of the performance lies above this sensory diversion. The *loa*'s intellectual analysis of the correspondence between music and beauty is addressed specifically to Elvira's soul. Sor Juana's message to the vicereine is that, unlike those who can perceive her beauty only through the senses, specifically through the eyes, Sor Juana, creator of this work of art, is able to intellectually grasp the countess's true and inherent harmonic beauty.

When teaching this *loa*, I have the students prepare the cards with the letters of the musical notes. We imitate Sor Juana's poetic games and create new ones. We also speculate about the type of music that could have been used and even try to use known melodies or create new ones to sing some verses (invariably, when trying to find a melody for the section when each note is introduced, someone turns to Maria's do-re-mi lesson in *The Sound of Music*). I want the students to have, at least to some extent, a verbal and musical experience that will entertain their senses. When the fun is over, we delve into the intellectual core of the work: the lesson on musical aesthetics. Once they have grasped the main concepts presented in the *loa*, I challenge them to find the aesthetic implications of this musical lesson in Sor Juana's *ars poetica* in general. They are asked to search for other examples in Sor Juana's works in which Sor Juana denounces the deceitful nature of the senses, the intellectual superiority of the soul, and the use of music to represent beauty.

The approaches to teaching Sor Juana and music here suggested are a response to Sor Juana's call to seek in one art what we cannot grasp from another: "Yo de mí puedo asegurar que lo que no entiendo en un autor de una facultad, lo suelo entender en otro de otra que parece muy distante; y esos propios, al explicarse, abren ejemplos metafóricos de otras artes" ("For my part, I can say with certainty that what I do not understand in one author on a certain subject, I usually understand in another author who treats what appears to be a very distant subject. And in turn these very authors, once understood, can unlock the metaphorical examples employed in still other arts" [4: 450; 59]). Sor Juana's interest in a wide variety of disciplines is by itself an invitation to us as readers, students, and teachers to revisit her texts through interdisciplinary approaches. The study of the musical settings of Sor Juana's poetry and her music-theory lessons allows us to explore the musical dimension of her work and gives us a valuable insight into her cultural milieu in general and to her *ars poetica* in particular.

NOTE

[1]The first two lines are from *Primero sueño* (1: 335), whereas the third is based on the closing words of her testament: "Yo, la peor del mundo" ("I, the worst woman in the world" [4: 523]). All translations, except for those from the *Answer*—where I cite Arenal and Powell—are mine.

Sor Juana, an Official Habit: Twentieth-Century Mexican Culture

Emily Hind

The Mexican actor Susana Zabaleta poses for a red-carpet shot; she wears an elegant black evening gown with a red bolero jacket and feathered purse. I ripped the photo out of the Sunday gossip magazine included in a Mexico City newspaper, because written on the gown across Zabaleta's abdomen and pelvis are the words "Hombres necios que acusáis a la mujer sin razón" ("Stubborn men who wrongly accuse woman" [*M Magazine*].[1] The newspaper caption calls the outfit "inspiring" and does not pass up the chance to pun on the "quills" of Zabaleta's handbag. If the Sunday paparazzi photos are any indication, professors should rejoice when it comes time to study Sor Juana. The poet commands attention—even when printed in latitudes other than the pelvic. Sor Juana's personal struggle and literary work offer the stuff of potentially Oscar-worthy epic films. What's more, her baroque spirit facilitates ever-relevant conundrums. Does turning Sor Juana's feminist poetry into high fashion imply a bourgeois defusing of an otherwise noncommercial message? Or is Sor Juana's appliqué-able irony appropriately sported across one's lower abdomen? While the present essay tenders more questions than answers, it does assert Sor Juana's continued significance in contemporary society.

Students outside Mexico studying Sor Juana as an icon may benefit from a preliminary Internet search. By using the image-search option on the *Google* Web site and the keywords "Sor Juana" one can locate traditional portraits and more contemporary depictions of the poet. One page on the Web employs Sor Juana's likeness as a portal to nun-themed pornography. Clearly, viewer discretion—or perseverance—is advised. Instructors may also ask students to bring to class a list of national heroes who appeared in one way or another in their elementary education. On the list, students should jot some notes about the women role models who engrossed or repelled them. Ideally, a professor will explain the assignment by modeling it. I would mention my former obsession with biographies of the United States and British female medical workers Clara Barton, Florence Nightingale, and Elizabeth Blackwell; this interest was facilitated by the texts available in the school library. I repeatedly read these biographies for juicy anecdotes, such as the night during the Civil War when the exhausted Barton slept in a stream. Now, as then, I find this detail preposterous. The depiction of Barton's heroically solitary yet intelligent and community-minded renunciation casts her in the same mold that official representation in Mexico makes of Sor Juana and Chile makes of Gabriela Mistral. In fact, an interesting parallel may be found in Elizabeth Horan's study of iconic treatment of Gabriela Mistral on Chilean stamps, currency, and other forms of official homage. An in-class discussion might list the names mentioned by students and then descriptors of these women on a chalkboard. Students might then extrapolate roles from these official descriptors.

Discussion may pass from students' individual experiences and meditation on which characteristics in a given woman role model benefit the state to a review of recent uses of Sor Juana's image, using the findings from the Internet search as illustrations. Instructors should emphasize that the previous discussion, instead of merely structuring study of Sor Juana, should undergo revision as students reexamine their knowledge through meditation on the iconic Mexican poet. In the paragraphs that follow, I will explore the consequences of a twentieth-century Mexican official culture that idealizes Sor Juana as first among women and the application of Sor Juana's image by the Mexican citizenry at large and by assorted cultures beyond Mexico to serve causes such as Chicana identity and lesbian rights.

Official national history, often termed Mexico's secular religion, imagines Sor Juana as a saintlike figure. The religious meaning of the word *canonization* comes to mind when contemplating Sor Juana's evolution from colonial celebrity to required reading. Why has Sor Juana in particular come to serve official needs so prominently? Of course, her technically and thematically sly opus supplies one reason for continued interest in her work. On the other hand, Sor Juana functions as an image more than as a quotable notable in official usage. Thus, conveniently for governmental deployment of Sor Juana in a racist society, portraits of Sor Juana present her as light-skinned. In fact, this point receives special attention in a reading in the sixth-grade free textbooks from the series Libros de Texto Gratuitos ("Free Textbooks") that by law all Mexican schoolchildren must receive. Though many of the textbooks have been issued in a third reincarnation, the sixth-grade literature textbooks from 1972, drafted during the second wave of revisions, have yet to be updated. A germane passage, by the aforementioned Nobel Prize–winning Chilean author Gabriela Mistral describes the famous portrait by Miguel Cabrera of Sor Juana, an image that is also found on Mexico's current two-hundred-peso bill.

The description of Sor Juana comes from an essay included in Mistral's textbook for women, *Lecturas para mujeres* ("Readings for Women"), commissioned by the secretary of education José Vasconcelos and first published in 1923 during a project of citizen- and nation-building. In the excerpt reproduced in free textbooks, Mistral stresses Sor Juana's white face, like "una almendra desnuda" ("a naked almond"), and the contrast between her pale face and black hair and eyes as "muy hermoso" ("very beautiful"). Mistral assures us that Sor Juana's figure is "muy bella" ("very beautiful"). From the beginnings of the modern, postrevolutionary Mexican nation to the beginnings of the twenty-first century, then, generations of Mexican students have learned that Sor Juana's "esbeltez" ("slenderness") and "palidez" ("paleness") should incite reverence (qtd. in Ruiz de Bravo Ahuja 93). Indeed, in the original series of free textbooks published in 1960, the third-grade "national tongue" text describes the books that members of a fictional family peruse: the mother reads a cookbook; the little boy reads a history of aviation; the little girl reads a story about a worm; and the father reads a biography of Sor Juana. The text also reproduces a poem by Sor Juana (Domínguez Aguirre and León González). Twentieth-century national education thus posits Sor Juana as an important, though abbreviated, literary touchstone.

Besides Sor Juana's skin color, her vows of chastity may explain her official appeal over other women in Mexican history. For example, unlike La Malinche, Hernán Cortés's translator and lover, Sor Juana did not procreate with the ambivalently viewed Spaniards. By not having children with mortal men, Sor Juana may compete for top purity prizes in the Mexican canon with the iconically ubiquitous, though often darker-skinned, Virgin of Guadalupe. As Ermilo Abreu Gómez observes, Sor Juana stands as a woman without sex; instead of having her head cut off, Sor Juana's sacrifice is her body (177, 174). Indeed, in the official Mexican version, derived from colonial labels, Sor Juana as the "tenth muse," the "phoenix of America," and a secular madonna seems cerebral, virginal, and borderline superhuman.

Elsewhere, I have suggested that a "Sor Juana archetype" in Mexican women's twentieth-century works exists; this archetype divorces the female intellectual or artist from biological maternity and prevents the intellectual woman character from attaining professional success. The archetype demonstrates the relevance of Sor Juana's desexed image, even for Mexican intellectuals who are also mothers themselves. For example, in the short novels *Antes* ("Before") and *Duerme* ("Sleep"), and the longer *Cielos de la tierra* ("Heaven's Earths"), Carmen Boullosa creates a series of female characters whose characteristics sometimes overlap. For simplicity's sake, three patterns can be identified among these female figures: death from adolescence, the inability to menstruate, and the desire to become a man. Similarly, the novelist Ana Clavel, in *Los deseos y su sombra* ("Desire and Its Shadow"), turns her protagonist invisible and thus unlikely to enter into a normative sexual relationship that might lead to maternity. In the much-studied *Como agua para chocolate* ("Like Water for Chocolate"), Laura Esquivel allows her female protagonist to express her artistic side in culinary experiments. Perhaps because of the intellectual aspect of her domestic talents—the science of her kitchen that produces complex cuisine and functional matches—the character Tita cannot unite with her true love, Pedro, until the end of the novel, when sex with Tita kills him. Before this conclusion, Tita is able to nurse her sister's child through a nonnormative biological experience. Despite magical realism, Tita fails to achieve the conventional matrimony and maternity that she desires.

Earlier examples of a split between maternal and intellectual functions include *Los recuerdos del porvenir* ("Recollections of Things to Come") by Elena Garro. There, the mirroring characters, Julia and Isabel, do not engage in normative heterosexual, maternal roles. When Julia is rescued from her abusive lover and whisked into the sunrise on a white horse with Felipe, time stops, and Julia vanishes from the novel. The narrative picks up again with Isabel replacing

Julia as *querida* ("mistress"), although at the end of the novel instead of developing her talents or having children or escaping with a better partner, solitary Isabel turns to stone.

When an intellectual character does become pregnant, this often happens near the end of the text, as if to signal that the pregnant protagonist loses her hold on narrative interest. Ángeles Mastretta's *Mal de amores* (*Lovesick*) imagines an intellectual woman protagonist, a self-proclaimed bigamist with a medical career. Significantly, the character Emilia becomes pregnant and has her children in the last three pages of a 375-page novel. Before that, Emilia follows the Sor Juana archetype, exemplified by her aunt Milagros, who rejects most domestic and maternal activities: she dislikes sewing but skillfully designs her dresses, hates to cook, conspires in politics, travels, refuses to marry, never has children, and only in what appears to be late middle age agrees to cohabit with her lover. Emilia's mother, Josefa, on the other hand, suffers preternaturally regular and painful periods that always coincide with a certain phase of the moon and enjoys a contented domestic existence with her husband. As a tribute to maternal biology, Josefa anticipates her daughter's eventual motherhood and turn from the Sor Juana archetype.

The lack of narrative focus on protagonists' maternal roles in works by Mexican female authors hints at internal censure among women. Rosario Castellanos's play "El eterno femenino" ("The Eternal Feminine") addresses this repression of women by women and casts Sor Juana as herself or, at least, as an archetype. A cross-dressed Sor Juana woos her friend Celia, although the poet stops short of a kiss. Before correctly identifying her interlocutor, Celia believes she speaks to a male suitor and describes Sor Juana in contrast to her own fertile reproductive system. According to Celia, Sor Juana will give birth only to literary tropes and cobwebs. In the midst of Celia's explanation, Sor Juana offers the word "sterile" as a description of herself (404). Sor Juana fails to match Celia's maternal ideal, and in consequence Castellanos indicates a mind-maternal split based on a perceived brain-body division embodied (or cerebralized?) in Sor Juana.

The power of the Sor Juana archetype over Mexican women writers may stem from a generalized cultural inhibition concerning women's sexuality. In her self-representation in the partially autobiographical bildungsroman *Rito de iniciación* ("Rite of Initiation" [written 1964, published 1997]), Castellanos portrays her fictional alter ego as sexually repressed. Near the end of the novel, the solitary, frigid Cecilia turns down a marriage proposal from the homosexual Sergio, who senses her corresponding nonnormativity.

If Mexican women throughout the twentieth century find acceptance of female sexuality a difficult literary task, one perhaps complicated by the ubiquitous and impossible-to-imitate role model of the Virgin Mother in Mexico, the Sor Juana archetype does not challenge the dichotomy as much as it facilitates the image of an intellectual asexual woman. Should students find it taxing to relate to a culture that condemns women's sexuality and separates the maternal from the intellectual, a review of parallel phenomena in their cultures may prove helpful. For example, most universities tend to keep children away from campus, thus isolating them from academic work, and companies such as Victoria's Secret advertise sexy lingerie by attaching angel wings to models, as if to legitimate female sexuality through asexuality. While on the subject of fashion, profitable mention might be made of darker-skinned models and celebrities in the United States and Europe, such as Naomi Campbell, Tyra Banks, and Beyoncé Knowles, who tend to straighten their hair and sometimes sport nearly blond locks. Even though some learners may not know the particulars of the Mexican context, they probably have had some contact with a society that squirms before issues of race and women's sexuality.

In trying to explain Sor Juana's image, the instructor can hardly overemphasize the importance of Sor Juana's skin color and absent (hetero)sexuality as a partial explanation for deployment of the poet's image in support of racist and sexist projects. Of course, Sor Juana can be made as sexual or as chaste as suits her readers' needs. Permissible for a general audience to watch are biographies, novels, and plays about the poet. Racier theatrical versions of Sor Juana exist, perhaps most notably by the performance artist and writer Jesusa Rodríguez, who has staged a striptease while reciting Sor Juana's poem *Primero sueño* ("First Dream"; see *Jesusa Rodríguez*). Rodríguez has also published a brief play that casts Sor Juana in the Mexican penitentiary Almoloya (see *Sor Juana en Almoloya*; for a translation, see Taylor and Ramírez-Cancio), where the poet asserts her lesbianism and mocks Octavio Paz's biography of her, *Las trampas de la fe* (*The Traps of Faith* [1982]). Rodríguez's Sor Juana also comes to assume contemporary relevance by critiquing the Mexican politics of the new millennium. Other works that celebrate Sor Juana as a lesbian include María Luisa Bemberg's Argentinian-produced film, *Yo, la peor de todas* ("I, the Worst of All," which, like Rodríguez's piece, shows a physical and sentimental attraction between Sor Juana and her patron the vicereine María Luisa Manrique de Lara y Gonzaga, Countess of Paredes.

With or without the lesbian representation, Sor Juana also plays an important role for many Chicana artists and intellectuals. For example, two historically significant articles in a university-level textbook that documents Chicana feminism offer biographical details of Sor Juana to propose a tradition of Mexican intellectual women (Rincón; NietoGómez, "Chicana Feminism" and "The Chicana"). Though the political goal favors Chicanas, the technique of celebrating Sor Juana as an unquestioned hero parallels the methods of the Mexican government. Of course, Chicana iconic applications of Sor Juana range beyond a biographical review. Amalia Mesa-Bains creates self-termed *domesticana* ("domestican") altars that incorporate iconic figures, such as Sor Juana, in an attempt to canonize alternatives to patriarchy. To return to the textual, the novel *Sor Juana's Second Dream* by the Chicana writer Alicia Gaspar de Alba creates a lesbian protagonist using Sor Juana's poetry. In that novel, a perspective coincident with Mexican official usage emerges from the first page, which reprints four signatures by Sor Juana. The signature both as truth claim and as sacred scripture points to the fetish that tends to develop around the charismatic figure of Sor Juana. The poet's survival not as herself but as a slogan of sorts marks probably an inevitable step in the veneration of any historical figure.

Perhaps more clearly than other artistic representations, the Mexican-born United States resident Katia Fuentes's depiction of herself as Sor Juana by projecting corresponding iconic imagery on her body expresses the tendency to appropriate Sor Juana and to make her into what the spectator turned creator wishes Sor Juana to incarnate. In the Internet journal in which her work appears, Fuentes comments, "The hypnotizing sensation that the projected light creates on my body is, I feel, similar to the power that seeing a real Saint might have for us." In other words, Sor Juana's image represents the sacred in the present tense and thus is inevitably contemporary, even when intended to connote "tradition" or the historic past.

Appropriation of the poet's figure was first practiced during Sor Juana's lifetime, and Sor Juana recognizes the process, as indicated in verses such as "diversa de mí misma / entre vuestras plumas ando, / no como soy, sino como / quisisteis imaginarlo" ("diverse from myself / I wander among your quills / not as I am, but rather / as you wanted to imagine" [1: 159]). Another reference to this process plays on the poet's nickname, "phoenix of America": "pues nunca falta quien cante: / *Dáca el Fénix, toma el Fénix,* / en cada esquina de calle" ("for someone croons or hollers / "Your Phoenix here! Get your Phoenix! / on every neighborhood corner" [1: 144; Arenal and Powell 173]). The omnipresence of Sor Juana's image expressed in these lines still affects Mexican daily life.

Consider the series of black-and-white newspaper ads for Dodge and Chrysler cars printed in 2004, which show the outline of a car wrapped in a two-hundred-peso bill, the edges and top of which disappear in order to fold around the automobile profile. The whole bill is not visible; it is Sor Juana's face that alerts the observer that the image refers to the general notion of money. Apparently, the most recognizable and encouragingly iconic bill for Mexicans is Sor Juana's. Printed on currency, the poet's image circulates, literally, as cultural capital. Does the poet-nun inspire trust in car salespeople? What kind of saint is Sor Juana anyway, if her image functions on legal tender and in car ads? Sor Juana seems so readily recognizable that a campaign for copyrights juxtaposes miniature typewritten pages whose light and dark patches of text combine to form the familiar outline of the poet. In this instance, Sor Juana represents all authors, the archetypical author, the one the reader should not want to rip off by photocopying illegally. Again, an ethical allusion seems to emerge through the visual reference to the poet-nun.

Though students may analyze the outcome of this iconic usage for themselves, it is my contention that official imagery and ethical reference to Sor Juana tend to domesticate a wittily independent, feminist thinker. It is challenging to think of Sor Juana as a rebellious writer when studying her docile portrait, reduced to a face and wimple-swathed neck on the two-hundred-peso bill, with a very small signature beneath Sor Juana's cropped image. The habit itself hints that the Mexican woman celebrated for her brain should be attractively feminine, but not sexy. Significantly, in view of the problem in Mexico of the "mujer pública" ("public woman")—a phrase that connotes a prostitute—the poet's lips remain closed; as Abreu Gómez puts it, when analyzing the complete portrait, "Sor Juana is always about to speak no more" (175). Despite Sor Juana's official docility, it is hard to get the best of her in official representation, where she functions as something other than, or more than, "woman." To explore this notion, I return to a series of free government textbooks, this time to the current history books edited by Felipe Garrido, beginning in 1994, which display a nearly absolute masculinist bias.

In the texts for fourth and sixth grades, the two levels that supply relevant subject matter, no woman appears on the detailed timeline at the bottom of each page, except in the dates marking Sor Juana's birth and the publication of her works. Excluding two sonnets by Sor Juana in the fourth-grade book, neither the fourth- nor the sixth-grade text includes an excerpt from a woman writer's text. Inclusion of Sor Juana as the sole female literary figure encourages the understanding of her not only as first among intellectual women in Mexican official history but also as having attained that honor by virtue of her nonnormativity: she is able to compete with men because she does not fit the category "woman." Establishing Sor Juana as the model of the woman intellectual seems to remind girls that they will need to be more than or other than women to achieve intellectual renown, a message that perhaps forestalls the aspiration.

Given Sor Juana's frequent presence in masculinist literary canons and her position in Mexican official culture as the symbol of the woman intellectual (that is, the nonnormative woman), some students may wonder whether Sor Juana's complaints about the seventeenth-century's attitude toward women register a drastically different social environment than today's context. Does the stubborn-men theory about *machista* ("sexist") hypocrisy—men who accuse women of the faults that men encourage—hold true in the present day? If so, is Sor Juana an ineffectual "first" female intellectual in Mexico? To transpose this question to other nationalities, does Sor Juana's identification of the double standard explicate the wink at sexual repression in the brand Victoria's Secret? After considering the degree of discrepancy among three categories: Sor Juana's major texts, the uses made of the poet's image, and the contemporary state of feminism, students may wish to contemplate the remarkable, if disquieting, power of interpretation. Do discussants feel that they too wield this power, or do they merely observe it?

As Jesusa Rodríguez's theater reveals, not all manipulation of Sor Juana's likeness turns her into a sort of intellectual Betty Crocker or a domesticated, one-dimensional saint. For example, the university housed in the remodeled convent where Sor Juana lived, Universidad del Claustro de Sor Juana, constantly markets itself through Sor Juana's name and likeness. The institution distributes images of Sor Juana on postcards and brochures that tweak the familiar image with everything from a superimposed Betty Boop head to wild makeup coloring to dot-matrix representation. During the summer of 2004, advertisements in select Cinemex movie theaters ran a black-and-white cartoon that publicized the twenty-fifth anniversary of the Universidad del Claustro de Sor Juana. In the cartoon, the poet first appears incognita in a hooded mask emblazoned with the number twenty-five and walks among a cheering crowd until she enters a wrestling ring, where she whips off her mask and tosses it toward the sky. Though not dressed in pants or a miniskirt, and more demure and blank than perky and white, Sor Juana as a *lucha libre* ("free fighting") wrestler connotes pop culture, and the Claustro seems to argue that Sor Juana is cool, a woman of the people—at least a woman of the cartoon figures who hold signs advertising majors in the liberal arts. Would the privileged, yet nonnoble woman born of unmarried parents have been amenable to such elbow rubbing with the masses? Would she embrace a connection between higher education and screaming crowds, rock music, and theatrical sport? Is the unmasking of Sor Juana an ironic striptease, given her nun's robe and her present inability to expose herself further?

It would seem that ownership of Sor Juana is still up for grabs. In fact, according to Francisco de la Maza, the poet's remains are buried in a common grave in the Universidad del Claustro de Sor Juana, marked by a marble plaque placed in 1964–65. The disparity between the commemorative plaque and more grandiose memorials, such as the Rotunda of Illustrious Men, renamed Rotunda of Illustrious Persons in 2003, suggests uneasiness with Sor Juana's physical presence in the pantheon of heroes. At one point, Maza grumbles, the convent architecture required visitors to step on the burial site, which was treated as unremarkable corridor flooring (*Sepulcro* 18). Such nonchalance toward Sor Juana's burial site seems pardonable. After all, in official and popular imaginations, Sor Juana is neither deceased nor exclusively leased. Study of Sor Juana's contemporary image offers an unpredictable treasure hunt that chronicles with remarkable sensitivity our ideological fantasies and agendas.

I would conclude class discussion with an enumeration of the following paradoxes surrounding the poet that mark how Sor Juana's image gauges our obsessions and hypocrisies: once a standard of rationality in a tradition proud of its mystics, she now serves as a saint in a system proud of its positivist progresses; once a feminist in an age of machismo, she now functions as a lesbian in a period of hotly contested homophobia; once an alternately rebellious and submissive woman in an age that feared her enough to wish to control her every observable move, Sor Juana now symbolizes a nearly gender-neutral being in a time of supposedly more permissive attitudes. The contradictions deepen: Sor Juana stands as religious heretic and secular saint, as a queerly oxymoronic female intellectual, as an image saturated with significance and yet "always about to never speak again." Sor Juana shows us up, shows us who we wish to become and what we wish we could have changed. The image of Sor Juana—well, let's just say it's the stuff of excellent student evaluations.

NOTES

Many thanks to Braulio González Vidaña for providing me publicity from the Universidad del Claustro de Sor Juana and to Emilie Bergmann and Stacey Schlau for their outstanding editing skills and suggestions for further research.

[1]All translations are mine unless otherwise indicated.

Traces of Sor Juana in Contemporary Mexicana and Chicana/Latina Writers

Sara Poot-Herrera

Sor Juana's thought predates a great deal of modern discourse regarding many contemporary issues, including women's rights, gender equality, education in Mexico, and the idea of a unique "New Spanish" cultured identity. Her name is nationally and internationally known and is quoted, at least in her homeland, in a myriad of social and cultural circles. From the erudite to the illiterate, it is common to hear her famous lines, "You foolish and unreasoning men / who cast all blame on women."[1] Those who read Sor Juana recognize not only her literary genius but also her intellectual and other flirtations, as well as a delightful irony and sense of humor.

Primero sueño ("First Dream")—her search for knowledge—and the *Respuesta* (*Answer*), her defense of intellectual freedom, are two of her works that have exerted the most influence on contemporary women's writing. In the *Respuesta*, women writing today discover, and at times re-create, narrative passages from Sor Juana's childhood: her arrival in Mexico City, the decision to assume the habit, daily life in the Convent of Saint Jerome, and her motivation for writing the document itself. Like her modern readers, Sor Juana well knew that knowledge translated into power; she lives on in the genius and timelessness of her work. Over the three centuries since her death on 17 April 1695, she has become the foremost Hispanic female literary figure of all time. This is exactly what allows us, as teachers, to use Sor Juana as a prototype and an antecedent when approaching the subject of contemporary women intellectuals. In this essay, I would like to highlight some key moments from her life and work that have inspired Latin American and Chicana/Latina writers, as well as demonstrate how her influence has found form.

Sor Juana Inés de la Cruz's legacy has had multiple repercussions, from references to her work found in titles, epigraphs, and phrases in contemporary creation—literary and other—to the implicit echo of her ideas. Continued interest in her work is expressed not only in scholarship but also in the work of the many women writers who have converted the Mexican nun-intellectual into a literary character and in the productions of artists who have represented and interpreted her in music, painting, cinema, theater, collage, and performances of varied types. All of these women are, first and foremost, her readers. Their recognition of Sor Juana's genius and wit makes her come alive for us and transforms her into a potential contemporary of her successors. Through the sympathetic act of reading, narrators, poets, and playwrights, as well as essayists, philosophers, and other women artists, revisit, rewrite, and reinvent her.

Twentieth-century women writers recover, from the *Respuesta*, the image of the young Juana of "yesterday," who before she was three years old accompanied her elder sister "in one of those girls' schools they call *Amigas*" (49). Juana thought that she had fooled the teacher by stating that her mother had authorized the lessons: "I learned to read in such a short time that I already knew how by the time my mother heard of it. . . . The woman who taught me (may Good keep her) is still living, and she can vouch for what I say" (49). This statement by Sor Juana may be used to motivate and inspire students, especially female and minority students and any who have undergone great hardship or obstacles to pursue their studies. Sor Juana's life and works can be used to establish a critical timeline for the concept of education as liberating process.

In the introduction to *La ética del placer* ("The Ethics of Pleasure"), Graciela Hierro says: "Feminist philosophy for Mexicans starts with our mother and teacher Sor Juana Inés de la Cruz, matures with Rosario Castellanos, and continues its way up to our days" (11–12). Both implicitly and explicitly, the work of the twentieth-century Mexican writer and feminist thinker Rosario Castellanos exemplifies Sor Juana's legacy. In *Juicios sumarios* ("Summary Judgments"), Castellanos dedicates two essays to Sor Juana: "Asedio a Sor Juana" ("Sor Juana Besieged") and "Otra vez Sor Juana" ("Sor Juana, Once Again"). The famous poet-nun is a fundamental reference in Castellanos's essay *Mujer que sabe latín* ("A Woman Schooled in Latin" [1973]), a character in the play "El eterno femenino" ("The Eternal Feminine" [1975]), versified in "Meditación en el umbral" ("Meditation on the Threshold" [1972]), and a literary and feminist frame in the short story "Family Album" (1971). Regarding Sor Juana's life, Castellanos states in "Mujer que sabe latín": "La ejemplaridad de Sor Juana es tan sospechosa ante el criterio de sus superiores que primero le hubieran prohibido que mandado que consignara su historia. Pero ella aprovecha la coyuntura de una reprimenda para escribir un alegato a su favor" ("The exemplarity of Sor Juana was so suspicious to her superiors that at first they would have prohibited rather than commanded her to consign her story. But she takes advantage of the occasion of a reprimand to write an allegation on her own behalf" [890–91]). This allegation would become her autobiography, as conceived and analyzed by the critic and Sor Juana scholar Margo Glantz in *Sor Juana Inés de la Cruz, ¿hagiografía o autobiografía?* ("Sor Juana Inés de la Cruz: Hagiography or Autobiography?").

Those who read and re-create Sor Juana from the *Respuesta* meet the child who years later said, "I would abstain from eating cheese, because I heard tell that it made people stupid, and the desire to learn was stronger for me than the desire to eat" (49). Another passage from the *Respuesta* refers to the sacrifice that the young Juana made when she cut her hair to see if the speed with which she expanded her knowledge and understanding would compete with the speed with which her hair grew: "And so my hair grew, but I did not yet know what I had resolved to learn, for it grew quickly and I learned slowly. Then I cut my hair right off to punish my dull-wittedness, for I did not think it reasonable that hair should cover a head that was so bare of facts" (51).

The anecdote concerning Sor Juana's hair is a necessary reference for the successors of the young and future poet who wish to reconstruct the image of Sor Juana as a woman who wanted to know more in order to be less ignorant. The poem "The Young Sor Juana," in *Communion* by Pat Mora states: "Again I'll feel my hair / rain softly on my clothes, gather" (78). It is precisely the intellectual significance of women's hair, traditionally associated with sensuality, that will intertwine a variety of contemporary women's writing in relation to the seventeenth century, when Sor Juana was known as the "tenth muse" and "phoenix of Mexico."[2]

Sor Juana braids several passages of her early life into the story of her desire for knowledge. She sacrifices the vanity of her hair and the pleasure of food and is willing to sacrifice her feminine identity to continue studying. Conscious from an early age of the obstacles to women's education, she says in the *Respuesta*:

> I heard that in Mexico City there were a University and Schools where they studied the sciences. As soon as I heard this I began to slay my poor mother with insistent and annoying pleas, begging her to dress me in men's clothes and send me to the capital, to the home of some relatives she had there, so that I could enter the University and study. (49)

Although Sor Juana could not attend the university because in the seventeenth century its doors were closed to women, in the twentieth century her former convent has become the University of the Cloister of Sor Juana, where men and women study together and where the faculty includes writers dedicated to her legacy.

In "Mujer que sabe latín," Castellanos synthesized several episodes taken from her foremother's life and writings, illustrative of the poet's passion for books and learning:

> El de Sor Juana no es camino de santidad sino método de conocimiento. Para conservar lúcida la mente renuncia a ciertos platillos que tienen fama de entorpecer el ingenio. Para castigar a su memoria por no retener con la celeridad debida los objetos que se le confían, se corta un pedazo de trenza. Sueña en disfrazarse de hombre para entrar en las aulas universitarias; intenta pasar, sin otro auxilio que el de la lógica, de la culinaria a la química. Desde su celda de encierro escucha las rondas infantiles y se pregunta por las leyes de la acústica. Desde su lecho de enferma, sin más horizonte que las vigas del techo, indaga los enigmas de la geometría. Lectora apasionada, aprende el alfabeto por interpósita persona y llega a su hora final reducida a la última desnudez: la de no poseer un solo libro. (891)
>
> Sor Juana's is not a road of sanctity but a method of knowledge. To keep a lucid mind she renounces certain dishes infamous for clogging talent. To punish her memory for not retaining the objects entrusted quickly

> enough, she cuts off a braid. She dreams of disguising as a man in order to enter university rooms; she tries to pass, with no help other than logic, from culinary to chemistry. From her cell she hears children's singing and wonders about the laws of acoustics. From her sick bed, with no horizon but the ceiling beams, she inquires about the enigmas of geometry. An impassioned reader, she learns the alphabet through an intermediary and reaches her final hour reduced to the ultimate nakedness: that of not possessing a single book.

The teacher and students may use this passage to explore the very nature of the act of reading while contemplating the concept of the reader's nakedness when separated from books.

Referring to Sor Juana's desire for education, Anna NietoGómez paraphrases the *Respuesta,* imagining the conflict between the privileged position of theology and Sor Juana's desire for scientific learning: " 'If the world's supposed to be a manifestation of God's great goodness, how can I understand that if I don't know anything about it? These are the prerequisites for my understanding of His great and beautiful powers.' So she advocated that women have the right to education" ("Chicana Feminism" 54). NietoGómez extends the teaching of Sor Juana to Chicana writers: "Sor Juana [Inés] de la Cruz will be given recognition for literary contributions to the world. *La Respuesta* . . . may become the symbol of the right of every Mexicana and Chicana to education and the fulfillment of her potential" ("The Chicana" 130).

In *A Library for Sor Juana: The World of Sor Juana Inés*, Mora, a Chicana writer, treats the child Sor Juana as a character in a world of books. If during most of her life the convent isolated her from the exterior world, her ample library and her epistolary friendships transported her, both psychologically and intellectually, far beyond the confines and limits of her cell. Indeed, her vital textual presence is evident in the historical context and literary texts of the twenty-first century. As a tribute to Sor Juana's love of books, there are libraries throughout Mexico with her name or the name of one of her texts, such as the Public Regional Library "Primero Sueño" in Amecameca, a town close to Sor Juana's childhood home.

After living in the palace as the viceroys' favorite, Juana changes residence and chooses life in the convent. She chooses books, her old friends, over marriage; she observes and learns from nature and all that surrounds her. In the *Respuesta,* Sor Juana ironically tells Sor Filotea:

> pero, señora, ¿qué podemos saber las mujeres sino filosofías de cocina? Bien dijo Lupercio Leonardo, que bien se puede filosofar y aderezar la cena. Y yo suelo decir viendo estas cosillas: Si Aristóteles huberia guisado, mucho más hubiera escrito. (4: 459–60)

> But in truth, my Lady, what can we women know, save philosophies of the kitchen? It was well put by Lupercio Leonardo that one can philosophize

> quite well while preparing supper. I often say, when I make these little observations, "Had Aristotle cooked, he would have written a great deal more." (75)

The Mexican writer Mónica Lavín's *Dulces hábitos: Golosinas del convento* ("Sweet Habits: Convent Tidbits") is redolent with the aroma of the philosophical kitchen of Sor Juana. Mora also refers to this passage in her work "Nepantla: Essays from the Land in the Middle":

> Obviously, Sor Juana lived a privileged life and knew that housework can be true drudgery when a woman has no options. But rather than focusing on the drudgery of work, her words present such work as a source of creativity. (293)

Beatriz Espejo proposes that Sor Juana is the exception to the rule, "the first female American intellectual"; she writes:

> Her books opened to her the doors of the world, since her eyes could only see the volcanoes in the valley from the windows of a monastery cell. She anticipated an era and within four walls she conceived the substantial part of her writings. Once in a while, like pieces lost here and there, she left personal signs. (45)

We continue to find phrases taken from Sor Juana in the titles of contemporary women writers. When Ángeles Mastretta received the 1997 Rómulo Gallegos Prize for her novel *Mal de amores* (*Lovesick*), she entitled her acceptance speech "El mundo iluminado" ("The Illuminated World"), an allusion to the last line of *Primero sueño*. She says:

> Less audacious than Sor Juana, further from her genius than from her determination, those of us who are fortunate to find a destiny in the will to name the world, share with her the daily disillusion of misunderstanding. That is why we write, ruled by that disenchantment and convoked by an ambition we imagine that while naming fire, fish, prudence, wind, stupor, death, we can for an instant understand what they are. (198–99)

El mundo iluminado also became the title of a collection of essays and personal tales that includes the speech that she delivered when she received the prize.

Sor Juana's lines are frequently used as titles and epigraphs in books by women writers. In 1985, María Elvira Bermúdez published *Detente, sombra* ("Halt, You Shadow"); the title is taken from the first line of Sor Juana's sonnet 165. María Rosa Palazón borrows a line from the same sonnet to create another title that immediately brings to mind the figure of Sor Juana: *Imagen del hechizo que más quiero. Autobiografía apócrifa de José Joaquín Fernández de*

Lizardi ("Image of the Enchantment I Love the Most: Apocryphal Autobiography of Joaquín Fernández de Lizardi").

As epigraphs for her short-story collection, *Ojos de papel volando* ("Confetti Eyes Drifting"), María Luisa Mendoza chose lines from Sor Juana's flattering ballad to the Countess of Paredes: "que tengo, de tu carencia, / cuaresmados los deseos" ("That I have, of your lack, / quarantined desires" [1: 81]) and the signature from her final self-condemnation, "Yo, la peor del mundo: Juana Inés de la Cruz" ("I, the worst in the world: Juana Inés de la Cruz" [4: 523]). These epigraphs constitute a sly wink at the reader, so that we may understand Mendoza's nine short stories in a new light, that of a poetic tradition centuries old. In the stories, there are instances of other poems by Sor Juana; for example the line "El viento sosegado, el can dormido" ("Calm wind, sleeping dog") from *Primero sueño* (1: 337, line 80), found in the short story "El día del amor" ("The Day of Love" [91–98]) or the line from sonnet 180, "Dices que yo te olvido, Celio, y *mientes*" ("You say that I forget about you, Celio, and you lie" [1: 295]), which appears in "Me olvido de olvidarte" ("I Forget to Forget You" [128–37]). These examples are clear opportunities for instructors to use Sor Juana's work to inspire new and more informed readings of twentieth-century Mexican literature.

One of the epigraphs in *El rastro* ("The Trace"), by Margo Glantz, comes from sonnet 164, "Esta tarde, mi bien, cuando te hablaba" ("This afternoon, my dear, when I spoke with you" [1: 287–88]). This epigraph frames the novel; other lines from sonnet 164 echo throughout the entire book: "mi corazón deshecho entre tus manos" ("my heart already exhausted in your hands" [30]); "pues entre el llanto, que el dolor vertía, / el corazón deshecho destilaba" ("So among the tears my pain poured, my torn heart distilled" [121]). Glantz quotes from Sor Juana's sonnet 152, "Verde embeleso de la vida humana": "que yo, más cuerda en la fortuna mía, / tengo en entrambas manos ambos ojos / y solamente lo que toco veo" ("because I, more sober in my fortune, have eyes between both hands and see only what I touch" [1: 280–81; 130]). In her use of Sor Juana's words and imagery, Glantz acknowledges the timeless relevance of the poet's work and offers a discursive tapestry that significantly enriches her own.

A few years before writing *El rastro*, Glantz published *Apariciones* ("Apparitions"). One of the two plots in the novel involves two cloistered nuns invoking mystical raptures, while in a final acknowledgment the novelist names Juana Inés de la Cruz among other "authors from whom," she says, "I have sometimes borrowed texts literally." Glantz's narrative and nonfiction works deeply reflect Sor Juana's presence, making this contemporary author a significant literary heir to the colonial Mexican poet.[3]

Copublished by Alfaguara and the University of the Cloister of Sor Juana, Glantz's *Apariciones* appeared in the erotic series Primero sueño ("First Dream"). The University of the Cloister of Sor Juana also printed the series El caracol ("The Snail"), in which Griselda Álvarez published her book of poetry titled *Erótica* (1999). Both collections bear Sor Juana's mark, as does the series

Diversa (Potpourri) by the National Autonomous University of Mexico, in which Graciela Hierro published *La ética del placer* ("The Ethics of Pleasure").

Sor Juana is also a model for characters in several works of fiction. In *Mistificaciones* ("Mystifications"), a short novel by Aline Pettersson, the narrator assumes the poet's character when she says: "I was Sor Juana," models her life after her, renames her lovers and signs a short story with names that appear in Sor Juana's secular love poetry: "Later on I was deepening into the abstractions, but now it was the words of her, Sor Juana, beyond which mine hid. And then, her beautiful image vested with the flowery night of her habit, in which conflicts collided" (11). This character, who "dreamed herself secluded in the convent praising the Lord" (58), says she adopted the persona of Sor Juana in order to save herself from the uncertainties of life.

Several Chicana writers also re-create the life of Sor Juana: Estela Portillo Trambley does so in her play, *Sor Juana*, and Alicia Gaspar de Alba, in her novel *Sor Juana's Second Dream*. Gaspar de Alba's "Author's Postscript" states: "Though this is the first to be published, it is actually the second English-language novel on Sor Juana's life. The first is Dorothy Schons's 'Sor Juana: A Chronicle of Old Mexico,' which the author calls a 'novelized' biography" (461). Before *Sor Juana's Second Dream*, the author informs the reader that she had already published "Interview with Sor Juana Inés de la Cruz" (Gaspar de Alba, "Politics"). Lastly, in 2004 Gloria Durán published *Catalina, mi padre* ("Catalina, My Father"), a historical novel that presents the fictionalized lives of Sor Juana and of Catalina de Erausto, the famous Monja Alférez.

This small sample demonstrates the impact of Sor Juana on contemporary women writers. It is clear that her life and work prefigure many issues that are still urgent for women. Some of the authors mentioned have established a conversation with Sor Juana; others simply refer to her. One even compares herself to the "tenth muse": the poet Paula Poniatowska Amor is known by some as the Eleventh Muse. After several interviews with Amor beginning in 1958, Elena Poniatowska wrote in *Las siete cabritas* ("The Seven Crazy Goats") that Amor "said and maintained she was superior to Sor Juana, 'because she is dead and I am alive' " (*Las siete* 51). Although we may certainly disagree with Amor, her comment makes it clear that Sor Juana is the benchmark for women who would wish to be famous and revered throughout the ages.

Poniatowska also quotes Sor Juana in many interviews and speeches. Referring to her own mother, she says in "Aleluya": "I will become refined later by her, by assaying her finenesses, in the way of Sor Juana" (13). In her cultural notes about theater published in the Mexican journal *La jornada*, Olga Harmony frequently quotes Sor Juana, while Vilma Fuentes speaks on Sor Juana in Paris and published in Mexico her article "Sor Juana, Garro, Castellanos, y María Luisa Mendoza."

In theatrical performances from the 1970s and 1980s, Ofelia Medina and Rita Guerrero and, before them in the 1960s, Amparo Ochoa stand out. In later years, Jaramar Soto and the groups Voices of Sor Juana and Women in Ritual continue the tradition of portraying Sor Juana on the stage. Marcela Rodríguez composed the arias of *Funesta* ("Mournful") and also *Primero sueño* ("First Dream") for chamber orchestra and soprano. Jesusa Rodríguez has continued to recite the 975 lines of *Primero sueño* by heart; the Chicana actress Rose Portillo recites Sor Juana's poetry in the United States; and Sandra Lorenzano does the same in Mexico. Marta Luna directed *Los demonios de la fe* ("Demons of Faith") in 2002 with the actresses Miriam Calderón, Andrea Ávila, and Magdalena Tenorio. In Mexican films Sor Juana has been played by Andrea Palma (Peón), Lupita Gallardo (Sevilla), and Ana Ofelia Murguía (Joskowicz). In the visual arts, she is a motif in the work of Maris Bustamante and, above all, in that of Perla Estrada de los Ríos. As can be seen from these varied references to her, Sor Juana may be used as a subtext in almost any course that focuses on Mexican women writers, as well as those on Mexican artists and feminist thinkers.

There are also intertwining glints of Sor Juana's presence woven into the works of others. In a one-page section titled "La historia" ("The Story") in María Luisa Puga's *La forma del silencio*, the narrator—the author's alter ego—speaks of herself using the third person: "When nobody was there she felt free. The first time she noticed that she trimmed her hair. . . . With scissors she trimmed: snip, snip. . . . That day there was drama. She learned not to show the results of that freedom she felt" (77). Like Sor Juana, the character uses the strategy of knowing in silence, enjoying her freedom without saying anything about it.

For Ana Clavel, in *Paraísos trémulos* ("Tremulous Paradises"), the cutting of the hair no longer relates to silence but to the character's freedom, although lost hair refers more to the loss of memory than to the challenge of acquiring knowledge:

> Cada vez que se cortaba el pelo perdía un poco de memoria. Ella no lo sabía y tampoco los que la rodeaban. . . . Observaba que el pelo le había crecido y que un mechoncillo rebelde se obstinaba en enfrentarla con la vida. Resolvía un nuevo corte. Y cada vez, el rechazo y el cabello rebelde hacían lo suyo. Un diá, decidió cortar por lo sano. El mundo prometió paraísos trémulos e inexplorados, palpitantes como su cabeza rapada. (9)
>
> Each time she trimmed her hair she would lose a little bit of her memory. She didn't know it, and neither did those around her. . . . She would then observe that her hair had grown and that a rebellious lock was requiring her to face life. She would then resolve to cut it again. And each time the rejection and the rebellious hair did their own thing. One day she decided to cut it all off. The world promised trembling and unexplored paradises, throbbing like her shaven head.

Of course there are literary prizes named after Sor Juana. For her 1962 novel *Oficio de tinieblas* ("The Office of Darkness"), Castellanos obtained the Sor Juana Inés de la Cruz Prize. There is also, among others, the State of Mexico Sor

Juana Inés de la Cruz Medal in Letters and Arts. Likewise, every year on International Women's Day the National Autonomous University of Mexico offers the Sor Juana Inés de la Cruz Prize to women distinguished in the fields of letters, humanities, and sciences. In 1993, the Sor Juana Inés de la Cruz Prize was established at the International Book Fair in Guadalajara for the best novel written by a woman author, although, ironically, as far as we know, Sor Juana never wrote a novel.[4] Two of the winning writers had published essays in the 1991 homage to Sor Juana: Margo Glantz ("Labores") and Angelina Muñiz-Huberman, who also won the prize for the novel *Dulcinea encantada* ("Dulcinea Charmed") in 1993. Other Mexican women writers contributed to *Los empeños: Ensayos en homenaje a Sor Juana Inés de la Cruz* ("The Trials: Essays in Homage to Sor Juana Inés de la Cruz" [Fernández and Quiarte]): Beatriz Espejo, Margo Glantz, Adriana González Mateos, Alessandra Luiselli, and Margarita Peña, who also edited the book *Cuadernos de Sor Juana* ("Sor Juana's Notebooks").

Not only literary prizes, schools, and libraries bear the name of Sor Juana. Writers' symposia have been dedicated to her, including the conference cycle in 2001 named El mundo iluminado y yo despierta ("The Illuminated World, and I Awake"), alluding to the closing line of *Primero sueño*. Demonstrating Sor Juana's relevance to all sectors of society, an association of sex workers in Mexico City gathers under the name of Sor Juana Inés de la Cruz Regional Coordination. More than three centuries ago, Sor Juana showed clear understanding of prostitutes when she absolved women of guilt and sentenced men in her *Sátira filosófica*: "¿O cuál es más de culpar, / aunque cualquier mal haga: / la que peca por la paga, / o el que paga por pecar?" ("Or which more greatly must be faulted, / though either may commit a wrong: / she who sins for need of payment, / or he who pays for his enjoyment?" [1: 229; 159]).

Women intellectuals of today, hand in hand with Sor Juana, or in her shadow, continue weaving her thought into the fabric begun in her classroom at one of the schools called "Amigas" ("school for girls") and continued in her cell at the Convent of Saint Jerome. The literary genius of Sor Juana, her ambition to seek the truth, and her consciousness of being a woman make her today, more than three centuries after her death, the most influential Latin American figure in writing, philosophy, and modern feminism.

NOTES

[1]With the exception of translations from Arenal and Powell's *The Answer / La respuesta*, translations are mine.

[2]A precursor for this work is Luciani's "Recreaciones."

[3]Among her many other publications, Glantz is the author of four books on Sor Juana (*Apariciones*, *Saberes*, *Hagiografía*, and *Comparación*).

[4]The Nicaraguan writer Milagros Palma conceived this prize, coordinated by the SOGEM School ("General Society of Mexican Writers School"). From the beginning, the Mexican writer Martha Cerda has actively participated in administering it.

NOTES ON CONTRIBUTORS

Gwendolyn Alker is associate teacher of theater studies in the Department of Drama at New York University, where she teaches classes on feminism and theater, sound theory, and Latin American performance. She is a former managing editor of *Women and Performance: A Journal of Feminist Theory* and has published in *Theatre Journal*, *TDR*, *Dance Research Journal*, and elsewhere. She is currently revising her dissertation on performances of silence for publication.

Electa Arenal is professor emerita of Hispanic and women's studies, City University of New York. She is one of the founders of the field of women's studies and a translator and a specialist in early modern Hispanic monastic women's culture and has focused much of her work on the writings of Sor Juana Inés de la Cruz and Marcela de San Félix. Her fourth book, an illustrated, critical edition of Sor Juana's *Neptuno alegórico* (written with Vincent Martin), is forthcoming and will be followed by a bilingual edition.

Emilie L. Bergmann is professor of Spanish at University of California, Berkeley. She coedited *Mirrors and Echoes: Women's Writing in Twentieth-Century Spain* (2007) and *¿Entiendes? Queer Readings, Hispanic Writings* (1995) and coauthored *Women, Culture, and Politics in Latin America* (1990). She has published on visual culture, gender, sexuality, and the maternal in early modern literature, including the poetry of Sor Juana Inés de la Cruz, and on twentieth-century Spanish women's writing.

Catherine Boyle is professor of Latin American cultural studies at King's College London. She has published widely on theater and cultural studies and is cofounder and editor of the *Journal of Latin American Cultural Studies*. Her translation of Sor Juana Inés de la Cruz's *Los empeños de una casa* as *House of Desires* premiered in the Royal Shakespeare Company in 2004.

Catherine M. Bryan is associate professor of Spanish at the University of Wisconsin, Oshkosh. She is also a member of the Latin American studies and women's studies teaching faculty. Her most recent publications focus on nostalgia, resistance, and the migrant subject in Peruvian narratives. Her current research and teaching projects include women writers of the political and aesthetic avant-garde; *indigenismos*; and, gender, class, and visual culture studies in Latin America and Brazil.

Jennifer L. Eich is professor of Spanish at Loyola Marymount University. She has published a study of Mexico's first female theologian, *The Other Mexican Muse: Sor María Anna Águeda de San Ignacio (1695–1756)*. Her current book project, " 'Honesty Opens My Lips': Cultural Affirmation and Resistance in Colonial Spanish American Conventual Narratives," focuses on colonial Spanish American women's religious narratives and analyzes narrative strategies, literary techniques, and cultural practices that conformed to and transcended political, geographic, and cultural boundaries.

Verónica Grossi is associate professor at the University of North Carolina, Greensboro. She has written on early modern Spanish poetry, Sor Juana Inés de la Cruz, and contemporary Latin American writers. She is the editor of *Escrito en México by Enrique Fierro* (1999) and the author of *Sigilosos v(u)elos epistemológicos en sor Juana Inés de la*

Cruz (2007). She is currently writing a book of poetry and a study of Ángeles Romero's script and theatrical performance titled *Sueño*.

Geoff Guevara-Geer is assistant professor of Spanish and Spanish American literature at Ripon College. His teaching interests include Spanish American literature and culture, literary theory, colonial literature, and comparative literature. He has written articles on Lazarillo de Tormes and Charlie Chaplin and is currently working on a book-length project on paranoia in Spanish American literature, as well as articles concerning Julio Cortázar's radical alterity and the ends of Homeric orality in Alejo Carpentier.

Tamara Harvey is assistant professor of English at George Mason University. She has published articles on early American women, including " 'My Goods Are True': Tenth Muses in the New World Market," in *Feminist Interventions in Early American Studies* and has edited *Washington's South* with Greg O'Brien. She is finishing a book project on the uses of functionalism by Sor Juana, Anne Bradstreet, Anne Hutchinson, and Marie de l'Incarnation, entitled "Modesty's Charge: The Body and Feminist Tactics in Early American Women's Discourse."

Emily Hind is assistant professor of Spanish at the University of Wyoming. She has published a book of interviews with Mexican women writers (2003), as well as articles on Mexican film, Rosario Castellanos's use of lesbian themes, Jean Franco's *Plotting Women*, and texts by José Emilio Pacheco and Mario Bellatín. She is currently studying experimental texts by Cristina Rivera Garza, Carmen Boullosa, and Ana Clavel.

Daniel P. Hunt is associate professor of Spanish at Idaho State University. He has published articles on Pedro Calderón de la Barca, Ricardo Palma, Isabel Allende, and Paco Ignacio Taibo II, as well as "A Field Study of Teeth in Hispanic Literature." His research is interdisciplinary and emphasizes comparative literature, politics, and the Hispanic mystery novel. He teaches all levels of language and literature in Spanish and honors humanities.

Stephanie Kirk is assistant professor of Spanish in the Department of Romance Languages and Literatures at Washington University in Saint Louis. She is the author of *Convent Life in Colonial Mexico: A Tale of Two Communities* (2007). Her main area of research is the study of gender and power relations in the early modern Hispanic world.

Asunción Lavrin is professor of history at Arizona State University. Among her research interests are the church and Mexican nuns in colonial Mexico, feminism, and women's history in the twentieth century. She has published several books, including *Monjas y beatas: La escritura femenina en la espiritualidad barroca novohispana, siglos XVII y XVIII*, edited with Rosalva Loreto López (2002), and *Feminism and Social Change in the Southern Cone, 1890–1940* (1995). In addition, she has published over eighty essays, including "Los hombres de Dios. Aproximación a un estudio de la masculinidad en Nueva España" in *Anuario Colombiano de Historia Social y de la Cultura* (2004). She is the author of a book on Mexican nuns and conventual life in Mexico (forthcoming from Stanford UP). Her current project focuses on masculinity and the Mendicant orders in colonial Mexico, 1550–1750.

Carol Maier is professor of Spanish at Kent State University. An affiliate of Kent's Institute for Applied Linguistics, she is the translator of work by Rosa Chacel, Severo Sarduy, and María Zambrano. Her research focus is translation theory, practice, and pedagogy. Currently she is translating books by Chacel and Sarduy, editing a volume that will be an homage to the late Helen R. Lane, and editing a collection of essays about teaching literature in translation with Françoise Massardier-Kenney.

Yolanda Martínez–San Miguel is associate professor of Romance languages at the University of Pennsylvania. She is author of *Saberes americanos: Subalternidad y epistemología en los escritos de sor Juana* (1999) and *Caribe Two Ways: Cultura de la migración en el Caribe insular hispánico* (2003). Her research and teaching focus on colonial Latin American discourses and contemporary Caribbean and Latino narratives, colonial and postcolonial theory, and migration and cultural studies.

Kathryn Joy McKnight is associate professor of Spanish at the University of New Mexico. She is the author of *The Mystic of Tunja: The Writings of Madre Castillo, 1671–1742* (1997) and has published articles on seventeenth-century Afro-Hispanic documentary narratives; she is currently preparing an anthology of these narratives.

Mariselle Meléndez is associate professor of colonial Latin American literatures and cultures at the University of Illinois, Urbana-Champaign. Her research focuses on issues of race, gender, and sexuality in colonial Spanish America; she has a special interest in the eighteenth century and cultural and visual studies. She is the author of *Raza, género e hibridez en* El lazarillo de ciegos caminantes (1999), as well as numerous articles, and coeditor of *Mapping Colonial Spanish America: Places and Commonplaces of Identity, Culture, and Experience* (2002).

Stephanie Merrim is Royce Family Professor of Comparative Literature and Hispanic Studies at Brown University. Among her publications on Sor Juana is *Early Modern Women's Writing and Sor Juana Inés de la Cruz* (1999). She is the author of "The 'Spectacular City' and the Work of the New World Baroque,in Colonial Mexican Literary Culture."

John A. Ochoa is associate professor at Pennsylvania State University. He is author of *The Uses of Failure in Mexican Literature and Identity* (2005), which examines several "monuments" of the Mexican canon, including Bernal Díaz del Castillo, J. J. Fernández de Lizardi, Alexander von Humboldt, José Vasconcelos, and Carlos Fuentes. He also has published on postcolonial theory and on border performance art.

Mario A. Ortiz is assistant professor of Spanish at Catholic University of America. His recent publications include "Villancicos de *negrilla*: Imaginando al sujeto afro-colonial," "Euterpe en los conventos femeninos novohispanos," and " 'Yo, (¿) soy quien soy (?)': La mujer en hábito de *comedia* en *Valor, agravio y mujer.*" He is currently editing a collection of essays on modern representations of Sor Juana. His research and teaching interests focus on Latin American colonial and postcolonial literature, poetry, musico-literary studies, and Latin American popular song.

Rosa Perelmuter is professor of Spanish at the University of North Carolina, Chapel Hill. She is the author of two books on Sor Juana: *Noche intelectual: La oscuridad idiomática en el* Primero sueño (1982) and *Los límites de la femineidad en sor Juana Inés de la Cruz: Estrategias retóricas y recepción literaria* (2004). Her research interests include Spanish American colonial literature, especially poetry; contemporary Spanish American narrative; and Latino literature and culture. Currently she is at work on a book-length study of the descriptions of nature in sixteenth- and seventeenth-century epic poems written in Spanish America.

Sara Poot-Herrera is professor at the University of California, Santa Barbara. Her publications include *Un giro en espiral: El proyecto literario de Juan José Arreola* (1992) and *Los guardaditos de sor Juana* (1999). She is also editor of and contributor to *"Y diversa de mí misma / entre vuestras plumas ando": Homenaje internacional a sor Juana Inés de la Cruz* (1993), *El cuento mexicano: Homenaje a Luis Leal* (1996), *Sor Juana y su mundo: Una mirada actual* (1995), and *En gustos se comen géneros: Congreso internacional de comida y literatura* (2003).

Amanda Powell is senior instructor of Spanish at the University of Oregon. She is editor and translator, with Electa Arenal, of Sor Juana's *The Answer / La respuesta* (1994) and is author, with Kathleen A. Myers, of *A Wild Country out in the Garden: The Spiritual Journals of a Colonial Mexican Nun* (1999). She has published translations: works of poetry and prose in *Untold Sisters* (Arenal and Schlau [1989]) and in María de San José Salazar's *Book for the Hour of Recreation* (2002). Her articles include (with Dianne Dugaw) "Sapphic Self-Fashioning in the Baroque Era: Women's Petrarchan Parody in Spanish and English, 1550–1700" and "A Feminist Road Not Taken: Baroque Sapphic Poetry."

Rocío Quispe-Agnoli is associate professor of Spanish American colonial and postcolonial studies at Michigan State University. She has published *La fe indígena en la escritura: Resistencia e identidad en los Andes coloniales* (2006), as well as several articles on Amerindian literacies and on women writers of early modern Spain and colonial Spanish America. She has edited a special issue of *Cuaderno Internacional de Estudios Hispánicos y Lingüística*, titled *Beyond the Convent: Colonial Women's Voices and Daily Challenges in Spanish America*. She also won three literary contests in fiction and published some short stories.

Lisa Rabin is associate professor of Spanish at George Mason University. She has written articles on Sor Juana, colonial Latin American narrative, and the ekphrastic poetry of *modernista* poets. Her research interests currently center on ideologies of literature in United States institutions. She and her literature students run a book club for "struggling" readers at Gunston Middle School in Arlington, Virginia. She will begin a long-term project on how this group affected the development of the participant children's literacy, schooling, and social agency. She is currently writing on this project as a model for service learning in university literature education.

Elias L. Rivers is Leading Professor of Hispanic and Comparative Literature Emeritus at Stony Brook University, State University of New York. He has edited, with Georgina Sabat de Rivers, a critical edition of Sor Juana's work, *Poesía, teatro, pensamiento: Lírica personal, lírica coral, teatro, prosa / Sor Juana Inés de la Cruz* (2004), as well as anthologies of early modern Spanish poetry, including *Renaissance and Baroque Poetry of Spain* (1966) and *Garcilaso de la Vega, Poesías castellanas completas* (1969). He also published *Things Done with Words: Speech Acts in Hispanic Drama* (1986), *Muses and Masks: Some Classical Genres of Spanish Poetry* (1992), and *El soneto español en el Siglo de Oro* (1993).

Stacey Schlau is professor of Spanish and women's studies at West Chester University. Her books include, authored with Electa Arenal, *Untold Sisters: Hispanic Nuns in Their Own Works* (1989); the critical edition, *Viva al siglo, muerta al mundo: Obras escogidas de María de san Alberto (1568–1640)*; and *Spanish American Women's Use of the Word:*

Colonial through Contemporary Narratives (2001). She has published articles on seventeenth- through twentieth-century Spanish and Spanish American women writers, especially of narrative, and is working on a book on women and the Hispanic inquisitions.

Nina M. Scott is professor emerita of Spanish from the University of Massachusetts, Amherst; recently she was acting chair of the Spanish department at Mount Holyoke College. She coedited *Breaking Boundaries: Latina Writing and Critical Readings* (1989) and *Coded Encounters: Race, Gender, and Ethnicity in Colonial Latin America* (1994); translated and edited Gertrudis Gómez de Avellaneda's *Sab* and *Autobiography* (1993); and published *Madres del verbo / Mothers of the Word*, a bilingual anthology of early Spanish American women writers (1999).

Lisa Vollendorf is associate professor of Spanish at California State University, Long Beach. Author of *Reclaiming the Body: María de Zayas's Early Modern Feminism* (2001) and *The Lives of Women: A New History of Inquisitional Spain* (2005), she has edited *Recovering Spain's Feminist Tradition* (2001) and *Literatura y feminismo en España* (2006). Her current book projects include "Sex and the Law in the Hispanic World" and, with James A. Parr, *Approaches to Teaching Cervantes's* Don Quixote. A volume edited with Daniella Kostroun titled "Women, Religion, and the Atlantic World (1600–1800)" is forthcoming.

Grady C. Wray is associate professor of Spanish at the University of Oklahoma, where he teaches Latin American literature. His book, *The* Devotional Exercises / *Los* Ejercicios Devotos *of Sor Juana Inés de la Cruz, Mexico's Prodigious Nun (1648/51–1695)* (2005), is the first critical study and bilingual annotated edition of Sor Juana's devotional work, and it closely examines devotional writing in New Spain in the late seventeenth century.

SURVEY PARTICIPANTS

Maureen Ahern, *Ohio State University*
Gwendolyn Alker, *New York University*
Electa Arenal, *City University of New York*
John Beverley, *University of Pittsburgh*
Julie Bosker, *De Paul University*
Catherine Bryan, *University of Wisconsin, Oshkosh*
Glenn Carman, *De Paul University*
Raquel Chang-Rodríguez, *City University of New York*
Jennifer Corry, *Berry College*
Alice Edwards, *Mercyhurst College*
Patricia Fernós, *Austin Community College*
Fernando Gómez, *Stanford University*
Alfonso González, *California State University, Long Beach*
Margaret Greer, *Duke University*
Verónica Grossi, *University of North Carolina, Greensboro*
Geoff Guevara-Geer, *Ripon College*
Tamara Harvey, *George Mason University*
Emily Hind, *University of Wyoming*
Daniel P. Hunt, *Idaho State University*
Ivan Jiménez-Williams, *Western Illinois University*
Stephanie Kirk, *Washington University*
Alessandra Luiselli, *Texas A&M University*
Yolanda Martínez–San Miguel, *University of Pennsylvania*
Kathryn J. McKnight, *University of New Mexico*
Carmen Millán de Benavides, *Pontífica Universidad Iberoamericana*
Anna More, *University of California, Los Angeles*
RoseAnna Mueller, *Columbia College*
Kathleen Myers, *Indiana University*
Kimberly Nance, *Illinois State University*
Daniel Nappo, *University of Tennessee, Martin*
John Ochoa, *Pennsylvania State University*
Mario Ortiz, *Catholic University of America*
Sarah Owens, *College of Charleston*
Rosa Perelmuter, *University of North Carolina, Chapel Hill*
Amanda Powell, *University of Oregon*
Rocío Quispe-Agnoli, *Michigan State University*
Lisa Rabin, *George Mason University*
Judith Rosenthal, *California State University, Fresno*
Diana Valencia, *Saint Joseph College*
Lisa Vollendorf, *California State University, Long Beach*
Grady C. Wray, *University of Oklahoma*
Elissa Weaver, *University of Chicago*

WORKS CITED

The following list consists of all the works by Sor Juana that are discussed and quoted from in the volume.

The Answer / La respuesta. Including a Selection of Poems. Ed. and trans. Electa Arenal and Amanda Powell. 1994.

Antología poética. 2004.

Autodefensa espiritual. Carta de la madre Juana Inés de la Cruz escrita al Rev. P. Maestro Antonio Núñez de la Compañía de Jesús. Ed. Aureliano Tapia Méndez. 1986.

Carta de sor Juana Inés de la Cruz a su confessor: Autodefensa espiritual. Ed. Aureliano Tapia Méndez. 1993.

The Divine Narcissus / El divino Narciso. Trans. Patricia A. Peters and Renée Domeier. 1998.

Enigmas ofrecidos a la Casa del Placer. Ed. Antonio Alatorre. 1994.

Fama y obras pósthumas. 1700. <http://www.ub.uni-bielefeld.de/diglib/delacruz/fama/>.

House of Desires. Trans. Catherine Boyle. 2004.

The House of Trials. Trans. David Pasto. 1997.

Inundación Castálida. 1689. Ed. Georgina Sabat de Rivers. 1982.

Libro de cocina: Convento de San Jerónimo. 1996.

Lírica. Ed. Raquel Asún. 1983.

Neptuno alegórica. Ed. Electa Arenal and Vincent Martin. Forthcoming 2007.

Obras completas. Porrúa edition. 1985.

Obras completas. Diccionario, galería y ediciones facsimilares. Ed. Guadalupe Correa and Tadeo Stein. 2004.

Obras completas de sor Juana Inés de la Cruz. Ed. Alfonso Méndez Plancarte and Alberto G. Salceda. 1951–57.

The Pathless Grove Sonnets. Trans. Pauline Cook. 1950.

Pawns of a House / Los empeños de una casa. Trans. Susana Hernández Araico. 2005.

Poems, Protest, and a Dream. Trans. Margaret Sayers Peden. 1997.

Poesía, teatro, pensamiento: Lírica personal, lírica coral, teatro, prosa. Ed. Elias L. Rivers and Georgina Sabat de Rivers. 2004.

Poesía lírica. Introd. José Carlos González Boixo. 1992.

Prime Sway: A Transduction of Primero Sueño *by Sor Juana Inés de la Cruz.* John M. Bennett. 1996.

The Sonnets of Sor Juana Inés de la Cruz in English Verse. Trans. Carl W. Cobb. 2001.

A Sor Juana Anthology. Trans. Alan S. Trueblood. 1988.

Sor Juana Inés de la Cruz, Poems: A Bilingual Anthology. Trans. Margaret Sayers Peden. 1985.

Sor Juana: Poet, Nun, Feminist, Enigma. Autodefensa Espiritual. *A Poet's Translation.* Trans. Alicia L. Galván. 1998.

Sor Juana's Dream. Trans. Luis Harss. 1986.

Sor Juana's Love Poems. Trans. Joan Larkin and Jaime Manrique. 2003.

Sor Juana's Love Poems / Poemas de Amor: A Bilingual Edition. Ed. and trans. Joan Larkin and Jaime Manrique. 1997.

El sueño. Trans. John Campion. 1983.

A Woman of Genius: The Intellectual Autobiography of Sor Juana Inés de le Cruz. Trans. Margaret Sayers Peden. 1982.

This list consists of all the works cited in the volume, including the works by Sor Juana listed above, here listed under the name of the editor or, when an editor is lacking, under the title.

Abreu Gómez, Ermilo. *Iconografía de sor Juana Inés de la Cruz.* Prólogo. J. de J. Núñez y Domínguez. México, DF: SEP, Publicaciones del Museo Nacional de México, 1934.

Achebe, Chinua. *Things Fall Apart.* London: Heinemann, 1958.

Ackerman, Diane. Preface. *Reverse Thunder: A Dramatic Poem.* New York: Lumen, 1988. N. pag.

Acosta, Leonardo. *El barroco de Indias y otros ensayos.* Cuadernos Casa 28. La Habana: Casa de las Américas, 1985.

Adorno, Rolena. "Reconsidering Colonial Discourse for Sixteenth- and Seventeenth-Century Spanish America." *Latin American Research Review* 28.3 (1993): 135–45.

Alatorre, Antonio. "La carta de sor Juana al P. Nuñez (1682)." *Nueva revista de filología hispánica* 35 (1987): 591–673.

———, ed. *Enigmas ofrecidos a la Casa del Placer.* By Sor Juana Inés de la Cruz. 1994. México, DF: Colegio de México, 1995.

Alatorre, Antonio, and Martha Lilia Tenorio. *Serafina y sor Juana (Con tres apéndices).* México, DF: Colegio de México, 1998.

Alciati, Andrea. *A Book of Emblems:* The Emblematum Liber *in Latin and English.* Ed. John F. Moffit. Jefferson: McFarland, 2004.

Aldridge, A. Owen. "The Tenth Muse of America: Anne Bradstreet or Sor Juana Inés de la Cruz." *Inter-American Literary Relations.* Intl. Comparative Lit. Assn. Congress. Vol. 3. New York: Garland, 1985. 177–88.

Aldridge, Alan. *The Beatles: Illustrated Lyrics.* London: Macdonald, 1990.

Amerlinck de Corsi, María Concepción, and Manuel Ramos Medina, eds. *Conventos de monjas: Fundaciones en el México Virreinal.* México, DF: Condumex, 1995.

Amor Poniatowska, Paula. *Nomeolvides.* Introd. and trans. Elena Poniatowska. México, DF: Plaza y Janés, 1996.

Anderson, W. Paul. *Hunger's Brides.* Toronto: Random, 2004.

Antología poética. By Sor Juana Inés de la Cruz. Introd. José Miguel Oviedo. Madrid: Alianza, 2004.

Arenal, Electa. "The Convent as Catalyst for Autonomy: Two Hispanic Nuns of the Seventeenth Century." *Women in Hispanic Literature: Icons and Fallen Idols.* Ed. Beth Miller. Berkeley: U of California P, 1983. 147–83.

———. "Del emblema al poema, 'Leyendo como una mujer la imagen de la Mujer.' " *Aproximaciones a sor Juana.* Ed. Sandra Lorenzano. México, DF: U del Claustro de Sor Juana, Fondo de Cultura Económica, 2005.

———. "Enigmas emblemáticos: *El Neptuno alegórico* de sor Juana Inés de la Cruz." López Portillo 85–94.

———. "Monjas chocolateras: Contextualizaciones agridulces." Moraña and Martínez–San Miguel 135–52.

———. "Sor Juana Inés de la Cruz: Speaking the Mother Tongue." *University of Dayton Review* 16.2 (1983): 93–105.

———. "Sor Juana's Arch: Public Spectacle, Private Battle." *Crossing Boundaries: Attending to Early Modern Women.* Ed. Jane Donawerth and Adele Seeff. Newark: U of Delaware P, 2000. 173–94.

———. " 'This life within me won't keep still.' A Dramatic Re-creation of the Life and Thought of Anne Bradstreet (1612–72) and Sor Juana Inés de la Cruz." *Reinventing the Americas: Comparative Studies of Literature of the United States and Spanish America.* Ed. Bell Gale Chevigny and Gari Laguardia. Cambridge: Cambridge UP, 1986. 158–202.

———. " 'What Women Writers?': Plotting Women's Studies in New York." *The Politics of Women's Studies: Testimony of Thirty Founding Mothers.* Ed. Florence Howe. New York: Feminist, 2000. 183–93.

———. "Where Woman Is Creator of the Wor(l)d; or, Sor Juana's Discourse on Method." Merrim, *Feminist Perspectives* 124–41.

Arenal, Electa, and Vincent Martin, eds. *Proyecto multidimensional de reconstrucción del "Neptuno alegórico" y edición bilingüe del mismo.* Introd. and notes Arenal and Martin. Trans. David Randall with Arenal and Martin. Madrid: Cátedra, forthcoming 2007.

Arenal, Electa, and Yolanda Martínez–San Miguel. "Refocusing New Spain and Spanish Colonization: Malinche, Guadalupe and Sor Juana." Castillo and Schweitzer, *Companion* 174–94.

Arenal, Electa, and Amanda Powell, eds. and trans. *The Answer / La respuesta. Including a Selection of Poems.* By Sor Juana Inés de la Cruz. New York: Feminist, 1994.

Arenal, Electa, and Stacey Schlau. *Untold Sisters: Hispanic Nuns in Their Own Works.* Trans. Amanda Powell. Albuquerque: U of New Mexico P, 1989.

Aristotle. *Poetics.* Trans. S. H. Butcher. 4 Oct. 2000. 2 Mar. 2007 <http://classics.mit.edu/Aristotle/poetics.html>.

———. The Rhetoric *and* The Poetics *of Aristotle*. Introd. Edward P. J. Corbett. Trans. W. Rhys Roberts and Ingram Bywater. New York: McGraw, 1954.

Armacanqui-Tipacti, Elia J. *Sor María Manuela de Santa Ana: Una teresiana peruana*. Cuzco, Perú: Centro de Estudios Regionales Andinos "Bartolomé de Las Casas," 1999.

Ashcroft, Bill, Gareth Griffiths, and Helen Tiffin. *The Empire Writes Back*. New York: Routledge, 2003.

———, eds. *Post-colonial Studies Reader*. New York: Routledge, 1995.

Austin, John L. *How to Do Things with Words*. New York: Oxford UP, 1962.

Avilés, Luis F. "Sor Juana en el punto de fuga: La mirada en 'Este que ves, engaño colorido.' " *Bulletin of Hispanic Studies* 77 (2000): 413–31.

Ayala Mallory, Nina. *El Greco to Murillo: Spanish Painting in the Golden Age*. New York: Harper, 1990.

Baker, Peter. *Deconstruction and the Ethical Turn*. Gainesville: UP of Florida, 1995.

Balbuena, Bernardo de. *La grandeza mexicana y compendio apologético en alabanza de la poesía*. Ed. and introd. Luis Adolfo Domínguez. México, DF: Porrúa, 1985.

Barbeito Carneiro, María Isabel. *María de Orozco (1635–1709)*. Madrid: Orto, 1997.

Barnstone, Willis. *Six Masters of the Hispanic Sonnet: (Francisco de Quevedo, Sor Juana Inés de la Cruz, Antonio Machado, Federico García Lorca, Jorge Luis Borges, Miguel Hernández): Essays and Translations*. Carbondale: Southern Illinois UP, 1993.

Barthes, Roland. *Image-Music-Text*. Ed. and trans. S. Heath. London: Paladin, 1977.

Bauer, Ralph. *The Cultural Geography of Colonial American Literatures: Empire, Travel, Modernity*. Cambridge: Cambridge UP, 2003.

Beckett, Samuel, trans. *Anthology of Mexican Poetry*. London: Thames and Hudson, 1958.

Behn, Aphra. Oroonoko, The Rover, *and Other Works*. Ed. Janet Todd. London: Penguin, 1992.

Bellido, Joseph. *Vida de la V.M.R.M. Maria Anna Agueda de S. Ignacio, primera priora del religiosissimo Convento de dominicas recoletas de santa Rosa de la Puebla de Los Angeles*. México, DF: Biblioteca Mexicana, 1758.

Bemberg, María Luisa, dir. *Yo, la peor de todas*. Icarus Films and First Run Features, 1990.

Bénassy-Berling, Marie-Cécile. "Actualidad del sorjuanismo (1994–1999)." *Colonial Latin American Review* 9 (2000): 277–92.

———. *Humanisme et religion chez sor Juana Inés de la Cruz. La femme et la culture au XVII siécle*. Paris: Editions Hispaniques, Publications de la Sorbonne, 1982.

———. *Humanismo y religión en Sor Juana Inés de la Cruz*. México, DF: U Autónoma de México, 1983.

Benítez, Fernando. *Los demonios en el convento: Sexo y religion en la Nueva España*. México, DF: Era, 1985.

Benjamin, Walter. *El origen del drama barroco alemán*. Trans. José Muñoz Millanes. Madrid: Taurus, 1990.

———. *Illuminations*. New York: Harcourt, 1968.

Bennett, Herman. *Africans in Colonial Mexico: Absolutism, Christianity, and Afro-Creole Consciousness, 1570–1640*. Bloomington: Indiana UP, 2003.

Bennett, John M. *Prime Sway: A Transduction of "Primero Sueño" by Sor Juana Inés de la Cruz*. Norman: Texture, 1996.

Bennett, Judith. " 'Lesbian-like' and the Social History of Lesbians." *Journal of the History of Sexuality* 9 (2000): 1–24.

Benson, Elizabeth. *Retratos: Two Thousand Years of Latin American Portraits*. New Haven: Yale UP, 2004.

Berger, John. *Ways of Seeing*. London: Penguin, 1972.

Bergmann, Emilie. "Abjection and Ambiguity: Lesbian Desire in Bemberg's *Yo, la peor de todas*." *Hispanisms and Homosexualities*. Ed. Sylvia Molloy and Robert McKee Irwin. Durham: Duke UP, 1998. 229–47.

———. "Amor, óptica y sabiduría en Sor Juana." Moraña and Martínez–San Miguel 267–81.

———. "Ficciones de sor Juana: Poética y biografía." Poot-Herrera, *"Y diversa de mí misma"* 171–83.

———. "Optics and Vocabularies of the Visual in Luis de Góngora and Sor Juana Inés de la Cruz." *Writing for the Eyes in the Spanish Golden Age*. Ed. Frederick A. de Armas. Lewisburg: Bucknell UP, 2004. 151–65.

———. "Sor Juana Inés de la Cruz: Dreaming in a Double Voice." *Women, Culture, and Politics in Latin America*. Seminar on Feminism and Culture in Latin Amer. Berkeley: U of California P, 1990. 151–72.

Bergmann, Emilie, and Leah Middlebrook. "La mujer petrarquista: 'Hollines y peces.' Poética renacentista de la óptica de sor Juana." *La mujer en la literatura española: Modos de representación desde la Edad Media hasta el siglo XVII*. Vol. 2 of *Breve historia feminista de la literatura española (en lengua castellana)*. Ed. Iris M. Zavala. Barcelona: Anthropos, 1995. 145–58.

Bermúdez, María Elvira. *Detente, sombra*. México, DF: U Autónoma Metropolitana, 1984.

Bernique, Juan de. *Idea de perfección y virtudes. Vida de la V. M. y sierva de Dios Catalina de Jesús y San Francisco. Hija de su tercera orden y fundadora del Colegio de las doncellas pobres de Santa Clara de la Ciudad de Alcalá de Henares*. Alcalá: Con licencia de Francisco García Fernández, Impresor de la U, 1693.

Bethell, Leslie, ed. *The Cambridge History of Latin America*. Vols. 1–2. Cambridge: Cambridge UP, 1984.

Beverley, John. *Una modernidad obsoleta. Estudios sobre el barroco*. Los Teques, Venezuela: Fondo Editorial A. L. E. M., 1997.

Bhabha, Homi K. *The Location of Culture*. New York: Routledge, 1994.

———. "Of Mimicry and Men: The Ambivalence of Colonial Discourse." *October* 28 (1984): 125–33.

———. "The Other Question . . . Homi Bhabha Reconsiders the Stereotype and Colonial Discourse." *Screen* 24 (1983): 18–36.

Bijuesca, K. Josu, and Pablo A. J. Brescia, eds. *Sor Juana and Vieira, trescientos años después*. Santa Barbara: Center for Portuguese Studs., Dept. of Spanish and Portuguese at the U of California, 1998.

Blanchot, Maurice. *The Space of Literature*. Trans. Ann Smock. Lincoln: U of Nebraska P, 1989.

Bonnet, Marie-Jo. "Sappho; or, the Importance of Culture in the Language of Love: Tribade, Lesbienne, Homosexuelle." *Queerly Phrased: Language, Gender and Sexuality*. Ed. Anna Livia and Kira Hall. Oxford: Oxford UP, 1997. 147–66.

Boone, Elizabeth Hill, and Walter Mignolo, eds. *Writing without Words: Alternative Literacies in Mesoamerica and the Andes*. Durham: Duke UP, 1994.

Boullosa, Carmen. *Antes*. México, DF: Vuelta, 1989.

———. *Cielos de la tierra*. México, DF: Alfaguara, 1997.

———. *Duerme*. Madrid: Santillana, 1994.

———. *Llanto: Novelas imposibles*. México, DF: Era, 1992.

Boyer, Augustín. "Programa iconográfico en el *Neptuno alegórico* de sor Juana Inés de la Cruz." *Homenaje a José Durand*. Ed. Luis Cortest. Madrid: Verbum, 1993. 37–46.

Boyle, Catherine, trans. *House of Desires*. By Sor Juana Inés de la Cruz. London: Oberon, 2004.

Brading, David A. *The First America: The Spanish Monarchy, Creole Patriots, and the Liberal State, 1492–1867*. Cambridge: Cambridge UP, 1991.

———. *Mexican Phoenix: Our Lady of Guadalupe: Image and Tradition across Five Centuries*. Cambridge: Cambridge UP, 2001.

Bradstreet, Anne. *The Tenth Muse (1650)*. Delmar: Scholars' Facs., 1978.

Bramón, Francisco. *Los sirgueros de la Virgen*. 1944. Ed. Agustín Yáñez. México, DF: U Nacional Autónoma de México, 1994.

Braudy, Leo, and Marshall Cohen, eds. *Film Theory and Criticism: Introductory Readings*. 6th ed. New York: Oxford UP, 2004.

Bravo Arriaga, María Dolores. "El arco triunfal novohispano como representación." *Espectáculo, texto y fiesta. Juan Ruiz de Alarcón y el teatro de su tiempo*. Ed. José Amezcua and Serafín González. México, DF: U Autónoma Metropolitana Iztapalapa, 1990. 85–93.

———. "Búsqueda del origen: La narración de fábulas en el *Neptuno alegórico* de sor Juana." Moraña and Martínez-San Miguel 243–54.

———. "Festejos, celebraciones y certámenes." Chang-Rodríguez 85–111.

———. "Signos religiosos y géneros literarios en el discurso de poder." Poot-Herrera *Sor Juana* 93–139.

Brilliant, Richard. *Portraiture*. Cambridge: Harvard UP, 1991.

Brokaw, Galen. "The Poetics of Khipu Historiography." *Latin American Research Review* 38.3 (2003): 111–47.

Brooten, Bernadette. *Love between Women: Early Christian Responses to Female Homoeroticism*. Chicago: U of Chicago P, 1996.

Burgess Noudehou, Lisa Maria. *Maps of Difference: Literature in the English and*

Spanish Colonies. Diss. U of Pennsylvania, 1995. Ann Arbor: UMI, 1995. AAT 9615101.

Burkholder, Mark A., and Lyman L. Johnson. *Colonial Latin America*. 4th ed. New York: Oxford UP, 2001.

Burns, Kathryn. *Colonial Habits: Convents and the Spiritual Economy of Cuzco, Peru*. Durham: Duke UP, 1999.

Butler, Judith. *Gender Trouble: Feminism and the Subversion of Identity*. New York: Routledge, 1990.

Calhoun, Cheshire. "The Gender Closet: Lesbian Disappearance under the Sign 'Woman.' " *Lesbian Subjects: A Lesbian Studies Reader.* Ed. Martha Vicinus. Bloomington: Indiana UP, 1996. 209–32.

Calleja, Diego. *Vida de sor Juana*. Ed. Emilio Abreu Gómez. México, DF: Antigua Librería Robredo, 1936.

Campion, John, trans. *El sueño*. By Sor Juana Inés de la Cruz. Austin: Thorp Springs, 1983.

Carrera, Magali M. *Imagining Identity in New Spain: Race, Lineage, and the Colonial Body in Portraiture and Casta Paintings.* Austin: U of Texas P, 2003.

Carvajal, Mariana de. *Navidades de Madrid*. Ed. Catherine Soriano. Madrid: Comunidad de Madrid, 1993.

Casares, Julio. *Diccionario ideológico de la lengua española.* Barcelona: Gili, 1990.

Casey, James. *Early Modern Spain: A Social History*. New York: Routledge, 1999.

Castellanos, Rosario. "Asedio a Sor Juana." Castellanos, *Poesía* 462–67.

———. *El eterno femenino*. Castellanos, *Poesía* 363–454.

———. *Juicios sumarios*. Castellanos, *Poesía* 457–742.

———. *Mujer que sabe latín*. Castellanos, *Poesía* 873–987.

———. "Otra vez Sor Juana." Castellanos, *Poesía* 467–70.

———. *Poesía, teatro y ensayo*. Ed. Eduardo Mejía. México, DF: Fondo de Cultura Económico, 1998. Vol. 2 of *Obras completas.* 2 vols.

———. *Rito de iniciación*. México, DF: Alfaguara, 1997.

Castelló Yturbide, Teresa. "Encuentro entre el conde de la Cortina y el capellán del convento de San Jerónimo." López Portillo 175–78.

Castillo, Susan, and Ivy Schweitzer, eds. *Companion to* The Literatures of Colonial America. Malden: Blackwell, 2005.

———, eds. *The Literatures of Colonial America: An Anthology*. Malden: Blackwell, 2001.

Castillo Grajeda, José del. *Compendio de la vida y virtudes de la venerable Catarina de San Juan.* México: Ediciones Xochitl, 1946.

Catalá, Rafael. "El *Neptuno alegórico* de sor Juana: Ontogenia de América." *Plural, Revista Cultural del Excelsior* 151 (1984): 17–27.

———. *Para una lectura americana del barroco mexicano: Sor Juana Inés de la Cruz y Sigüenza y Góngora*. Minneapolis: Prisma, 1987.

Catalog of Visual Materials. Assn. for Hispanic Classical Theater. 18 Dec. 2002. 23 May 2006 <http://www.trinity.edu/org/comedia/catalog.html>.

Cátedra, Pedro M., and Anastasio Rojo. *Bibliotecas y lecturas de mujeres. Siglo XVI*. Salamanca: Inst. de Historia del Libro y de la Lectura, 2004.

Cavendish, Margaret. *Paper Bodies: A Margaret Cavendish Reader*. Ed. Sylvia Bowerbank and Sara Mendelson. Orchard Park: Broadview, 2000.

———. *The Worlds Olio*. London: Martin and Allestrye, 1655.

Cerone, Pietro. *El melopeo y maestro: Tractado de musica theorica y pratica*. 1613. Introd. Alberto Gallo. Bibliotheca Musica Bononiensis, Sezione 2, no. 25. Bologna: Forni, 1969.

Cervantes, Miguel de. "El rufián dichoso." *Obras completas*. 16th ed. Ed. Angel Valbuena Prat. Madrid: Aguilar, 1970. 387–437.

Chang-Rodríguez, Raquel, ed. *La cultura letrada en la Nueva España del siglo XVII*. Vol. 2 of *Historia de la literatura mexicana*. México, DF: Siglo, 2002.

Chanticleer. *Mexican Baroque*. Teldec, 1994.

Chávez Leyva, Yolanda. "Breaking the Silence: Putting Latina Lesbian History at the Center." Zimmerman and McNaron 145–52.

Checa Cremades, Fernando. "Arquitectura efímera e imagen del poder." Poot-Herrera, *Sor Juana y su mundo* 251–305.

Chiampi, Irlemar. *Barroco y modernidad*. México, DF: Fondo de Cultura Económica, 2000.

Christine de Pizan. *The Book of the City of Ladies*. Trans. Earl Jeffrey Richard. New York: Persea, 1982.

Cicero, Marcus Tullius. Brutus, *with an English translation by G. L. Hendrickson and* Orator, *with an English translation by H. M. Hubbell*. London: Heinemann, 1939.

———. *De inventione. De optimo genere oratorum. Topica*. Cambridge: Harvard UP, 1949.

———. *De partitione oratoria*. Trans. Horace Rackham. Cambridge: Harvard UP, 1976–82. Vol. 2 of *De oratore. English and Latin*.

———. *Rhetorica ad Herennium*. Trans. Harry Caplan. Cambridge: Harvard UP, 1981.

Cirlot, J. Eduardo. *A Dictionary of Symbols*. Trans. Jack Sage. New York: Routledge, 1971.

Clamurro, William H. "Sor Juana Inés de la Cruz Reads Her Portrait." *Revista de Estudios Hispánicos* 20 (1986): 27–43.

Clavel, Ana. *Los deseos y su sombra*. México, DF: Alfaguara, 1999.

———. *Paraísos trémulos*. México, DF: Alfaguara, 2002.

Clendinnen, Inga. *Aztecs: An Interpretation*. New York: Cambridge UP, 1991.

Cobb, Carl W., trans. *The Sonnets of Sor Juana Inés de la Cruz in English Verse*. Lewiston: Mellen, 2001.

Cohn, Deborah N. "La construcción de la identidad cultural en México: Nacionalismo, cosmopolitismo e infraestructura intelectual, 1945–1968." *Foro hispánico* 22 (2002): 89–103.

Cook, Pauline, trans. *The Pathless Grove Sonnets*. By Sor Juana Inés de la Cruz. Prairie City: Decker, 1950.

Cornejo Polar, Antonio. *Escribir en el aire: Ensayo sobre la heterogeneidad socio-cultural en las literaturas andinas*. Lima: Horizonte, 1994.

Coro Exaudi de Cuba. *Esteban Salas: Baroque Cantatas from Santiago de Cuba*. Jade, 1998.

———. *Esteban Salas: Un barroco de Cuba*. Jade, 2003.

———. *El gran barroco: Musique baroque latinoamericaine XVII et XVIII siécles*. Jade, 2003.

———. *El gran barroco de Bolivia*. Jade, 2000.

———. *El gran barroco del Perú*. Jade, 2000.

Corominas, Joan de. *Diccionario crítico-etimológico castellano e hispánico*. Madrid: Gredos, 1980.

Correa, Guadalupe, and Tadeo Stein, eds. *Obras completas. Diccionarios, galería y ediciones facsimilares*. By Sor Juana Inés de la Cruz. CD-ROM. Rosario, Arg.: Nuevo Hélade, 2004.

Cottino-Jones, Marga. "The Myth of Apollo and Daphne in Petrarch's Canzoniere: The Dynamics and Literary Function of Transformation." *Francis Petrarch, Six Centuries Later: A Symposium*. Ed. Aldo Scaglione. Chapel Hill: Dept. of Romance Langs., U of North Carolina, 1975. 152–76.

Covarrubias y Horozco, Sebastián de. *Emblemas morales*. 1610. Ed. Juan de Dios Hernández Miñano. Cáceres, Spain: U de Extremadura, 1998.

———. *Tesoro de la lengua castellana o española*. 1611. Madrid: Turner, 1979.

Cruz, Anne J. "Willing Desire: Luisa de Carvajal y Mendoza and Female Subjectivity." Nader 177–94.

Cuadriello, Jaime. *Juegos de ingenio y agudeza. La pintural emblemática de la Nueva España*. México, DF: Equilibrista/Turner, 1994.

Culler, Jonathan. *Literary Theory: A Very Short Introduction*. Oxford: Oxford UP, 2000.

Cummins, Tom. "Representation in the Sixteenth Century and the Colonial Image of the Inca." Boone and Mignolo 188–219.

Cunningham, Gilbert, trans. "The Dream." By Sor Juana Inés de la Cruz. *Literatura Mexicana* 6 (1995): 600–12.

Curtius, Ernst Robert. *European Literature and the Latin Middle Ages*. New York: Harper, 1953. Princeton: Princeton UP, 1973.

Cypess, Sandra Messinger. "Los géneros re/velados en *Los empeños de una casa* de sor Juana Inés de la Cruz." *Hispamérica* 22.64–65 (1993): 177–95.

D'Aragona, Tullia. *Dialogue on the Infinity of Love*. Ed. and trans. Rinaldina Russell and Bruce Merry. The Other Voice in Early Modern Europe. Chicago: U of Chicago P, 1997.

Daston, Lorraine. "The Image of Objectivity." *Representations* 40 (1992): 81–128.

Daston, Lorraine, and Peter Galison. "Baconian Facts, Academic Civility and the Prehistory of Objectivity." *Annals of Scholarship* 8 (1991): 337–63.

———. "Objectivity versus Truth." *Wissenschaft als kulturelle Praxis, 1750–1900*. Ed.

Hans Erich Bödeker, Peter Hanns Reill, and Jürgen Schlumbohm. Göttingen, Ger.: Vandenhoeck, 1999. 17–32.

Davis, Natalie Zemon. *Women on the Margins: Three Seventeenth-Century Lives*. Cambridge: Belknap–Harvard UP, 1995.

DeLamotte, Eugenia C., Natania Meeker, and Jean F. O'Barr, eds. *Women Imagine Change: A Global Anthology of Women's Resistance from 600 B.C.E. to Present*. New York: Routledge, 1997.

Demarest, Donald, and Coley Taylor, eds. *The Dark Virgin: The Book of Our Lady of Guadalupe, a Documentary Anthology*. Freeport: Taylor, 1956.

Descartes, René. *Discourse on Method, Optics, Geometry, and Meteorology*. Trans. Paul J. Olscamp. Indianapolis: Bobbs-Merrill, 1965.

———. Discourse on the Method*; and,* Meditations on First Philosophy. Ed. David Weissman. New Haven: Yale UP, 1996.

Díaz Balsera, Viviana. "Cleansing Mexican Antiquity: Sor Juana Inés de la Cruz and the *Loa* to *El Divino Narciso*." Castillo and Schweitzer, *Companion* 292–305.

Diccionario de autoridades. 1726–39. 3 vols. Madrid: Editorial Gredos, 1990.

Domínguez Aguirre, Carmen, and Enriqueta León González. *Mi libro del tercer año. Lengua Nacional*. 1960. 9th ed. México, DF: Libros de Texto Gratuitos, 1967.

Dorantes de Carranza, Baltasar. *Sumaria relación de las cosas de la Nueva España con noticia individual de los descendientes legítimos de los conquistadores y primeros pobladores españoles*. 1902. Ed. José María de Agreda y Sánchez. México, DF: Medina, 1970.

Douay-Rheims Bible. *Douay-Rheims Catholic Bible*. 2004. 2 Mar. 2007 <http://www.drbo.org>.

Duby, Georges. *The Three Orders: Feudal Society Imagined*. Trans. Arthur Goldhammer. Chicago: U of Chicago P, 1980.

Dugaw, Dianne, and Amanda Powell. "A Feminist Road Not Taken: Baroque Sapphic Poetry." *Reason and Its Others: Italy, Spain, and the New World*. Ed. David Castillo and Massimo Lollini. Nashville: Vanderbilt UP, 2006. 123–42.

———. "Sapphic Self-Fashioning in the Baroque Era: Women's Petrarchan Parody in English and Spanish, 1650–1700." *Studies in Eighteenth-Century Culture* 35 (2006): 129–63.

Durán, Gloria. *Catalina, mi padre*. México, DF: Planeta, 2004.

Eco, Umberto. *Mouse or Rat? Translation as Negotiation*. London: Phoenix, 2004.

Egido, Aurora. "La página y el lienzo: Sobre las relaciones entre poesía y pintura." *Las fronteras de la poesía en el barroco*. Barcelona: Crítica, 1990. 164–97.

———. "La poética del silencio en el siglo de oro. Su pervivencia." *Las fronteras de la poesía en el barroco*. Barcelona: Crítica, 1990. 56–84.

Eich, Jennifer L. *The Other Mexican Muse: Sor María Anna Águeda de San Ignacio (1695–1756)*. New Orleans: UP of the South, 2004.

Espejo, Beatriz. *Oficios y menesteres (Crónicas)*. México, DF: U Autónoma Metropolitana, 1988.

Esquivel, Laura. *Como agua para chocolate*. México, DF: Planeta, 1989.

Faderman, Lillian, ed. *Chloe plus Olivia: An Anthology of Lesbian Literature from the Seventeenth Century to the Present.* New York: Viking, 1994.

———. *Surpassing the Love of Men: Romantic Friendship and Love between Women from the Renaissance to the Present.* New York: Morrow, 1981.

Fama y obras pósthumas. U of Bielefeld. 23 May 2006. 2 Mar. 2007 <http://www.ub.uni-bielefeld.de/diglib/delacruz/fama/>.

Fanon, Franz. *The Wretched of the Earth.* Trans. Constance Farrington. Harmondsworth: Penguin, 1967.

Fernández, Sergio, and Vicente Quiarte, eds. *Los empeños: Ensayos en homenaje a sor Juana Inés de la Cruz*. México, DF: U Nacional Autónoma de México, 1995.

Fernández de Santa Cruz, Manuel. "Carta de sor Filotea de la Cruz." Méndez-Plancarte and Salceda 4: 694–97.

Findlen, Paula, ed. *Athanasius Kircher: The Last Man Who Knew Everything*. New York: Routledge, 2004.

Flores, Kate, and Angel Flores, eds. *The Defiant Muse: Hispanic Feminist Poems from the Middle Ages to the Present.* New York: Feminist, 1986.

Fonte, Moderata. *The Worth of Women*. 1600. Ed. and trans. Virginia Cox. Chicago: U of Chicago P, 1997.

Foucault, Michel. *An Introduction*. Trans. Robert Hurley. New York: Pantheon, 1978. Vol. 1 of *The History of Sexuality*. 3 vols.

———. *Power/Knowledge: Selected Interviews and Other Writings*. Ed. Colin Gordon. New York: Pantheon, 1980.

———. "The Subject and Power." *The Essential Foucault: Selections from the Essential Foucault, 1954–1984.* Ed. Paul Rabinow and Nicholas Rose. New York: New, 2003. 126–44.

Franco, Jean. *Plotting Women: Gender and Representation in Mexico*. New York: Columbia UP, 1989.

———. "Sor Juana Explores Space." Franco, *Plotting Women* 23–54.

Fuchs, Barbara. *Mimesis and Empire: The New World, Islam, and European Identities*. Cambridge: Cambridge UP, 2001.

Fuentes, Katia. "Self-Portrait of a Mexican Saint." *Caveat Lector* 16.1 (2005). 2 Mar. 2007 <http://www.caveat-lector.org/1601/html/1601_art_fuentes2.htm>.

Fuentes, Vilma. "Sor Juana, Garro, Castellanos y María Luisa Mendoza." *Jornada* (2000). 2 Mar. 2007 <http://www.jornada.unam.mx/2000/12/12/opinion.html>.

Gallardo, Bartolomé José, ed. *Ensayo de una biblioteca española de libros raros y curiosos.* Vol. 4. Madrid: Tello, 1889.

Galván, Alicia L., trans. *Sor Juana: Poet, Nun, Feminist, Enigma.* Autodefensa espiritual: *A Poet's Translation*. San Antonio: Galvart, 1998.

Gaos, José. "El sueño de un sueño." *Historia Mexicana* 10.1 (1960): 54–71.

Garayta, Isabel. " 'Womanhandling' the Text: Feminism, Rewriting, and Translation." Diss. U of Texas, Austin, 1998.

García, Alma M., ed. *Chicana Feminist Thought: The Basic Historical Writings*. New York: Routledge, 1997.

García Canclini, Néstor. *Hybrid Cultures: Strategies for Entering and Leaving Modernity.* Trans. Christopher L. Chiappari and Silvia L. López. Minneapolis: U of Minnesota P, 1995.

Garcilaso de la Vega. *Poesías castellanas completas*. Ed. Elias Rivers. Madrid: Clásicos Castalia, 1972.

Garrido, Felipe. *Historia. Cuarto Grado.* 1994. 2nd rev. ed. México, DF: Libros de Texto Gratuitos, 2001.

———. *Historia. Sexto Grado*. 1994. 2nd rev. ed. México, DF: Libros de Texto Gratuitos, 2001.

Garrido, Gabriel. Liner Notes. *Phénix* 34–35.

Garro, Elena. *Los recuerdos del porvenir*. México, DF: Mortiz, 1963.

Gaspar de Alba, Alicia. "The Politics of Location of the Tenth Muse of America: An Interview with Sor Juana Inés de la Cruz." *Living Chicana Theory*. Ed. Carla Trujillo. Berkeley: Third Woman, 1998. 136–65.

———. *El segundo sueño*. Trans. Bettina Blanch Tyroller. Barcelona: Mondadori, 2001.

———. *Sor Juana's Second Dream: A Novel*. Albuquerque: U of New Mexico P, 1999.

Gauntlett, David, and Ross Horsley. *Web Studies*. 2nd ed. New York: Oxford UP, 2004.

Gibaldi, Joseph. *MLA Style Manual and Guide to Scholarly Publishing*. 2nd ed. New York: MLA, 1998.

Gilroy, Paul. *The Black Atlantic: Modernity and Double Consciousness*. 1993. Cambridge: Harvard UP, 1995.

Gimbernat González, Ester. "Speaking through the Voices of Love: Interpretation as Emancipation." Merrim, *Feminist Perspectives* 162–76.

Glantz, Margo. *Apariciones*. México, DF: Alfaguara–U del Claustro de Sor Juana, 1995.

———. "El cuerpo monacal y sus vestiduras." Moraña, *Mujer* 171–82.

———. "El elogio más calificado." Glantz, *Comparación* 157–210.

———. "Labores de manos: ¿Hagiografía o autobiografía?" Poot-Herrera, *"Y diversa"* 21–33.

———. *El rastro*. Barcelona: Anagrama, 2002.

———. *Sor Juana: La comparación y la hipérbole*. México, DF: Conaculta, 2000.

———. *Sor Juana Inés de la Cruz, ¿hagiografía o autobiografía?* México, DF: Grijalbo, 1995.

———. *Sor Juana Inés de la Cruz, saberes y placeres*. Toluca, Mex.: Inst. Mexiquense de Cultura, 1996.

Góngora y Argote, Luis de. *Obras completas*. Ed. Juan Millé y Giménez and Isabel Millé y Giménez. Madrid: Aguilar, 1967.

———. *Sonetos completos*. Ed. Biruté Ciplijauskaité. Madrid: Castalia, 1969.

Gonzalez de la Vara, Fernán, ed. *Cocina mexicana a través de los siglos*. 10 vols. México, DF: Clío, 1996.

González Echevarría, "BdeORridaGES (Borges and Derrida)." *Jorge Luis Borges*. Modern Critical Views. Ed. Harold Bloom. New York: Chelsea, 1986. 227–34.

Trans. of "BdeORridaGES (Borges y Derrida)." *Isla a su vuelo fugitiva: Ensayos críticos sobre literatura hispanoamericana.* Madrid: Porrúa Turanzas, 1983. 205–15.

———. "Colonial Lyric." *Discovery to Modernism.* Cambridge: Cambridge UP, 1996. 191–230. Vol. 1. of *The Cambridge History of Latin American Literature.* 3 vols.

———. *Myth and Archive: A Theory of Latin American Narrative*. Cambridge: Cambridge UP, 1990.

González García, José M. "Emblemas políticos en el barroco: Lectura de la imagen, visualización de la palabra." *Teoría de la interpretación. Ensayos sobre filosofía, arte y literatura*. Ed. María Herrera Lima. México, DF: U Nacional Autónoma de México–Consejo Nacional de Ciencia y Tecnología, 1998. 225–50.

Gortari Krauss, Yuri de, and Edmundo Escamilla Solis. *Guisos y golosos del barroco*. Cocina virreinal novohispana 3. México, DF: Clio, 2000.

Gournay, Marie de. "The Equality of Men and Women" 1622. Trans. Maya Bijvoet. Wilson and Warnke 14–15.

———. "The Ladies' Grievance." 1626. Trans. Maya Bijvoet. Wilson and Warnke 23–26.

Granado, Diego. *Libro del arte de cocina, por Diego Granado*. 1599. Ed. Joaquin del Val. Madrid: Sociedad de Bibliófilos Espanoles, 1971.

Graves, Robert. *The Crowning Privilege: Essays on Poetry*. Garden City: Doubleday, 1956.

Greenblatt, Stephen. "Learning to Curse: Aspects of Linguistic Colonialism in the Sixteenth Century." *First Images of America: The Impact of the New World on the Old.* Ed. Fredi Chiapelli, Michael J. B. Allen, Robert L. Benson, and Robert S. Lopez. Berkeley: U of California P, 1976. 561–80.

———. *Renaissance Self-Fashioning: From More to Shakespeare.* Chicago: U of Chicago P, 1980.

Greene, Roland. *Post-Petrarchism: Origins and Innovations of the Western Lyric Sequence*. Princeton: Princeton UP, 1991.

Gregory I. *Forty Gospel Homilies*. Trans. David Hurst. Kalamazoo: Cistercian, 1990.

Greimas, Algirdas Julien, and J. Courtés. *Semiótica. Diccionario razonado de la teoría del lenguaje.* Trans. Enrique Ballón and Hermis Campodónico. Madrid: Gredos, 1982.

Grossi, Verónica. "Claves políticas y epistemológicas en la *Carta de Monterrey* de sor Juana Inés de la Cruz." Moraña and Martínez–San Miguel 225–41.

———. "De la fiesta pública al claustro silencioso: Alegorías de conocimiento en sor Juana Inés de la Cruz." *Bulletin of Spanish Studies* 80.6 (2003): 665–93.

———. "Figuras políticas y epistemológicas en el *Neptuno alegórico* de sor Juana Inés de la Cruz." *Romance Quarterly* 51.3 (2004): 183–92.

———. *Sigilosos v(u)elos epistemológicos en sor Juana Inés de la Cruz*. Colección Nexos y Diferencias. Madrid: Vervuert-Iberoamericana, 2007.

Gruzinski, Serge. *La guerra de las imágenes: De Cristóbal Colón a "Blade Runner" (1492-2019)*. Trans. Juan José Utrilla. México, DF: Fondo de Cultura Económica, 1994.

———. *Images at War: Mexico from Columbus to* Blade Runner *(1492-2019)*. Trans. Heather MacLean. Durham: Duke UP, 2001.

Hall, Stuart. "Encoding, Decoding." *The Cultural Studies Reader*. Ed. Simon During. New York: Routledge, 1999. 507–17.

Hansen, Leonhard. *Vita mirabilis et mors pretiosa Maria Limensis / Exterio ordine S. P. Dominici excerpta et collecta per eximium P. F. Leonardum Hansen.* . . . Rome: Typis Nicolai Angeli Tinassij, 1664.

Haraway, Donna. *Simians, Cyborgs, and Women. The Reinvention of Nature.* New York: Routledge, 1991.

Harris, Max. "Disguised Reconciliations: Indigenous Voices in Early Franciscan Missionary Drama in Mexico." *Radical History Review* 53 (1992): 13–25.

Harrison, Regina. *Signs, Songs, and Memory in the Andes.* Austin: U of Texas P, 1989.

Harss, Luis, trans. *Sor Juana's* Dream. By Sor Juana Inés de la Cruz. New York: Lumen, 1986.

Harvey, Tamara. " 'My Goods Are True': Tenth Muses in the New World Market." *Feminist Interventions in Early American Studies*. Ed. Mary C. Carruth. Tuscaloosa: U of Alabama P, 2006. 13–26.

———. " 'Now Sisters . . . Impart Your Usefulness, and Force': Anne Bradstreet's Feminist Functionalism in *The Tenth Muse* (1650)." *Early American Literature* 35.1 (2000): 5–28.

Hebreo, León. *Diálogos de amor*. Trans. Inca Garcilaso de la Vega. Buenos Aires: Espasa Calpe, 1947.

Hernández Araico, Susana, trans. *Pawns of a House / Los empeños de una casa*. By Sor Juana Inés de la Cruz. Tempe: Bilingual, 2005.

Hierro, Graciela. *La ética del placer*. México, DF: U Nacional Autónoma de México, 2001.

Higgins, Antony. *Constructing the Criollo Archive: Subjects of Knowledge in the Biblioteca Mexicana and the Rusticatio Mexicana*. West Lafayette: Purdue UP, 2000.

Hill, Ruth. *Scepters and Sciences in the Spains: Four Humanists and the New Philosophy (ca. 1680–1740)*. Liverpool: Liverpool UP, 2000.

Hind, Emily. "The Sor Juana Archetype in Recent Works by Mexican Women Writers." *Hispanófila* 47.3 (2004): 89–103.

Holler, Jacqueline. *"Escogidas Plantas": Nuns and Beatas in Mexico City, 1531–1601*. New York: Columbia UP, 2005.

Hollywood, Amy. "On the Materiality of Air: Janet Kauffman's Bodyfictions." *New Literary History* 27.3 (1996): 503–25.

Horan, Elizabeth. "Mirror to the Nation: Posthumous Portraits of Gabriela Mistral." *Gabriela Mistral the Audacious Traveler*. Ed. Marjorie Agosín. Athens: Ohio UP, 2003. 224–49.

Ibsen, Kristine. *Women's Spiritual Autobiography in Colonial Spanish America.* Gainesville: UP of Florida, 1999.

Ingber, Alix, trans. *Sonetos del Siglo de Oro / Golden Age Sonnets.* 7 Apr. 2006. 2 Mar. 2007 <http://sonnets.spanish.sbc.edu/>.

Irigaray, Luce. *This Sex Which Is Not One*. Trans. Catherine Porter and Carolyn Burke. Ithaca: Cornell UP, 1985.

Irisarri, Ángeles de. *América: La aventura de cuatro mujeres en el Nuevo Mundo*. Barcelona: Random, 2002.

Jacobsen, Jerome V. *Educational Foundations of the Jesuits in Sixteenth-Century New Spain*. Berkeley: U of California P, 1939.

Jay, Martin. "Scopic Regimes of Modernity." *Vision and Visuality.* Ed. Hal Foster. Seattle: Bay, 1988. 3–23.

Jed, Stephanie. "The Tenth Muse: Gender, Rationality, and the Marketing of Knowledge." *Women, "Race," and Writing in the Early Modern Period*. Ed. Margo Hendricks and Patricia Parker. London: Routledge, 1994. 195–208.

Jesusa Rodríguez. Hemispheric Inst. Web site. 30 Mar. 2007 <http://hemi.nyu.edu/cuaderno/holyterrorsweb/jesusa/>. Path: Performances; Sor Juana, El Primero Sueño (2002).

Jones, Amelia, ed. "Introduction: Conceiving the Intersection of Feminism and Visual Culture." *The Feminism and Visual Culture Reader.* New York: Routledge, 2003. 1–7.

Jones, Ann Rosalind. *The Currency of Eros: Women's Love Lyric in Europe, 1540–1620.* Bloomington: Indiana UP, 1990.

Jones, Cyril. "El negro en los juegos religiosos de villancicos en México y España." *Estudios de literatura hispanoamericana en honor a José J. Arrom.* Chapel Hill: U of North Carolina, Dept. of Romance Langs., 1974. 59–69.

Jones, Joseph R. "*La Erudición Elegante*: Observations on the Emblematic Tradition in Sor Juana's *Neptuno alegórica* and Sigüenza's *Teatro de virtudes políticas*." *Hispanófila* 65 (1979): 43–58.

Jones, Willis Knapp, trans. Loa *from* El divino Narciso. By Sor Juana Inés de la Cruz. *Spanish-American Literature in Translation.* Vol. 1. Ed. Jones. New York: Unger, 1966. 301–08.

Jordan, Constance. *Renaissance Feminism: Literary Texts and Political Models*. Ithaca: Cornell UP, 1990.

Joskowicz, Alfredo, dir. *Constelaciones*. Perf. Ana Ofelia Murguía. Written by Joskowicz and Belarmino Kepler. Nova, 1980.

Judovitz, Dalia. *The Culture of the Body: Genealogies of Modernity*. Ann Arbor: U of Michigan P, 2001.

Kaminsky, Amy Katz. Introduction. *Water Lilies / Flores del agua: An Anthology of Spanish Women Writers from the Fifteenth through the Nineteenth Century*. Ed. Kaminsky. Minneapolis: U of Minnesota P, 1996. 1–14.

Kantaris, Geoffrey. "Difference and Indifference: The Poetry of Sor Juana Inés de la Cruz." 1992. Cambridge U. 3 Feb. 2005 <http://www.latin-american.cam.ac.uk/SorJuana/SorJuana2.htm>.

Kirk, Pamela. "God among Nations." Kirk, *Sor Juana* 27–36.

———. *Sor Juana Inés de la Cruz: Religion, Art, and Feminism*. New York: Continuum, 1998.

Kittel, Muriel, trans. "Arguing That There Are Inconsistencies between Men's Tastes and Their Censure When They Accuse Women of What They Themselves Do Cause." By Sor Juana Inés de la Cruz. Flores and Flores 21–22.

Klor de Alva, José Jorge. "The Postcolonization of the (Latin) American Experience: A Reconsideration of 'Colonialism,' 'Postcolonialism,' and 'Mestizaje.' " *After Colonialism: Imperial Histories and Postcolonial Displacements*. Ed. Gyan Prakash. Princeton: Princeton UP, 1995. 241–75.

Kubayanda, Josaphat. "On Colonial/Imperial Discourse and Contemporary Critical Theory." *1992 Lecture Series*. College Park: U of Maryland, 1990.

Kügelgen, Helga von. "The Way to Mexican Identity: Two Triumphal Arches of the Seventeenth Century." *World Art: Themes of Unity in Diversity. Acts of the XXVIth International Congress of the History of Art*. Vol. 3. Ed. Irving Lavin. University Park: Pennsylvania State UP, 1989. 709–20.

Langer, Ullrich. "Gunpowder as Transgressive Invention in Ronsard." *Literary Theory / Renaissance Texts*. Ed. Patricia Parker and David Quint. Baltimore: Johns Hopkins UP, 1986. 96–114.

Lanser, Susan. "Befriending the Body: Female Intimacies as Class Acts." *Eighteenth-Century Studies* 32 (1998–99):179–98.

Larkin, Joan, and Jaime Manrique, trans. *Sor Juana's Love Poems*. Madison: U of Wisconsin P, 2003.

Lavín, Mónica. *Dulces hábitos: Golosinas del convento*. Cocina virreinal novohispana 1. México, DF: Clío, 2000.

———. *Sor Juana en la cocina*. Cocina virreinal novohispana 4. México, DF: Clio, 2000.

Lavrin, Asunción. "Unlike Sor Juana? The Model Nun in the Religious Literature of Colonial Mexico." Merrim, *Feminist Perspectives* 61–85.

———. "Vida conventual: Rasgos históricos." Poot-Herrera, *Sor Juana* 35–91.

León, Tonia. "Sor Juana Inés de la Cruz's 'Primero sueño': A Lyric Expression of Seventeenth-Century Scientific Thought." Diss. New York U, 1989.

Leonard, Irving A. *Baroque Times in Old Mexico: Seventeenth-Century People, Places, and Practices*. Ann Arbor: U of Michigan P, 1966.

———. *La época barroca en el México colonial*. México, DF: Fondo de Cultura Económica, 1986.

Lezama Lima, José. *La expresión americana*. México, DF: Fondo de Cultura Económica, 1993.

Libro de cocina: Convento de San Jerónimo. Selección y transcripción atribuidas a sor Juana Inés de la Cruz. Toluca, Mex.: Inst. Mexiquense de Cultura, 1996.

Lienhard, Martin. *La voz y su huella*. México, DF: Pablos, 2003.

Lindenberger, Herbert. Foreword. *MLA Style Manual and Guide to Scholarly Publishing*. Joseph Gibaldi. 2nd ed. New York: MLA, 1998. xv–xxvi.

Lipski, John. *A History of Afro-Hispanic Language: Five Centuries, Five Continents*. New York: Cambridge UP, 2005.

López Portillo, Carmen Beatriz, ed. *Sor Juana y su mundo: Una mirada actual.* México, DF: U del Claustro de Sor Juana, Fondo de Cultura Económica, 1998.

López Poza, Sagrario. "La erudición de sor Juana Inés de la Cruz en su *Neptuno alegórico.*" *Perinola* 7 (2003): 241–70.

Loreto López, Rosalvo, and Ana Luisa Benitez Muro. *Un bocado para los ángeles: La cocina conventual novohispana.* Cocina virreinal novohispana 2. México, DF: Clio, 2000.

Luciani, Frederick. "El amor desfigurado: El ovillejo de sor Juana Inés de la Cruz." *Texto Crítico* 34.5 (1986): 11–48.

———. "Anamorphosis in a Sonnet of Sor Juana Inés de la Cruz." *Discurso literario* 5 (1988): 11–18.

———. "Emblems, Optics and Sor Juana's Verse: 'Eye' and Thou." *Calíope* 4.1–2 (1998): 157–72.

———. *Literary Self-Fashioning in Sor Juana Inés de la Cruz.* Cranbury: Associated UP, 2004.

———. "Recreaciones de sor Juana en la narrativa y teatro hispano/norteamericanos, 1952–1988." Poot-Herrera, *"Y diversa de mí misma"* 395–408.

Ludmer, Josefina. "Tricks of the Weak." Merrim, *Feminist Perspectives* 86–93.

Luna, Marta, dir. *Los demonios de la fe.* Perf. Miriam Calderón. 2002.

Luschei, Glenna. "The *Enigmas* of Sor Juana." *Prairie Schooner* 80.4 (2006): 18–20.

———. "Translating Sor Juana." *Prairie Schooner* 80.4 (2006): 21–24.

Maclean, Ian. *The Renaissance Notion of Woman: A Study in the Fortunes of Scholasticism and Medical Science in European Intellectual Life.* Cambridge: Cambridge UP, 1980.

Maier, Carol. Rev. of *The Answer / La respuesta,* by Sor Juana Inés de la Cruz. Trans. Electa Arenal and Amanda Powell. *Comparative Literature* 47.1 (1995): 79–82.

Makowski, Elizabeth. *Canon Law and Cloistered Women:* Periculoso *and Its Commentators, 1298–1545.* Washington: Catholic U of America P, 1997.

M Magazine. Reforma 3 Oct. 2004: 43.

Manrique, Jorge Alberto. "El manierismo en la Nueva España: Letras y artes." *Anales del Instituto de Investigaciones Estéticas* 45 (1976): 107–16.

———. *Manierismo en México.* México, DF: Textos Dispersos, 1993.

Maravall, José Antonio. *La cultura del Barroco: Análisis de una estructura histórica.* Barcelona: Ariel, 1975.

———. *Culture of the Baroque: Analysis of a Historical Structure.* Trans. Terry Cochran. Minneapolis: U of Minnesota P, 1986.

———. *Teatro y literatura en la sociedad barroca.* Madrid: Seminario y Ediciones, 1972.

Martin, John Rupert. *Baroque.* New York: Harper, 1977.

Martín, Luis. *Daughters of the Conquistadores: Women of the Viceroyalty of Peru.* 1983. Dallas: Southern Methodist UP, 1989.

Martínez del Río Redo, María Josefa, and Teresa Castelló Yturbide. *Delicias de antaño: Historia y recetas de los conventos mexicanos*. México, DF: Océano, 2000.

Martínez Montiño, Francisco. *Arte de cocina, pasteleria, vizcocheria y conserveria*. 1611. Barcelona: Sierra y Marti, 1823.

Martínez–San Miguel, Yolanda. *Saberes americanos. Subalternidad y epistemología en los escritos de sor Juana*. Pittsburgh: Instituto Internacional de Literatura Iberoamericana, 1999.

Mastretta, Ángeles. *Mal de amores*. México, DF: Alfaguara, 1996. Trans. as *Lovesick*. Trans. Margaret Sayers Peden. New York: Riverhead, 1997.

———. "El mundo iluminado." *El mundo iluminado*. México, DF: Cal y Arena, 1998. 197–200.

Maza, Francisco de la. *Arquitectura de los coros de monjas en México*. México, DF: U Nacional Autónoma de México, 1985.

———. *La mitología clásica en el arte colonial de México*. México, DF: U Nacional Autónoma de México, 1968.

———. *El sepulcro de sor Juana Inés de la Cruz: Breve crónica del Templo de San Jerónimo y de la restauración de sus coros*. México, DF: n.p., 1967.

———, ed. *Sor Juana Inés de la Cruz ante la historia. Biografías antiguas. La fama de 1700. Noticias de 1667 a 1892*. Rev. Elías Trabulse. México, DF: U Nacional Autónoma de México, 1980.

Mazzotti, José Antonio. *Coros mestizos del Inca Garcilaso. Resonancias andinas*. Lima: Bolsa de Valores de Lima, 1996.

McKnight, Kathryn Joy. *The Mystic of Tunja: The Writings of Madre Castillo, 1671–1742*. Amherst: U of Massachusetts P, 1997.

Medina, Ofelia. *Sor Juana hoy*. Miami: WEA Latina, 1995.

Melammed, Renée. *Heretics or Daughters of Israel? The Crypto-Jewish Women of Castile*. New York: Oxford UP, 1999.

Memoria del Coloquio Internacional sor Juana Inés de la Cruz y el pensamiento novohispano. Toluca, Mex.: Instituto Mexiquense de Cultura, 1995.

Ménage, Gilles. *The History of Women Philosophers*. 1690. Trans. Beatrice H. Zedler. Lanham: UP of America, 1984.

Méndez, María Águeda. "La comida en el claustro novohispano: Sustento corporal y espiritual." Poot-Herrera, *En gustos se comen géneros* 439–58.

Méndez Plancarte, Alfonso. "Estudio liminar." Méndez Plancarte and Salceda 2: vii–lxxviii.

———, ed. *Poetas novohispanos. Primer siglo (1521–1621)*. 1942. México, DF: U Nacional Autónoma de México, 1991.

———, ed. *Poetas novohispanos. Segundo siglo (1621–1721)*. 1945. Vol. 1. México, DF: 1995.

Méndez Plancarte, Alfonso, and Alberto G. Salceda, eds. *Obras completas de sor Juana Inés de la Cruz*. Vols. 1–3, ed. Méndez Plancarte. Vol. 4, ed. Salceda. México, DF: Fondo de Cultura Económica, 1951–57. 4 vols.

Mendoza, María Luisa. *Ojos de papel volando*. México, DF: Mortiz, 1985.

Menocal, María Rosa. *Shards of Love: Exile and the Origins of the Lyric*. Durham: Duke UP, 1994.

———. *Writing in Dante's Cult of Truth: From Borges to Bocaccio*. Durham: Duke UP, 1991.

Merkl, Heinrich. "Juana Inés de la Cruz y Carlos de Sigüenza y Góngora en 1680." *Iberoromania* 36 (1992): 21–37.

Merrim, Stephanie. *Early Modern Women's Writing and Sor Juana Inés de la Cruz*. Nashville: Vanderbilt UP, 1999.

———, ed. *Feminist Perspectives on Sor Juana Inés de la Cruz*. Detroit: Wayne State UP, 1991.

———. "Hemispheric Colonial Studies, 'The Garden of Forking Paths,' and Sor Juana Inés de la Cruz." "Incomparable Americas: Colonial American Studies after the Hemispheric Turn." Ed. Lisa Voigt and Eric Slauter. Forthcoming.

"Toward a Feminist Reading of Sor Juana Inés de la Cruz: Past, Present, and Future Directions in Sor Juana Criticism." Merrim, *Feminist Perspectives* 11–37.

Mesa-Bains, Amalia. "*Domesticana*: The Sensibility of Chicana *Rasquachismo*." *Chicana Feminisms: A Critical Reader*. Ed. Gabriela F. Arredondo, Aída Hurtado, Norma Klahn, Olga Nájera-Ramírez, and Patricia Zavella. Durham: Duke UP, 2003. 298–315.

Mignolo, Walter. *The Darker Side of the Renaissance: Literacy, Territoriality, and Colonization*. Ann Arbor: U of Michigan P, 1995.

———. *Local Histories / Global Designs: Coloniality, Subaltern Knowledges, and Border Thinking*. Princeton: Princeton UP, 2000.

Mínguez, Víctor. *Los reyes distantes. Imágenes del poder en el México virreinal*. Barcelona: Biblioteca de les Aules, 1995.

Mirzoeff, Nicholas. "Introduction to Part Four." Mirzoeff, *Visual Culture Reader* 593–600.

———. *An Introduction to Visual Culture*. London: Routledge, 1999.

———, ed. *The Visual Culture Reader*. 1998. 2nd ed. London: Routledge, 2002.

———. "What Is Visual Culture?" Mirzoeff, *Visual Culture Reader* 3–13.

Mistral, Gabriela. *Lecturas para mujeres*. 1923. 2nd ed. México, DF: SEP, 1987.

Mitchell, W. J. T. *Iconology. Image, Text, Ideology*. Chicago: U of Chicago P, 1986.

———. *Picture Theory: Essays on Verbal and Visual Representation*. Chicago: U of Chicago P, 1995.

Monaco, James. *How to Read a Film: The World of Movies, Media, Multimedia*. 3rd ed. London: Oxford UP, 2000.

Montero Alarcón, Alma. *Monjas coronadas*. México, DF: Consejo Nacional para la Cultura y las Artes: Dirección General de Publicaciones, 1999.

Mora, Pat. *A Library for Sor Juana: The World of Sor Juana Inés*. New York: Knopf, 2002.

———. "Nepantla: Essays from the Land in the Middle." García 292–94.

———. "The Young Sor Juana." *Communion*. Houston: Arte Público, 1991. 77–78.

Moraga, Cherríe, and Barbara Smith. "Lesbian Literature: A Third-World Feminist Perspective." Zimmerman and McNaron. 23–33.

Moraña, Mabel. ed. *Mujer y cultura en la Colonia hispanoamericana*. Pittsburgh: Biblioteca de América, 1996.

———. *Viaje al silencio. Exploraciones del discurso barroco*. México, DF: U Nacional Autónoma de México, 1998.

Moraña, Mabel, and Yolanda Martínez–San Miguel, eds. *Nictímene . . . sacrílega: Estudios coloniales en homenaje a Georgina Sabat-Rivers*. México, DF: U del Claustro de Sor Juana, 2003.

Moreto y Cavana, Agustín, and Francisco Lanini y Sagredo. *Comedia famosa: Santa Rosa del Peru*. Madrid: Fernández Buendía, a costa de Manuel Meléndez, 1671.

Mujica, Bárbara, ed. Preface. *Sophia's Daughters: Women Writers of Early Modern Spain*. New Haven: Yale UP, 2004. ix–lxxix.

Muñiz-Huberman, Angelina. "Las claves de Sor Juana." Poot-Herrera, *"Y diversa"* 315–25.

Muriel, Josefina. *Cultura femenina novohispana*. 1982. México, DF: U Nacional Autónoma de México, 1993.

———. *Las mujeres de Hispanoamérica. Êpoca colonial*. Madrid: Mapfre, 1992.

Muriel, Josefina, and Alicia Grobet. *Fundaciones neoclásicas; la marquesa de Selva Nevada, sus conventos y sus arquitectos*. México, DF: U Nacional Autónoma de México, 1969.

Muriel, Josefina, and Manuel Romero de Terreros. *Retratos de monjas*. Mexico: Jus, 1952.

Myers, Kathleen Ann. *Neither Saints nor Sinners: Writing the Lives of Women in Spanish America*. New York: Oxford UP, 2003.

———, ed. and introd. *Word from New Spain: The Spiritual Autobiography of Madre María de San José (1656–1719)*. Liverpool: Liverpool UP, 1993.

Myers, Kathleen Ann, and Amanda Powell. *A Wild Country out in the Garden: The Spiritual Journals of a Colonial Mexican Nun*. Bloomington: Indiana UP, 1999.

Nader, Helen, ed. and introd. *Power and Gender in Renaissance Spain. Eight Women of the Mendoza Family, 1450–1650*. Urbana: U of Illinois P, 2003.

Nava y Saavedra, Jerónima. *Jerónima Nava y Saavedra (1669–1727): Autobiografía de una monja venerable*. Ed. and introd. Angela Inés Robledo. Calí, Colombia: U del Valle, 1994.

Navarrete, Ignacio. *Orphans of Petrarch: Poetry and Theory in the Spanish Renaissance*. Berkeley: U of California P, 1994.

NietoGómez, Anna. "Chicana Feminism." García 52–57.

———. "The Chicana—Perspectives for Education." García 130–31.

Noble, Andrea. "Latin American Visual Cultures." *The Companion to Latin American Studies*. Ed. Philip Swanson. New York: Oxford UP, 2003. 154–71.

Nola, Roberto de. *Libro de cozina [por] Roberto de Nola*. Ed. Carmen Iranzo. 1525. Madrid: Taurus, 1969.

Novo, Salvador. *Cocina mexicana, o historia gastronómica de la cuidad de México*. México, DF: Porrúa, 1967.

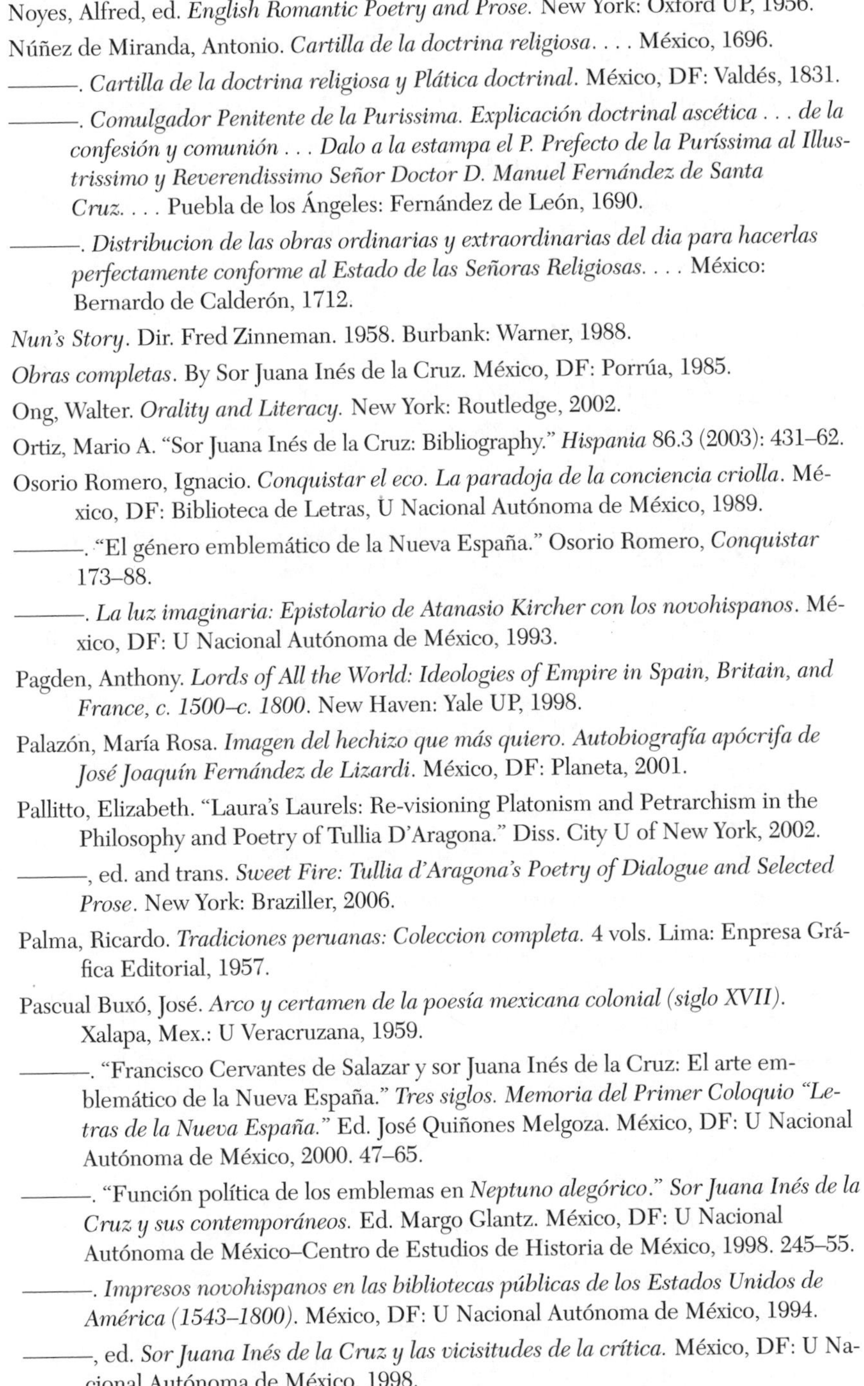

Noyes, Alfred, ed. *English Romantic Poetry and Prose.* New York: Oxford UP, 1956.

Núñez de Miranda, Antonio. *Cartilla de la doctrina religiosa. . . .* México, 1696.

———. *Cartilla de la doctrina religiosa y Plática doctrinal.* México, DF: Valdés, 1831.

———. *Comulgador Penitente de la Purissima. Explicación doctrinal ascética . . . de la confesión y comunión . . . Dalo a la estampa el P. Prefecto de la Puríssima al Illustrissimo y Reverendissimo Señor Doctor D. Manuel Fernández de Santa Cruz. . . .* Puebla de los Ángeles: Fernández de León, 1690.

———. *Distribucion de las obras ordinarias y extraordinarias del dia para hacerlas perfectamente conforme al Estado de las Señoras Religiosas. . . .* México: Bernardo de Calderón, 1712.

Nun's Story. Dir. Fred Zinneman. 1958. Burbank: Warner, 1988.

Obras completas. By Sor Juana Inés de la Cruz. México, DF: Porrúa, 1985.

Ong, Walter. *Orality and Literacy.* New York: Routledge, 2002.

Ortiz, Mario A. "Sor Juana Inés de la Cruz: Bibliography." *Hispania* 86.3 (2003): 431–62.

Osorio Romero, Ignacio. *Conquistar el eco. La paradoja de la conciencia criolla.* México, DF: Biblioteca de Letras, U Nacional Autónoma de México, 1989.

———. "El género emblemático de la Nueva España." Osorio Romero, *Conquistar* 173–88.

———. *La luz imaginaria: Epistolario de Atanasio Kircher con los novohispanos.* México, DF: U Nacional Autónoma de México, 1993.

Pagden, Anthony. *Lords of All the World: Ideologies of Empire in Spain, Britain, and France, c. 1500–c. 1800.* New Haven: Yale UP, 1998.

Palazón, María Rosa. *Imagen del hechizo que más quiero. Autobiografía apócrifa de José Joaquín Fernández de Lizardi.* México, DF: Planeta, 2001.

Pallitto, Elizabeth. "Laura's Laurels: Re-visioning Platonism and Petrarchism in the Philosophy and Poetry of Tullia D'Aragona." Diss. City U of New York, 2002.

———, ed. and trans. *Sweet Fire: Tullia d'Aragona's Poetry of Dialogue and Selected Prose.* New York: Braziller, 2006.

Palma, Ricardo. *Tradiciones peruanas: Coleccion completa.* 4 vols. Lima: Enpresa Gráfica Editorial, 1957.

Pascual Buxó, José. *Arco y certamen de la poesía mexicana colonial (siglo XVII).* Xalapa, Mex.: U Veracruzana, 1959.

———. "Francisco Cervantes de Salazar y sor Juana Inés de la Cruz: El arte emblemático de la Nueva España." *Tres siglos. Memoria del Primer Coloquio "Letras de la Nueva España."* Ed. José Quiñones Melgoza. México, DF: U Nacional Autónoma de México, 2000. 47–65.

———. "Función política de los emblemas en *Neptuno alegórico.*" *Sor Juana Inés de la Cruz y sus contemporáneos.* Ed. Margo Glantz. México, DF: U Nacional Autónoma de México–Centro de Estudios de Historia de México, 1998. 245–55.

———. *Impresos novohispanos en las bibliotecas públicas de los Estados Unidos de América (1543–1800).* México, DF: U Nacional Autónoma de México, 1994.

———, ed. *Sor Juana Inés de la Cruz y las vicisitudes de la crítica.* México, DF: U Nacional Autónoma de México, 1998.

———. " 'El sueño' de sor Juana: Alegoría y modelo del mundo." *Las figuraciones del sentido. Ensayos de poética semiológica*. México, DF: Fondo de Cultura Económica, 1984. 235–52.

Pasto, David, trans. *The House of Trials*. By Sor Juana Inés de la Cruz. New York: Lang, 1997.

Paz, Octavio. Foreword. Trueblood vii–xii.

———. *Sor Juana Inés de la Cruz o las trampas de la fe*. Barcelona: Seix Barral, 1982. México, DF: Fondo de Cultura Económica, 1995.

———. *Sor Juana; or, The Traps of Faith*. Trans. Margaret Sayers Peden. Cambridge: Belknap–Harvard UP, 1988.

Peden, Margaret Sayers. "Building a Translation, The Reconstruction Business: Poem 145 of Sor Juana Inés de la Cruz." *The Craft of Translation*. Ed. John Biguenet and Rainer Schulte. Chicago: U of Chicago P, 1989. 13–27.

———, trans. *Poems, Protest, and a Dream*. London: Penguin, 1997.

———, trans. *Sor Juana Inés de la Cruz, Poems: A Bilingual Anthology*. Binghamton: Bilingual, 1985.

———, trans. *A Woman of Genius: The Intellectual Autobiography of Sor Juana Inés de la Cruz*. 1982. 2nd ed. Salisbury: Lime Rock, 1987.

Pedraza, Pilar. "El silencio del príncipe." *Goya* 187–88 (1985): 37–46.

Peña, Margarita, ed. *Cuadernos de sor Juana*. México, DF: U Nacional Autónoma de México, 1995.

Peón, Ramón, dir. *Sor Juana Inés de la Cruz*. Perf. Andrea Palma. Written by Peón, Armando Vargas de la Mazo. La Mexicana, 1935.

Perea, Héctor. "Angulos oscilantes en el rostro de sor Juana." *Artes de México* 25 (1994): 30–37.

Perelmuter [Pérez], Rosa. "La bella (sor Juana) Inés, el jamón y berenjenas con queso." Poot-Herrera, *En gustos se comen géneros* 459–81.

———. *Los límites de la femineidad en sor Juana Inés de la Cruz: Estrategias retóricas y recepción literaria*. Biblioteca Áurea Hispánica 29. Madrid: U de Navarra-Iberoamericana / Vervuert, 2004.

———. *Noche intelectual: La oscuridad idiomática en el* Primero sueño. México, DF: U Nacional Autónoma de México, 1982.

Pérez San Vicente, Guadalupe. "Sor Juana y su libro de cocina." *Memoria del Coloquio Internacional sor Juana Inés de la Cruz y el pensamiento novohispano, 1995*. Toluca, Mex.: Inst. Mexiquense de Cultura, 1995. 341–49.

Perry, Mary Elizabeth. *Gender and Disorder in Early Modern Seville*. Princeton: Princeton UP, 1990.

———. *The Handless Maiden: The Moriscos and the Politics of Religion in Early Modern Spain*. Princeton: Princeton UP, 2005.

Peters, Patricia, and Renée Domeier, trans. The Divine Narcissus / El Divino Narciso. By Sor Juana Inés de la Cruz. Albuquerque: U of New Mexico P, 1998.

Petition. Ms. Legajo 850, sección 5. Audiencia de México, Ramo eclesiàstico. Archivo de las Indias, Sevilla.

Petrarch, Francesco. *Petrarch's Lyric Poems: The "Rime Sparse" and Other Lyrics*. Ed. and trans. Robert M. Durling. Cambridge: Harvard UP, 1976.

Pettersson, Aline. *Mistificaciones*. México, DF: U Autónoma Metropolitana, 1996.

Pfandl, Ludwig. *Juana Inés de la Cruz, die zehnte Muse von Mexico, ihr Leben, ihre Dichtung, ihre Psyche*. München: Rinn, 1946.

Le phénix du Mexique: Villancicos de sor Juana Ines de la Cruz mis en musique à Chuquisaca au XVIIIe siecle. Perf. Ensemble Elyma, Cor Vivaldi, and Els Petits Cantors de Catalunya. Cond. Gabriel Garrido. Les Chemins du Baroque, 1999.

Picón Salas, Mariano. "El barroco de Indias." Picon, *Conquista* 121–46.

———. *De la conquista a la independencia*. 1944. México, DF: Fondo de Cultura Económica, 1994.

Pilcher, Jeffrey. *Que Vivan los Tamales: Food and the Making of Mexican Identity*. Albuquerque: U of New Mexico P, 1998.

Poblete, Juan, ed. *Critical Latin American and Latino Studies*. Minneapolis: U of Minnesota P, 2003.

Poesía lírica. By Sor Juana Inés de la Cruz. Introd. José Carlos González Boixo. Madrid: Cátedra, 1992.

Poniatowska, Elena. "Aleluya." Amor Poniatowska 11–15.

———. *Las siete cabritas*. México, DF: Era, 2000.

Poot-Herrera, Sara. "La caridad de Serafina, fineza de sor Juana." *Literatura: De la Edad Media al siglo XVIII*. Ed. Martha Elena Venier. México, DF: Colegio de México, 1997. 331–68. Vol. 2 of *Varia lingüística y literaria. 50 años del CELL*. 3 vols.

———. "Una carta finamente calculada, la de Serafina de Cristo." Bijuesca and Brescia 127–41.

———, ed. *En gustos se comen géneros*. 3 vols. Mérida: Inst. de Cultura de Yucatán, 2003.

———, ed. *Sor Juana y su mundo: Una mirada actual*. México, DF: U del Claustro de Sor Juana, 1995.

———, ed. *"Y diversa de mi misma entre vuestras plumas ando": Homenaje internacional a sor Juana Inés de la Cruz*. México, DF: Colegio de México, 1993.

Portús, Javier, ed. *The Spanish Portrait: From El Greco to Picasso*. London: Scala, 2004.

Pozzi, Edna. *El ruido del viento*. Buenos Aires: Lohlé, 1989.

Preminger, Alex, et al. *The New Princeton Encyclopedia of Poetry and Poetics*. Princeton: Princeton UP, 1993.

Puga, María Luisa. *La forma del silencio*. México, DF: Siglo XXI, 1987.

Quevedo, Francisco de. *Obra poética*. Ed. José Manuel Blecua. Madrid: Castalia, 1969.

———. *Poesía original completa*. Ed. José Manuel Blecua. Barcelona: Planeta, 1990.

———. *Poesía varia*. Ed. James O. Crosby. Madrid: Cátedra, 1982.

Quijano, Aníbal. "Coloniality of Power, Eurocentrism, and Latin America." *Nepantla* 1.3 (2000): 533–80.

Quintilian. *The* Institutio Oratoria *of Quintilian*. London: Heinemann, 1953.

Rabasa, José. "Reading Cabeza de Vaca; or, How We Perpetuate the Culture of Conquest." *Writing Violence on the Northern Frontier*. Durham: Duke UP, 2000. 31–83.

Rama, Angel. *La ciudad letrada*. Hanover: Norte, 2002.

Ramos, Alonso. *Segvnda parte de los prodigios de la omnipotencia y milagros de la gracia en la vida de la venerable sierva de Dios Catharina de S. Joan, natural del Gran Mogor, difunta en esta imperial ciudad de la Pvebla de los Angeles en la Nueva España*. México, DF: Fernández de León, 1690.

Reyes, Alfonso. *Memorias de cocina y bodega*. México, DF: Fondo de Cultura Económica, 1953.

Rigolot, François. "Nature and Function of Paronomasia in the *Canzoniere*." *Italian Quarterly* 18 (1974): 29–36.

Rincón, Berenice. "La Chicana: Her Role in the Past and Her Search for a New Role in the Future." García 24–28.

Rivers, Elias L., ed. *Renaissance and Baroque Poetry of Spain with English Prose Translations*. 1966. Prospect Heights: Waveland, 1988.

Rivers, Elias L., and Georgina Sabat de Rivers, eds. *Poesía, teatro, pensamiento: Lírica personal, lírica coral, teatro, prosa.* By Sor Juana Inés de la Cruz. Madrid: Espasa-Calpe, 2004.

Robbins, Jeremy. *The Challenges of Uncertainty: An Introduction to Seventeenth-Century Spanish Literature.* London: Duckworth, 1998.

Rodríguez, Jesusa. Home page. 29 Jan. 2007 <http://www.hemi.nyu.edu/cuaderno/holyterrorsweb/jesusa/nav.html>.

Rodríguez, Marcela. *Funesta*. N.p.: Urtext, 2000.

Rodríguez Hernández, Dalmacio. *Texto y fiesta en la literatura novohispana (1650–1700).* México, DF: U Nacional Autónoma de México, 1998.

Romero, Angeles. "*Sueño:* A Multimedia Play Based on the Life of Sor Juana Inés de la Cruz." MA thesis. Ohio State U, 2003.

Rose, Gillian. *Visual Methodologies: An Introduction to the Interpretation of Visual Materials*. London: Sage, 2003.

Ross, Kathleen. *The Baroque Narrative of Carlos de Sigüenza y Góngora: A New World Paradise*. New York: Cambridge UP, 1993.

Rubial García, Antonio. *La plaza, el palacio y el convento: La ciudad de México en el siglo XVII*. México, DF: Consejo Nacional para la Cultura y las Artes, 1998.

———. "Varones en comunidad. Los conventos urbanos de los mendicantes en el siglo XVII novohispano." *Tepotzotlán y la Nueva España.* Ed. María del Consuelo Maquívar. México, DF: Instituto Nacional de Antropología e Historia, 1994. 162–174.

Ruiz de Bravo Ahuja, Gloria. *Español. Sexto Grado. Lecturas*. 1972. 27th ed. México, DF: Libros de Texto Gratuitos, 2000.

Sabat de Rivers, Georgina. "Amarilis: Innovadora peruana de la epístola horaciana." *Hispanic Review* 58.4 (1990): 455–67.

———. *En busca de sor Juana*. México, DF: U Nacional Autónoma de México, 1998.

———. “A Feminist Rereading of Sor Juana’s Dream.” Merrim, *Feminist Perspectives* 142–61.

———. Introduction. Sabat de Rivers, *Inundación* 9–71.

———, ed. *Inundación Castálida*. By Sor Juana Inés de la Cruz. 1689. Madrid: Castalia, 1982.

———. “El *Neptuno* de sor Juana: Fiesta barroca y programa político.” *University of Dayton Review* 2 (1983): 63–73. Rpt. in Sabat de Rivers, *Busca* 241–61.

———. “Sor Juana lnés de la Cruz: Imágenes femeninas de su científico *Sueño*.” *Estudios de literatura hispanomamericana: Sor Juana Inés de la Cruz y otros poetas de la colonia*. Barcelona: Promociones y Publicaciones Universitarias, 1992. 305–26.

———. “Sor Juana y sus retratos de poéticos.” *Revista Chilena de literatura* 23 (1984): 39–52. Rpt. in Sabat de Rivers, *Busca* 57–78.

———. “Sor Juana y su *Sueño*: Antecedentes científicos en la poesía española del Siglo de Oro.” *Cuadernos Hispanoamericanos* 31 (1976): 186–204.

Said, Edward. *Orientalism.* London: Routledge, 1978.

Saint-Saëns, Alain. “Homoerotic Suffering, Pleasure, and Desire in Early Modern Europe, 1450–1750.” Saint-Saëns and Delgado 1–86.

Saint-Saëns, Alain, and María José Delgado, eds. *Lesbianism and Homosexuality in Early Modern Spain: Literature and Theater in Context*. New Orleans: UP of the South, 2000.

Sáinz, Gustavo. *Retablo de inmoderaciones y heresiarcas*. México, DF: Mortiz, 1992.

Salazar Simarro, Nuria. “Muebles y objetos en los espacios femeninos novohispanos.” *Barroco iberoamericano. Territorio, Arte, Espacio y sociedad.* Ed. Ana María Aranda et al. Vol. 1. Sevilla: Giralda, 2001. 191–211. 2 vols.

Salceda, Alberto G. Introduction. Méndez Plancarte and Salceda 4: vii–xlviii.

Salmerón, Pedro. *Vida de la venerable madre Isabel de la Encarnación*. . . . México, DF: Rodríguez Lupercio, 1675.

Sampson Vera Tudela, Elisa. *Colonial Angels: Narratives of Gender and Spirituality in Mexico, 1580–1750.* Austin: U of Texas P, 2000.

Sánchez, Miguel. “Imagen de la virgen María, Madre de Dios de Guadalupe. Milagrosamente aparecida en a ciudad de México. Celebrada en su historia, con la profecía del capítulo doce del Apocalipsis.” *Testimonios historicos guadalupanos*. Ed. Ernesto de la Torre Villar and Ramón Navarro de Anda. México, DF: Fondo de Cultura Económica, 1981. 152–281.

Sánchez Lacy, Alberto Ruy, ed. *El retrato novohispano*. Spec. Issue of *Artes de México* 25 (1994): 1–93.

Sautman, Francesca Canadé, and Pamela Sheingorn. Introduction. *Same-Sex Love and Desire among Women in the Middle Ages.* Ed. Sautman and Sheingorn. New York: Palgrave, 2001. 1–47.

Sawicki, Jana. *Disciplining Foucault: Feminism, Power, and the Body*. New York: Routledge, 1991.

Scher, Steven Paul. "Literature and Music." *Interrelations of Literature*. Ed. Jean-Pierre Barricelli and Joseph Gibaldi. New York: MLA, 1982. 225–50.

Schlau, Stacey. *Spanish American Women's Use of the Word: Colonial through Contemporary Narratives*. Tucson: U of Arizona P, 2001.

Schloder, John E. *Baroque Imagery*. Cleveland: Cleveland Museum of Art, Indiana UP, 1984.

Schmidhuber de la Mora, Guillermo. With Olga Martha Peña Doria. *The Three Secular Plays of Sor Juana Inés de la Cruz*. Trans. Shelby Thacker. Lexington: UP of Kentucky, 2000.

Schons, Dorothy. "The First Feminist in the New World." *Equal Rights* 31 Oct. 1925: 11–12.

Schurman, Anna Maria van. *The Learned Maid; or, Whether a Maid May Be a Scholar? A Logick Exercise.* London: Redmayne, 1659.

———. *Whether a Christian Woman Should Be Educated and Other Writings from Her Intellectual Circle*. Trans. Joyce L. Irwin. Chicago: U of Chicago P, 1998.

Scott, Nina M. " 'If you are not pleased to favor me, put me out of your mind . . . ': Gender and Authority in Sor Juana Inés de la Cruz." *Women's Studies International Forum* 11.5 (1988): 429–38.

———, ed. and trans. *Madres del verbo / Mothers of the Word. Early Spanish American Women Writers: A Bilingual Anthology*. Albuquerque: U of New Mexico P, 1999.

———. " 'Ser mujer, ni estar ausente, no es de amarte impedimento.' " Poot-Herrera, "*Y diversa de mí misma*" 159–69.

———. "The Tenth Muse." *Américas* 30.2 (1978): 13–20.

Searle, John. *Speech Acts: An Essay in the Philosophy of Language*. London: Cambridge UP, 1969.

Seed, Patricia. *Ceremonies of Possession in Europe's Conquest of the New World, 1492–1640*. New York: Cambridge UP, 1998.

Sevilla, Raphael J., dir. *El secreto de la monja.* Perf. Lupita Gallardo. Written by Iñigo de Martino. 1939.

Shannon, Laurie. *Sovereign Amity*. Chicago: U of Chicago P, 2002.

Sidney, Philip. "Poem 71." *Astrophel and Stella*. Ed. R. S. Bear. *Renascence Editions: An Online Repository of Works Printed in English between the Years 1777 and 1799*. U of Oregon, 1995. 28 Mar. 2007 <http://darkwing.uoregon.edu/~rbear/stella.html>.

Sigüenza y Góngora, Carlos. *Paraíso occidental.* México, DF: Consejo Nacional para la Cultura y las Artes, 1995.

———. *Primavera indiana, poema sacro histórico. Idea de Maria Santissima de Guadalupe de México, copiada de flores*. México City: Vargas Rea, 1945.

Siria, Antonio. *Vida admirable y prodigiosas virtudes de la V. sierva de Dios D. Anna Guerra de Jesús.* Guatemala, 1713.

Smith, Hilda L., and Berenice L. Carroll, eds. *Women's Political and Social Thought: An Anthology*. Bloomington: Indiana UP, 2001.

Smith, Paul Julian. "The Rhetoric of Presence in Lyric Poetry." *Writing in the Margin: Spanish Literature of the Golden Age.* Oxford: Clarendon, 1988. 43–77.

Socolow, Susan Migden. *The Women of Colonial Latin America.* Cambridge: Cambridge UP, 2000.

Sontag, Susan. "Notes on 'Camp.' " *Susan Sontag Reader.* Harmondsworth: Penguin, 1983. 105–19.

Sor Juana en Almoloya. By Jesusa Rodríguez. 2 Mar. 2007 <http://www.hemi.nyu.edu/cuaderno/holyterrorsweb/jesusa/sorjuanaalmoyatext.html>.

Sor Juana Inés de la Cruz (Juana de Asbaje). Ed. Geoffrey Kantaris. 2 Mar. 2007 <http://www.latin-american.cam.ac.uk/culture/SorJuana>.

Sousa, Lisa, Stafford Poole, and James Lockhart, eds. and trans. *The Story of Guadalupe: Luis Laso de la Vega's "Huei tlamahuiçoltica" of 1649.* By Luis Laso de la Vega. Stanford: Stanford UP, 1998.

Spadaccini, Nicholas, and Luis Martín-Escudillo, eds. *Hispanic Baroques: Reading Cultures in Context.* Nashville: Vanderbilt UP, 2005.

Spengemann, William. *A New World of Worlds: Redefining Early American Literature.* New Haven: Yale UP, 1994.

Spivak, Gayatri. "Can the Subaltern Speak?: Speculations on Widow Sacrifice." *Wedge* 7/8 (1985): 120–30.

———. In Other Worlds: Essays in Cultural Politics. New York: Routledge, 1987.

Stam, Robert. "From Hybridity to the Aesthetics of Garbage." *Social Identities* 3.2 (1997): 275–90.

Starr–LeBeau, Gretchen. *In the Shadow of the Virgin: Inquisitors, Friars, and Conversos in Guadalupe, Spain.* Princeton: Princeton UP, 2003.

Stevenson, Robert. "Sor Juana Inés de la Cruz's Musical Rapports: A Tercentenary Remembrance." *Inter-American Music Review* 15 (1996): 1–21.

———. "Sor Juana's Mexico City Musical Coadjutors: José de Loaysa y Agurto and Antonio de Salazar." *Inter-American Music Review* 15 (1996): 23–37.

Sturken, Marita, and Lisa Cartwright, eds. *Practices of Looking: An Introduction to Visual Culture.* New York: Oxford UP, 2002.

Suárez, Úrsula. *Relación autobiográfica de Ursula Suárez (1666–1749).* Ed. Mario Ferrecio Podestá. Santiago, Chile: Academia Chilena de Historia, 1984.

Suárez Briones, Beatriz. "De cómo la teoría lesbiana modificó a la teoría feminista (y viceversa)." *(Trans)formaciones de las sexualidades y el género.* Ed. Mercedes Bengoechea and Marisol Morales. Alcalá de Henares: U de Alcalá, 2001. 55–67.

Taibo, Paco Ignacio. *Encuentro de dos fogones.* 2 vols. México, DF: Promoción e Imagenes, 1992.

Tapia Méndez, Aureliano, ed. *Carta de sor Juana Inés de la Cruz a su confesor: Autodefensa espiritual.* By Sor Juana lnés de la Cruz. Monterrey, Mex.: Monterrey, 1993.

———. "Planos, documentos y retratos." *Carta de Sor Juana Inés de la Cruz a su confessor. Autodefensa Espiritual.* Ed. Tapia Méndez. Monterrey: U de Nuevo Léon, 1981. 183–253.

Tavard, George H. *Juana Inés de la Cruz and the Theology of Beauty: The First Mexican Theology.* Notre Dame: U of Notre Dame P, 1991.

Taylor, Diana, and Marlène Ramírez-Cancio, trans. "Sor Juana in Prison: A Virtual Pageant Play." *Holy Terrors: Latin American Women Perform*. Ed. Taylor and Roselyn Constantino. Durham: Duke UP, 2003. 211–15.

Tello, Aurelio. "Sor Juana Inés de la Cruz y los maestros de capilla catedralicios o de los ecos concertados y las acordes músicas con que sus villancicos fueron puestos en métrica armonía." *Pauta: Cuadernos de teoría y crítica musical* 16 (1996): 5–26.

Theodoro, Janice. *América Barroca: Tema e variações.* São Paolo: Edusp–Nova Fronteira, 1992.

Thompson, E. N. S. *Literary Bypaths of the Renaissance*. New Haven: Yale UP, 1924.

Todd, William Mills, III. *The Familiar Letter as a Literary Genre in the Age of Pushkin*. Princeton: Princeton UP, 1976.

Todorov, Tzvetan. *The Conquest of America: The Question of the Other.* Trans. Richard Howard. New York: Harper, 1984.

Toussaint, Manuel, ed. *Loa con la descripción poética del arco que la catedral de México erigió para honrar al Virrey, conde de Paredes, el año de 1680. Imaginó la idea del arco y lo describió sor Juana Inés de la Cruz. Reprodúcela en facsímile de la primera edición El Instituto de Investigaciones Estéticas como homenaje a la excelsa poetisa en el primer centenario de su nacimiento*. México, DF: U Nacional Autónoma de México, 1952.

Trabulse, Elías. *Los años finales de sor Juana: Una interpretación (1688–1695).* México, DF: Centro de Estudios de Historia de México, 1995.

———. *Carta de Serafina de Cristo 1691*. By Sor Juana Inés de la Cruz. Introd. and transcribed by Trabulse. Toluca, Mex.: Inst. Mexiquense de Cultura, 1996.

———. "Carta de Seraphina de Christo." Bijuesca and Brescia 183–93.

———. "El mayordomo: Don Mateo Ortíz de Torres." *Sor Juana Inés de la Cruz y sus contemporáneos.* Ed. Margo Glantz. México, DF: U Nacional Autónoma de México, Centro de Estudios de Historia de México, Condumex, 1998. 21–28.

———. *La muerte de sor Juana.* México, DF: Centro de Estudios de Historia de México, Condumex, 2000.

———. "El silencio final de sor Juana." Bijuesca and Brescia 143–55.

———. "El universo científico de sor Juana Inés de la Cruz." *Colonial Latin American Review* 4.2 (1995): 41–50.

Trambley, Estela Portillo. Sor Juana *and Other Plays*. Ypsilanti: Bilingual, 1983.

Traub, Valerie. "Desire and the Differences It Makes." *The Matter of Difference: Materialist Feminist Criticism of Shakespeare*. Ed. Valerie Wayne. Ithaca: Cornell UP, 1991. 81–114.

———. *The Renaissance of Lesbianism in Early Modern England.* Cambridge: Cambridge UP, 2002.

Trueblood, Alan S., ed. and trans. *A Sor Juana Anthology.* Fwd. Octavio Paz. Introd. Trueblood. Cambridge: Harvard UP, 1988.

Turner, Steve. *A Hard Day's Write*. New York: Carlton, 1999.

Vega, Lope de. *El arte nuevo de hacer comedias en este tiempo*. Ed. Juana de José Prades. Assn. for Hispanic Classical Theater. Ed. Eric W. Vogt and Vern

Williamsen. 8 Nov. 2006 <http://www.coh.arizona.edu/spanish/comedia/misc/artnue.html>.

———. *The New Art of Writing Plays*. Trans. William T. Brewster. Introd. Brander Matthews. New York: Dramatic Museum of Columbia U, 1914. 28 Mar. 2006 <http://www.broadviewpress.com>. Path: Links; Adjunct Materials; Broadview Press Adjunct Website for Drama.

———. *Nuevo Mundo descubierto por Cristobal Colón / The New World Discovered by Christopher Columbus: Una edición crítica y bilingüe*. Ed. Robert M. Shannon. New York: Lang, 2001.

Vicinus, Martha. "Lesbian History: All Theory and No Facts or All Facts and No Theory?" *Radical History Review* 60 (1994): 57–75.

Vickers, Nancy. "Diana Described: Scattered Woman and Scattered Rhyme." *Writing and Sexual Difference*. Ed. Elizabeth Abel. Chicago: U of Chicago P, 1982. 95–108.

Vieira, António. *Sermón del padre Antonio Vieira en la Capilla Real, año 1650*. Méndez Plancarte and Salceda 4: 673–94.

Villar, Luis M. "The Sor Juana Inés de la Cruz Project." Online posting. 23 Jan. 2005. <http://www.dartmouth.edu/~sorjuana/>.

Villa Sánchez, José de. *Justas, y debidas honras, que hicieron, y hacen sus proprias obras, a la M. R. M. Maria Anna Agueda de S. Ignacio*. . . . México, DF: Biblioteca Mexicana, 1758.

Vitoria, Baltasar de. *Primera parte del teatro de los dioses de la gentilidad. Autore el P. Fr. Baltasar de Vitoria, Predicador de San Francisco de Salamanca, y natural de la mesma Ciudad*. . . . Imprenta Real, 1673.

Vollendorf, Lisa. *The Lives of Women: A New History of Inquisitional Spain*. Nashville: Vanderbilt UP, 2005.

Wahl, Elizabeth. *Invisible Relations: Representations of Female Intimacy in the Age of Enlightenment*. Stanford: Stanford UP, 1999.

Warnke, Frank J., ed. and trans. *Three Women Poets (Renaissance and Baroque): Louise Labé, Gaspara Stampa, Sor Juana Inés de la Cruz*. Lewisburg: Bucknell UP, 1986.

Weber, Alison. *Teresa de Avila and the Rhetoric of Femininity*. Princeton: Princeton UP, 1989.

Wellek, René, and Austin Warren. "Image, Metaphor, Symbol, Myth." *Theory of Literature*. 3rd ed. New York: Harcourt, 1956. 186–211.

Williams, Raymond. *Marxism and Literature*. Oxford: Oxford UP, 1985.

Wilson de Armas, Diana. *Cervantes, the Novel, and the New World*. Oxford: Oxford UP, 2001.

Wilson, Katharina M., and Frank J. Warnke, eds. *Women Writers of the Seventeenth Century*. Athens: U of Georgia P, 1989.

Wilson, Leslie. "La Poesía Negra: Its Background, Themes, and Significance." *Blacks in Hispanic Literature: Critical Essays*. Ed. Miriam DeCosta. Port Washington: Kennikat, 1977. 90–104.

Wollstonecraft, Mary. *A Vindication of the Rights of Woman*. 1792. Ed. Charles Hegelman, Jr. New York: Norton, 1967.

Worthen, William B., ed. *The Wadsworth Anthology of Drama*. Boston: Thomson/ Wadsworth, 2004.

Yo, la peor de todas (1990) ("I, the Worst of All"). Ed. Irina Negrea, Audrey Gibbs, Nicole Robertson. May 2001. 29 Jan. 2007 <http://www.lehigh.edu/~ineng/ icn2/icn2-title.html>.

Young, Robert. *Colonial Desire: Hybridity, Theory, Culture and Race.* London: Routledge, 1995.

Zamora, Margarita. "América y el arte de la memoria." *Revista de crítica literaria latinoamericana* 21.41 (1995): 135–48.

Zayas y Sotomayor, María de. *Desengaños amorosos*. Ed. Alicia Yllera. 2nd ed. Madrid: Cátedra, 1993.

———. *The Enchantments of Love*. Trans. H. Patsy Boyer. Berkeley: U of California P, 1990.

———. *Novelas amorosas y ejemplares*. Ed. Julián Olivares. Madrid: Cátedra, 2000.

Zimmerman, Bonnie, and Toni A. H. McNaron, eds. *The New Lesbian Studies: Into the Twenty-First Century*. New York: Feminist, 1996.

INDEX OF NAMES

INDEX OF WORKS BY SOR JUANA INÉS DE LA CRUZ

Modern Language Association of America

Approaches to Teaching World Literature

Joseph Gibaldi, series editor

Achebe's Things Fall Apart. Ed. Bernth Lindfors. 1991.
Arthurian Tradition. Ed. Maureen Fries and Jeanie Watson. 1992.
Atwood's The Handmaid's Tale *and Other Works*. Ed. Sharon R. Wilson, Thomas B. Friedman, and Shannon Hengen. 1996.
Austen's Emma. Ed. Marcia McClintock Folsom. 2004.
Austen's Pride and Prejudice. Ed. Marcia McClintock Folsom. 1993.
Balzac's Old Goriot. Ed. Michal Peled Ginsburg. 2000.
Baudelaire's Flowers of Evil. Ed. Laurence M. Porter. 2000.
Beckett's Waiting for Godot. Ed. June Schlueter and Enoch Brater. 1991.
Beowulf. Ed. Jess B. Bessinger, Jr., and Robert F. Yeager. 1984.
Blake's Songs of Innocence and of Experience. Ed. Robert F. Gleckner and Mark L. Greenberg. 1989.
Boccaccio's Decameron. Ed. James H. McGregor. 2000.
British Women Poets of the Romantic Period. Ed. Stephen C. Behrendt andHarriet Kramer Linkin. 1997.
Brontë's Jane Eyre. Ed. Diane Long Hoeveler and Beth Lau. 1993.
Emily Brontë's Wuthering Heights. Ed. Sue Lonoff and Terri A. Hasseler. 2006.
Byron's Poetry. Ed. Frederick W. Shilstone. 1991.
Camus's The Plague. Ed. Steven G. Kellman. 1985.
Cather's My Ántonia. Ed. Susan J. Rosowski. 1989.
Cervantes' Don Quixote. Ed. Richard Bjornson. 1984.
Chaucer's Canterbury Tales. Ed. Joseph Gibaldi. 1980.
Chaucer's Troilus and Criseyde *and the Shorter Poems*. Ed. Tison Pugh and Angela Jane Weisl. 2006.
Chopin's The Awakening. Ed. Bernard Koloski. 1988.
Coleridge's Poetry and Prose. Ed. Richard E. Matlak. 1991.
Collodi's Pinocchio *and Its Adaptations*. Ed. Michael Sherberg. 2006.
Conrad's "Heart of Darkness" and "The Secret Sharer." Ed. Hunt Hawkins and Brian W. Shaffer. 2002.
Dante's Divine Comedy. Ed. Carole Slade. 1982.
Defoe's Robinson Crusoe. Ed. Maximillian E. Novak and Carl Fisher. 2005.
DeLillo's White Noise. Ed. Tim Engles and John N. Duvall. 2006.
Dickens' David Copperfield. Ed. Richard J. Dunn. 1984.
Dickinson's Poetry. Ed. Robin Riley Fast and Christine Mack Gordon. 1989.
Narrative of the Life of Frederick Douglass. Ed. James C. Hall. 1999.
Early Modern Spanish Drama. Ed. Laura R. Bass and Margaret R. Greer. 2006
Eliot's Middlemarch. Ed. Kathleen Blake. 1990.
Eliot's Poetry and Plays. Ed. Jewel Spears Brooker. 1988.
Shorter Elizabethan Poetry. Ed. Patrick Cheney and Anne Lake Prescott. 2000.

Ellison's Invisible Man. Ed. Susan Resneck Parr and Pancho Savery. 1989.
English Renaissance Drama. Ed. Karen Bamford and Alexander Leggatt. 2002.
Works of Louise Erdrich. Ed. Gregg Sarris, Connie A. Jacobs, and James R. Giles. 2004.
Dramas of Euripides. Ed. Robin Mitchell-Boyask. 2002.
Faulkner's The Sound and the Fury. Ed. Stephen Hahn and Arthur F. Kinney. 1996.
Flaubert's Madame Bovary. Ed. Laurence M. Porter and Eugene F. Gray. 1995.
García Márquez's One Hundred Years of Solitude. Ed. María Elena de Valdés and Mario J. Valdés. 1990.
Gilman's "The Yellow Wall-Paper" and Herland. Ed. Denise D. Knight and Cynthia J. Davis. 2003.
Goethe's Faust. Ed. Douglas J. McMillan. 1987.
Gothic Fiction: The British and American Traditions. Ed. Diane Long Hoeveler and Tamar Heller. 2003.
Hebrew Bible as Literature in Translation. Ed. Barry N. Olshen and Yael S. Feldman. 1989.
Homer's Iliad *and* Odyssey. Ed. Kostas Myrsiades. 1987.
Ibsen's A Doll House. Ed. Yvonne Shafer. 1985.
Henry James's Daisy Miller *and* The Turn of the Screw. Ed. Kimberly C. Reed and Peter G. Beidler. 2005.
Works of Samuel Johnson. Ed. David R. Anderson and Gwin J. Kolb. 1993.
Joyce's Ulysses. Ed. Kathleen McCormick and Erwin R. Steinberg. 1993.
Works of Sor Juana Inés de la Cruz. Ed. Emilie L. Bergmann and Stacey Schlau. 2007.
Kafka's Short Fiction. Ed. Richard T. Gray. 1995.
Keats's Poetry. Ed. Walter H. Evert and Jack W. Rhodes. 1991.
Kingston's The Woman Warrior. Ed. Shirley Geok-lin Lim. 1991.
Lafayette's The Princess of Clèves. Ed. Faith E. Beasley and Katharine Ann Jensen. 1998.
Works of D. H. Lawrence. Ed. M. Elizabeth Sargent and Garry Watson. 2001.
Lessing's The Golden Notebook. Ed. Carey Kaplan and Ellen Cronan Rose. 1989.
Mann's Death in Venice *and Other Short Fiction*. Ed. Jeffrey B. Berlin. 1992.
Marguerite de Navarre's Heptameron. Ed. Colette H. Winn. 2007.
Medieval English Drama. Ed. Richard K. Emmerson. 1990.
Melville's Moby-Dick. Ed. Martin Bickman. 1985.
Metaphysical Poets. Ed. Sidney Gottlieb. 1990.
Miller's Death of a Salesman. Ed. Matthew C. Roudané. 1995.
Milton's Paradise Lost. Ed. Galbraith M. Crump. 1986.
Milton's Shorter Poetry and Prose. Ed. Peter C. Herman. 2007.
Molière's Tartuffe *and Other Plays*. Ed. James F. Gaines and Michael S. Koppisch. 1995.
Momaday's The Way to Rainy Mountain. Ed. Kenneth M. Roemer. 1988.
Montaigne's Essays. Ed. Patrick Henry. 1994.

Novels of Toni Morrison. Ed. Nellie Y. McKay and Kathryn Earle. 1997.
Murasaki Shikibu's The Tale of Genji. Ed. Edward Kamens. 1993.
Pope's Poetry. Ed. Wallace Jackson and R. Paul Yoder. 1993.
Proust's Fiction and Criticism. Ed. Elyane Dezon-Jones andInge Crosman Wimmers. 2003.
Puig's Kiss of the Spider Woman. Ed. Daniel Balderston and Francine Masiello. 2007.
Novels of Samuel Richardson. Ed. Lisa Zunshine and Jocelyn Harris. 2006.
Rousseau's Confessions *and* Reveries of the Solitary Walker. Ed. John C. O'Neal and Ourida Mostefai. 2003.
Shakespeare's Hamlet. Ed. Bernice W. Kliman. 2001.
Shakespeare's King Lear. Ed. Robert H. Ray. 1986.
Shakespeare's Othello. Ed. Peter Erickson and Maurice Hunt. 2005.
Shakespeare's Romeo and Juliet. Ed. Maurice Hunt. 2000.
Shakespeare's The Tempest *and Other Late Romances*. Ed. Maurice Hunt. 1992.
Shelley's Frankenstein. Ed. Stephen C. Behrendt. 1990.
Shelley's Poetry. Ed. Spencer Hall. 1990.
Sir Gawain and the Green Knight. Ed. Miriam Youngerman Miller and Jane Chance. 1986.
Song of Roland. Ed. William W. Kibler and Leslie Zarker Morgan. 2006.
Spenser's Faerie Queene. Ed. David Lee Miller and Alexander Dunlop. 1994.
Stendhal's The Red and the Black. Ed. Dean de la Motte and Stirling Haig. 1999.
Sterne's Tristram Shandy. Ed. Melvyn New. 1989.
Stowe's Uncle Tom's Cabin. Ed. Elizabeth Ammons and Susan Belasco. 2000.
Swift's Gulliver's Travels. Ed. Edward J. Rielly. 1988.
Thoreau's Walden *and Other Works*. Ed. Richard J. Schneider. 1996.
Tolstoy's Anna Karenina. Ed. Liza Knapp and Amy Mandelker. 2003.
Vergil's Aeneid. Ed. William S. Anderson and Lorina N. Quartarone. 2002.
Voltaire's Candide. Ed. Renée Waldinger. 1987.
Whitman's Leaves of Grass. Ed. Donald D. Kummings. 1990.
Wiesel's Night. Ed. Alan Rosen. 2007.
Woolf's To the Lighthouse. Ed. Beth Rigel Daugherty and Mary Beth Pringle. 2001.
Wordsworth's Poetry. Ed. Spencer Hall, with Jonathan Ramsey. 1986.
Wright's Native Son. Ed. James A. Miller. 1997.